WILDLIFE MANAGEMENT ON YOUR LAND

The Practical Owner's Manual on How, What, When, and Why

Charles L. Cadieux

*Photos by Author
unless otherwise credited*

Stackpole Books

Copyright © 1985 by Stackpole Books

Published by
STACKPOLE BOOKS
Cameron and Kelker Streets
P. O. Box 1831
Harrisburg, PA   17105

Printed in the U.S.A.

Library of Congress Cataloging in Publication Data

Cadieux, Charles L.
   Wildlife management on your land.

   1. Wildlife management—United States.   I. Title.
SK361.C28   1985   639.9   84-16189
ISBN 0-8117-1877-8

Contents

Foreword   ix

1   **Don't Let the Language Scare You**   **1**
       Definitions of Terms

2   **Principles of Wildlife Management**   **10**

3   **Upland Game Birds**   **13**
       Needs of Upland Game Birds
       The Quail Family
          Bobwhite Quail
          Mountain Quail
          Gambel's Quail
          Scaled Quail
          California Quail
          Harlequin Quail
          Cooking Quail
       The Ring-necked Pheasant
          Management for Pheasant
          Cooking Pheasant

The Grouse Family
Ruffed Grouse
Blue Grouse
Spruce Grouse
Sage Grouse
Management for Sage Grouse
Pinnated Grouse
Management for Pinnated Grouse
Sharp-tailed Grouse
Management for Sharptails
Cooking the Pinnated and Sharp-tailed Grouse
The Introduced Partridges
Hungarian Partridges
Chukar Partridges
Cooking the Introduced Partridge
The Wild Turkey
Management for Wild Turkeys
Doves
Mourning Doves
Management for Mourning Doves
White-winged Doves
Management for White-winged Doves
Cooking Doves
Band-tailed pigeons

4   Migratory Waterfowl   99
The Canada Goose
Cooking the Goose
Wild Ducks
All Dabblers Follow the Mallards
Management for Dabblers and Mallards
Cooking Wild Ducks
Woodies—The Different Ducks
Management for Wood Ducks
Habits and Problems of Waterfowl
Migration of Birds
Feeding versus Baiting
Lethal Lead
Botulism

5   Small Game Animals   134
Squirrels
Fox and Gray Squirrels
Cooking Fox or Gray Squirrels

Red Squirrels
Flying Squirrels
Kaibab Squirrels
Tassel-eared Squirrels
Management for Squirrels
Cottontail Rabbits
Management for Rabbits
Cooking Rabbits
Raccoons
Cooking Raccoons

6   Life in the Watery World   158
Trout
Rainbow Trout
Brook Trout
Brown Trout
Cutthroat Trout
Lake Trout
Improving a Trout Stream
Beaver and Trout
Pan Fish
Bluegill Sunfish, King of Pan Fish
Lots of Sunfish
Crappies
Yellow Perch
Walleyes
Northern Pike
Bullheads
Bass
Largemouth Black Bass
Smallmouth Black Bass
Spotted Bass
White Bass
Channel Catfish
Minnows and Bait Fish
Minnow Farming
Pond Construction
Control of Rough Fish

7   The Farm or Ranch Fish Pond   197
Compatible Fish Populations
Harvesting the Crop of Fish
Feeding the Fish
Winterkill
Summerkill

8   Fish Farming for Profit   204

   Caged-Fish Production
      Feeding Caged Catfish
      Sickness
      What Do They Weigh?
      Do You Have to Raise Only Catfish?
   Fish Farming Is Another Matter Entirely!
   Look Before You Leap
   Minnow Ranching

9   Deer   212

   The White-tailed Deer
      What Do We Know About Whitetails?
      Management for the White-tailed Deer
   The Mule Deer
   Proper Care of Venison
      Cooking Venison

10   Other Big Game Animals   235

   The Pronghorn Antelope
      Management for the Pronghorn
   Elk
      What Happened to the Elk?
      Management for the Elk
   Moose
      Cooking Moose

11   Exotic Big Game as a Cash Crop   248

   Getting into the Exotics Business

12   Managing Nongame Birds on Your Land   255

13   Predator Control   263

14   Crawfish as a Farm Crop   267

   Through the Year with the Crawfish
      Food Requirements
      Water Quality
      Want to Try Crawfish Farming?
      Cooking the Crawfish

15 **State and National Departments and Agencies** **273**
    The United States Fish and Wildlife Service
      Regional Offices
    State Conservation Agencies
    Other Sources of Information
      Suggested Reading

16 **Trapping** **281**

17 **Posting Land Against Trespass** **285**

18 **Censusing Wildlife** **288**
    How Many Have You Got?
      Aerial Counts of Deer or Elk
      Aerial Counts of Fur Bearers
      Counting Grouse
      Fish Index
      Waterfowl
    For What It's Worth Department
    Worthless Trivia

19 **Trees and Wildlife** **293**
    Some Wildlife-Preferred Trees
    Managing the Woodlot
    Suggested Reading

20 **About Scientific Names** **303**
    Birds
    Animals
    Fresh-Water Fishes

Index **307**

Foreword

Sometimes I'm pessimistic about the future of wildlife in America. That semi-cynicism probably comes from 25 years in natural-resource management, where you notice the effects of mankind's proliferation. People are scattered all over, and more come to fill the gaps. Lower life forms retreat while intensive agriculture, subdivisions, shopping malls, highways, energy developments, and other evidences of *Homo sapiens* unfold. Wildlife habitat is destroyed, and wild creatures disappear.

Then again I can be somewhat optimistic. Although the bell tolls for wildlife, it sounds softly. Animal living places normally are not deleted in huge chunks, thereby roiling public anxiety. Instead, they vanish here and there and bit by bit. Few people notice the change.

Today, you see a brushy fencerow filled with pheasants. Tomorrow, it may be plowed and planted to wheat. A secluded hollow that shelters white-tailed deer soon becomes a reservoir or landfill. And that weed patch hiding bobwhites at the edge of town could turn to asphalt streets and manicured lawns within a year. The process is insidious, but there is time to reverse the trend and thus reason for hope.

We are fortunate that the chronic nature of habitat loss allows an opportunity to fight back. That gift of time must be used judiciously. This book can help carry the battle. It has the appeal and authority to capture landowner interest and thereby make good things happen for wildlife on the ground where it counts. It is an excellent tribute to the wildlife-management background and superb writing talent of Chuck Cadieux. He knows wildlife, and he knows how to write about it interestingly.

Chuck learned the nuts and bolts of wildlife management during better than three decades with various state and federal natural-resource agencies. He worked on farms, forests, and rangelands across America and knows what makes the land and landowners hum. He was stationed in Washington, D.C. and other big cities long enough to discover the opportunities that exist for wildlife enhancement in metropolitan and suburban areas. Consequently, there are few people with his breadth of experience and knowledge on how to entice landowners to grow wildlife on their property.

Chuck's knack for the written word was honed to a sparkling edge during those decades of learning. He is among the few writers who can transform boring wildlife-management principles into engaging prose. Thus, his books are as entertaining as they are informative.

A man known for his interest in the economics of a situation, Chuck offers landowners more than aesthetics for their investments. He recommends ways to make fish and wildlife into cash crops. The popular white-tailed deer, for example, is a bigger money-maker than domestic livestock for landowners in some parts of the country. Other game and fish species can turn a profit too if managed properly. This is an important feature for the many landowners who must make a living from the land first and worry about wildlife second.

For landowners who want more wildlife on their property, here are the essential facts on how to do it. For each landowner that reads and follows some of the suggestions offered, wildlife will be a cut better off. And as the habitat improvements accumulate, the future of wildlife and its many recreational uses will brighten.

The lessons on these pages remind us semi-cynics and inform novices that wildlife can be created as well as eliminated. But more importantly, they offer practical techniques and advice that landowners can understand and use economically to build habitat the same way it was lost . . . bit by bit.

Lonnie L. Williamson
Wildlife Management Institute

1

Don't Let the Language Scare You

Wildlife managers use a special language, almost as hard to understand as that spoken by medical doctors or lawyers. A few wildlife managers use this special language to insulate themselves from the real world. But most of them use it because it enables them to say exactly what they mean. In this book, I'm going to use a much simpler language—plain English. But there are special terms I'll use often, and you'll understand the book much more easily if you know the meaning of these terms. So in the first chapter of *Wildlife Management on Your Land*, I will define some of our most important wildlife terms by telling you what they mean to me.

You should read through these definitions before you start to use *Wildlife Management on Your Land*. If you don't, you may not get the right message, and you won't know what this book is trying

to tell you. Don't try to memorize these definitions. When you run across a term that's new to you, just turn back to this first chapter and refresh your memory.

DEFINITIONS OF TERMS

Age Ratio means the proportion of old to young in any wildlife population. For example, we might say that the old-young ratio of a pheasant population in the early fall is about 1:6, and prospects for hunting would be good. If the age ratio had fallen to about 1:2, it would be better not to hunt hens at all and to go easy on the roosters, for the population would not be in very good shape.

Allowable Harvest is the percentage of the total population that can be harvested by hunters without hurting the chances of that population reproducing itself in

1

satisfactory numbers in the next breeding season.

Altricial means helpless at hatching and requiring a lot of parental care. The opposite meaning is the word *precocial*. Young robins are altricial, of course, as they must have food brought to them for several weeks. Young pheasants are precocial. Although young humans are definitely not hatched, they are altricial in that they require parental care for a long time.

Balance of Nature. According to ancient theories of wildlife management, there was a dynamic balance between eaters and the life forms they ate. It was felt that the foxes ate the meadow mice until the meadow mice became scarce, then they shifted their attention to other food sources. If there were too few foxes, the mice would explode in numbers, and the foxes would come hurrying back to do their job of controlling numbers of meadow mice. The entire concept sounds wonderful; too bad it isn't true.

We humans upset that balance of nature many centuries ago, when we became the first species in the history of the world to grow so powerful that we had the ability to control our own destiny. If there ever was a balance of nature in North America, it was upset when the first white settlers came. The only way to restore the balance of nature would be for us to bulldoze our cities, tear up our highways, and eliminate all humans except those who could earn their food with the sweat of their brow or those who could hunt and kill enough other life forms to keep body and soul together.

A temporary balance of nature can be achieved in a controlled environment. For example, it is possible, in a wide-spectrum way, to achieve a balance in a fish-bowl. It may even be possible to effect this result in a small body of water, such as a stock pond. Other than that, forget the concept of balance of nature. It no longer exists, if indeed it ever did, and has not existed since man became supreme among life forms on this planet.

Biota is dictionary-defined as the "total fauna and flora" of an area or region. I will use the term to mean the total of all life forms in an area, region, or time period. For example, the total biota of a pond will include the fishes, amphibians, snakes, turtles, polliwogs, green algae, ducks, geese, bass—every living thing, plant or animal, in the pond.

Browse is both a verb and a noun. As a verb, to browse means to feed by biting off the leaves and tender parts of trees and forbs, as opposed to grazing, which means to feed by biting off grasses. Many big game animals, such as the mule deer, are both browsers and grazers. As a noun, browse means the food that is eaten by a browsing animal.

Capon is the name that we give to a castrated male bird. This is usually done in the belief that it will improve the flavor of the bird when used as food. It is also used by wildlife managers to make sure that the male bird does not breed, to avoid hybridization, for example.

Carnivorous means meat-eating. A fox is a carnivore, because he enjoys eating mice and songbirds and they are meat. You and I are nearly all carnivores, because most of us enjoy eating meat. When primitive man began eating meat, he got his necessary protein quickly, because meat contains much more protein per pound than does grass or fruit. As a result, man had the pleasure of getting the essential food-gathering out of the way in a short time and had more time to think.

This is why man did a lot of thinking and why he advanced in the arts and in civilization. It is also why he achieved dominion over all other living things. Whether this was good or bad is still an open question. But it is my belief that, because man was a hunter and a killer of meat, he became a thinking animal and this led him into thinking about lots of things, such as civilization.

Carrying Capacity means the number of a given species that can exist in a given place, from one generation through the next generation of that species. For example, we might say that the quail carrying capacity of McDonald's Farm is about three coveys of fifteen birds per covey. We might say that the pond on McDonald's Farm has a bass carrying capacity of 100 pounds of bass.

It matters little that 300 ring-necked pheasants are living on a North Dakota prairie farm in late August, if the total lack of winter cover allows the blizzard to kill them off in January. In that situation, the carrying capacity of the farm is not 300, but zero. The pheasant that died in January obviously will not nest in late April. In other words, the realistic concept of carrying capacity speaks of the number of individuals of that species that can exist in that area, all through the year.

Because this carrying capacity concept is important to all wildlife management, let's take a pair of examples. In example one, 50,612 catfish hatch in the slough behind McDonald's dam and cruise happily in his stockwater reservoir for five months. They find lots of food and they grow to a length of 6 inches by late February. Then, when the reservoir freezes over, there is no wind or wave action to put new supplies of oxygen in the water.

It becomes difficult to find enough oxygen to pass through their gills (which is how a fish breathes), and 47,802 catfish die of suffocation. This leaves 2,810 catfish. By late March, decaying vegetation under the ice is producing a lot of rotten egg gas and using a lot more oxygen. All of the catfish die except 14, which find a supply of oxygen where a small stream trickles into the water, bringing oxygen to them under the ice. When the ice melts, there are 14 catfish, and when the water warms up, they pair off and spawn but produce very few young, simply because they are immature spawners. What was the carrying capacity of that pond for catfish? If you said 14, you get a gold star.

Example number two takes us to a small lake. Redhead ducks nest on this lake, and this year a pair brings off a large brood and successfully rears ten of them to flight stage. They fly off south and the next spring, nine of them are still alive—the old pair and seven of the young ones. Three pairs of redheads fly to our small lake, looking for nesting sites. Surely there is enough food there to carry twenty nesting pairs, for the vegetation is lush and of just the right kinds. But redheads are highly territorial in their demands for nesting room. They will fight to keep a big water area for their exclusive use. The second pair of nesters that arrives on the small lake will find themselves driven out. The first pair have a dog-in-the-manger attitude toward "their" lake. The final result is that again there is only one pair of nesting redheads. Carrying capacity for redhead ducks? One nesting pair.

Climax Species are the final result of a process known as climax succession. For example, if we log off a piece of ground, plow it up, and seed it to grasses, we create one kind of habitat. If we then abandon that plot and make no attempt to keep it in grass, it will go through a series of vegetation changes (climax succession) in which the grass loses out to forbs, which lose out to larger woody plants, which in turn lose out to trees. Of course, this all depends upon which kind of plants are best suited to the soil and water conditions found on that plot. In a different situation, grass may take over and be the climax species. It all depends upon which is best at existing in that environment after some change has given them all a chance at taking over.

Commensal comes from the Latin *com*, meaning "with," and *mensa*, meaning "table." So a commensal species is one that eats from man's table. This surely applies to rats and mice when they live in our homes. But in a more limited sense, it also applies to animals that eat man's crops as a regular part of their life. This means mule deer feeding on alfalfa fields in New Mexico, whitetails eating apples in a Vermont orchard, and pheasants eating wheat in South Dakota or mallards dining on corn in Iowa or Illinois.

Cover means the vegetation that protects a part of a wildlife species' life. Nesting cover for a mallard duck is simply tall grass or forbs within a short distance of a water area. Escape cover for a cottontail rabbit may mean a brush pile, which he can dive into or under to escape his enemies. Winter cover for a white-tailed deer may mean a tamarack swamp's thick vegetation in Vermont.

Cyclic means repeating itself in a (sometimes) predictable cycle. Ruffed grouse seem to be cyclic in northeastern United States, their numbers rising and falling in cycles that can be predicted for the future by studying the past. Reasons for such cycles are not well known, for wildlife management is not an exact science.

Depredation means a damaging of something that man wants, when that damage is done by wildlife. For example, when mallard ducks discover swathed wheat, they dive in and do considerable damage in their yen for the finer foods, and that is called depredation. Winter-hungry elk commit depredations upon ranchers' haystacks. Beaver cutting down apple trees to provide food and building material for their dams are also committing a depredation.

Ecology is one of the most-often misused words in the English language. The word comes from the Greek *logos,* "the study of." In the case of ecology, we mean the study of the ecosystem, and the ecosystem is the sum total of all things that affect the situation. We can study the ecology of our pair of redhead ducks, for example, and we would find that we were studying their food habits and food requirements, their reproductive cycle, their nest-building habits, the predators that prey upon them, the food plants they may kill out by overeating, the insects that they eat, and the insects that pester the hen as she sits on her eggs. We would be studying everything that affects the redhead. The bumper sticker that says SAVE THE ECOLOGY is the product of ignorance. Are you really trying to save the study of something? I think what they mean to say is SAVE THE HUMAN ENVIRONMENT. If so, I agree heartily with their sentiments.

Edge is an important concept to wildlife managers. By edge we mean any place where two different types of cover exist in close proximity. We have found that we can increase white-tailed deer numbers by increasing the amount of edge in the environment of the white-tailed deer.

The edges between forest and shrub belts of vegetation are important places for deer to feed. The edges between cultivated fields and grasslands are important places for upland game birds to feed, to nest, and to escape their enemies. All other things being equal, the more edge, the more wildlife in a given area.

Environment is the niche in which a particular individual animal finds itself. Our environment includes our home, our town, our job, the air we breathe, the food we eat, our friends and relations, and the things that affect us adversely or beneficially. We can be environed by bad influences, or we can be environed by good things. So can a grebe, a coyote, or a ring-necked pheasant.

Eutrophication is dictionary-defined as the process that amasses nutrients in a lake or pond, thereby supporting a lush growth of plant and animal life whose decay finally uses up the oxygen in the body of water, making it sterile for life forms that depend upon dissolved oxygen in the water. What the dictionary doesn't go on to say is that this is a normal process of aging in most bodies of water. This has special meaning for the fishery manager. It means that a reservoir left to its own natural processes has a finite life. This aging can be slowed by proper soil conservation, which slows soil erosion and subsequent silting. It can be delayed by ''flow-through'' currents that carry nutrients along with them, both into and out of the reservoir. However, we must remember that most reservoirs serve the purpose of slowing down running water or even stopping its movement entirely. Reduced current velocity means that solids settle to the bottom.

Feral simply means gone wild or acting like a wild animal. We lose many nesting birds each year to feral house cats. The process of becoming feral may be partial or complete. If a house cat abandons all pretense of living with humans, it is feral, but we also refer to animals that go wild during the night but return to humans in the daytime as being feral.

Food Chain is a term we use to describe the movement of nutrients through the environment. For example, a typical farmland food chain starts when the nutrients in plants are eaten by meadow mice. The nutrients are neither created nor destroyed, but they are changed in form. Now those nutrients are part of the body of the mouse. Along comes a coyote and eats the mouse, thus transferring those same nutrients into the flesh of the coyote. The coyote is shot by a hunter, and his body lies there on the prairie. Before it decomposes, parts of those nutrients are eaten by other carnivores—a badger, for example. The rest of the coyote's carcass decomposes, returning those nutrients to the soil. Microorganisms in the soil combine with the bacteria of decay to change the form of those nutrients again, making them available to the growing plants. The food chain led from soil organisms to plants to mice to coyotes to soil organisms again, completing the food cycle, or food chain.

In a pond, a simple food chain would be this: Insects feed on tiny plankton. Minnows eat the insects, and the minnow is in turn eaten by a crappie, which is in turn eaten by a largemouth black bass. In this particular pond, the bass is the top of the food chain. The bass dies, and his decaying body releases nutrients into the water and into the soil at the bottom of the pond. These nutrients are fed upon by plankton, and the cycle starts anew.

Humans are at the top of the food chain in almost all instances. The only exception is when that human is fed upon, directly, by a larger meat eater, such as a shark or a man-eating tiger.

In most cases, humans are not fed upon directly. However, the nutrients stored in our perishable bodies are never lost. In one way or another, they are always returned to the never-ending food chain, for nutrients are neither created nor destroyed.

Gallinaceous is a term that means "like chickens." Pheasants, grouse, and partridges are gallinaceous birds.

Harvest in biological terms means man's use of the available species. For example, a hunter harvests part of the available crop of quail produced on McDonald's Farm every year, just as Mr. McDonald harvests his crop of apples or wheat or corn, or white-tailed deer. In the case of a hunter's harvest, the word is simply a euphemism for the word *kill*.

Herbivorous means feeding on plants. Cows are herbivores, so are deer. So are humans, who are also carnivorous. In many animal species, the distinction is not hard and fast. Crows, for example, eat plants such as corn, and they also eat meat, such as a road-killed squirrel. Bears eat great quantities of grass, and they also relish fish and carrion.

Hibernation is a process of suspended animation, used as a method of getting through periods of extreme cold or periods of time in which food is not available to the hibernating species. In true hibernation, the animal goes into a very deep sleep, with greatly reduced heart beat and even lowered body temperature. Sometimes hibernation is a sleep so deep that the hibernating animal, if cut, will not bleed. Because of its lowered metabolism rate, the demands upon the body fat are very small, enabling the animal to survive months without feeding. Some species hibernate for short periods,

interspersed with periods of outside activity, but the true hibernators enter their winter den, go to sleep, and stay asleep until spring. Bears even give birth to their young while hibernating.

Irruption means an explosion in numbers of a particular species or many species of wildlife. For example, cotton rats go on periodic irruptions, or unaccountable increases in population. Jackrabbits have attracted attention by several irruptions in Utah and other desert states. An irruption is a population increase significantly greater than the usual fluctuations of cyclic populations.

Lek is a term useful in the study of gallinaceous birds. A lek is a dancing ground, a place where male birds of the sage, pinnated, and sharp-tailed grouse species gather to perform their mating rituals and courtship dances. Attachment to these dancing grounds (leks) may be so ingrained in the birds that they will refuse to leave the ground even when it becomes the landing strip of an air base. In Texas, Attwater's prairie chickens refused to leave an ancestral lek simply because it was now paved and used by jet airplanes for landing. Collisions between plane and chicken were commonplace, causing great financial loss, to say nothing of the disruption of the ancient courtship dance.

Mast means the fruit of oaks, beeches, and other fruit- and nut-bearing trees that are used as food by wildlife species. Acorns are the most common component of mast, but all nuts, and many fruits, can also be lumped under the collective term *mast* in the wildlife dictionary. Mast is an important food for squirrels, deer, turkeys, javelina, wild hogs, and many large birds.

Monogamous means breeding with only one individual during a given breeding season. For example, the Baltimore oriole is monogamous, as they form a pair bond and breed only with each other during the breeding season.

Omnivorous means that the species will eat everything. Have you noticed that humans fall in this category? Obviously, if a species is omnivorous, it must also be carnivorous and herbivorous.

Pair Bond means that attraction that holds a male and female of a species together for longer than the time needed for the male to inseminate the female. Sometimes this pair bond is developed out of necessity, as when it takes both parents to feed the young, which are dependent over a long period of time. Humans are examples of this pair bonding. Because the human young is dependent for perhaps a dozen years or more, it is necessary that the male stay with the female long enough to rear the young. There is no pair bond in polygamous species, where the male breeds with the female and then departs. There is a short-lived pair bond in the case of fox squirrels, where the pair remains together from the actual time of mating until shortly before the young are born. There is another kind of pair bond among quail, wherein the male remains near the nesting hen all through incubation, although he does not incubate the eggs himself. When the young are hatched, the male plays a part in rearing the young.

Usually polygamous species have no pair bond, and their young are precocious, ready to make their own way in the world within a short time after birth, and/or hatching. Turkeys are a good example.

Polygamous means breeding with more than one individual during a breeding season. A pheasant rooster is certainly polygamous, for he will service as many as twenty hens during a breeding season. Mule deer, elk, fur seals, and turkeys are all examples of polygamous species. In most polygamous species it is possible to harvest a large percentage of the available males during the hunting season, for all females will be bred anyway, despite the scarcity of males.

Precocial means that the newly hatched young are able to follow their mother within hours of having been hatched. The dictionary definition says that they are free to move about soon after birth. This would apply to most of the gallinaceous birds, of course, with the pheasant and ruffed grouse being prime examples. In a more far ranging definition, we could speak of the deer family as being precocious (if not precocial) as they are able to follow their mother within hours after birth. Rabbits are definitely not precocial; hares definitely are precocious.

Predator is a term we use for any organism that beats us to the harvest of another organism. For example, a coyote is a predator because he eats the sheep we intended to eat ourself. A bobcat is a very efficient predator, preying on rabbits, birds of all kinds—anything smaller than the bobcat. Man, obviously, is the greatest of all predators, for he has it in his power to kill any and every other species.

Prey includes those organisms that the predator feeds upon. To a coyote, sheep and fawns are prey, so are gophers, birds, rabbits, squirrels—even grasshoppers. To a mountain lion, deer are a favorite prey species. To man, all living organisms are prey, intentionally or accidentally.

Raptor, for our purposes, means a flying meat eater, for example, hawks or owls.

Reproductive Potential means the ability of that species to reproduce itself. This ability to reproduce is determined by (a) number of young produced at one time, (b) age of the species at first breeding, (c) length of gestation period, (d) number of times per year that they reproduce, (e) survivability of the young produced.

Thus, the whooping crane, which doesn't breed until four years old, which lays but two eggs and often hatches just one, has a very *low* reproductive potential. The mourning dove, which nests at one year and produces multiple broods per year, has an excellent reproductive potential, a very *high* potential.

Sex Ratio is usually thought of as the proportion of males to females. For example, a pheasant population with a sex ratio of 1:3 is in excellent shape, for surely all three hens will find a willing male during the breeding season. A quail population with a sex ratio of 1:16 would be in terrible shape, because fifteen of those hens would not find mates.

Stockpiling of game species is usually used to describe the futile attempt to have more of a given species by not harvesting any this year. In fact, it is most often used by biologists who say, "You cannot stockpile game; it doesn't work." They are right, of course. If we do not shoot any quail this year, in an attempt to have more next year, we find that winter mortality removes the birds that the hunter did not remove. It is true; you cannot stockpile short-lived species. If we close the season on canvasbacks in the hope that more of them will breed next year, we are only kidding ourselves. The duck doesn't live long enough to make that kind of wildlife management work. Remember, you cannot stockpile game.

Stratification is the formation of different layers, or strata, in a body of water, by reason of different temperatures. Water of different temperature has a different density. This prevents the two waters from mixing. Warmer water is on top, colder water below in the normal situation of stratification. I saw this graphically illustrated one day on the Colorado River where it flows past the Willow Beach National Fish Hatchery. A decision was made to stock 9- and 10-inch rainbow trout every month of the year. The cold Colorado, which flows into Lake Mohave, underlies the sun-warmed surface layers. To stock into those hot surface waters in July would mean instant death to the valuable fish. So the Fish and Wildlife Service developed a stocking barge that featured an elongated delivery tube that reached down through the hot water and into the cold river below.

Using scuba gear, we hung on the bottom end of the delivery pipe and watched the trout come out with the water from the transport tanks on the barge above. Naturally, these fish were considerably agitated from being handled with nets, loaded into tanks and transported down river, then discharged through the pipe. They shot out of the tube at high speed, swimming in every possible direction. But those that shot upward seemed to ricochet off the invisible barrier that was the line between cold water below and hot water above. No trout went through into that hot water. All bounced downward and disappeared in the colder, darker depths. Stratification prevented them from moving into gradually warmer water above them. It also prevented them from quickly dying in the water that was too hot to sustain rainbow trout life.

Sustained Yield is defined as the allowable harvest that can be repeated, year after year, without harming the resource. This may refer to the harvest of 200 saw logs from a woodlot or the shooting of five deer from that same woodlot. In each case, the harvest must be low enough so that the resource can continue to reproduce itself and repeat the harvest, year after year.

Sympatric means "the same fatherland." If two species are sympatric, that means that they live in the same areas. For example, scaled quail and Gambel's quail are sympatric species.

Thermocline is the name we give to that layer of water in a lake or pond where the temperature gradient is greater than that of the warmer water above or the colder water below. In other words, this is where hot and cold water meet, without mixing to any appreciable degree.

When this thermocline is disrupted by seasonal changes in the weather or by a physical movement of the water, we refer to the lake "turning over," when what we actually mean is that the thermocline has been broken and the water temperature layers are mixing, or reversing, top to bottom.

Warbles are the encysted larva of certain flies, such as the botfly larva, that develop under the skin of host animals. When it is ready for the next stage in its metamorphosis, it comes out of the host animal and usually pupates in its next stage of development. Although ugly, these warbles are almost never harmful to the animal serving as a host.

2

Principles of Wildlife Management

It is easy to write glowing generalities about what you should do to help wildlife. But it is much harder to write these when you are forced to consider the obvious fact that the landowner must earn a living, not just provide a living for wildlife.

Let's start out by recognizing a few facts.

Fact 1. The landowner is *the* most important single factor in the future of all species of wildlife. The greater part of the United States is privately owned. It is owned by people like you, not by the federal or state governments. In a state where 90 percent of the land is privately owned, management must, perforce, take place on privately owned land. This management can only succeed with the cooperation of the landowner.

Fact 2. There is no free lunch. For every value you wish to gain, there is an equal and opposite loss. Sometimes it is difficult to recognize, but the opposing loss is there. For example, a farmer can decide to clear the brush and small trees out of a field corner and plow that corner to add three bushels of wheat per year to the yield of his land. That added wheat crop is a plus, but the loss of winter cover for that covey of quail is a loss. Wildlife managers are quick to note that loss, but the farmer's pocketbook is just as quick to notice the gain.

Conversely, if we replace ten acres of soybeans with ten acres of shelterbelt or windbreak, there are both gains and losses. It is easy to point to the obvious gain—that we now have prime cover for pheasants, rabbits, squirrels, and deer, along with a greatly improved wildlife food supply. That's a plus. But we have ten acres less in production, and that loss of cash income is definitely *not* a plus. But we also have increased moisture-holding in the lee of the shelterbelt, improved subsoil moisture conditions, and, usually, improved yield per acre. Those things are harder to measure, but the profits and losses are there. Even more difficult to measure is the plus of decreased soil erosion. That must be measured over decades or even centuries. It may mean a plus for your great-grandson if he farms the land. It is up to the intelligent landowner to assess accurately the pluses and minuses and then make an intelligent decision—*insofar as is possible*. Sometimes we know what we *should* do for the benefit of wildlife and even for the benefit of future generations, but we simply cannot do it, because we must feed our family first and that takes precedence over long-range benefits for the future.

Fact 3. No one action takes place by itself. All living things are interrelated in a great, complicated web of action, reaction, and interaction. When we push in on the web of life in one place, it obviously must bulge out in another place. We make decisions as humans, and our decisions are not subject to review by nonhuman life forms—so nonhuman life forms suffer. For example, if we kill a bull snake—just because of a revulsion toward all snakes—we destroy one of the most efficient mousers that we can ever find. Mice increase in numbers, which may lead to increased crop damage by rodents. It may also result in greater survival rates in small bird species, or even improve the chances for quail eggs or baby quail in their first few days of life.

Fact 4. Unnatural changes in the environment may have unexpected and far-reaching effects. The most obvious ex-

ample is the introduction of DDT into the environment. Universally hailed as the greatest insecticide the world had ever seen, DDT was responsible for great reductions in disease-carrying insect populations all over the world. It resulted in greatly improved crop yields, in lice-free children in primitive countries—it was thought to be an unmitigated blessing. Then, almost too late for some species, we found out that it was affecting all other life forms above insects in the food chain. Entire species of birds (for example, the brown pelican) were almost exterminated because DDT residues, working their way from insect to fish to pelican, made it impossible for the brown pelican to manufacture egg shell! The peregrine falcon, which fed on insect-eating birds, suffered a similar decrease in numbers.

Fact 5. What *You* do on your land affects your neighbors, both near and far. If you use a chemical spray on your crop, you will affect your neighbor. You may be guilty of letting the spray drift over to a neighbor's land and kill some crop, bird, or animal that he did not want killed. If the breeze doesn't carry it across the fence line, perhaps surface run-off will. But even if you are a good manager and keep the chemicals inside your fences, you cannot keep the neighbor's birds or animals from coming over onto your land and being affected. This is not a plea for complete abstinence from agricultural chemicals— we are not that silly. The American farmer is the most productive in the world, in part due to the excellent chemicals he has to help him. I know that you will continue to use these chemicals. But I hope that they will be used wisely and that a careful watch will be kept for unexpected results—near or far.

Fact 6. You do not own your land in an

absolute manner. You have inherited, or
gained by your efforts, the stewardship
of that land. No one can say you nay in
most management decisions, but you are
only the steward of that land, and you
must hold it in trust for your sons and
daughters, or for future generations. The
land is yours, in fee title, but there are
serious limitations to ownership. This is
perhaps best expressed in the beautiful
words of a prayer written by Margaret
Menamin and adopted as the official
prayer of the Outdoor Writers Association of America. It says:

> God, give me stillness, give me
>   time to stand
> Unpressed by creeds and credits,
>   undefiled
> By dust of industry, and be a child
> Reminded of my oneness with the
>   land.
> Let me stop running and be
>   reconciled
> To feel my feet send roots into the
>   sand;
> Let me put forth fresh blossoms
>   from my hand.
> Let me not lose my kinship with
>   the wild.
> And if I call this mine, remind me,
>   God,
> That it is only as my blood and
>   bone
> Are mine; not mine to waste, not
>   mine to own,
> But mine to be. I am the
>   goldenrod,

> The grain, the granite; I am stream
>   and glen,
> Remind me to preserve myself,
>   Amen.

Fact 7. You operate under many con-
straints in your management of wildlife.
You cannot, for example, harvest your
white-tailed deer crop any time you want
to, as you can your beef crop. You must
operate under state and federal laws. You
do not own wildlife; no one ever does
own wildlife until it is dead. Wildlife is
the property of the state. This is galling
to many landowners, for they are forced
to suffer the depredations of elk on their
haystacks without shooting the elk—because the state owns the elk. It is also
irritating to many landowners to be told
that they "have a sacred duty to protect
and foster wildlife." Let's forget the
preachments of city folks in this regard
and look only at what is good for us and
what is good for wildlife. In this book, I
will try to consider the needs of wildlife
first, the needs of the landowner second,
the hunter or fisherman third, and the
general public last. But I will try to consider all needs, because no man is an island, no farm is self-sufficient and independent of other farms and other farmers,
no species is confined entirely to one
landowner's property.

The most important consideration in
the future of wildlife in America is the
landowner. I have tried not to forget that
in writing this book.

3

Upland Game Birds

You would like to have more quail on your farm? Your first impulse is to buy some and turn them loose on your land. But that is not smart.

There used to be many ring-necked pheasants on your farm, especially along the creek bottom, but they've all been shot out and you want more? Do you buy some and turn them loose? No!

More money and effort has been wasted on "turned-loose" game birds than in any other form of wildlife management, with the possible exception of bounty payments on slain predators. Let's put it another way. If you are a farmer and you find that ten out of eighteen of your cows have starved to death, despite the fact that you kept them in a good-looking pasture, would you go out and buy ten more and put them in the same pasture? No.

First of all, you'd find out why they died. Second, you'd correct the condition that caused the loss of those expensive cows. *Then* you'd replace the cows you lost and hope for better things.

You live in the northern part of the country and all of your chickens froze to death during a severe storm, the worst you'd ever seen. Do you immediately replace the chickens with those hatched from an incubator and hope that you won't have another storm like that in your lifetime? No, you have more sense than that. You replace the broken windows in the henhouse, you do a lot of things to make it warmer during the next storm, and then—only then—do you replace the lost chickens.

But we do not seem to be that smart about our wildlife. Perhaps we do not

13

adopt the basic dollars-and-cents attitude toward our wildlife. But we definitely should!

NEEDS OF UPLAND GAME BIRDS

It is basic to ask ourselves *Why* we do not have the population of wildlife species that we would like to have. Is there something missing? If the situation looks perfect for the species, then you must ask, "Why aren't they there?" Wildlife is very good at finding and filling the proper niche for its existence.

Let's look at a few examples. In the days of the Soil Bank program, Dakota farmers put a lot of land into the bank, and much of that land was overgrown with uncut sweet clover. This lush growth provided near-perfect winter cover for ring-necked pheasants. The pheasant knew a good thing when she saw it, and the hens chose the sweet clover for nesting cover. In addition, the clover itself provided a lot of food for the seed-eating pheasants.

Farms that never had a pheasant on their acres before suddenly found themselves with thousands! Nobody turned loose any pheasants on those acres, the pheasants simply came to the improved conditions represented by the sweet clover.

The agricultural subsidy policies changed, and there was no profit in leaving land in the soil bank. The clover disappeared under the plow. It didn't take any genius to predict that the pheasants would also disappear from that land. The carrying capacity of a section of land that is plowed to the barbed wire on all four sides is almost zero for wildlife. It *is* zero for pheasants facing a northern winter. Now, noticing that the pheasants were gone, did the farmer turn loose some more pheasants to replace those that had disappeared?

Of course not.

Southern Arizona has some high plains that provided some of the world's best pasturelands at the turn of the century. But the lure of year-round pasture in warm climates lured too many livestock operators to bring too many cows and sheep to those lands. They overgrazed the land, causing damage that is not yet healed. Many of the native game species disappeared. For example, the masked bobwhite, common in those lands prior to the coming of the cloven-hooved livestock, disappeared.

They were thought extinct for several decades. Then seed stock was found in Old Mexico and the Patuxent Wildlife Research Center in Maryland produced thousands of masked bobwhites.

But turning loose those quail on their ancestral lands did little good. The tall grass that they favored for nesting cover was still absent. The only success the restocking program had was when the "turning loose" followed years of systematic efforts to improve the ground cover. After improving the grasslands habitat, the reintroduction was tried once again.

The first masked bobwhite quail restocked into southern Arizona were pen-raised birds, of course. They were quickly eaten by the raptors (hawks and owls that winter in southern Arizona) because they did not have innate caution bred into them.

Then a smart biologist thought up the idea of releasing the very young birds with a broody male Texas bobwhite that had been captured from the wild and caponized. The wary, wild-trapped male readily accepted parental duties and taught the young quail how to freeze when he sounded the alarm, how to run for cover when told to do so—in other words, how to live. It worked. And the male bobwhite could not hybridize with the wild population, because he was caponized.

To study a particular habitat and see if it is suited to the species you want, or to find out why it is not suited, you must start by recognizing that all species of wildlife require (1) water, (2) food, and (3) places to live. You will note that "places" is plural. Hardly any species can exist from generation to generation with only one place to live. A place to live may be a complicated thing. To sum up the arguments about replacing missing game with "turned loose" game, just remember the logical steps to take when facing a "missing species" situation. . . .

1. Find out what is missing. Is it food; water; or escape, nesting, or winter cover?

2. Provide that which is missing.

3. Wait for nature to provide the species you want. If the necessaries are all there, nature will usually fill the vacant niche.

4. If you still do not have the species population you want, check again to see what is missing and try to remedy it.

5. If you still wish to restock, try to get wild-trapped animals with which to stock. Pen-raised species are doubly handicapped, because they do not know how to exist in the wild.

6. When you "turn loose" game, do it the gentle way. Allow the game to walk free, or fly free, on its own timetable. Dumping causes panicky flight.

THE QUAIL FAMILY

The Western hemisphere can boast of ten species of quails, all of which were native to this land before Columbus and Company brought their European-style dog-and-pony show to the shores of the Caribbean Isles. Seven varieties are found in the United States.

1. mountain quail, *Oreortyx picta*
2. California quail, *Lophortyx californica*
3. Gambel's quail, *Lophortyx gambelii*
4. scaled quail, *Callipepla squamata*
5. harlequin quail, *Cyrtonyx montezumae,* also called Montezuma's, Mearns'
6. masked bobwhite quail, *Colinus virginianus ridgewayii*
7. bobwhite quail, *Colinus virginianus*

The fact that the bobwhite quail is listed last doesn't mean a thing. He is the bird that most people are referring to when they say "quail" or sometimes when they say "pa'tridge" or usually when they say "birds." The bobwhite is the bird most often pursued by gentlemen hunting the antebellum plantations over a brace of highly trained pointers. They are also the birds most often pursued by the high-school boy who is sneaking in a weekend morning hunt when he ought to be doing his chores. The bobwhite is the reason for existence of pointers and most setters. He is a cheerful companion on your land, and his whistled call gives him his name—"bob-bob-white" sometimes, sometimes just "bob-white," with the emphasis on the "white" end of the call. Let's look at the bobwhite quail.

Bobwhite Quail

He may be mighty and fabled in song and story, but the bobwhite is a small bird. Birds shot during hunting season

Male bobwhite quail. *U.S. Fish & Wildlife photo.*

vary in weight from a low of 5.7 ounces in both Texas and Florida, all the way up to huge bobwhite quail weighing 8.2 ounces in Massachusetts. These are averages, and the "farther north they're bigger" theory is borne out by the 6.5 ounces that is average for all of the country, with its smallest farthest south and its biggest farthest north.

Should you then buy birds from up north and turn them loose down in Florida? No! That's been tried, and in a generation or two the new strain weighs in at the same weight as the old (native) birds.

As further proof that quail are small birds, ponder this: It will usually take 5½ dressed quail to weigh in at 1 pound! That means that the dressed quail weighs in at under 3 ounces.

But we aren't interested in quail as a source of meat. We value them highly as a great game bird, the reason for countless enjoyable hours spent outdoors, a cheerful harbinger of spring, a destroyer of weeds and insects, and a fine neighbor on our lands.

Bobwhite quail are indigenous to the southeastern United States. To roughly define their "good" range, let's extend the Mason-Dixon line westward all the way to Plattsmouth, Nebraska, then drop that line south to Galveston, Texas. Everything southeast of that line is well within the range of the native bobwhite. But there are places within that range where the bobwhite does not find what he wants in habitat, climate, and food. So there are no bobs in those places. Also, outside of that southeastern states loop described above, there are many places where the bobwhite finds the climate, food, and habitat just what he wants, and he is found in those places. For example, he seems to be doing well in the Willamette Valley of Oregon but is not able to expand his range there.

What prevents the rest of the United States from being bobwhite quail country? Probably the most important limiting factor is the arid nature of the lands to the west of this favored loop. The quail requires water to drink. Dew on the grass helps, but the quail requires free water to drink at least part of the time. In addition, the hatchability of eggs is lowered when the humidity drops. During the time that the baby quail is using its egg tooth to peck a circle around the big end of the egg shell so that it can emerge into the world, it is important that the membrane remain soft and pliable. This "pipping" and pecking its way out of the shell may take the better part of a day. If it is exceptionally dry during that period, the membrane becomes hard and stiff when exposed to the air, and this greatly reduces hatchability.

Lack of humidity limits the bobwhites' expansion westward, and cold limits its expansion northward. Now, it is important to realize that the degree of this limitation caused by cold weather is dependent upon the availability of good winter cover and good winter food. Cold weather dooms the bob in an unprotected field, where drifting snow covers both food and cover. But the hardy little birds can prosper in below-zero weather if sufficient winter food and winter cover are available. For example, I've known bobwhite coveys to prosper during a sub-zero winter month in southern Minnesota when they had access to ample corn (above the snows) and to dense thickets of winter cover . . . cover so dense that there was less than an inch of snow on the ground beneath the branches, although 3 feet of the white stuff drifted hard over the exposed stubblefields.

The importance of winter climate is emphasized by the fact that the bobwhite quail was never native to North Dakota with its severe winters, but is found at just as high latitudes in Vermont, Massachusetts, and Maine, if good habitat exists for his use.

Wildlife management authority Durward L. Allen says, "Snow and ice are the most destructive climatic agents to the bobwhite quail on the northern edge of its range." We all agree on that, for we have seen bobwhite coveys the day before a severe storm and failed to see them ever again after the storm subsided. Some researchers say that snow and the simple act of flushing are a deadly combination to some bobs on the northern

edge of their range. It seems that when the bird flies, it causes snow to hit the inner feathers under the wing and to lodge there. Then, when the bird lands and folds its wings, that snow melts, causing a lowering of the body temperature. That slight lowering can be the final blow that takes life from the bobwhite.

On the southwestern edges of his natural range, the bobwhite quail often intermingles with the scaled and Gambel's quail, as well as inhabiting the same coverts with the Mearns'. Hybridization is very rare. Hybrids of almost every possible combination have been noted in captivity and occasionally in the wild. However, this hybridization is not the norm and is not prevalent enough to be statistically significant. In other words, it doesn't matter on those rare occasions when it does happen.

Nesting

Although some male bobwhites will start calling as early as mid-March, especially after a spell of unusually warm weather, the birds don't get serious until the last week in April in most areas. Like most gallinaceous males, the bobwhite quail rooster defends a territory. But it is hard to determine whether he is defending a calling site, a nesting territory, a feeding range territory, or only the area immediately around his chosen hen. The last idea, that he is defending only his hen and the territory around her, is most logical, for quail are definitely monogamous. Both sexes help to build the nest, which is usually started by scratching out a shallow, 5- or 6-inch-diameter bowl. Then the birds line this shallow bowl with dead grass and small leaves. Most bobwhite quail nests are near edges—the edge of a pond, the edge of a road or path, the edge of a forest plantation. They are seldom more than 60 feet from such an edge. The nest must be in grass that is easy for the nesting hen, and for her chicks, to walk through. In other words, it must be sparse vertical growth so that it can be parted easily. The eggs, usually between 12 and 15 of them, are usually deposited on a one-per-day laying schedule. Incubation doesn't start until the last egg is laid. Usual incubation period is twenty-three days. When the young hatch out, they are allowed a couple of hours to get their eyes accustomed to the bright light,

dried under the brooding hen, and then are ready to leave the nest, usually never to return.

Unless the hen is lost, the male doesn't incubate eggs (normally) but that doesn't mean he has forsaken his mate. If the hen is lost, the male bird may complete the incubation and rear the brood successfully. More often, he leaves the incubation to her while he remains nearby, and usually has a date with his mate when she leaves the nest to feed herself. They forage together, and then the gallant little cock escorts her part of the way back to the nest. They part at a distance from the

Bobwhite quail pair. *U.S. Fish & Wildlife photo.*

nest—probably an inherited trait to limit calling attention to the nest—and she returns to her nest, he to his dustbathing or just plain loitering. Inasmuch as the nest is usually roofed over with grass, by virtue of being built in the grass in the first place, the quail nest is very hard to find.

Mortality

At least 70 percent of all quail in a given population will die in any single year! Most females do not live long enough to breed! We cannot save birds from this year to hunt next year.

About two-thirds of all quail nests are failures! Terrestrial predators such as opossums, skunks, red and grey foxes, cotton rats, raccoons, weasels, mink, bobcat, several kinds of snakes, ground squirrels, and all types of tree squirrels relish quail eggs, and many nests are destroyed in this manner. Flooding due to unseasonable spring rains or to very heavy spring run-off ruins quail nests. Spring burning of the wrong kind can destroy many nests, along with improperly timed disking or harrowing or chopping of nesting cover areas.

This should not be interpreted to mean that only one-third of the nesting quail bring off broods. Far from it. Quail are eager renesters and will almost always try again if their nest is destroyed or the eggs are eaten. Sometimes, quail will try nesting for the third time if they lose their first two attempts. But average clutch size goes down and hatching percentage drops in later clutches. Renesting may be very important for other reasons, such as providing a second age class in the same year if the first age class is lost through climatic catastrophe.

The same group of terrestrial predators will eat young quail, and when the bobs are walking about they face other dangers from above. Cooper's, sharp-shinned, and marsh hawks; horned and barred owls; blue jays; crows; and even turkeys, both domestic and wild; all these will kill and eat the very small bobwhites.

By the end of the first hour after hatching, young bobwhite quail have been observed "freezing" upon hearing the signal from their parent. When they heed the signal "stop and don't move," they will instinctively hold their position even when approached very closely—sometimes even when picked up by man. This instinctive behavior serves them very well, for a small quail—immobile—is almost invisible on the usual forest floor litter.

The parents and their young form the normal covey, and they stick together until time for "covey splitting" in the early spring, when the young roosters start roaming off by themselves, leaving the covey. However, it must be remembered that coveys do a lot of shuffling about in the late fall and winter. If the covey gets too small, it will usually join another covey.

If food for the coming winter seems abundant, and if winter cover seems to be plentiful, the coveys will shift about much less than they will if they are instinctively hunting for better wintering sites.

It is also worthy of note that hunting serves to disperse the coveys and to increase the "shuffling" of birds between coveys.

One interesting reason for the formation of larger coveys is this. Bobwhite quail normally roost in a circle, or disk formation, with all heads pointing out and tails pointing inward to the center of the circle. Although the romantic notion is that this method of roosting allows the birds to move out of there faster when alarmed, the real reason is that this formation conserves body heat better than any other formation. Birds usually walk to their roosting site, although some coveys regularly fly to the roosting site. They usually roost on the ground but may use the horizontal branches of low vegetation.

History of Bobwhites

The bobwhite quail has been around a very long time. Believe it or not, they evolved from the flying reptiles—they still have teeth, in fact—way back in the Pliocene Age. The scientists named the fossil quail *Colinus,* which is an adaptation of the Nahuatl word for quail, which is *colin.* Their fossil remains have been identified in rock formations dated to one million years ago. The bobwhite quail was here when we got here, and we must do our part to make sure that the bobwhite is here after we are gone.

Pre-Columbian Indians did not feed heavily on the quail, for they wanted a bigger chunk of meat for their stewpots, and rabbits, deer, turkeys, and other sources of protein were deemed to be more worthy targets for Indian arrows. Early European settlers felt the same way, for flintlocks and early percussion guns were not suitable for killing the small, fast-flying quail. When the Indians ate quail, they trapped them, which is still true in the desert Southwest and in most of Mexico.

DeSoto was probably the first European to eat quail in this country. In 1557 he was presented a meal of bobwhites by the Indians in what is now Laurens County, Georgia. That's the first recorded quail dinner by Europeans, but I find it hard to believe that none of the settlers dined on quail in the years before 1557, when DeSoto freeloaded off the poor Indians. In any event, a very great number of quail dinners have been enjoyed in Laurens County from 1557 to the present day. Early settlers trapped bobwhite quail for food and for profit. In 1854, 12 tons of bobwhite quail were shipped from Beloit, Wisconsin, to eastern markets, according to freight billing records. In 1905 it was reported that a half a million bobs went to market from the famous Black Belt of Alabama and Mississippi. For the information of "nawthuners," the Black Belt is so named for the depth and fertility of its soil, not for its racial composition.

In fact, the European colonization of this continent did little to harm the bobs and a lot to help them. Primeval forest was not good quail habitat. As the forests were cleared and the fields cultivated, the bob took advantage of the great increase in edge habitat. He also took to cultivated grains and to the more easily accessible weed seeds that were available in great quantities around the family farm homestead.

Domestic poultry even scratched up some foods for quail, foods that would have been otherwise unavailable. Domestic livestock opened up several new vistas for quail food, from undigested seeds in cattle droppings to the development of feed crops for livestock. Quail also found these food plantings and profited from them.

But there is a point of diminishing returns in almost every operation. As the clearing of lands continued, it reached this point of diminishing returns for the bobwhite quail about 1850 in the south and about 1890 in the northern part of the quails' range.

The aristocrats of the Old South had already developed a worship cult for the bobwhite by that time, and they did not want to see anything limit the mushrooming growth of bobwhite populations. They decided that they could increase the population of bobs by buying more to turn loose. They bought them from Mexico starting in 1910, and until the Mexican government put a stop to the exportation in 1948, more than a quarter of a million quail were restocked into the United States from Mexico. Nobody followed up on these plantings to see if they were successful, because it was so logical that they would succeed. Logical but wrong. The subspecies *Colinus texanus* was the one they bought from Mexico. It was obviously not suited to the more humid coverts of the Deep South, because it was perfectly adapted to the drier parts of Mexico. In most informed opinions this was money wasted.

As deep forests gave way to a mixture of cultivated fields and lighter stands of timber, bobwhite quail increased greatly. When large tracts of timber were harvested, it was found that the bob increased on that area for about the next five years, then the changes were no longer profitable to quail. As cattle-watering devices such as windmills, water tanks, and stock dams with a reservoir of water opened the semiarid plains to cattle, the bobwhite gladly extended his range.

From 1492 until about 1940, the bobwhite quail flourished along with his nearest neighbor, man! It is now becoming increasingly more difficult for the neighborly quail to hold his own in the face of increasingly bad land use, increasingly heavy hunting, and deterio-

ration of habitat. Deterioration of habitat is the worst enemy of the quail, and that is something you can control on your land. "Clean" farming, where the land is plowed right up to the barbed wire on both sides, and then the wire is lifted and the land plowed under the barbed wire, is the worst enemy the quail ever had.

Quail Foods

Three-quarters of the quails' food is seeds and plant forms; the other quarter is insects. This holds true during the spring, summer, and fall quarters when insects are readily available. In winter, the seed proportion goes up to more than 90 percent.

In one of the earliest-known food studies, Margaret M. Nice estimated that one quail would eat 56,430 insects and 5,379,168 weed seeds in a year. These seemingly astronomical figures are still being borne out in modern-day studies, which find an individual quail eating more than 560 mosquitoes at a single meal or gulping down 168 grasshoppers to fill one tiny, but bulging, crop. Among favorite insect foods are the cotton boll weevil (hurray for our side), the chinch bugs, mosquitoes, grasshoppers, potato beetles, aphids, flies, slugs, crickets—none of which will win a popularity contest with us landowners.

Plant foods of greatest importance are different in each area, of course, but the cultivated crops leading the roll are corn, lespedeza, and millet. Sorghums are good quail food, but the kernels are soft and don't remain available long once they hit the ground. Before they hit the ground, blackbirds usually beat the quail to the harvest of sorghums.

Clean cultivation is often an enemy of

bobwhite quail, as it prevents the growth of weed crops between the rows, such as in tobacco and corn fields. Quail can be surprising in their choice of cultivated crops. For example, Bicolor lespedeza is excellent quail food, but clover seeds are seldom eaten by choice, and alfalfa is seldom utilized by quail.

Most of our information about quail food habits results from examination of the crops of birds taken during hunting season. This leaves us pretty much in the dark as to spring and summer foods. Hunting-season food habits studies in Alabama (a great quail state) showed that wild beans, beggarweeds, two kinds of partridge peas, greenleaves, loblolly pine seeds, milk peas, lespedeza, butterfly peas, and corn were the important items in quail crops.

In Oklahoma, another good quail state, similar studies listed ragweed, sunflower, acorns, sorghum, trailing wild bean, sweet gum, panic grass, Florida dogwood, nut rush, and oak as most important.

Another hunting season study, this time in Missouri, listed the five most important items as: lespedeza, corn, common ragweed, sorghum, and acorns.

Bobwhite quail like sprouted seeds and the first green leaves in the spring.

What Makes Good Quail Country?

There are few givens in this equation. There are a few generally accepted rules of thumb that are worthy of mention.

1. Bobs prefer habitat where the division between exposed ground and upright cover is about half and half.

2. Bobs cannot use matted ground cover. They cannot travel through it.

3. Open forest growth where sunlight reaches most of the ground below is good habitat; tall "canopied" forests are not.

4. Water must be available. Dew helps, but is not a total substitute for free water.

5. Best of all is the combination of one-third open or cultivated fields; one-third transitional area, nesting cover, and some food, easily traveled through; and one-third open canopy forest. It may be necessary to disk or chop the transitional area every three or four years; otherwise it will go through the climax succession, resulting in a mature forest of trees, which is not what we want in our transitional area. Prescribed burning can achieve the same result of keeping our transitional area in transition, but great care must be exercised in both the timing and the extent of prescribed burning. For if everything is burned, the quail population usually disappears with it. Unless you are experienced in controlled burning, it is a good idea to talk it over with your County Agricultural Extension Agent before you light that match.

Populations seem to expand during the periods when tenant farming leaves lots of edges, lots of weedy fields, lots of unfarmed corners. Populations disappear with the advent of agri-business with its large, "clean-cultivated" fields.

Bobs do better in a mixed woods and grasses environment than they do in a sylvan monoculture, such as row-planted trees intended for lumber.

Bobs do better when hardwoods are killed off, allowing sunlight to reach the ground where once everything was shaded.

Bobwhites do better where insecticides are not needed. This means that corn is a better crop than soybeans, from the point of view of a bobwhite quail.

Bobwhites do better where swamps are drained but where small water areas are still present than they did in the original swampy area.

Best Food and Cover Plants

There are many plants that provide both food and cover for bobwhite quail. These plants are: beautyberry, blackberry, dogwood, holly-gallberry, hawthorn, honeysuckle, roses, sassafras, sumac, viburnum, wild cherry, and wild grape. You know which plants will do best in your area, so choose accordingly. If you do not know which of these combination food and cover crops are suited to your area, talk to your County Agent again. He is supposed to know, and usually does.

Black locust provides food but little cover. The same is true of prickly pear cactus, a favored escape cover plant for Texas bobwhites, but not a source of food for quail. If your desires lean toward oaks, be sure to get the kinds of oaks that provide small acorns, not the golf-ball-sized ones that turkeys love but quail cannot eat whole. Multiflora, once considered the answer to all quail questions in some of our southern states, is now considered only as a very good cover plant—especially escape and loafing cover—but provides no food. Lopping off undesirable trees by cutting them almost through at waist height will provide a lot of good escape cover and loafing cover for the quail when waiting for cover plantings to mature.

Sericea is a good cover crop in the northern part of the quail range, and its seed is also a food of last choice for quail. It is good management to fence all food patches to keep livestock out. Remember that some food patches may produce plant by-products that are toxic to livestock.

Artificial Feeding

If lack of food is the limiting factor—and this is seldom true—you may want to go to supplemental feeding. Ground feeds are good, so are the wheats, oats, sorghums, and cracked corn. Food should be made available where the birds are not exposed to raptor predation while feeding. Put the feeder back in under the multiflora rose or in a thicket of some kind, not out in the open. It is also wise to keep the feeder away from domestic poultry. Remember that artificial feeding will localize your quail coveys—keep them anchored to one area when natural foods are scarce. This can work to your advantage if your aim is to keep the birds at home on your land. It can work against the quails if it exposes them to predation or if it furthers the spread of disease or parasites through crowding.

As a general rule, it is much smarter to plant food crops for quail than to provide artificial feeding.

How many quail can you expect to have in good habitat? What is a goal to be aimed for? Extremely favorable habitat in Missouri can be expected to have as many as one quail to every two acres. One quail per four acres is pretty darned good. And anything up to one quail per each twelve acres is considered huntable population.

Although the bobwhite quail occupies by far the greatest range in the United States of any quail species, it is also true that the desert southwest sports all six United States species of quail. The other five—after the bobwhite—are much less amenable to management than the adaptable little bob. Each of these five species is beautifully adapted to a particular type of habitat found in the Southwestern states of (western) Texas, New Mexico, Arizona, California, and Nevada.

Mountain Quail

The mountain quail looks very much like his close relative, the Gambel's quail.

However, the Gambel's has a topknot feather that bends forward and even curves downward at the front end, while the mountain quail sports a stiff, erect topknot. There are other, minor, differences in coloration, but the stiff topknot will serve to identify the mountain species.

Oreortyx picta is found on the Pacific slopes of the mountains from British Columbia all the way south to the southern end of the Baja California peninsula, and—because it has been introduced there—it is also found in Idaho and Nevada—at least temporarily.

Largest of all the United States quail, the mountain variety lays the fewest eggs, with a clutch size that averages about 8 eggs. With such a small clutch, the male evidently feels that each egg is worth a lot to the future of his race, for he shares the incubation duties with his mate.

The specialized habitat chosen by the mountain quail consists of very dense brush, high on the mountainside. His preferred foods are very different from those of other quail. He is not as dependent upon seeds, especially weed seeds, as the others are. He eats such things as acorns, as do other species, but he is also very fond of mushrooms, and he digs the bulbs of many plants to feed himself.

Another difference is that, in most environments, the mountain quail performs an annual migration. They breed and nest in the higher conifer country and then winter in the lower chapparal zones.

Because they prefer running to flying when danger approaches, the mountain quail has not been very popular with sport hunters who want a difficult flying target. But his large size and excellence on the dinner table has earned him a devoted following of scatter-gunners who have learned to appreciate the big fellow and who have studied the mountain quail's

habits well enough to know how to bag them with consistency.

Unless you own a very large piece of Pacific Coast territory, it is almost certain that your mountain quail will be with you only part of the year, because of their habit of migrating. If you want to do something to improve the lot of your birds, it may be difficult. However, as with almost all wildlife species, we can make sure that the three essentials—food, water, and cover—are available in the same small area. Take a careful look at your mountain quail habitat to see if something is missing. Are food plants located close to water supplies, or do they at least have good escape cover separating them? If not, the birds may be threatened by the necessity of traveling long distances without cover to reach food supplies or water. The absence of any of the three necessities will usually mean that the mountain quail are also absent.

If you have a goodly population of mountain quail, your best bet to increase that population is to control mortality—which will probably mean curtailing the hunting of the birds until the optimum population is reached. However, do not be overoptimistic or ask too much of the birds. Perhaps they are already at the optimum population level for the type of habitat offered by your property.

If curtailing mortality does not increase your population in two years, it is time to change tactics. Check with the State Game and Fish Department of your state as to what food and cover plants are best for the mountain quail *in your area,* and see if it is possible for you to increase the supply of those food and cover plants.

At the same time, or perhaps first, check on the availability of water for the birds. You may find that it is possible to increase the "inhabited range" of the birds by supplying water at different spots around your land. And make sure that water is *really* available. I have seen metal watering tanks that did not have anything for the birds to light upon inside the steel walls. The water level was too low to be reached by birds perching on the rim. There were no leaks. Here there were 10,000 gallons of water in sight and not a drop to drink.

A good-sized piece of lumber—big enough to float three or four birds if they alight upon it at the same time—floating in a metal tank will make the water available to the quail. Make sure that your float rides low enough in the water so that the birds can reach the water it is floating upon. Better yet, a leak will make a trickle of water available to the quail on the ground level—but most of us hate to see water wasted in the desert Southwest. One of the best systems for metal water tanks is a slanted walkway inside the tank, which allows the quail to reach the water no matter what the depth is. A perfect watering system is one which allows the birds to reach water without exposing themselves to their worst enemies, the Cooper's and sharp-shinned hawks.

Gambel's Quail

In appearance, this beautiful quail resembles the mountain variety, but he has a bouncy, curved-forward topknot instead of the stiff one sported by the mountain quail. This species has chosen the desert environment rather than the higher mountains, and because there is so much arid territory in the southwest, it has a very large range, which runs across Arizona and New Mexico into Texas and quite a bit farther north.

Like the mountain variety, the Gam-

bel's often roosts in the lower branches of trees and small shrubs. Brush is the important word for the Gambel's quail, and the brush types it prefers are mesquite, chamisa, catclaw, creosote bush, tamarisk, and the prickly pear cactus, which is important escape cover for so many species.

Unlike the mountain, the male Gambel's quail does not help with the incubation duties; like the bobwhite, he does help rear the young when they hatch out.

Life in the desert can be harsh, and the Gambel's quail, as well as the scaled quail, is very well adapted. Reproduction seems to depend upon the availability of green feed for the breeding adults and for the newly hatched young. Valgene Lehmann did some very interesting research into this phenomenon in Texas—not only for quail but for all species of wildlife—on the sprawling King Ranch in south Texas. He studied the vitamin content of foods available to wildlife and correlated it with their reproductive success.

The Gambel's quail is a realist. When chances for reproductive success seem very poor—as in a very dry year—they simply skip the effort entirely. They do not nest nor try to bring off a brood. Conversely, in a very good year, when it is apparent that there will be plenty of green food and the resultant insect food for the hatchlings, the Gambel's quail may even succeed in bringing off a second brood. In other words, the superbly adapted Gambel's makes the most of good conditions and shrugs his shoulders and sits it out when the chances are poor.

How to Help the Gambel's Quail

The one management practice that seems to hold out hope for increasing Gambel's quail populations is the reduction of grazing. Overgrazing has removed this beautiful bird over much of its range; controlled grazing can improve the nesting and escape cover and help increase populations. It would seem logical that an increase in watering areas would be beneficial, but it is not possible to find hard evidence that this is true. The bird is superbly adapted to its desert home.

Scaled Quail

This is the most widely distributed of the southwestern quail species, running from western Texas all the way to California, with a huge sweep of territory to the south in Mexico and ranging well up into southern Colorado, Utah, and Nevada. It has also been introduced into the state of Washington, with indifferent results.

A pale, silvery gray and buff-brown bird, it gets its name from the brown edging on breast feathers, which give it the appearance of wearing fishlike scales instead of feathers. Both sexes also sport a topknot of feathers, but the feature is much less evident than in the mountain or Gambel's quails. New Mexico is the proud possessor of the biggest population

See where the scaled quail gets its name? This one was photographed in New Mexico.

of any state in most years. Here the birds are often called cottontops.

Scaled quail populations fluctuate wildly, like the Gambel's with which it often shares the range. Like the Gambel's, it requires green stuff for successful reproduction. When that green stuff is not present—due to lack of spring rainfall—young birds of the year will be very scarce that fall.

Scaled quail are superbly adapted to the desert environment where they are found, and their worst enemy in the hundred years since intensive ranching came to the desert southwest has been the grazing of cattle. When desirable cover plants, such as atriplex, are heavily grazed, the population suffers—and sometimes disappears.

A good-sized quail, the scaled produces individuals that reach a half pound in weight. Like the other species, the scaled quail seems to be monogamous, but it is not known whether or not they mate for life. The male is quite a gentleman, as he shares the duties of incubation with his mate.

Populations of scaled quail normally contain more males than females, which ensures every young quail female a mate, even if she is the ugliest one on the mesa. The mated pair build their nest on the ground and do an excellent job of hiding it. Normal clutch size is somewhere between 9 and 16 eggs, with 13 being the most common number. Incubation takes from twenty-one to twenty-three days. Nesting success is very low, with probably three-quarters of all nests being destroyed or lost to natural catastrophe or predators. However, in a good year, the scaled quail will almost always renest. New Mexico biologists feel that a very large percentage of pairs succeed in

bringing off a brood before the season ends, despite the high percentage of nest destruction. Nesting may continue through the May-to-September season, resulting in a great disparity in age of young of the year. However, scaled quail do not bring off two broods in a year.

Scaled quail chicks are very precocious, following their parent closely from the first hour of their life outside the egg shell. They are able to find and get their own food after one day of life and evidently find lots of food, for they grow rapidly.

Coveys stay together until they are full-grown, then the common practice is for two or more coveys to merge, forming groups of as many as 100 birds. The largest grouping I ever saw was in extreme southwestern New Mexico in the first week of December. In a walk of less than one mile, I was constantly flushing scaled quail and estimated that I had seen at least 500 birds in that one mile. In that same territory, there were also large numbers of Gambel's quail. It is also worthy of note that that same territory had perhaps the greatest number of coyotes I had ever seen and heard in a small area. Evidently the coyote is not the limiting factor on scaled quail numbers.

Cottontops love to run and hate to fly when pursued by hunters, which does not endear them to the shotgunner. But if the hunter is successful in getting the covey to fly, it will spread out quite a bit and then the singles can be sought and flushed much more easily than the covey could be flushed.

Perhaps the most mobile of all quail species, the scaled may roam for as much as a mile from roosting spots during the day's feeding. Although they move about a lot, they are not to be considered migratory in any sense of the word. They walk long distances but almost always come back to the same roost area before darkness.

Like the Gambel's, with which it is often sympatric, the scaled quail just doesn't bother to try nesting in extremely dry years. As a result, one or more very dry springs can result in a terrific drop in the population. However, some pairs evidently succeed in bringing off a brood, for the population does not disappear. Remember that this species, like all quails, suffers a turnover of about 70 percent in its numbers every year!

It is obvious that the availability of green stuff and insect foods are the limiting factors when scaled quail reproduction is concerned.

Because they range over tremendous areas of land, and because it is difficult to hunt them, hunting pressure probably ranks pretty low on a list of mortality factors. Superbly adapted to its chosen home, the scaled quail will be with us for many years. It inhabits areas ranging from about 1,000 feet to 7,000 feet in elevation, wherever its particular cover is found. That cover is usually sparse vegetation, such as creosote bush, atriplex, sagebrush, cenisa, prickly pear cactus, and catclaw. In the southern part of its range we can add ocotillo, lecheguilla, tasajillo, and saguaro cactus. In the higher elevations, it ventures into the pinyon-juniper vegetation, but does not seem to prosper there.

Although it is perhaps the quail most suited to life in the desert, the scaled quail seem to prefer to live near water supplies. Hunters often take advantage of this fact by searching only that part of the scaled quails' range near windmills or stockwater dams.

How to Help the Scaled Quail

There is only one obvious thing that man can do to help the scaled quail—besides leaving them alone—and that is to provide water at widely separated points. This allows the quail to range farther afield and to spread out, thus reducing its losses to predation, parasites, and disease. But unless man learns to control the climate, there is really very little we can do to influence the populations of scaled quail. Overgrazing is their worst enemy—but few ranchers are willing to face up to the fact that they are overgrazing a piece of land.

California Quail

Also called valley quail, the California was originally found in the Pacific Coast states from southern Oregon to Baja California, hence its name of California quail. In Oregon its original range was only those counties that bordered both California and Nevada. Transplanting has increased its range until it is now found in almost every county in the state. The first settlers in present-day California found this bird in great numbers, far more than other quail. It seems to fill *suitable* habitat rapidly. It is now fairly well established in Washington, Idaho, and Nevada in addition to its historic range. It has been widely used in restocking, with considerable success in the western states.

This was the favorite bird for the market hunters in the early days, with as many as 177,366 being shipped out of California in 1895–1896 alone.

Although it prefers roosting in low tree branches rather than on the ground, the California species is quite similar to the Gambel's in many respects. It is unusual in that it has a very high reproductive potential. In good years, the male often rears the first clutch, while the hen lays and incubates a second clutch of eggs. Clutch size falls in the range of 12 to 15.

More so than the Gambel's or scaled, the California quail needs available water, especially for the growing young birds in their first two weeks after hatching.

After they are almost fully grown, the coveys will often merge into larger social groups in early winter. These coveys often reach 100 in number. Highly gregarious, the California quail doesn't seem to require a lot of individual space, and good cover can easily support a population as dense as two birds per acre.

Good habitat includes lots of food plants, of course, and favored foods are acorns, which they love, clovers, filarees, lupines, lotus, fiddleneck, and a hundred other sources of seed and insect meals.

How to Help the California Quail

Reduction of overgrazing, preservation of blocks of prime nesting habitat, provision of widely separated watering places, construction of gallinaceous guzzlers that provide water during extreme drought condition—these are helpful measures.

Harlequin Quail

Also called Montezuma's quail and Mearns' quail, the harlequin is the rarest of the desert southwestern quail. A very fast-flying bird, it holds well for a pointing dog, which is very unlike the Gambel's and scaled, and it is very good to eat.

Sounds like a prime candidate for the title of "best" southwestern quail, but there is one thing wrong with that scenario. The harlequin seems to prefer tall, dense understory habitat in the pine-oak woodlands, at considerable elevation. This touchiness about where it wants to live narrows the choice down so much that this elite bird is found only in a constantly shrinking habitat. Its prognosis in the United States is not good. Originally it was found over a very large part of the continent, ranging from southern Arizona and New Mexico, all the way down the tremendous length of Mexico to about the present city of Oaxaca. It is still found *in* that range, but the range is far from solid. Rather, it is made up of isolated pockets of harlequins found in suitable habitat only. The dense understory it prefers is hard to find in today's heavily grazed southwest. Since 1910, it has steadily declined in numbers.

Easily recognized, the harlequin seems to be a round, bowling-ball-shaped bird, with no apparent tail. The male wears a complicated pattern of black and white bars and carries white dots on its sides, which make it easy to recognize. They are monogamous; the male does not help with incubation; and they make a very elaborate nest, which is extremely difficult to find in the tall grass habitat they choose for their home. Clutch size is in the usual range, being described as 8 to 14 in number.

Their diet is unusual, and the bird has a very strong foot, suited to digging out the tubers that form a large part of their diet. The tuber of chufa flatsedge is especially sought after, and they dig it up from several inches under the surface of the ground. In addition, they eat almost every food taken by the other southwestern quail, when available.

Today's hunting regulations seldom allow for the harvest of harlequin quail, reflecting the fact that they are not abundant in any part of their range lying inside the borders of the United States.

How to Help the Harlequin Quail

Reduction of grazing pressure will assist this species, as will fencing off desirable nesting habitat from domestic cattle and sheep. Given good habitat, the harlequin quail seems very able to maintain its numbers.

Cooking Quail

Around our house it is considered sacrilegious to take the skin off a quail. The reason is very obvious; they are small birds and they tend to dry out quickly. The skin prevents drying out. However, I have to admit that one of my close hunting buddies simply "breasts out" the quail and makes some wonderful dishes with those chunks of quail. He is always treating us to another new marinade, and they are all good. Also, he prepares quail breasts in a thick, creamy gravy that is out of this world.

However, the best quail I ever ate in my life were cooked for me by Pilar, the fine cook in the restaurant at the Los Mochis Trailer Park, Los Mochis, Mexico. The hunting for quail and white-winged and mourning doves out of Los Mochis is amazingly good, year after year, and Pilar has had lots of practice.

Quail à la Pilar

Use six to eight whole birds, which have been carefully cleaned and washed, keeping the skin intact. The whole birds are cooked slowly in a tightly covered *tres pes,* which is the old three-footed dutch oven favored by outdoorsmen in Mexican climes. There is a half-inch of water in the bottom of the pan, and the quail are placed on their backs, so the breasts, in effect, steam their way to tenderness.

Next, when the breasts are tender to the fork, coat the breasts with a heavy layer of olive oil. Then sprinkle a tiny bit of garlic on each breast and put them under the broiler for a short minute and a half to brown the breasts. That's all there is to it.

Many people like to eat quail roasted with a strip of bacon laid across the breast. I do not. If I wanted bacon, I'd fry up some bacon. This time I want quail.

Roast Quail

Use six or eight birds, huddled together they don't dry out so much. Put a gob of butter inside each bird. Rub the outside with butter, salt liberally, then brown the birds in a hot frying pan, doing it quickly. Again smear the outside with butter and wrap them in heavy foil. Put the foil-wrapped birds in a 400°F oven for about 20 minutes or until tender. That's all. Variations on this theme include marinating the birds overnight in a mixture of olive oil, tarragon (about two teaspoons), and a bit of thyme, then cook as before.

Barbecued Quail

In her excellent *The Bounty of the Earth Cookbook,* Sylvia Bashline presents a recipe for barbecued quail that is right tasty.

6 *quail, with skins on*
¼ *cup chopped onion*
¼ *cup chopped green pepper*
¼ *cup butter*
¼ *cup water*
¼ *cup catsup*
½ *teaspoon dry mustard*
¼ *cup dry red wine*
½ *teaspoon salt*
  parsley sprigs
6 *tablespoons prepared barbecue*
  sauce

Split each quail in two. Sauté the onion and green pepper in the butter. Add liquids and seasonings and simmer for 10 minutes. Preheat oven to 450°F. Butter a shallow baking dish and arrange quail, skin side up, in the dish. Brush some butter on the quail and add a tablespoon of prepared barbecue sauce to each bird. Bake 25 minutes, basting with the sauce during the cooking. Serve on a heated platter, surrounding a bed of hot buttered rice. Ladle the pan juices over the rice. Serves three or four at Sylvia's house, only two or three at my house. I'm a heavy eater when it comes to game birds.

Broiled Quail

Quail can be broiled, deliciously, if you cut them in half and smear liberally with either olive oil or melted butter. If you use butter you have to keep repeating the basting; olive oil lasts a bit longer. Broil them quickly and eat them hot, with the juices bubbling out of the meat.

THE RING-NECKED PHEASANT

The Chinese ring-necked pheasant, introduced from far-off Asian coverts, is at times the most intelligent and at times the dumbest of all game birds.

In 1953, as an employee of the North Dakota Game and Fish Department, I worked with a pheasant-rearing program at Spiritwood Lake. We had approximately 5,000 young pheasants in big pens with 10-foot ceilings. A visitor to the game farm slammed the door of his car, which was not visible to the pheasants. Instantly, 5,000 young pheasants rocketed into the air, flying straight upward in panic. No less than 15 birds hung themselves by sticking their necks through the wire mesh and died there; another 200 scraped large patches of skin off their heads, fighting to get out through the wire. Many of those birds died. In that rearing and restocking program, we lost hundreds of young birds in an icy rain, although they were standing 5 feet from shelter that they used all day long. Too dumb to come in out of the rain?   .

About those same years, I was privileged to watch an adult rooster running along ahead of a line of hunters that sought to put him into the air so that he could be dropped with a shotgun blast. He had his long tail stretched out on the ground, his head only an inch above the frozen cornfield as he skulked along. The end of the cornfield was just ahead, and then his cover would disappear; he'd have nothing to do but take to wing. The rooster stopped beside a tumbleweed that had been blown up against a standing stalk of corn. Carefully he stretched his neck up alongside the cornstalk to take a good look at the line of oncoming hunters. Then he ducked his head down to the ground and wiggled his way in under the tumbleweed. Only the last two inches of his tail stuck out. Without moving a feather, he waited while the hunters came to the end of the cornfield. Two hens, illegal targets at that time, rocketed into the air and the hunters held their fire. "Damn!" said one hunter. "I would have sworn I saw at least one rooster in that field." Smart, huh?

Early settlers in eastern America stocked English pheasants into American coverts many times, but these attempts failed to get a foothold. Then the American consul in China, Judge Owen H. Denny, shipped pheasants from Asia and had them released in the Willamette Valley of Oregon. Judge Denny, I hope you have a star in your crown in heaven for that act, and even at this late date, I want to thank you, sir! You have given American hunters more pleasure than any other human being ever did.

The pheasant has been repeatedly stocked into every single one of the fifty states. In most cases, the stockings were wasted. But where he gets a foothold, the ringneck can explode in numbers. He reached his population highs during the days of the Soil Bank laws, which paid farmers for leaving farmland in sweet clover and other cover crops, which were left uncut. These plantings provided superb nesting cover and unparalleled escape cover. Those same patches of mature sweet clover provided snug winter

Chinese ringneck pheasant rooster. *South Dakota Game, Fish and Parks photo.*

homes for the ringnecks. In South Dakota, undeniably the top pheasant state, a small stocking in 1911 got a foothold, and the birds took off. In 1944, conservative estimates put the numbers of pheasants in South Dakota at sixteen million! Yes, South Dakota topped all pheasant states, and South Dakota never had a pheasant-rearing and stocking program.

During the same period (1913–1939), North Dakota had made several attempts to get the gaudy big game birds started in that state. No luck. Then, just before the onset of World War II, the roosters walked across the state line and became established in the southeastern corner of the state. North Dakota's pheasant stock came free of charge; it just walked into the state and homesteaded. A period of good weather allowed the Chinese ringneck to spread over almost all of the state, and when I came back to my home state of North Dakota at the end of World War II, the hunting opportunity was unbelievable.

In fact, home on leave a year before the end of the war, I brought along a case of 10-gauge shotgun shells—the only shotgun fodder I could find—from San Francisco. Borrowing an ancient 10-gauge double with big hammers, I walked out from my hometown of Jamestown and shot a limit of birds each and every day of the open season. I don't remember how many birds were allowed in the daily bag, but it was considerable. In fact, if the limit had been 100 per day, the average shotgunner would have had no trouble in filling out his limit in those days of shell shortages and pheasant plethoras. We often flushed as many as 100 pheasants at one time.

The ring-necked pheasant is an avid explorer and does a good job of spreading his range into new coverts. By trial and error through the first half of this century, the pheasant found out where he could live and where he could not. At the risk of oversimplification, it can be said that the ringneck lives where corn is grown, and certainly he reached his greatest numbers in the cornfield and brush habitats of a big arc stretching from western Pennsylvania and eastern Ontario, across the corn belt states of Illinois, Indiana, Wisconsin, Minnesota, Iowa, Nebraska, and the two Dakotas. However, the situation changes when you go west. The pheasant occupies good habitat in Idaho, Washington, Oregon, and California, and here his existence does not seem to be predicated upon the availability of corn. With this one difference, the pheasant of California and the pheasant of the glory years in the Dakotas, Iowa, and Nebraska are the same bird. Where the southern edge of good corn country meets the northern edge of milo maize and grain sorghum country, the pheasant marks out its southern limit. Why the pheasant does not take to the more southerly climes is still a mystery. New Mexico and Texas have populations of ringnecks, but the New Mexico ringneck is limited almost exclusively to river bottom habitats. For years I have felt that the absence of humidity during the incubation season limited the New Mexico pheasant. Commercial hatching operations have proved to us that eggs do not hatch well in a very dry environment. This makes sense in the desert and semiarid coverts of New Mexico and Arizona, but the argument goes all to pieces when you ask why the pheasant doesn't succeed in humid Louisiana or Mississippi or Georgia. Whatever the reason, the pheasant is a northerner to a far greater extent than the bobwhite quail is a southerner.

Tracing the ancestry of this game bird

would be impossible. He is part Chinese ringneck to be sure. But he also carries a strain of the black Mongolian pheasant, bits of English pheasant, even bits of Lady Amherst, Afghan whitewing, and other (even more) exotic pheasants. During the pen-raising period of North Dakota pheasant management, we experimented with the black Mongolian strain. These birds did not establish themselves for any appreciable period of time, but that is not to say that they did not add to the gene pool of the state's pheasants. We used the "quiet release" method of putting the fully grown pen-raised birds into the wild. We put the crates down near excellent escape cover just before nesting time in the spring and then we opened the back door of the crates and walked quietly away. While we watched, the birds slowly got the idea that the back door was open

and they meandered out to look at this brave new world. Because it was the height of the breeding season, we kept the cock birds separate from the hens. Under crate conditions the amorous males would claw all the feathers off the backs of the poor hens in their attempts to copulate. So it happened that we released a crate containing eight randy roosters who had been cooped up for at least eight hours enroute to the release point. One hundred yards away, two crates of just released hens were slowly adjusting to their newly found freedom.

We watched with binoculars from 200 yards away, anxious to count out the eight roosters and pick up the crates and head for home. Just as the first Mongolian rooster came out of the crate, a native pheasant hen came strolling along, pecking here and there, totally unaware of

The near-perfect gamebird, the Chinese ringneck pheasant, flushes from underfoot. *South Dakota Game, Fish and Parks photo.*

what was about to happen. What happened was that eight lusty roosters hit that poor hen all at once, and all eight bred that hen in quick succession. Then the eight roosters all crowed, shook their feathers and went walking away. The hen looked fearfully over her shoulder as she scurried away. I feel that those eight roosters probably made quite a contribution to the gene pool of pheasants in that county, even though the roosters themselves were not smart enough in the ways of the wild to survive through the next winter.

Such hybridization may be the key to the remarkable vigor of the ring-necked pheasant at the present time. Its reproductive potential is probably the highest of any game bird in the continental United States.

Strictly polygamous, the pheasant rooster gathers harems of hens during the breeding season. They come to him on his crowing territory for breeding. One rooster can fertilize as many as fifty hens, and they stay fertile for as long as forty days after copulation! Potent is the word for pheasant papas!

When standing at stud, the cock pheasant is a magnificent-looking bird. He postures and struts, showing off his very long tail feathers to their best advantage, and crows his raucous challenge to the world. This brassy call sounds to me like ''cohnk-cok'' with no interval at all between the ''cohnk'' and the shorter ''cok.'' The sound can be heard for miles on a quiet spring morning. The challenge is a sign that he is available, but even more, it is a sign to other roosters to stay out of his territory. If another cock challenges seriously—which is rare—the ensuing fight is something to behold. Using the hard spurs on the backs of their legs, the cocks

rowel each other unmercifully, pecking and pulling feathers with their beaks, swatting lustily with their wings. The fights can end in death, although this is very rare. When he's in a romantic mood in the springtime, the cock pheasant is very belligerent and has been known to chase away a curious house cat, swatting at the cat with his wings and even following it for 20 or 30 yards.

The rooster is perhaps the most brilliantly colored of all game birds, with an iridescent sheen to his feathers in many parts of his gaudy body. His head features iridescent green on top, bright red decorations around and under the yellow eye, more iridescent blue and green feathers on the neck, down to the starkly white collar that gives him his name. As if this were not enough color, the rooster's body is a coppery reddish brown, flecked with black and tans. On the rump, ahead of that 2-foot-long, stiff-feathered tail, there is a patch of greenish iridescence that reminds you of the peacock's coloration. The lower abdomen is often almost entirely black.

Much more drably colored, the hen is an overall tan, brown, buffy-cream coloration, which blends in perfectly with her surroundings, making her almost invisible on the nest.

Hens usually nest on the crowing territory of the rooster, but this is not a hard and fast rule. At times the pheasant hen rivals the Leghorn in egg production. The first eggs are laid anywhere the hen happens to be when the urge hits her. These ''accidental'' eggs are almost never incubated and are seldom fertile—which is amazing, considering the virility of the pheasant cock. At this stage of egg-laying, the hens often establish dump nests, where as many as seven different hens dump their excess egg production into a common nest—which is not incubated and does not hatch, naturally. But when she gets down to serious nesting, the pheasant lays a clutch of from 7 to 13 eggs, on average. Clutches as big as 23 eggs have been successfully hatched, however. The hen does all of the incubating; his Lordship is still off on the breeding grounds, crowing lustily and hoping for a late hen to show up. Twenty-three days after incubation starts, the precocial chicks pip their egg shells and come into the world, ready to follow their mother wherever she may walk.

One of the biggest causes of mortality occurs during the nesting period. Pheasants nest on the ground and they love to locate their nests in alfalfa fields. But the time for the first cutting of alfalfa is the same time the pheasant hen is in the latter stages of incubation and very reluctant to leave the nest. The mower bar comes slicing through her world and she hunkers down even lower, hoping to be passed by. But the mower bar doesn't pass anything by, it cuts the entire field. So she stands up to flush at the last second, and the mower bar cuts off her feet or legs. The hen often flies away, without feet and bleeding badly. Naturally, she is not able to return to the nest. This happens so often that it may actually be the largest single cause of pheasant mortality. In some years, in the Dakotas, Iowa, and Nebraska, mower mortality actually exceeded the hunter kill in some areas.

The pheasant chicks dine 100 percent on insects during the first part of their life, with grasshoppers being an important part of the diet. They follow the mother and learn the ways of the wild from her, which means that they slowly adapt their diet to become predominantly seed eaters. In midsummer and fall, both adults and young go on grasshopper binges at times, consuming unbelievable numbers of hoppers.

Unlike some other upland game birds, the ring-necked pheasant has no chance to bring off two broods in a summer. Consider the arithmetic. After serious egg-laying starts, the hen deposits an egg every day—let's say for fourteen days. Then she starts incubation, which lasts twenty-three days; that's thirty-seven days from start to hatching time. During the first two weeks of their life, the chicks badly need that mother. She broods them, protecting them from the cold rains, keeping them alive long enough for their protein-rich insect diet to give them strength. If she is required for only ten days, we have now kept her occupied for forty-seven days. Do that twice in one year? Not likely! When you see very small pheasant chicks late in the season, it means a second attempt at nesting after the first one failed. It does not mean a second successful brood.

The greatest population densities ever recorded in the annals of North American pheasant history occurred in Ontario and the two Dakotas. In other words, on the *northern* edge of their range.

Given good winter cover, the grain-eating pheasant has no fears of wintry blizzards. But without that cover, the ringneck population of an area can be completely eliminated by blizzards. It is not the cold temperatures that do the damage, but the blowing snow. Wind-driven snow enters the birds' feathers, is melted by the body heat, and lowers the body temperature. Wind-driven snow lodges in the partly opened beak and freezes there. More and more wind-driven snow adds to the mouthful, until the birds have difficulty in breathing, or even suffocate because their mouth is full of ice. If they are able to get out of the wind, or able to minimize its effects by sheltering in weedy cover, the ringneck can last out any blizzard without harm. A healthy, well-fed pheasant can go without food for more than three weeks! The birds are big and strong and can scratch their way down to food, if necessary. Their beaks are strong, enabling them to peck frozen corn from the cob or to pick their food loose from the frozen ground. Although grains, such as corn and wheat, are their preferred food, they will eat the seeds of almost all weeds and simply do not starve to death. Winter-killed birds didn't starve; they died from lowered body temperatures, which can be attributed directly to the lack of good cover.

During the Soil Bank years, when cover was abundant over the northern part of North Dakota, a good population of pheasants lived there. Now there are no pheasants in the northern part of North Dakota—except in a few isolated pockets of good cover. The loss of Soil Bank cover forced the pheasant to reduce its range, shrinking back from the northern edge. But it was not cold that took away those ringnecks; it was the lack of cover that would have allowed them to ride out the winter storms. There have been instances where as many as 300 dead pheasants were counted in a skimpy shelterbelt in North Dakota after a particularly bad blizzard. Half a mile away, 600 live pheasants greeted the new day in a healthy shelterbelt that bordered a tall stand of sweet clover. The same storm hadn't bothered them a bit.

Cover! It cannot be emphasized too

Swinging a shotgun on a ringneck rooster. *South Dakota Game, Fish and Parks photo.*

The importance of winter cover to the ringneck pheasant can not be overstated, as witness this crowded bit of woody cover. *South Dakota Game, Fish and Parks photo.*

strongly that cover is the key to pheasants. Nesting cover is important; winter cover is vital.

Alfalfa and oats are preferred nesting sites, being chosen in preference to weedy fencerows and lowland marshy vegetation. But the mower makes alfalfa a poor choice. Mower mortality can be greatly reduced, if *you* will make the effort by placing a horizontal bar across the front of the tractor, as far ahead of the mower blade as possible. Several 3-foot-long heavy chains are hung on this horizontal bar, extending to the ground. As the mowing operation starts, the chains flush nesting hen pheasants ahead of the deadly mower bar. Although it is not 100 percent successful, due to the devotion with which the hen sticks to her nest, it has been able to reduce nesting mortality to a great degree.

Provision for nesting cover is all-important, for the new crop must be saved if we are to continue to enjoy healthy pheasant populations. Sweet clover, left unmowed until about July 15, is the best

bet for nesting pheasants. If it can be left unmowed through the winter, it will serve a double purpose. It is one of the most successful winter covers when a big blizzard hits. It is a good idea to clothe the land with clover, because the pheasant has no chance on a landscape left naked to the winter.

Recognizing that the absence of winter cover was the limiting factor in pheasant production in North Dakota, that state's Game and Fish Department undertook a big program of planting woody cover in the very early 1950s. Their well-conceived program attempted to "build to" the existing shelterbelts that changed the landscape of the Dakotas in the 1930s. Originally conceived to stop soil erosion, the shelterbelts were a good beginning upon which pheasant winter cover might be built. Russian olive and other fast-growing woody shrubs and plants were planted in astronomical numbers. Research proved that the program did improve the lot of the ringneck. However, the cost proved too great for the small

At the height of the Soil Bank program, pheasants increased to almost unbelievable numbers in some areas. *South Dakota Game, Fish and Parks photo.*

population state to handle. Even in 1984, the beneficial aspects of this program can still be found by anyone taking a pheasant census.

Why is the pheasant the darling of most Game and Fish Departments within the pheasant range? Because pheasant management is so easy—easy to plan, not easy to carry out. Consider the fact that the roosters can easily be distinguished from the hens, which makes a "roosters only" season a practical regulation. Compare what would happen if the regulations said that we could shoot only male quail! Such a regulation would be impossible to enforce, naturally, but with the rooster pheasant it is hard to say that you made a mistake.

How many roosters can you safely allow the hunter to harvest? For practical purposes, you can shoot all of them. In

practice, it has proved impossible to shoot out a rooster population. The birds become very wary and elusive when hunted hard. The increasing difficulty of bagging a rooster makes hunting less attractive, and hunters stop pursuing the roosters.

Several states have researched this by hiring paid hunters to keep on after the roosters in a research sample area, trying to see if they can kill the roosters down to the point where they could not fertilize the hens the next spring. In every case, it proved impossible to harvest more than 75 percent of the available roosters, no matter how intensively they were hunted. In the most common results, it proved impossible to take even half of the available roosters.

Nebraska first recognized the value of this fact. They offered longer seasons than South Dakota, with more generous bag

During the lush years of the Soil Bank bonanza, ringnecks brought smiles to the faces of millions of hunters, demonstrating the effect of good habitat on a gamebird population. *South Dakota Game, Fish and Parks photo.*

limits, although no one would claim that Nebraska had as many pheasants as South Dakota. Nebraska recognized that their liberalized regulations would not harm the pheasant, so they used their generous regulations to entice the nonresident hunter who financed a large part of their wildlife management programs.

Unlike the wild turkey, the pheasant is easily stocked, easily pen-reared, easily wild-trapped. The pen-raised wild turkey never becomes completely wild. The pen-raised pheasant never becomes completely tamed or domesticated. Some good

can be expected to result from stocking even pen-raised birds in good coverts. Using wild-trapped birds, stocking success is assured in good habitats.

At home around man, the pheasant thrives in the intensively farmed lands— *if* winter cover is available to supplement nesting cover. Once again, *cover* is the key to pheasant abundance.

Add to the factors of easy sex differentiation, ease of stocking, high virility of males, and adaptability to human surroundings, the fact that the rooster pheasant can survive heavy hunting pressure and can live through the coldest winters (in good cover), and you begin to see why the ring-necked pheasant is very nearly perfect in the eyes of the wildlife administrator.

Of course, the ringneck provides another attraction . . . he is one of the best-tasting birds in the entire world. Totally without that flavor that some people call a "wild taste," the pheasant is great on the table.

Management for Pheasants

First, let's assume that you are within known pheasant range and that there are some pheasants in your area, but that you want more, or at least you want them on your land. You know that pheasants can become an economic liability in that they do eat a lot of corn and other grains, that they have been known to pull up sprouting corn to eat the tender morsel at the bottom, that they do occasionally peck their way into the occasional ripe tomato, that they got so numerous in South Dakota that some hardhearted farmers paid boys to find and "stomp" pheasant nests. You know that they will eat from your feedlot mangers when the winter snows cover their other foods. You are aware that they will not only peck with your chickens but will actually attempt to breed your chickens when the spring madness hits them? But you still want pheasants? I agree with you 100 percent.

Let's take a hard look at your farm or ranch and see what is missing from the equation that spells pheasant success. Let's check off the requirements:

1. Winter cover
2. Nesting cover
3. Escape cover
4. Grainfields available in close proximity to winter and escape cover.
5. Water, in the heat of summer. Snow will do all right in the winter.

If you have all of those needs, chances are that you already have pheasants. But you may want to improve the situation to have more pheasants.

Start with winter cover, because this is the limiting mortality factor throughout most of the pheasants' range. Provide uncut sweet clover patches, close to grainfields, close to water, close to nesting cover. If possible, provide travel lanes of tall grass (weeds are better) or clover, leading from one requirement to another.

If you can afford to leave a row or two of uncut corn standing, leave it on the outside edge of the field, where it will be easily available to birds in their winter cover.

If you can afford to provide large areas of good grass or clover cover for nesting purposes, it is recommended that you mow "hunting strips" through the very heavy cover, in order to help hunters get the birds into the air. After all, cropping your harvest is a part of management. Odd-shaped nesting cover parcels are much to be preferred over long, thin strips provided along the edges of your fields. A long, thin strip is a preferred travel way for skunks, foxes, badgers, coyotes, or any other carnivore you might have around. While the high reproductive potential of the pheasant is more than a match for predation under normal conditions, you may upset this balance by forcing the pheasant into nesting where predators are most apt to travel.

Delay mowing of prairie hay and alfalfa until well past the hatching time. Most farmers are well aware of what is going on on their land and can tell when the first pheasant broods show up. That is the time to make those first cuttings, not before, if you want to help pheasants.

Look far down the road that stretches ahead. Are your shelterbelt plantings or other woody cover getting to the over-mature stage? You should anticipate replacement plantings well before the need occurs, for it takes several years to produce even the fastest-growing woody plants. Look ahead, and plant replacements early.

If summer-fallowing land is a normal part of your crop management plan, please take the pheasant into account in planning that rotation. Plowed land offers very little to the pheasant, and it will help greatly if lands are summer-fallowed in a rotation that will allow the pheasant access to stubble every year. Waste grains are the insurance policy for the pheasant, the certain foods available in the last stages of winter when the need is greatest.

If standing corn is the winter food of first preference, check occasionally to see that the pheasants can reach the food and are making use of it. It might be necessary to "roll down" a bit of the standing corn to make it available to wintering birds. If possible, make this winter food available close to wintering cover. Every time the pheasant has to venture far from cover to feed, his danger is multiplied.

Speaking of dangers—what are they? Although we are quick to blame predators, they have never been significant on a statewide scale. Predation has always been with the pheasant, yet it has never defeated it. Foxes pick up and carry to their dens the inedible portions of pheasants that died of other causes, thus giving themselves a reputation they do not deserve. Great horned owls take a few

pheasants, but they hunt at night, and the pheasant roosts in dense cover—*if cover is available*—thus minimizing his exposure to the big owls.

Most of our pheasant losses are lost to machinery . . . the mower is probably number one, but the speeding auto racks up a terrific number of road-killed pheasants in any given year. In known pheasant territory, it is a good idea to keep a sharp lookout for flying pheasants. I saw one hit the front windshield (safety glass) of a car that was traveling about 70 miles an hour. The cock probably weighed 3½ pounds. Get out your slide rule and figure out the force of impact. Or better yet, look at the results. The windshield literally exploded and the rooster ended up, considerably the worse for wear, on the ledge behind the back seat. Luckily, that one hit on the passenger side. If it had exploded that glass in front of the driver, at 70 mph, there would have been little chance of staying on the road. Strangely enough, it is often the mother hen that is hit by the car, leaving the youngsters to fend for themselves. If they are less than fourteen days old, their chances are very poor.

Remember that management includes harvest of the crop. Do not be afraid that you might "overshoot" the flock if you adopt a roosters-only regulation. If you want to reduce the numbers of birds, you will have to shoot hens—just exactly the same as you must shoot does if you wish to reduce deer numbers.

Encourage the use of enough gun to do a good job on pheasants. To my mind, that means a 12-gauge, nothing less. Of course, a magnum 20 in the hands of an expert will do the job. For the average hunter, the 12 is not too much gun. The pheasant sports an unbelievably heavy coat of soft feathers, which soak up the impact of lead and allow the birds to fly on, even after sustaining direct hits with quite a few pellets. Worst of all, the wounded pheasant lands running, and no man can catch one on foot—a dog has a hard enough time. A wounded pheasant will hide very cleverly, and it takes the dog's nose to find it.

To my ears, the ringing challenge of a crowing pheasant is the finest harbinger of spring. To make it possible for the cock to crow in the springtime, we must provide cover in the winter time. Put simply, cover means ringnecks!

Cooking Pheasant

Any dish you can prepare using chicken will be even better with pheasant. At least, that's my opinion. In my earliest pheasant-eating days in North Dakota, we almost always dredged the pieces of pheasant in egg and then in flour, browned them in a frying pan, and then set the whole works to cooking very slowly in a covered pan. The results were some of the best eating I can ever remember. If a bit of sliced onion was sautéed in the pan first, it just helped a tiny bit more than somewhat.

If pheasant flesh has any problem at all, it is a tendency to dry out if cooked too long. Avoid that and you can hardly go wrong.

Here are a few recipes for those who want to do something a little fancier with this wonderful eating bird.

Pheasant in Cream

> *1 Pheasant, cut into serving-size pieces*
> *1 teaspoon monosodium glutamate*
> *¼ cup flour*
> *salt and pepper to taste*
> *1 teaspoon paprika*
> *¼ cup cooking oil*
> *1 small can mushroom bits and pieces*
> *1 small onion, chopped*
> *½ cup sour cream*

Dredge pheasant pieces in mixture of monosodium glutamate, flour, salt and pepper, and paprika, and set aside to dry. Heat the cooking oil in frying pan to about 360°F. Brown pheasant, using kitchen tongs to turn. Browning takes about 15 minutes. Transfer browned pieces to shallow casserole in a single layer. Brown mushrooms and onions and add to casserole, spreading evenly. Spread the sour cream evenly over the pheasant pieces and bake in a 325°F oven for about 45 minutes or until birds are tender to the fork. If you have a young bird, do not cover. If it is an old bird, cook covered for 40 minutes, then uncover to crisp the meat again. Add more cream to make sure that the bird does not dry out.

We mention different techniques for old and young pheasants. How to tell them apart? Well, the spur on the back of the leg, just above the foot, is white or gray on the end in a young bird, and you can dent it easily with the thumbnail. On a mature cock, the spur is shiny black and very stiff and hard; you cannot dent it with a fingernail. Also, the young roosters may still have some pin feathers; the adult bird will not.

Although pheasants have an amazing number of feathers, and plucking one is a long and laborious job, I prefer to cook pheasants with the skin on. This is important in order to avoid drying out. However, if you don't have time to pluck the bird, or if you intend to use only the legs and breasts, it is very easy to skin the bird. Simply rip the skin over the breastbone and peel it back to expose the entire white-meated breast. Using a sharp knife alongside the breast bone, slice down and under the breast, lifting it off the carcass. Then peel the skin off the very large legs and thighs, and break the joint where the leg hooks onto the back. You now have four pieces of pure meat, and you have wasted very little eating meat.

If you have skinned the pheasant and removed the breasts, you may wish to try these recipes.

Pheasant Kiev

> boned pheasant breast
> chunks of butter, 1/4 inch square
>   and 3 inches long
> flour
> equal portions of milk and egg,
>   beaten together
> cracker crumbs

Cut each boned breast in two. Score the outside of each piece with a sharp knife, and carefully pound the meat into patties about 1/2-inch thick. Place a stick of butter on each patty, season with pepper and parsley flakes, and roll up the patty. Coat it with flour, dip in milk-egg combination, and roll in cracker crumbs. Deep-fry in 350°F cooking oil until the pieces float. Good, friend, good!

Sweet and Sour Pheasant

> 3 pheasant breasts
> 3 tbsp. cooking oil
> 13 1/2 ounce can pineapple chunks
> 1 cup chicken broth

> 1/4 cup white vinegar
> 2 tbsp. soy sauce
> 1/4 cup brown sugar
> 3 tbsp. corn starch
> 1 large bell pepper, cut in
>   chunks
> 4 small tomatoes, cut up fine

Skin and bone the pheasant breasts, cut the meat into 1/2-inch strips. Cook pheasant in preheated oil in skillet over high heat. Stir often while cooking. Add syrup from pineapple, half of the chicken broth, vinegar, soy sauce, and brown sugar. Bring to boiling, combine corn starch and remaining chicken broth, and add this to the sauce while stirring. Cook until thickened. Add pineapple chunks, bell pepper, and tomatoes, and cook over low heat until heated through. Serve over chow mein noodles. Makes 4 to 6 servings, but two of us eat it all at our house.

Pheasant in Beer

> 1 pheasant, cut into serving
>   pieces
> 2 cans beer (any brand)
> 1/2 cup soy sauce
> 1 tbsp. sugar

Put cut-up pieces of pheasant in large pot; pour 1 can of the beer over the meat. Start drinking the other can, slowly. Add soy sauce and sugar. Boil briskly, uncovered, while continuing to sip the second can of beer. Watch carefully! When sauce starts to caramelize, turn the heat down low and turn the pheasant pieces to coat them with the syrup. Finish drinking the second can of beer. Approximate cooking time is 30 minutes.

All of the above recipes for cooking pheasant come from the South Dakota

Department of Game, Fish and Parks. If a South Dakotan doesn't know how to cook pheasant, nobody does.

Pheasant can be baked, broiled, barbecued, broasted, even boiled (sacrilegious, in my opinion). Pheasant can be fried, grilled, stewed, even shish-kebabed (although it has a tendency to dry out on a spit). Pheasants are wonderful eating. Look in your recipe book and try anything that can be tried with chicken. The only difference is that pheasant tastes better.

THE GROUSE FAMILY

In the contiguous forty-eight states, we have six species of the grouse family. Technically, we should also include the members of the ptarmigan family, but we see little chance of affecting their status through management procedures that can be applied by a landowner, so we'll just stick to the six more familiar, more widespread species.

Three of these species, the ruffed, blue, and spruce grouse, are forest dwellers. They are never found very far from trees.

The other three, the sage, pinnated, and sharp-tailed grouse, are ground-dwelling species who love the open prairies and sagebrush flats of our nation.

The sage grouse male—the mighty Cock of the Plains—is the biggest North American grouse. The female ruffed grouse is undoubtedly the smallest.

All grouse put on a fascinating display at mating time, but no two species perform alike.

The ruffed grouse occupies the largest range—the pinnated, probably the smallest range.

The Attwater's subspecies of pinnated grouse is probably in most danger of extermination; the ruffed is the most certain of a good future.

Sage grouse occupy a very specialized niche in nature's scheme of things, and evolution has taught us that specialization is dangerous.

In size they run from the big sage grouse; the not-quite-so-big blue grouse; the pinnates and sharptails, which are about equal in size; down to the spruce and ruffed grouse, which are the smallest of the six.

Let's meet the members of the grouse family—typically North American—one at a time.

Ruffed Grouse

In New England they call ruffed grouse "patridges" or just "pats." Early settlers called them fool grouse and were able to kill a brace with a stick or a thrown stone. That was in colonial times. The only foolish grouse I ever met were in the Val d'Or region of northern Quebec, where they seldom saw a hunter. I walked into a cover that had a ruff behind every bush and they all sat and looked at me with a stupid expression, or even walked closer to me, coerced by curiosity. I shot a trio, the only ones I was able to force into flight—forcing them to fly far enough away so that a load of chilled sixes wouldn't mangle the meat.

They tasted good, but that was their only resemblance to the lordly ruffed grouse I knew from hunting trips in the lower forty-eight.

The hunt I shall never forget was in the Pembina Hills of North Dakota, right up against the Canadian border. There was a skift of snow on the ground, the wind was cutting cold, but the sun shone brightly. There were plenty of grouse, and we hunted them over a Weimaraner

Attwater's prairie chicken on the dancing ground in Texas.

who seemed to have mastered the style of the ruff. It was late in the season, and the birds were skilled at flushing from behind a dense clump of brush, at dodging behind a heavy tree trunk the same split millisecond you squeezed the trigger, and other escape tricks well-known to the family of hard-hunted ruffs. At the end of six hours of good dog work, and after firing about thirteen shots each, two of us had our limit of three ruffed grouse. I well remember that day's sport and I also remember the delightful flavor of those birds. They'd been feeding on frozen highbush cranberries for about two months.

The naive birds of Northern Quebec and the postgraduate grouse of the Pembina Hills had a lot in common, for they were the same species. But that's where the similarity ended. Their different reactions to human intrusion pointed up the obvious—which is that ruffed grouse learn quickly. Where they are hunted hard, they are a supreme test for the scatter-gunner on an October afternoon, wily, artful, and slick. A wing shot who hits nine out of ten pheasants and seven out of ten quail will find himself scoring about four out of ten on hard-hunted grouse.

Not that they are fast fliers, for they are not. But they are expert at using the cover to effect their getaway. Most charges of shot end up in the trunks of trees, which the artful dodger has just put between he and thee at the exact moment you pulled the trigger. His flight is noisy—unless it suits his purpose to be quiet—then he can glide through the woods without a sound. In noisy flight, his short wings beat very rapidly, and the extra large tail allows him to dodge and maneuver in surprising fashion.

He's an expert aerial acrobat in his favorite woods, but a weak flier over any distance. He seldom flies more than a few hundred yards, and a sustained flight of a mile or more is beyond his capabilities, according to most authorities.

The ruffed grouse today occupies the largest range of any native North American game bird, stretching from Georgia northward through Quebec and westward across "forested" Canada all the way into the Yukon and on into Alaska. He calls British Columbia home and is found down the backbone of the Rockies into the northern half of Wyoming. A bird of the forests, his range extends down only to the northernmost fringe of North

Prime ruffed-grouse country, a road lane between stands of mixed conifers and hardwoods. *U.S. Forest Service photo.*

Dakota, but he has a big chunk of Minnesota in his domain. He is native to all of the United States except the desert Southwest and is also found in almost all of forested Canada.

The males outweigh females by a little bit, but even the heaviest macho male seldom tops 1½ pounds. About 19 inches total length from tip of tail to tip of beak, and about a 23-inch wingspread—that's about the size of the ruffed grouse.

Dark brown sprinkled with white and brown on the topside, white with horizontal brown and black bars on the underside, the ruffs—both male and female—sport a "ruff" of extra-long feathers on the neck. During courtship, the male

displays this ruff fully erected, with much head shaking and pirouetting to call it to your attention. Male birds have longer tail feathers than do females. In addition, the male sports a dark brown *unbroken* band across the end of his tail. That same band is broken in the middle in the case of the female.

All grouse put on an interesting courtship display, but that of the ruff is perhaps the classiest. The male bird selects a drumming spot—usually a 20- to 28-inch log that is downed. Positioning himself atop this log, he flattens his stiff tail feathers down against the wood to brace himself, gives his head a few preliminary shakes and then starts to flap his wings

Male ruffed grouse getting ready to start drumming.
Ed Bry, North Dakota Game and Fish photo.

went off and the grouse was caught in the act. Ed has considerably refined his techniques since those early attempts, but drumming grouse photographs still require a lot of woods skill and patience.

The purpose of the drumming is to announce to the world in general and to any receptive hens in particular, that he, the drummer, is claiming ruffed grouse rights to this particular piece of grouse woods, that he is interested in sex, and that he is, indeed, a very impressive fellow. At this stage of the proceedings, males will fight for drumming territories, and the fights are for real, not just a ritualistic display.

Breeding males also strut, turkey gobbler-wise, with ruff stiffly extended, with curved wings brushing sibilantly against the ground, with much shaking of heads and dancing about, regally prancing for all the world to see. The bragging male seems to lose all fear at this stage and will often attack a human who comes close to his dancing ground, although the majority of times he will slip silently away to live and strut another day.

Most ruffed grouse drumming takes place in the magic hour that straddles sunrise and again at the sunset hour. However, at the peak of the season, drumming can often be heard at every hour of the night and day.

The hens shrug off this display with an indifference that is almost convincing. They try to give the impression that they don't even notice. But when a hen comes into the well-defined (to a grouse) courtship area, the strutting male immediately becomes a solicitous suitor. He follows meekly behind the female at times, at other times he turns on her and puts on a ferocious display that seems ill-suited to a grouse marriage proposal.

as rapidly as he can. The wings moving through the air create a booming sound, which sounds for all the world like a heavy engine starting up. The "whoom, whooms" come closer and closer together until the sound melds into a steady thunder. It is amazing how much noise can come from such a small bird.

Ed Bry, well-known wildlife photographer of the North Dakota Game and Fish Department, has captured this unusual courtship display in pictures probably better than any other photographer. His earliest attempts used a flash gun attached to an ancient Graphic camera, and the shutter release triggered by a line wound out from a fishing reel. With his camera prefocused on the precise drumming spot, Ed would climb into his sleeping bag and prepare to spend the night in the icy woods of early spring. When he heard the drumming, he took up the slack and struck with the rod tip. The flash gun

This sequence shows how the ruffed grouse produces the drumming sound. *Ed Bry, North Dakota Game and Fish photo.*

Whatever the system, it works well. Grouse are monogamous, and mated pairs stay together throughout the breeding season. The hen lays an average of 11 eggs, in a very well concealed nest. Their eggs seem much more able to withstand cold rain and freezing temperatures than the eggs of any other gallinaceous bird. The hen does all of the incubating, and for twenty-four days she is really bound to the nest, leaving it only for a very short period after dawn and again in the late afternoon. During those times, she hurries to feed, eats her fill, and gets back on the nest as fast as she can.

Young ruffed grouse are very precocial, leaving the nest to follow the hen within a couple of hours of their hatching. They seem to understand the soft, clucking commands of the mother grouse right away, and learn to stay very close. If one strays away, he is condemned to death, for his mother cannot count, nor will she go searching for lost young'uns.

At the hen's command, the youngsters learn to flatten themselves against the forest litter and stay perfectly still. This defense mechanism is singularly effective, because protective coloration makes the immobile young almost invisible.

In a good year, about 60 percent of all ruffed grouse eggs will hatch. When the nest is destroyed, *some* grouse will renest, although the second clutch will be smaller, with a lower percentage of fertile eggs and reduced hatching success. Third attempts are very rare, if they exist at all.

This is a period of high mortality for the ruffs. Cold rains cause heavy losses, both directly and by eliminating the supply of insects that provide the high protein for rapid growth. Almost every predator in the woods takes a toll of the young grouse when they are smaller than tennis balls. But they don't stay small very long, for the world they hatch out into is filled with luscious small insects to be chased down, picked up, and eaten. When two weeks old, they can fly weakly and are extremely agile.

By late September, the ruffed grouse brood is breaking up in spectacular fashion. Nature has designed a unique mechanism for "shuffling the deck" of young ruffs, making them move from their home range and become acquainted with future mates from different broods. This mechanism is called the "Crazy Flight," and it happens every fall. The birds of the year, moved by some inner compulsion, take off in a flight that can only be described as "unsupervised." They fly into the sides of cars and houses, and large plate glass windows take a heavy toll at times. When this crazy flight is over, the brood will never be reunited, and the birds will be shuffled throughout the grouse woods, in position to find their own mates. Whatever the explanation of the crazy flight, it does a good job of preventing line inbreeding in the grouse families.

The food of the ruffed grouse is amazingly varied through most of the year, but in winter it becomes almost a "single source" proposition. All berries, small acorns, fruits, apples, buds, rose hips, and cranberries are utilized as they become available through the year, supplemented always with tremendous quantities of insects. But when winter snows blanket the normal food supplies and insects are all dormant and unavailable, the ruffed grouse turns to its winter survival rations, the buds of the aspen, or poplar tree. These buds are always available, no matter how deep the snows may become, and the ruffed grouse's dependence upon poplar buds explains why the presence of these trees is the one constant in the grouse equation. Without poplars, there would be no ruffed grouse.

Therefore, perfect ruffed grouse habitat must start with the presence of aspen. After that first requirement, we can find a tremendous variety in grouse country. Abandoned farmsteads are favored in New England, and volunteer seed supplies that arise near old barns and other buildings are a favored food. Add small-acorn oaks, blackberries, thornapples, cranberries, blueberries, and a thousand grassy plant seeds, and you know what the ruff needs. To set up a paradise for ruffed grouse, we would have small—one- or two-acre—food plots interspersed with ten-acre chunks of conifers and aspens, preferably aspens which are cut over one fourth of their range every ten years. Uneven stands of timber are perfect for grouse, which means that the farm woodlot designed for fuelwood production is a good place to find the grouse.

Winter holds few terrors for the ruff. His winter staple food is high above snow drifts and always plentiful. When the ambient temperature gets too low to suit him, he simply builds an igloo. Like the Eskimo, he has learned that snow has wonderful insulating qualities. The grouse actually pitches head first into soft snow, burrows and pushes and shoves his way down deeper into the drifted snow, and then waits out the blizzard in a burrow which is often forty or even fifty degrees warmer than the outside air. It would seem that the birds would be in great danger from predation at this time, but such is not the case. The few birds taken by the opportunistic fox, coyote, or bobcat, are more than offset by the number of birds that make it through the blizzard in this

way. The storm they evade is much more of a peril than the predator who might find them. Having a "snowed-in" grouse erupt out of the snow at your feet is one of the biggest surprises of the winter northwoods. Once experienced, it will not soon be forgotten.

Cyclic changes in population are noteworthy in the ruffed grouse life history. These are of two kinds—the annual and the boom-and-bust cycle. It is impossible to stockpile any game species, but this is even more true of the ruffed grouse. Mortality factors will cause a loss of 70 percent of the flock between October 1 and next spring's drumming season. It has been proved by research that the mortality chalked up to human hunters only substitutes for the natural mortality of the winter months. If you don't shoot them, they'll be lost to another mortality factor, and in either case they won't be there at drumming time.

"One year there were grouse in every bush—the next year, we couldn't find a bird!" That's the boom-and-bust cycle in operation. For reasons we do not even pretend to understand, the total population of a huge area of grouse country will suddenly collapse, and it will be difficult to find even a single bird. For two or three years, birds will be scarce—although food and cover are everywhere. Then the population begins to build again and for four or five years, we have more and more grouse. Then . . . boom! The population disappears again. We have seen such cyclic collapses start in Nova Scotia and spread westward all the way across the continent. At other times, the various regional cycles seem to operate independently and without correlation one to the other.

There is only one lesson in this cyclic

business—when the grouse are there, it will pay you to hunt them, for they are going to disappear whether you hunt or do not hunt.

The ruffed grouse, *Bonasa umbellus*, is one of the hardiest, most adaptable, sportiest birds ever to dodge a shot charge. He can live anywhere that his beloved winter food is available atop the aspens. He doesn't like to be too close to humans, for he has learned that long life is not compatible with human companionship. He prefers "dirty" farming, which is a misnomer for the preferred method of cultivating land—a way in which all wildlife gets a chance to live rather than only man. He doesn't seem to want any of man's crops—unless you can blame him for taking up residence in a farmstead after man moved out. The ruff probably looks at an abandoned farmstead and says to himself, "Well, humans didn't do too well on that hardscrabble piece of hilly land, but I think I'll do just fine."

And if we leave him alone, he usually does.

But if you want to give him a helping hand, take a good look at your forested lands. Can you do any of these things to improve the land for grouse?

1. Cut down tall, mature trees that form a canopy and shade out more desirable grouse plants?
2. Cut your aspens in an "uneven" schedule, so that there are always poplar buds at every stage of development?
3. Provide dense pine clusters amid immature hardwoods?
4. Provide wild crab and hawthorn trees?
5. Increase grapevines, greenbriers, small conifers, or thornapples?

6. Increase the supply of small acorns?
7. Add juneberries or witch hazel?
8. Increase the "edge effect?"

If you can do any of these things, Ol' Ruff will appreciate it.

Blue Grouse

The scientist calls him *Dendragapus obscurus,* which gives credit to the shadowy places in the high mountains this hardy bird calls home. He is called by many names, such as hooter, pine chicken, pine grouse, even dummy grouse.

The blue grouse lives in some of the most beautiful country on the face of the earth, the great open spaces and coniferous forests between 5,000 and 12,000 feet above sea level. The destiny of the blue is tied to the Douglas fir tree, almost to the same extent that the ruffed grouse is tied to the poplar. But not quite—the blue has learned how to get along without the Douglas fir in some of the Rocky Mountains and some of the northern California parts of its range. However, there is a big difference. The ruffed grouse absolutely must have the poplar tree, for its buds are the sole winter food of the ruff. The blue grouse does not depend upon the Douglas fir for food; it is simply a case of both the tree and the bird being well suited to the same beautiful mountainside.

Its overall range extends from southeastern Alaska, across southern Yukon and into Alberta, then follows the Coastal range of mountains southward into northern California. Its range also follows the tops of the Rockies southward to New Mexico, where it is an important part of the game bird scene.

Largest of all the U.S. forest grouse, and second in size only to the sage grouse overall, the blue has no fears of winter weather. In fact, it breeds at lower elevations, then slowly works its way upward until it winters at the very highest elevations. In some parts of Colorado, that means a seasonal elevation migration from 5,000 feet upward to 10,000 feet when the wintry winds blow.

Both sexes sport slate-gray upper bodies mottled with brown and black, and white markings on the flanks and breast. Both sexes have long, square-ended tails, which are not barred. The males have colored eye combs—wattlelike patches of skin above the eyes—which become prominent in courtship display. These eye combs vary in color with the family, or subspecies, the bird belongs to. Some are yellow, almost orange in breeding excitement, while others are purplish.

Preferred habitat is the grassy parks and open spaces between deep coniferous forests and aspen patches. If that habitat also contains snowberry, bromegrass, and vetch, as well as a few water seeps or springs, it is blue grouse heaven. Adult birds will drink from springs or creeks when free water is available, but the bird doesn't seem to be limited by the availability of water—except when the hen is brooding a very young brood. Then she is seldom found more than half a mile from water.

The food of the blue grouse is heavily plants, with insects being taken only by newly hatched birds for the first three weeks of their lives. Young birds are very precocious, and usually leave their mother to go it on their own after seven days! Such early splitting up of the family group is a sign of things to come, for the blue grouse spends most of its life in solitary splendor.

Year around, the food of the blue grouse is 63.8 percent conifer needles, 17 percent berries, 17.2 percent miscellaneous plant materials, and only 1.7 percent animal matter. In areas where the Douglas fir is prominent, that tree's needles furnish 100 percent of its winter food! The white fir is a preferred roosting species of tree, and its needles are also eaten, as are all firs, hemlock, and Ponderosa pine.

I have opened the crops of blue grouse taken during an early September hunting season in New Mexico and found rose hips, dandelion heads, and wild currants, mixed with a goodly amount of pine needles.

Obviously, the food requirement is not the limiting factor in blue grouse population economics, for its favorite foods are always available. Why then, are we not up to our proverbial hip pockets in blue grouse?

The loss of cocky young birds, old enough to feed by themselves and anxious to get out from Mom's apron strings, is very great. Cold storms—in a high country where it can snow any day of the year—take a toll of inexperienced young birds. Predation by coyotes, foxes, raccoons, Cooper's hawks, sharp-shinned hawks, and goshawks is heavy. Nest destruction by snakes, crows, ravens, and skunks increases mortality. There are good years for reproduction and there are bad years, and we really don't know much about the reasons for this. The blue grouse population fluctuates wildly, yet we do not classify the population dynamics of the blue grouse as being cyclic. It is not that predictable.

When springlike temperatures turn the young grouse's fancy to thoughts of love, the males strut to their "hooting" posts. Only the oldest males seem to do the breeding, with younger males hooting their hearts out on territories around the periphery of the mating area.

"Hooting" is a collective term for the sound and visual display of the courtship season. Males return to the same hooting positions each year. Once in place, they proclaim their territoriality and also proclaim their masculine availability by making a hooting sound with their throat and a small gular pouch—small, at least, in comparison with the sage grouse. At the same time, they put on a display of their masculinity, wings curved and stiffly held out from the body in turkey-gobbler style, tail spread and held stiffly in a fan-like position, head thrust skyward with a series of jerky thrusts, gular pouch displayed, and white feathers rimming the pouch held stiffly erect. While maintaining this posture, the cock bird makes a series of intimidating rushes straight ahead, as if to frighten off an unseen rival.

In some parts of the range, the blue grouse cock may even add some flight displays to his repertoire, leaping upward and dropping back to the ground in a manner designed to attract attention from any female in the area.

While all this is going on, the female approaches the strutting lord and master and demonstrates her submissiveness by compressing her feathers tightly against her body, so as to appear as small as possible while he is being as big as possible. She enters his boudoir and copulation takes place.

The hen makes a typical "grouse-type" nest, well hidden, and lays an average 6 to 7 eggs therein. Incubation seems to be twenty-six days, and the eggs all hatch at once. The chicks follow the hen away from the nest that same day, never to return. A week later, they are on their own, living the solitary life in the most beautiful country in the world.

Young birds of the year are definitely not wary. They often demonstrate how they got the name of dummy, or fool hen, by holding very close for the hunter, allowing him to approach within arm's length, before taking flight—flying 50 feet to a branch at head height for a man and perching there while they inspect this curious newcomer into their realm.

The bird that has overwintered in the high country, however, is a different matter entirely. That adult is suspicious and wary, flushes well ahead of the hunter, and takes off in a long, curving glide down the mountainside to alight a quarter of a mile away.

The disparity in savvy between young and old works with another disparity—young birds are delicious; old birds are apt to be strong-tasting from that insufferable diet of pine needles, so if you go for the sporty birds, you get poor eating. If you go for the good eating, you bag inexperienced youngsters which are hardly a challenge for the shotgunner.

I solve that problem by going to the high country for a wonderful day of communing with nature at its best, and if I happen to bag three young grouse for a very delicious dinner, I figure that as an added dividend from a day well spent.

Most authorities say that there is little in the way of management that will affect the birds' numbers in years to come. There is no shortage of food, so we don't need to supplement their diet. Predation has never appeared to be the limiting factor with blue grouse populations, so we need not work in that area to help the grouse. Winter cover seems to be ample, with the birds well versed in the intricacies of staying alive under the thick branches of a big conifer, up against the trunk out of the wind, clothed in a feathered, insulated suit.

Unless you own a very large piece of real estate in the mountain area, there is small chance that you will own both the summer and winter range of the blue grouse individual. This further reduces the chances that you can do anything to help the blue grouse.

Hey, I've got an idea! Let's leave them strictly alone, except in hunting season. Then, we'll harvest a few succulent young birds, walk a few miles at 8,000 feet, and enjoy the beauty all around us. The blue has gotten along for millennia without our manipulations in his behalf. Maybe he can make it a few more years if we molest him only at harvesttime.

Spruce Grouse

This little grouse, tied with the ruffed as the smallest of the North American grouse, is a brightly marked little dandy. Expert at surviving in the northern winter, a dramatic actor in courtship time, he has much to recommend him to the lover of wildlife. One thing is wrong. . . .

Because of his diet of strong-tasting conifer needles throughout most of the year, the spruce grouse is inedible by our standards. The very first one I ever saw was while hunting ruffed grouse in Quebec. I had dropped a ruffed grouse and was walking directly to it to retrieve the bird, afraid to take my eye off the spot where it fell because they are notoriously hard to locate on the forest floor. Just as I saw the bird lying against a pine log, another grouse rocketed out of the brush just behind me. Instinctively I pivoted, aimed, and fired—and in the split millisecond of firing, I noticed a strange bit of white on the target. It was the brightly marked black and white of the spruce grouse.

Although I knew of their reputation—or lack of it—on the dinner table, I prepared the spruce grouse exactly as I did the ruffed grouse, and, in fact, I couldn't tell which was which as I presented the "oven-ready" birds to the cook. I was served the whole spruce grouse, and I took one experimental bite. I chewed it, tasted it, and got rid of it. I've never killed another spruce grouse.

His scientific name is *Dendragapus canadensis,* which can be translated as "tree-loving Canadian." And that is a good description. His range extends from central Alaska across Canada below the tree line all the way to lovely Cape Breton Island, Nova Scotia. The southern extremities of his range lie in the northern edges of New York, New Hampshire, Maine, and Vermont.

In addition, there is a subspecies called Franklin's (*C. franklinii*) that inhabits the tops of the Rockies, all the way down into Idaho, Montana, and into the Yellowstone Park area of Wyoming. As his scientific name indicates, he is a forest dweller and is never found very far from conifers. Historically, his range probably extended much farther down into the contiguous forty-eight states. However, this is a very trusting, unwary bird, and he was undoubtedly killed off by man—even though man scorns him as an entree.

Male and female differ greatly in coloration. The male is an overall black and gray topside, is barred on his breast with solid white and black, and has a black abdomen. The female is mostly barred on head and underparts, with black, gray, and buff; the sides are ocherous, and the underparts mostly creamy white. Both sexes have legs that are feathered to the toes, a particularly good adaptation to the northern climate. Although the color dif-

Dorsal side of a spruce grouse, from Quebec. Markings are easy to identify.

ference ensures that you don't confuse ruffed with spruce grouse, there is another big difference—the spruce has a much shorter tail than the ruffed grouse.

The preferred habitat of the spruce grouse is an interspersion of spruce and jack pine with aspen, birch, and alder understory, mixed with arbutus. If it also contains some blueberry, cranberry, or other berry bushes, so much the better.

The food requirements of the spruce grouse are usually easily met. It dines heavily on the needles of jack pine, white spruce, and larch, with a side dish of tamarack and lodgepole pine. These are the staples. In springtime, add the leaves and fruits of many berries, especially blueberry. Newly hatched chicks eat heartily of insect life, with the emphasis on arthropods. As they grow rapidly on this high protein food, they switch gradually to plant food, and by October the youngsters are living almost entirely on jack

pine needles. This switch to jack pine needles is a good move, for that's the only food available during the coldest winter months.

Like all grouse, the spruce puts on a great courtship display—although the purpose of this display seems to be as much for staking out male territories as it is for attracting the females. The dandies fan their tails like a turkey gobbler, arch their wings, and stretch their heads up as high as they can—in this position, they make a series of aggressive rushes forward and back, strutting, displaying, threatening, bragging.

Often the spot chosen for this display is on a high limb of a tree. At times the courtship display terminates with a short up and down flight, starting from the display post and ending on the ground. During this display flight, the bird will drum its wings rapidly, making a series of thudding sounds. It does not "drum" its wings rapidly as does the ruffed grouse, but it does put on a spectacular performance. All the while it is posturing and bragging about its abilities, it is stabbing its head upward into the sky, shaking its neck from side to side and moving its feet in an intricate dance pattern.

The hen hides her nest remarkably well, under pine branches, often cushioned deep into the moss. Favorite location is at the base of a single pine tree. The average clutch size, as ascertained by researchers, is remarkably small, varying from 4.7 eggs in Minnesota to 7.5 in Alaska. If the nest is lost, renesting does occur, but we do not know to what extent the spruce grouse can be relied upon to try again.

Because the spruce grouse is to some extent sympatric with both the ruffed and the blue grouse, it would seem wise for the wildlife manager to spend his time and effort on improving things for those more edible species, secure in the knowledge that what benefited the other two species would also benefit the spruce grouse.

It would be a terrible tragedy if the trusting, tame, almost simple-minded spruce grouse would vanish from the face of the earth due to man's neglect. After all, he is not sought for food; he has lived with all other predators for millennia— and is still here. Let's make sure that man is not blamed for his disappearance also.

He's a fun bird to have for a neighbor.

Sage Grouse

Largest of the North American grouse, the lordly Cock of the Plains may weigh as much as 8 pounds. When the first European came to this continent, the sage grouse occupied a very tightly defined niche across the Great Plains and Great Basin states. Wherever the sage plant (*Artemisia tridentata*) was found, there was the sage grouse. Elimination of sage brush and conversion of the land to irrigated farming has spelled doom for the big sage chicken in many areas.

Today the sage grouse is found in its favored sage habitat westward from North Dakota, across southern Canada, but not into British Columbia. If you draw a line slanting southwesterly from the western Dakotas across to eastern California, you'll include the best sage grouse habitat in Nevada, Utah, Wyoming, Montana, and Colorado. Within this range, we must exclude the cultivated land, the coniferous forests, and intensively used grazing lands.

New Mexico lost its sage grouse population generations ago, and repeated attempts to introduce them to the same co-

verts have not been effective to date, although rumors persist that there is a relict population in the vicinity of Taos, New Mexico.

Remember that this range we have described is not fully inhabited by sage grouse. In fact, their populations have become discrete in most cases, isolated pockets of good habitat, with good populations of birds, scattered across a huge territory largely empty of sage grouse.

Centrocercus urophasianus is the scientific name for this grouse. The cocks are much larger than the hens when adult. However, without the size differential, it would be difficult to tell the sexes apart. Both have narrow, pointed tails. Both have a variegated pattern of gray-brown-buff and black on the upper parts, shading down to paler flanks and a black abdomen.

As with other grouse, the male sage grouse comes equipped with gular pouches, which are inflated during the elaborate courtship ritual. The bare skin shown at this time is often a bright yellow. Eye combs of wattle material growing over the eyes are also yellow, and this appendage becomes dilated and bright yellow in color during the spring booming season.

The very precocial young come into this world with a salt-and-pepper down covering their young bodies. They leave the nest immediately upon hatching and follow the hen for about ten days, then become much more independent. The family groups, however, hold together until well into fall.

The settlement of the intermountain west exactly paralleled the decline of the big grouse. Overgrazing hurt the range and drouth eliminated local populations in many instances. State after state was forced to close the hunting season on sage grouse because of declining populations. By 1937, hunters sought the big birds only in Nevada, Montana, and Idaho. Federal land use programs, begun during the dust bowl years, helped to restore the sage grouse to some of its abused range. Taylor Act lands, managed by the Bureau of Land Management, were removed from overgrazing, and the plant growth slowly recovered. When the sage had recovered to its former status, the sage grouse reappeared in habitats from which it had long been absent.

In 1964, North Dakota opened a limited hunting season on sage grouse, the first such legal hunting since 1922. The gradual decline in numbers caused by land abuse (overgrazing and erosion caused by overgrazing) was arrested by improved range management, and the sage grouse began a gradual recovery. Although spraying to control sage still hurts the big grouse, his recovery in numbers seems to be continuing. With the increase in populations has come a liberalization in hunting seasons. Today the national take of sage grouse by hunters exceeds 100,000, with about 40,000 of that kill coming on the wide sagebrush flats of Wyoming.

The sage grouse is at his most spectacular in the springtime, when he joins other mature males on the leks, or spring booming grounds. The lek is usually situated on a windswept place, which will be free of snow earlier than the surrounding terrain. This may be a stony ridge or simply an opening in the sage brush beloved of the sage grouse.

As the mating urge grows, the males undergo a transformation in appearance. The big skin flap that covers their upper front seems to swell and hang in a pendulous fold nearly to the ground. The feathers of this frontal area now seem almost entirely a snowy white. Two large gular sacs appear in the neck skin, growing to the size of apples when inflated with air and glowing yellow in the bright morning air. At the same time, the rooster spreads his tail in a fan shape, each feather stiffly erect. With wings held out from the sides and curving downward until the ends of the flight feathers touch the ground, the bird presents a formidable appearance. Each posturing cock is lord of a small territory and will fight viciously to drive another cock away from his territory. Unless the challenger cock actually trespasses on his small breeding territory, however, the fighting is more ritual than real, with the cocks each proclaiming his belligerence and his ability to defeat any other sage cock in the world.

The males fly into the lek before the first glint of sunrise appears on the prairie horizon. They begin their performance, mostly for the edification of other males, by going into the dance, swelling up the gular sacs and then letting the air out of those sacs in an explosive "plop!" which can be heard for miles on a quiet spring morning. With the sounds of scolding challenges and booming of gular pouches, the lek becomes a noisy place.

Enter the hens, quietly walking past the subordinate males that posture on the outer edges of the lek, past the challenger cocks that will be next year's dominant breeding males, and on into the territories of the Cock of the Plains, the breeding roosters. All the while they are walking into their assignation with the big rooster, the hens adopt a submissive posture, compress their plumage, and try to disappear. Once at the breeding ground, however, they are impatient for their moment with the top rooster and may actually fight among themselves for first access to the males.

This sequence shows a strutting sage grouse, the "cock of the plains." *Ed Bry, North Dakota Game and Fish photo.*

Strictly a polygamous species, the male plays no part in incubation or the rearing of the young. The hens usually lay 7 or 8 eggs in a ground nest. Most nests are located where there is some tall sage, but where the ground is not actually covered by sage. In fact, research shows that the sage hen does not like it when the ground is more than 35 percent covered by sage. Incubation takes twenty-six days, and this is the most dangerous period of the life of the sage grouse. Of 503 nests studied in one research project, 47 percent were lost to predation with skunks, coyotes, ground squirrels, and badgers being the culprits in most cases.

Food is seldom a problem to the sage grouse. Year around, 62 percent of all its food is sage leaves and buds. Insects are taken readily by the young chicks, but they quickly switch to plant food. Ninety-seven percent of all food used by adults is plant in origin. In summertime, dandelions and alfalfa are added to the diet, but in winter months, sage is 100 percent of the diet.

As a result of their diet, young birds are quite good on the dinner table, while the older birds are apt to be strong and "sage" tasting.

The sage grouse does not rank high on my list as a sporty bird. The cocks are so large that they appear closer than they actually are, causing some misses. However, their flight is slow and ponderous and they make an easy target when within normal shotgun range.

Management for Sage Grouse

Good range management is good management for sage grouse, in most cases. However, the bird simply must have its sagebrush. If your range management plans include elimination of sage, you are

sounding the death knell for the sage grouse.

To keep sage grouse populations on your land, you should:

1. Preserve the sagebrush.
2. Hold spraying, insecticides or herbicides, at a minimum or eliminate entirely.
3. Prevent overgrazing. Grasses interspersed with sagebrush is the best habitat for sage grouse.
4. Provide openings in the sage, or bulldoze out some of the sage periodically. Tall, mature sage plants are not good grouse range, if they occupy more than 35 percent of the total area.
5. Regulate or control hunter caused mortality. Close the season when the population seems down, open it when the numbers are up.

A newspaper story dated May 10, 1984, quoted Gerald D. Kobriger, upland game bird biologist for the North Dakota State Game and Fish Department, as saying, "Sage grouse dancing ground surveys showed a 22 percent increase over the year before." He said that the state's sage grouse range is limited by the availability of black sage, a habitat type increasingly threatened by modern land use practice. Major population growth, Kobriger maintains, is mostly a function of suitable habitat and not of removal by hunters of annual surpluses. Limited fall seasons have been held over the years with no negative impacts on the population of the trophy-size birds. End of news story. We couldn't have said it better.

Pinnated Grouse

When Grandfather Lou Cadieux first hunted on the wide prairies of North Dakota, the only native grouse was the sharptail. During the lifetime of Ken Cadieux, my father, the pinnated grouse (AKA Ol' Yellowlegs and prairie chicken), swept in behind the plow and the moldboard, increasing in numbers as the tall grass prairie was broken and put into crops. When I first started hunting those same North Dakota prairies, there were more pinnates than sharptails. During my lifetime, the pinnate has almost disappeared, leaving the sharptail once again alone in his favored coverts. Sadly, the numbers of sharptails are greatly reduced from what they were before the days of the plow that broke the plains.

What are these birds we are talking about? The sharptail seems to be the only one of his kind, a strikingly marked creamy white and rufous brown bird, with a dull white breast broken by a series of small brown vee markings. His feet are feathered down to the toes with white, hairlike feathers. He shows a bright orange inflatable sac on the neck, which plays an important part in his courtship antics.

Pinnates, on the other hand, are recognized in three separate races. One is the greater prairie chicken—which was once the most numerous bird in the Dakotas and Nebraska—Old Yellowlegs, the bird that loved the newly plowed farmland combination of small grain crops and unbroken grassland. When I was a child, it was easy for a good wingshot to bag 50 "chickens" in a day. They were often found in huge flocks in the fall, with as many as 150 birds per covey group. I have fond memories of driving the side roads with my Dad, looking out the windows of the Model T and watching for the curious chickens to stick their heads up high. While feeding in the stubble fields, they were almost out of sight, but curiosity was their undoing. I remember Dad

holding up his thumb to show my brother and me what the chicken's head looked like. When we spotted the birds, we parked the Model T and walked directly toward them. Because they got up in singles, twos, and threes, it was an easy matter for the shotgunner to pick his targets and drop a very high percentage of the flushed birds. Even when the last bird had flushed, Dad would warn, "Let's look for the Tail-End Charleys!" He meant the one or two birds which would hug the ground and hold, only to get a case of the nerves and take off while we were picking up their downed brothers.

This was the greater prairie chicken, which gained its greatest numbers in the Dakotas, Minnesota, western Iowa, and Nebraska.

A sportier bird was the lesser prairie chicken, whose range was mostly in the southern part of the Great Plains. They were found from Wisconsin and Indiana westward across the grasslands of Kansas and Oklahoma and down into the great grass seas of southern Texas. The lesser was warier, flew much farther when alarmed, liked taller grass than his big brother. Because of the taller cover he inhabited, the lesser was more apt to fly than to walk when moving about his prairie range.

At the southern extremity of his range, he overlapped with an interesting subspecies, the Attwater's prairie chicken. This bird is now confined to a few prairies on the Gulf Coast of Texas and receives its greatest protection on and near the Aransas National Wildlife Refuge, home of the endangered whooping crane.

Of the three chickens—greater, lesser, and Attwater's, the greater is now the most numerous. It probably numbers half a million birds, with the greatest population being found in Kansas (200,000),

Chuck Cadieux holds aloft a sharp-tailed grouse.

followed by Nebraska's 70,000 and South Dakota's 40,000. Missouri estimates about 9,000; Oklahoma, 8,000; Colorado, 3,000; Minnesota and Wisconsin, 2,000 apiece; and my native state of North Dakota—where they once attained their greatest population densities—is down to less than 1,000 pinnates.

The lesser prairie chicken, which I consider a more sporting species than the greater, likes taller grass, flies more than the greater (instead of walking), and flushes at a greater distance. It probably numbers less than 60,000 birds in the whole world, with Kansas boasting of 18,000, the same population as claimed by Texas. Add about 10,000 in New Mexico and a few in Oklahoma, and you have the total lesser prairie chicken world population. Some 5,000 lessers are shot each year out of the average population of 50,000. Remember, please, that the hunter mortality in this case merely substitutes for the regular mortality that would occur, even without a hunting season.

The Attwater's, which once was nearly extirpated, is now doing quite well on a very limited range, under intensive protection and management, in the magnificent empire of Texas. Their range includes Aransas and Refugio counties on the coast, and inland to parts of Colorado and Austin counties. Part of the sprawling Aransas National Wildlife Refuge, acquired to protect the winter home of the whooping crane, is prime Attwater's habitat. With active state and federal programs assisting, the Attwater's is holding its own in numbers in this restricted range. The lesser is also holding its own, while the prognosis for the greater is not so good. The greater is increasing in numbers only in Wisconsin, where large sums of money have been spent on acquiring habitat for this grand bird.

The prairie chickens differ from the sharptail in possessing rich, reddish-brown horizontal bars over most of their feathered body; shorter, rounded tails instead of the spike tail of the sharp-tailed grouse; and no feathers on their yellowish legs.

Although all three subspecies eat strikingly similar diets, geographic considerations dictate the differences. For example, the availability of domestic feed grains near tall grass cover is the limiting factor with the greater prairie chicken in the northern parts of its range. Both the Attwater's and lessers eat more insect food than does the greater and seem to depend less upon cultivated grain crops.

Mast crops are utilized by all three subspecies, consisting of poplar, elm, pine, apples, birches, hazelnuts, and acorns. Mast crops, however, are not used by the pinnates to the same extent that they are used by the ruffed grouse. Grains are more important than mast crops as winter survival food. Sorghum, oats, wheat, and corn are preferred winter foods when available. Ragweed and lespedeza are also used by all three subspecies.

As with all other grouse, the young of the pinnates rely heavily on grasshoppers

and other insects during the first month of their life, and grasshoppers add up to a surprising 14 percent of all foods for pinnates the year around! The greater eats less insects than the other two pinnates.

Pinnate coveys stay together well into late fall, then they join with other coveys to form large flocks, which seem to stay together until the next spring's nesting season causes a dispersion. Fifty years ago in North Dakota, winter flocks commonly numbered as many as 200 birds. This was before the threshing machine was replaced by the combine. Straw stacks stood everywhere on the broad grain fields of the prairie states, and the pinnates used them as permanent food supplies during the worst of the winter.

Pinnates formed leks each spring, and the strutting, booming, posturing, displaying cocks put on a truly remarkable show.

We called these leks "booming grounds," and that is not a good name, for the sound made by the quick release of air from the dilated gular sacs cannot be called a boom. It was loud enough to be heard for a mile or more on a quiet morning, however. The pinnate display consisted of expanding his yellow gular sacs, arching his stiffly held wings outward until the tips touched the ground, bowing deeply, then making a series of dance steps ahead and back with the head held low toward the ground. As with all grouse, the purpose seemed to be to impress the other males more than to gain access to the females. Each strutting cock occupied his own carefully delineated territory and displayed aggressive intolerance of any infringement upon his territory by other males. Every morning the adjoining males met at the fringes of their respective territories, and each did his

Five-shot sequence of pinnates on "booming ground" (lek) in spring. *Ed Bry, North Dakota Game and Fish photo.*

level best to scare the other cock farther away. Intimidation never seemed to work, and they frequently resorted to short fights to settle the pecking order and redefine the limits of the territory. These fights consisted of threatening rushes, squatting with outstretched head and neck held close to ground level, hissing, and then a frontal charge. When they really got serious, they jumped into the air like fighting cocks, clawing at each other—rather ineffectually—with their feet. Damage was usually limited to a few ruffled feathers.

Receptive hens came to the center of the lek where most of the breeding was done by a few dominant males.

All pinnates do a good job of hiding the nest, which usually contains 12 to 14 eggs. After a twenty-three to twenty-six-day incubation period, the precocial young followed their mother away from the nest and never came back. Hens brooded their young by covering them with outstretched wings and warming them under the breast for about two weeks. Then brooding slowly terminated, but the covey stayed together as the young birds grew rapidly on their high protein grasshopper diet and slowly switched over to the plant food preferences of the adult.

Management for Pinnated Grouse

By plowing up the plains and prairies and turning them into grain farms, we have made the pinnate dependent upon us for grain foods in the wintertime. Corn left standing is a good winter food, and if it is "rolled down" or otherwise made available to the hungry grouse, so much the better. Depending upon snow conditions, choose sorghum, oats, wheat, or corn crops to be left standing for the birds.

Make sure that this winter food supply is close to fairly extensive, *tall* grass cover. Grass cover must be permanent, existing over the years, before it is of much good to the tradition-bound pinnate. If there is a lek on your land, you are most fortunate. Do your best to protect tall grass cover and winter grain supplies near the lek. If there is no lek on your land, the chances of establishing one are almost zero. Without their traditional breeding ground and traditional display ground, the pinnate has no sense of belonging, no way to attract the females, no way to carry on their complicated life-style.

Management for the pinnates requires manipulation of vegetation over large areas of land. Whether it be on the salt grass prairies of the Texas Gulf Coast, the wheatlands of Kansas, the aspen-scrub oak-grasslands of Wisconsin, or the short-grass prairies of South Dakota and Nebraska's Sand Hill country, the pinnate needs a large, unbroken expanse of tall-grass nesting and escape cover, close to wheat, corn, or sorghum grains, which are available through the winter. Given those givens, the pinnate will do all right. Without any part of that habitat, they will disappear.

Sharp-tailed Grouse

About the same size as the pinnated grouse, and sympatric with the pinnate over much of the western range of both of these birds, the sharp-tailed grouse is easily differentiated from his pinnated cousins.

The sharptail appears much paler, almost white, in comparison with the darker brown pinnate. The sharptail has a pattern of vees of dark on his creamy white underbelly, while the pinnate sports a solid barred appearance on his lower side. The pinnate has a short, blunt, rounded tail; the sharptail has a longer, sharper pointed tail, with several very long feathers in the exact center of that tail. The pinnates have yellow legs, completely without feathers on the lower part and without feathers on the feet. The sharptail has a good set of insulated stockings that cover his legs down to and including the toes.

The sharptail is more independent than the pinnate. Sharptails do not seem to require farm grain crops at all, although they will live on wheat and corn when it is available. During the fall hunting seasons in North Dakota, I find a large part of my birds in cornfields. However, examination of several hundred craws tells me that the sharptail has fed only occasionally on corn. The rest of his craw is filled with weed seeds, gleaned from the cornfield. He also uses the soft earth of the cultivated field for dustbathing, and that takes up a considerable part of his time during the early afternoon.

When the winter snows cover most of his usual seed foods, the sharptail will switch greedily to corn left hanging from the stalk. As the snowdrifts get deeper, more and more corn comes within reach of the birds and is probably very important in carrying them through the worst of the winter.

However, corn is definitely not a requirement for sharptails. They are more numerous in the wide, rolling grasslands of the western half of North and South Dakota than they are in the cornfields of the eastern part of the state. Thornapples and wild rose hips are important foods during winter.

The sharptail ranges across the continent from central Alaska to central Quebec, then southward across a tremendous sweep of plains and prairie. Exclude the heavily forested areas, and you'll find sharptails almost everywhere else in a huge territory encircled by a line which runs roughly from upstate New York, across to southern Nebraska, and westward and northward to the northwest corner of Montana. Canadian provinces of Alberta, Saskatchewan, Manitoba, and Ontario hold good populations of sharptails. In fact, Canada's sharptails are doing much better than our sharptails are doing—probably because man has changed the face of the land less in still-developing Canada.

Although you won't notice any difference in appearance, there are actually two

Sharp-tailed grouse are easily identified by the dark vees of brown on the buff underbelly.

separate families of sharptails. Biologists like to refer to the prairie family of sharps—those that live in Ontario, Michigan, Wisconsin, and Minnesota. We estimate about two million birds in that family. A bigger range is occupied by the plains family of sharptails. These three million birds range across Saskatchewan, Alberta, Manitoba, and into the two Dakotas, Wyoming, Montana, Nebraska, and Colorado.

Although they look alike, the two families have different ideas about the kind of cover they prefer. The prairie family likes more brush and finds a land where woody cover blankets 30 percent of the land nearly perfect. The plains family can do all right with far less woody cover. In fact, in North Dakota, my favorite sharptail coverts in Bowman and Slope and Golden Valley counties exhibit less than 5 percent woody cover, yet the sharps are doing quite well, thank you. Far more important, it seems to me, is the sharptails' need for undisturbed prairie haylands where tall grasses grow. If there is an occasional clump of thornapple or a few box elders in the bottom of some of the intermittent watercourses, that is so much the better.

Far less dependent upon man for a grain handout than his cousin, the pinnate, the sharptail is more proficient in finding food during the winter. He knows enough to hole up and stay put during the blizzards that ravage the plains. With his insulated booties and his fluffed-feathers insulation, he sits motionless on the lower branches of a thornapple and watches the swirling snow, biding his time. When the sun comes out again, he goes foraging and seldom has a problem finding something to eat.

Willow buds are a good survival food

in many parts of the northern range of the sharptail, along with chokecherries that still hang on the tree, poplar buds, and rose hips. Young birds eat many insects, which comprise as much as 15 percent of their diet in summer. Like all the grouse, they gradually switch to plant food and eat very little insect food after they are six months old. For four months of the year, dandelions are a preferred food. In the summer, green stuff comprises as much as 90 percent of their food.

The sharptail is much more of a challenge to the hunter than is the pinnate—especially the greater prairie chicken. Like the ruffed grouse, he learns quickly that the sound of a shotgun means that one of his brood mates is dead. He quickly learns to flush far ahead of the hunter, to fly over the next horizon before landing, and then to lie low for the rest of the day. They are favored by professional dog trainers to work young dogs on, for they hold well to a dog of one of the pointing breeds. Where they are hard-hunted, sharptails become quite a challenge to the hunter. Windy days are es-

A well-trained retriever brings a sharp-tailed grouse out of thick cover in southwestern North Dakota.

pecially difficult, for the birds are much more restless then. Probably realizing that they will not be so apt to hear the approaching hunter, they are more alert and flush far out of danger when the wind is blowing.

The sharptail courtship display is very similar to that of the pinnates, with most of the theatrics taking place in the first 30 minutes after sunrise. Traditional leks are a necessity for sharptails, for they do not seem to know how to handle the matter of courtship and territoriality without the traditional dancing ground. For this reason, restocking with live-trapped sharptails from another area will seldom succeed. The birds may stay in the general area and find food and cover to their liking, but when it comes time for courtship in the spring, there is no tradition to guide them. Some researchers also feel that the courtship ground is a necessary learning device for the younger males. By setting up their own territories on the periphery of the breeding ground, they learn from the adult males who do the actual breeding. Take away this learning experience, and they simply don't seem to get the hang of it. In other words, for the

sharp-tailed grouse, sex is at least partly a "taught" skill rather than an inherited knowledge.

Perhaps this explains the loyalty to the dancing ground, which has been described by so many researchers in the study of sharptails. If the area of the dance becomes part of a main highway, the loyal sharptails will gather on the concrete of the new highway, ready and willing to start their courtship display the next spring. In any collision with automobiles, sharp-tailed grouse come out a distant second best. At times, destruction of a dancing ground can condemn an entire local population of sharptails to oblivion.

Sharp-tailed hens do a good job of hiding their clutch, which averages about 12 eggs. Incubation takes twenty-three or twenty-four days, and the precocial young follow their mother and remain in a tight covey well into fall. If there are enough sharptails present, the coveys will amalgamate into larger winter groups, usually limited to fifty or sixty, and not group up into the huge winter flocks known in the pinnate family.

Management for Sharptails

Preservation of tall grass cover in tracts of ten acres or more is very helpful. By all means, preserve the ancestral lek; it is vital to the sharptails' existence. Provide, or preserve, brushy cover in close proximity to the grasslands. Reduce the amount of grazing and the amount of "cattle use" in woody cover. Where shade is scarce, cattle often do a lot of damage to needed woody cover simply by lying in, or walking in, the scant shade of the short trees. Provide grain crops—left standing above the snow—in close proximity to the roosting areas. Reduce the

A good retriever helps to conserve gamebirds by minimizing the crippling loss. This sharp-tailed grouse was found in the tall grass of North Dakota.

Sequence of displaying sharptail roosters. *Ed Bry, North Dakota Game and Fish photo.*

Both age and sex of sharp-tailed grouse are indicated by the tail feathers.

frequency of disturbance by humans in the nesting season. Outside of that, our best advice to those who want to help their sharptails is simply this: Leave them alone as much as possible. They have survived much and they are still there, superbly adapted to survival in the wide grasslands and scrubby parklands of the northern plains and prairies.

Cooking the Pinnated and Sharp-tailed Grouse

There is only one problem with cooking these prairie grouse (this applies to the sage hen as well), and that danger is that the white meat will dry out. An overcooked grouse is a tough, dry piece of unpalatable meat. A properly cooked grouse, especially a younger bird, is a gastronomic delight and a joy to the palate of the discerning landowner.

For the final word on cooking these delectable treats, we go to the South Dakota Game Fish and Parks Department—after all, they probably have more prairie grouse than any other state and they ought to know how to cook them. To make sure we start out with a recipe that will not result in dry meat, let's go with this one.

Prairie Grouse en Casserole

> 4–5 *grouse breasts*
> *flour*
> *shortening for frying*
> 1 *can cream of chicken soup*
> 1 *tbsp. onion salt*
> 1/2 *cup diced celery*
> 1/2 *cup finely diced carrots*
> 4 *ounces canned mushrooms*
> *(bits and pieces do well)*
> 1/2 *cup melted butter*
> *salt and pepper*

Slice off the breasts in one piece. Cut breast meat lengthwise into fillets. Flour and brown in hot fat. Layer the browned pieces in casserole with all of the remaining ingredients. Bake for 1½ hours, covered, at 325°F. Remove cover for last 15 minutes to brown—but be careful—watch to make sure that it doesn't dry out.

Don't waste the remaining meat on the grouse carcass. Cook it in a pressure cooker to make the meat fall off the bones easily, and you have some fine soup makings or the basis of another casserole.

Braised Grouse

> 1/2 *cup shortening*
> 2 *grouse breasts*
> *salt and pepper*

1½ *cups cold water*
1 *small onion, sliced*
1 *small carrot, sliced*
1 *stalk celery, in 1-inch lengths*
2 *sprigs parsley*
½ *bay leaf*
4 *tbsp. flour*
¼ *cup canned tomatoes*
1 *tsp. minced parsley*
1 *tsp. lemon juice*
½ *cup sautéed mushroom slices*

Melt ¼ cup shortening in skillet, add grouse, and sauté until brown. Season with salt and pepper. Cover with water, add onion, carrot, celery, parsley, and bay leaf. Simmer until tender. Remove grouse and strain stock. Melt remaining fat, add flour, and blend. Add stock and tomatoes gradually, stirring constantly. Add parsley, lemon juice, and mushrooms, and season to taste. Reheat the grouse in the sauce.

Grouse Surprise

salt and pepper
8 *whole birds, marinated*
overnight in milk
1 *cup flour*
¼ *pound butter*
1 *onion, chopped*
½ *tsp. curry powder*
1 *can mushroom soup*
½ *cup white wine*

Salt and pepper the birds. Roll in flour. Brown in butter to which onion has been added. Place birds and drippings in baking dish. Sprinkle on curry powder. Add undiluted mushroom soup and wine. Cover and bake 1 hour at 350°F.

Marinated Prairie Chicken

2 *chickens, cut into serving*
pieces

1 *cup dry sherry*
½ *cup salad oil*
2 *tbsp. parsley flakes*
2½ *tsp. salt*
2 *tsp. paprika*
1½ *tsp. thyme leaves*
1½ *tsp. basil leaves*
1 *tsp. tarragon leaves*
½ *tsp. powdered garlic*
½ *tsp. curry powder*
⅛ *tsp. pepper*

Place cut-up grouse in a plastic bag. Combine all other ingredients and pour over the chicken. Close plastic sack tightly. Refrigerate for 24 hours in the refrigerator, turning at least twice. Remove the grouse pieces from marinade, place skin-side-up in roasting pan, and bake in preheated oven at 350°F until tender. Baste frequently with marinade.

Grouse with Orange Slices

4 *grouse*
salt and pepper
4 *thick orange segments, seeded*
and peeled
4 *slices bacon*
¼ *cup melted butter*
grated peel of one orange
2 *tbsp. orange juice*
1 *tsp. lemon juice*
chopped parsley

Season grouse inside and out with salt and pepper. Cover each breast with an orange slice and a bacon slice, fasten with string. Place grouse, breast up, in a baking pan. Roast in a preheated 350°F oven until tender to the fork test. Baste frequently with the mixture of combined butter, orange peel, orange juice, and lemon juice. Remove string, sprinkle with parsley, and serve. Good!

THE INTRODUCED PARTRIDGES

Hungarian Partridges

Also called the gray partridge, this beautifully marked partridge has been introduced into all of the northern half of our nation. He has become established wherever there are large expanses of prairie, for he shuns the mountain habitat. Right now, the "Hun" is an established game bird in the Dakotas, Montana, Idaho, Washington, and the eastern half of Oregon and reaches its greatest numbers on the endless prairies of Saskatchewan and Alberta.

In the Hun's "glory years," which were probably in the early 1950s, I have flushed a dozen covey groups—averaging well over 100 Huns per group—in a two-mile walk across the grasslands of southeastern Saskatchewan.

Gray, buff, and brown feathers clothe the Hun, with little difference between male and female. There's a large dark brown horseshoe on the abdomen of adults. Markings are the same for both sexes, except that the male has a plain light stripe on each scapular, while the same area on the female is cross-barred. They are larger than quail but smaller than the other introduced partridge, the chukar.

For some reason, they have ingratiated themselves with landowners all through their range. In Bowman County, North Dakota, I often heard landowners caution hunters, "Go get the pheasants and the sharptails, but if you want to come back here and hunt, leave my Huns alone!"

Of course, there was no reason for the landowner *not* to love the Huns. The greater part of their diet was seeds, which included a hundred different weed seeds.

However, the Hun did recognize the value of that wonderful wheat—the best seed of them all. However, the small (800 grams is big) birds didn't touch the wheat before it was harvested, for its heads towered above them. Once the combine had swept the fields, the Huns moved in and gleaned a lot of food from those combined acres.

Although he feeds on cultivated small grain fields, the Hun is a bird of the prairie grasses. He nests in that tall grass, feeds in it, and lives in it and usually scorns woody cover. This leaves him especially exposed to avian predators during hard winters, when drifting snows cover his beloved grass, leaving few places to hide. During the hard winter of 1951–1952, in Morton County, North Dakota, I watched a covey of fourteen Huns that had shifted their winter home into a small clump of thornapple—the only brush rising above the bare prairie snowdrifts for several miles in every direction. They seemed to be getting along famously despite the below-zero temperatures and strong winds, until a new predator moved in. This was a snowy owl.

These owls drift down from their normal subarctic home during hard winters when food is scarce up north. This particular owl took up permanent residence on a branch at the top of the thornapple clump and held the covey of Huns hostage—with nowhere to go. Mr. Snowy Owl ate one Hun per meal until they were all gone. I think it took him twenty-one days to catch and eat the fourteen Huns. Once the Huns were all gone, the owl disappeared, probably seeking another covey of Huns.

But that was definitely unusual. In most habitats and in most years, the Hun seems to hold his own very well against a host of hungry predators. He can restock his habitat quite well by himself, given a chance, for his reproductive potential is good. Average clutch size is big, in the range of 15 to 17 eggs, with a maximum of 20 reported. There is no help coming from the male with incubation chores, but hatching success is usually very high.

All that is necessary for the Hungarian partridge to succeed is large areas of tall grass prairie, interspersed with wheat and cornfields. After that, it seems to be up to the climate, for the Hun does suffer from heavy snows and high winds in a long winter.

Because it holds well to the dog, the Hun is a favorite with sportsmen, and many have found out that the little rusty-tailed birds are not easy to hit. Although they are strong fliers, they usually travel less than a quarter of a mile when first flushed. If the covey is not split up, they are much more apt to flush at long range the second time they are approached. Singles are much more easily "walked up" than are coveys.

Let's take a look at Saskatchewan, the top habitat for this sporty little partridge. In a personal communication to me, ecologist Ross Melinchuk stated that the Huns were increasing in number over each of the five years leading up to 1984. He also made the following interesting observation: "It is virtually impossible to overshoot Hungarian partridge, due to their behavior and reproductive potential. This realization has been with us for some time, but now seems an appropriate time to translate it into liberal hunting regulations, given high partridge populations and short supplies of some other game birds. Doubling the bag limit was endorsed several years ago by a major Hun researcher working in Montana. It is the course of action proposed for the main Saskatch-

ewan Hun range. It would provide more recreational and harvest opportunity but would probably not produce a dramatic upswing in hunting pressure because of the traditional role of the Hun as a secondary or tertiary species.

"The biology of the Hungarian partridge is conducive to the increased bag limit proposal. Research, including work done here in Saskatchewan, suggests that the territoriality of this species results in populations being limited by the amount of spring cover. The results of our abandoned farmstead surveys reinforce this. Typically, an abandoned farmstead will support a fixed number of pairs—often one—year after year. There may be a brood of sixteen there in the fall, declining slowly in size during the winter, but only one pair left in the final analysis. The normal population turn-over of 70 to 80 percent is exaggerated during periodic severe winters. The bottom line applicable to most situations is simply 'use 'em or lose 'em'."

The reference to abandoned farmsteads is not an accidental one. The Hun seems to love the weedy yards left when a farm is abandoned. The extra shelter of dilapidated buildings is often used by the Hun, although he still prefers his grassland.

Chukar Partridges

It is very easy to identify the chukar partridge, for he will usually introduce himself with his ringing call of "chuk-chur—chuck-churr." Add to that his brightly colored appearance, and the identity crisis is resolved. He has a black-barred mask, which encircles his blue and cream-colored head with its bright vermillion colored beak, on a white and slate-blue body with distinctive black barring on the sides and chest. In addition, he has feet and legs that are brighter red than a "northern" mallard duck's. Males are slightly larger, but both sexes are colored the same. They'll average 12 to 14 inches long and weigh in at about 1¼ pounds, which makes them bigger than a quail and smaller than a ruffed grouse.

Chukars were introduced into almost all of the western states. Washington, Idaho, Oregon, and Nevada are the top states in chukar numbers right now. Nevada killed more than 115,000 chukars in the 1958 season and has probably killed more than a million of the red-legged partridges since the introduction in 1935. The chukar claimed his own niche, a huge stretch of terrain that was often unpopulated by other gallinaceous birds. His choice was the sagebrush and rocky

Chukar partridge. *Oregon Game photo.*

country of the Great Basin states, and he is now well established in those spots from eastern Washington to southern Colorado. Another identifying aspect of chukar country is the presence of steep slopes, for the chukar is definitely not a flatlander. The third identifier is that the bird seems to pick areas with lots of cheatgrass, which it evidently puts at the top of the list of its favorite foods. That list includes most seeds and green sprouts, waste grains, and wild fruits. Insects are heavily used in the summertime.

Alectoris graeca is a large bird, weighing in at up to 800 grams, which makes him attractive to the shotgunner. But hunting chukars is an invitation to a heart attack from overexertion. The human frame lacks a lot when it comes to being adapted to vertical transport in the mountains and cliff sides. The chukar is evidently perfectly adapted to this chore. When approached, the chukar prefers to run rather than fly. And it prefers to run uphill! Humans do not share this love of uphill running. The chukar is a strong flier, although it prefers to run like blue and white and black racehorses straight up the slipping, sliding talus slopes that make up a good bit of its preferred habitat. One of life's greatest frustrations is experienced by the hunter who chases them uphill for a mile or so, then watches them flush out of range and fly a mile and a half down slope, getting in position to do it all over again.

The most promising technique of wildlife management in the case of the chukar is the gallinaceous guzzler. The guzzler is a construction that provides free water in an area where it was not available before. In the hot deserts of Arizona and southern California, gallinaceous guzzlers are often constructed to shunt sparse

Readying a "gallinaceous guzzler" for use. These devices collect scanty rainwater and preserve it through the dry months. Reduced evaporation makes water available through the hot period. *Oregon Game photo.*

rainfall into caves, where evaporation is reduced by the shading, yet where the water is still available to such species as the desert bighorn, the white-winged dove, and many species of quail and partridge. This same technique is working in the Great Basin states to help chukars along. In a wet season, chukar coveys will scatter widely and be hard to find. When it is very dry, they will be found near the available waterholes.

Cooking the Introduced Partridge

Both the Hungarian and the chukar partridge are good eating. They are tasty table birds, but must be protected against drying out in all cooking methods. Shortly after World War II I carried a lunch box to work each day. During hunting season in North Dakota, that lunch box often contained a whole partridge—Hungarian of course, and that did make a royal lunch. Hot, the bird was even tastier. Here are some good ways to cook your pats:

Creamed Hungarian Partridge

> 2 partridges, cut in serving
>   pieces
>   flour
> 1/4 pound salt pork, diced and
>   fried (bacon can be used)
> 1 1/2 cups thick cream
> 1 large can evaporated milk

Flour the pats, and cook them in the shortening resulting from frying the salt pork. When the meat is done, put it into a pot. Add the crisp fat pork or bacon.

Pour the cream and evaporated milk into the skillet containing the rendered fat. Stir until well mixed and heated through. Then pour that mixture over the Huns and the salt pork in your pot. Bring to near boil, basting occasionally by stirring. Not only is the meat tasty, but the gravy is delicious.

Barbecued Chukar

    4 or 5 Huns or chukars
        2 cups catsup
        1 tsp. salt
      ¾ cup onion, chopped finely
      ¾ cup sweet pickle relish
        3 cups brown sugar

Place cut-up birds in casserole dish. Mix together all other ingredients and stir well, then add them to the casserole over the meat. Bake about 3 hours at 375°F, covered for first 2 hours, then uncovered. Watch to make sure it doesn't get too dry.

Partridge in Wine Sauce

        3 whole partridge breasts
        1 onion, sliced thin
        1 tbsp. chopped celery
          pinch dried tarragon
      ½ cup white wine
        4 tbsp. butter
        3 tbsp. flour
      ½ tsp. salt
        1 dash pepper
        2 tbsp. butter
        1 egg yolk, beaten
        4 tbsp. heavy cream

Cut breasts in half along breast bone, pull off skins. Put meat, onion, celery, tarragon and wine in large saucepan. Add just enough boiling water to cover the breasts. Cover and simmer for 30 minutes. Remove the breasts and keep them warm. Strain the liquid and boil to reduce to 2 cups. Melt the 4 tbsp. butter and stir in flour, salt, and pepper. Slowly add the partridge broth, stirring constantly. Keep on stirring while you cook until the mixture is smooth and thick. Add the 2 tbsp. butter, and simmer slowly. Combine egg yolk and cream, stir into hot sauce. Serve breasts covered with sauce. About enough for three, or two *hungry* men.

Any recipe that works with ruffed grouse or any of the prairie grouse will do well with either partridge. Just don't overcook this delicate meat.

THE WILD TURKEY

The wild turkey, king of the game birds, is not only one of the most sought-after prizes for North American hunters, it is also the subject of one of wildlife management's greatest success stories.

No one has even an educated guess as to how many wild turkeys existed in what is now the United States back when Columbus led the immigration from Europe that caused our wildlife species to comment, "Well, there goes the neighborhood!" However, there must have been a lot of wild turkeys, for the big birds were native to most of the states. They were absent, as far as we know, in California, Nevada, Utah, Idaho, Washington, both Dakotas, and Minnesota. We also know that wild turkeys were rare in Michigan, Vermont, New Hampshire, and Maine.

For decades, biologists blamed the decline of the wild turkey on the elimination of turkey habitat. Undoubtedly, this played a part. But we might just as well

Wild turkey gobbler. *U.S. Fish & Wildlife photo.*

They have enough other wildlife to compensate even for this terrible misfortune.

In 1983, it was estimated that 1½ million Americans went wild turkey hunting!

Our two million-plus wild turkeys are all of one species, good old *Meleagris gallopavo*. The wild turkey is slimmer and more streamlined than his domestic cousin. The tips of the tail feathers of wild turkeys are deep chocolate brown, while the tips of tail feathers in our barnyard birds are white. Another easy-to-see difference is that the legs of a wild turkey are a bright pink, while the tame ones sport gray or black legs. The wild species is divided into five subspecies—Florida, Eastern, Merriam's, Rio Grande, and Mexican.

Although individual weights vary greatly, the Eastern is slightly the largest subspecies, with adult toms weighing in

admit that the real cause of the declining populations was hunting. Turkeys were shot over all of their range and hunted very hard, indeed! We hunters lowered the population almost to the danger point. We hunters also paid for the research and the management that has brought the wild turkey back.

In 1930 there were roughly 20,000 wild turkeys in existence. They occupied turkey habitat in only twenty-one states!

But 1930 proved to be the nadir. In the next half a century, the numbers of wild turkeys increased 10,000 percent. In 1980 we counted more than two million wild turkeys in forty-nine states. Only Alaska is without wild turkeys. They've even taken root in Hawaii. Incidentally, grieve not for Alaskans, without wild turkeys.

Wild turkey carrying transmitter for radio-tracking study. *New Mexico State Game and Fish photo.*

at near 20 pounds on the average. Merriam's come second, with Rio Grande turkeys a close third; toms of both subspecies weigh over 17 pounds. Florida and Mexican subspecies weigh their adult gobblers at around the 14 or 15-pound range. All wild turkeys, obviously, are large birds.

In passing, we should note that there is another species, the ocellated turkey of Mexico's Yucatan jungles. A strikingly colored bird, the ocellated is becoming very much a disappearing species because of uncontrolled hunting on the part of the descendants of the Ancient Maya. But the only ocellated turkeys in the United States are on exhibit, not roaming the woods.

Now some folks claim that the gobbler is polygamous, that he gathers a big harem and mates with those hens exclusively. That is obviously not true. It is

hard to gather and hold a harem when the hens come and go as they please and only return to the gobbler's call when they are receptive to mating. The rest of the time they roam where they please. It would be much more honest to say that the gobbler is promiscuous, rather than polygamous. The male wild turkey has nothing whatsoever to do with incubating or caring for the young. If he is seen with the poults, it is only an accident.

The hen lays an average of 11 eggs in a well-hidden nest, and twenty-five to twenty-eight days later she hatches a bunch of chicks that are ready to leave the nest and forage with Momma within a few hours. Strange thing about turkey eggs—they weigh in at about 2½ ounces when laid and will sink in water. In a week or so, when the growing embryo has used up some of the stored food and a lot of carbon dioxide has been lost

Nesting wild turkey. *Jack Dermid, North Carolina Game photo.*

through the shell, the egg has lost weight to about 2 ounces, and it will now float.

What do turkeys eat? Everything they can catch that isn't too big to swallow! One food habits study of Eastern wild turkeys decided that no less than 354 species of plants were identified in the crops of these hungry birds. Although plants added up to the greater percentage, Eastern wild turkeys ate enough insects to make up as much as 16 percent of their diet in summer. Merriam's turkeys boosted that percentage of insect food up to 20 percent during peak times of spring and summer.

For Eastern turkeys, the food list is most impressive. Number one in order of importance is the acorn. In winter, the acorn made up 47 percent of their food in one study! But the turkey's taste is definitely catholic. Among its foods are wild black cherry, dogwood berries, black gum berries and seeds, sumac, smilax, pine seeds, hackberry, grass leaves and seeds, wild grapes, blackberry, blueberry, smartweed flowers, clover, bluegrass, sheep sorrel, panic grasses, crabgrass, paspalum, bristle grasses, alfalfa, wedge grass, black gum, buckwheat, wild oatgrass, sedges, mulberries, roses, docks, moss, pecan, hickory, chufa, crotons, pawpaw, elm seeds, beech, wheat, corn, ferns, oats, violets, foxtail, wild rye, hawthorns, buttercups, poison ivy, green briers, boneset, burdock, vetch, persimmon, lespedeza, peanuts, hemlock, and don't forget the insects . . . grasshoppers by the thousands, beetles, grubs, spiders, caterpillars, newts if small enough to swallow, crawfish, lizards, and even baby frogs. Nesting hens show a surprising knowledge of nutrition as they eat large quantities of snails when forming egg shells, the snails being high in calcium.

Rio Grande turkeys will definitely eat any of that menu, if they can find it. One Arizona study found that insects in summer made up as high a share of the diet as 61 percent, although it was more often 20 percent. The western birds, Rio Grande, Merriam's, and Mexican subspecies, ate a lot of other things, too, that were not available to their Eastern cousins. In order of importance, the food of the westerners was listed as pine seeds, grass, oats, acorns, muhly grasses, barley, dandelion, bluegrasses, lovegrasses, wheat needlegrass, dropseed grasses, sunflowers, smartweed, clover, bearberry, juniper, timothy, corn, wild oats, and chufa.

Young and old wild turkeys all eat insects, with grasshoppers most popular on the menu. But 90 percent of all of their food, year-round, is plant material. Cultivated plant favorites are corn, chufa, oats, millet, and cowpeas. With a varied *à la carte* menu like theirs, it is obvious that the wild turkey is not going to go hungry in most parts of the nation. Wild turkeys almost never die of starvation in the wild. If you find an emaciated bird, it is certain that it is suffering from some turkey disease, not from an empty stomach caused by lack of food.

In fact, wild turkeys of all subspecies are good at going without food. The adult gobbler feeds very little during the breeding season. He is so busy catering to other appetites and showing off for the younger toms that he forgets about eating. During that time he will lose as much as 2½ pounds. To get ready for that ordeal, he has stored about 2 pounds of fat on his breast meat, giving him rather a potbellied silhouette, but readying him for the demands of his many mates.

Researchers have documented the fact

that a healthy wild turkey can go without food of any kind for as long as seven days, and in extreme cases have survived twenty-three days without food, although the starved bird lost more than 30 percent of its body weight while with the weight watchers.

The hens take this love business with a little more savoir faire than do the strutting gobblers. They eat all during the mating season, which is good, because their bodies have to provide egg shell and living tissue material from which the embryo grows. No job for a victim of *Anorexia nervosa*. Hens usually nest in the first full year of their lives, and hatching success is excellent, running about 90 percent, proving that the hen did a good job of eating for herself and for the young birds.

For reasons that we do not understand yet, hatching success and reproductive potential are at their highest when the population is under a downward stress factor. For example, if the population has suffered from a very bad winter (not a good choice of examples, as the wild turkey can handle cold and snow quite well) or from overharvesting during the fall hunting season, then the population is under a stress, and the species rises to the occasion with excellent hatching success on large clutches of eggs under the incubating hen.

Most experienced hunters say that it is more difficult, on average, to bag a wily old tom turkey than it is to shoot a white-tailed buck! Which is high praise indeed!

So Now You Want Turkeys on Your Land!

Can't you just order some turkeys by mail, turn them loose on your land, and enjoy *wild* turkeys forever after?

No, you cannot!

If you can buy turkeys, they are not wild turkeys, so you don't want them.

If they are wild turkeys, it is against the law to buy or sell them.

There is only one source of truly wild birds for restocking purposes and that source is the state game and fish department of your state. There are no exceptions to this statement.

Can't you use partly domesticated birds, and let them "go wild"?

No, you cannot!

The history of turkey restocking with partly wild, partly tame birds is a long and sorry story. Summarized, it says that this method has been tried a total of 354 times, releasing 350,000 game-farm "wild" turkeys. These efforts resulted in 331 "total wipe-out" failures and doubtful successes in the other 23 cases. Sometimes the seeming success of "game farm" turkeys turned out to be a disaster for the native population, as it introduced poultry diseases lethal to the really wild birds.

The history of repeated failures finally enabled biologists to stop the politically motivated and very wasteful programs for stocking these "half-wild, half-tame" turkeys. Pennsylvania was the last state to convince its politicians, in 1980, when they stopped "put and take" stocking of "wild game farm" turkeys.

But remember that 10,000 percent increase in wild turkey numbers? It came about through restocking! Restocking with wild-trapped, truly wild birds. It works. It is still working. In 1972–1973, Massachusetts released a total of 37 birds wild-trapped in New York State. In 1983, this planting had increased to more than 4,000 birds.

Summarizing the restocking with wild trapped birds, we come to the conclusion that 841 attempts were made, using only

26,500 wild trapped birds, and we find 685 success stories, resulting in the great explosion of wild turkey numbers. This explosion took the king of game birds into every state except Alaska, including a bunch of marginal states. North Dakota, which was never home to native wild turkeys, now boasts of a huntable population of wild turkeys. Missouri, a good turkey state, feels that 15,000 acres of turkey habitat in each bloc is about the minimum, and they specify that that bloc of land must contain 70 percent woodland and 30 percent semi-open habitat. North Dakota would have a hard time finding many blocs of 15,000 acres that would meet these qualification standards. Yet restocking worked in North Dakota, and a wild population was established in far less desirable habitat than Missouri feels is necessary. These many success stories were accomplished with wild-trapped birds.

Why the catastrophic results with game-farm birds and the huge success with wild-trapped birds? Millennia of experience in escaping predators, including man, have endowed the truly wild turkey with a very big caution bump, a wariness that enables him to avoid trouble, to hide from hawks and eagles, to run from hunters' calls. The game-farm bird lacks this entirely. Most of them can still be killed by a boy with a stick, even a month after release, if they live that long.

How about the advertised situation where the birds are partly wild, and you hope that they will become totally wild after release? Sad experience has shown that it simply doesn't work that way. Instead of the tame birds becoming wild, it often happens that the wild birds become tame! Remember that a tame gobbler mating with five wild hens will produce about fifty poults, all of whom are half

tame, instead of being wild enough to survive in the wild. Cattlemen are fond of reminding us that the bull is one half of the herd, when it comes to genetic results. The same thing is true of the male turkey.

State game and fish departments have stopped entirely the useless release of game farm turkeys. However, there are still well-meaning people who listen to the lies of the game farm turkey breeders and release semi-tame turkeys into the wild. At times, they kill the existing population of wild birds by this action. In addition to introducing the bred-in stupidity and slow reaction time of the tame bird, they also introduce diseases and parasites for which the wild birds have no defenses. Domestic turkeys, immune to blackhead, will introduce blackhead to the wild population. This can cause a catastrophic die-off.

What's the Answer to Restocking?

Don't!

If there are wild-trapped birds available through your state conservation department, you can restock. If there are no birds available from your state department, you can *not* restock.

Management for Wild Turkeys

First of all, you must work at improving the habitat and at controlling mortality of wild turkeys. Prevent grass fires that eliminate needed nesting cover and reduce food supplies. This does not apply to controlled—managed—burning, which can do a good job of spurring growth of tender plants that are needed by the young turkeys. For advice on controlled burning for turkey food production, see your County Extension Agent.

Protect nest areas from flooding, which is self-explanatory habitat improvement.

Plant food plants, annual food plants—more about this later.

Use the mower in the same way you used controlled burning to encourage new growth and to reduce unwanted woody growth.

Plan your timber cutting to maximize the environment for turkeys. Monoculture—growing only one species of tree—is not good turkey management. Clearcutting of large tracts of land is not good for turkeys. If area-cutting of trees is necessary, make the cutover area as narrow and long as possible, so that it does not unduly hurt turkey habitat. Leave oak and other "mast" trees where they will provide accessible food for the turkeys in the winter. In chapter 21, we will learn more about woodlot management.

Use fertilizer in appropriate ways to maximize production of tender green plants in the spring, when the poults need that food the most.

Keep pesticide and herbicide spraying to an absolute minimum, both because some sprays will kill the poults directly, and because all insecticides reduce the amount of valuable protein food available to the growing poults.

Control Mortality Factors

First and foremost, you must control the percentage of your turkey flock that is killed by humans every year. This is essential to any plan for increasing the numbers of turkeys. Poaching must be eliminated, for *you* intend to manage your flock. You could not manage your beef herd if outsiders came in and trucked off cows whenever they had the chance. Neither can you properly manage a tur-

key flock if poachers take units out of that flock.

Equally important, you must control the legal hunting mortality. If you wish the flock to hold its own, you must never kill more than 25 percent of the available hens in any one year. (Remember that illegal kill must be figured in here, if it exists.)

If you wish the flock to increase in numbers, rule out the killing of hens entirely.

In any harvest system, allow only one hen to be harvested for each four gobblers that are killed.

Reduce mortality due to crippling and unretrieved mortality due to hunting by insisting on the use of guns with sufficient power. The turkey is a tough customer, and at fair range, his feathers will turn away a lot of pellets. Most authorities recommend allowing only 10-gauge or 12-gauge magnum shotguns, full choke, shooting pellets no larger than number 4. When rifles are used, rule out the .22 rimfire entirely, for it can result in birds being wounded and escaping to die elsewhere. When this happens, the hunter goes on to kill another bird and you have doubled your mortality, to the benefit of the foxes and crows, not to your benefit.

In any discussion of mortality causes, hunting must take first place. Remember to add illegal hunting to legal hunting, if there is poaching on your land. But remember that the wild turkey can withstand considerable hunting pressure in good habitat—without decreasing the population. Missouri opened their first spring season after an excellent habitat improvement and restocking program (with wild birds, of course). In 1960 hunters killed 94 turkeys. In 1964, they killed 369; in 1971 the number taken was up to

2,864 and in 1979 the kill totaled 13,741, and the turkey was still increasing in overall population in Missouri.

Another way to reduce mortality is by controlling the numbers of predators that beat you to the turkeys you want to harvest. This project is of minor importance, according to most turkey experts. Although feral cats and dogs kill many young turkeys, and although opossums and skunks do a number on turkey eggs in the nest, no one has ever proved that predation is *the* limiting factor on turkey production. Turkeys do a good job of hiding their nests, which allows most nests to hatch successfully despite a high population of predators. Second, it must be remembered that the turkey hen will usually renest when she loses her first clutch to predators. This loss of the first nest may result in no loss of young bird production at all.

Should You Feed Your Turkeys?

If you can honestly say that food is in short supply on your land, you probably do not have any turkey habitat. Supplemental feeding is almost always harmful in the long run. First of all, it concentrates the birds, thus increasing their exposure to predators, disease, and parasites. For example, if domestic poultry feed at the same feeder that you put out for your wild turkeys, there is an excellent chance that the wild birds will pick up cecal worms, which are carriers of blackhead, a known wild turkey killer.

By teaching your birds to rely on the feeders, you are cheating them out of the chance to become self-reliant and able to survive in the wild without the feeder. They may choose the tastier cracked corn and fail to learn that blueberries, rose hips, and grasshoppers are excellent food and good for them to boot.

If you insist on using artificial feeders (it isn't smart, my friend) please move the artificial feeders every month so that the birds are not continually feeding over contaminated ground with its crops of parasites and diseases.

Is There a Right Way to Feed Wild Turkeys?

There certainly is! Go out and plant feed crops, cultivated and wild, for the use of the birds. But make the birds do the harvesting, teach them to scratch for themselves instead of carrying the food to them on a golden platter.

Plant cultivated crops, such as chufa, oats, fescues, field peas, clover, alfalfa, corn, and wheat. Chufa is a good choice, but remember that it must be moved after a couple of years and seeded into new ground, otherwise it will develop root problems.

All the clovers are good, with ladino, crimson, and white leading the group as turkey foods. Consult your local extension agent. Corn is a good turkey food, but useless while standing. You must knock down the corn to make it available to the turkeys.

Winter wheat is a good choice as a supplemental food, for it provides green stuff when that commodity is in short supply and because it is accessible in early spring.

We also recommend soybeans, the grain sorghums, peanuts, bahia grass, ryegrass, cowpeas—you know your land and your soil, plant that which will do best. And if you want long-term results, why not plant a few oaks? Why not plant a row of oak down the lane, but not the busy road lane. Your grandson will enjoy better turkey hunting because of those oaks.

Planting food crops is always a good idea, but be sure to get good, qualified advice from your state conservation department or your county agricultural agent. It is easy to make general recommendations, but specific instructions are what you need. For example, Missouri Conservation Department says "More permanent food plots can be established in forest clearings by applying recommended amounts of limestone, rock phosphate, and fertilizer and seeding in the fall with a half bushel per acre of wheat and 2 pounds per acre of orchard grass. Then overseed one half of the plot in the fall or winter with 2 pounds per acre of Ladino clover and 2 pounds per acre of red clover, and the other half with 10 pounds per acre of Korean or Summit lespedeza." That is excellent advice for Missouri soils and for the needs of Missouri wild turkeys. Your state may be very different. Get professional advice, and then plant.

No matter what you plant, try to keep it away from heavily used roads or commonly visited buildings as much as possible. Although turkeys do a good job of adjusting to humans, they still prefer privacy. Fence livestock away from plantings that are intended solely for turkeys. But remember that turkeys hate to fly over a barbed wire fence or a hog-tite fence. Split rail fences are perfect, as they allow the bird to fly to the top of the fence, perch for a second, then hop on over—which is preferred turkey methodology. Swing gates into these planting areas should have a wooden bar along their top, to provide that same kind of "easy over" for the turkeys.

Remember that fertilizer will greatly increase food production on these food plant areas intended for turkeys.

Treated seeds will reduce the incidence of raccoons and other "varmints" digging up the seed and eating it.

By all means, try to keep wild turkeys away from domestic birds, from domestic poultry of all kinds. This is an absolute necessity to minimize the effects of domestic poultry diseases and parasites.

Another important way to improve habitat for wild turkeys is to provide waterings at different points around your land. Don't force the wild turkey to water with domestic poultry; give him his own watering place, far from domestic flocks. Watering spots for cattle opened up great areas of the semiarid southwest mountain forest to the wild turkey—you can open up big portions of your land by providing water where there is none at the start.

Stockwater or detention dams intended to hold water for turkeys should be deep, 8 or 10 feet if possible. The deeper pond will not dry up in late summer, when the water requirement is greatest. Such ponds need not be large, but there should be at least one water source per section of turkey habitat.

Just as tree claims and shelterbelts opened up the Great Plains states for wild turkeys, so judicious use of tree planting and woody cover planting can open your land for wild turkeys.

There are so many ways in which you can help your wild turkey population to prosper. The royal road to more wild turkeys lies in habitat improvement and mortality control. The wrong road is through restocking with game farm turkeys. *Don't do it!*

If you want more detailed information about wild turkeys, read *The Book of the Wild Turkey,* by Lovett Williams, available from Winchester Press. Equally interesting is *The Complete Book of the Wild Turkey,* by Dr. Roger Latham. Dr. Latham completed his monumental work way back in 1955, and Lovett Williams is obviously more up to date. Nevertheless, both books are highly recommended and highly readable.

DOVES

Mourning Doves

A slim, graceful, buff and gray colored, pigeonlike bird, the mourning dove has a tan-gray upperside, a buffy-tan underside, a faint scattering of red and blue iridescent feathers on head and neck, a long pointed tail, scimitar-shaped wings, and a darting, erratic, and very fast flight, and is found in every one of the forty-eight states. The bird is only 13 inches long, with a wingspan of about the same length. It drinks by sucking water *up* into the throat, rather than bobbing its head like most birds. It is a remarkably fast flier and the male bird gives milk!

The mourning dove might well be called the "Pittman-Robertson bird." Most

Turkey feeder used in hill country of Texas. Note metal sheathing, which prevents mammals from climbing the legs.

Simple deer and turkey feeder used in Texas hill country.

A mourning-dove broods two young. *U.S. Fish & Wildlife photo.*

wildlifers will recognize the reference to Pittman-Robertson, a pioneer piece of legislation that earmarked the excise tax on arms and ammunition for wildlife restoration work. A great part of the good wildlife management work done by the fifty State Game and Fish Departments has been financed by Pittman-Robertson moneys.

The mourning dove generates a great part of that Pittman-Robertson money. Shotgun shells fired at rocketing gray shapes seldom encounter dove feathers—at least a very high percentage of shotgun shells fired at mourning doves are misses. Because the ratio of hits to shells expended is so low, the mourning dove hunter buys lots of shells, paying lots of excise tax. So the dove is the main producer of P-R money. God bless their feathered little souls, the mourning dove has done far more to generate money for wildlife than any other species.

Because more hunters are after his little 4½-ounce body every year than any

other game bird, the mourning dove must have a secret of success, for he certainly is not decreasing in numbers. That secret is explained in one word—fecundity! Now fecundity is described as the "capacity of producing young in great numbers," and the mourning dove lays only 2 eggs at a time. How can this be fecundity?

Mourning doves lay their 2 eggs very early in the breeding season. They hatch those two eggs in only fourteen days. Two weeks later, the two young hatchlings are on the wing, following mother mourning dove out to feed, or perching on the end of the same branch upon which mother mourning dove has built her second nest, laid her second 2 eggs and is busily incubating them. The same rush to reproduce continues as long as the weather holds any promise of putting the latest brood on the wing before the winter snows put a stop to this orgy of breeding. Theoretically, as many as six broods are possible, and this has been recorded as far north as Pennsylvania or North Dakota. However, two successful broods per summer per female dove is about average. This means that each nesting pair puts four more doves on the wing with them that fall. And that seems to add up to fecundity.

When I was a United States Game Management Agent in Sioux City, Iowa, in the early fifties, the U.S. Fish and Wildlife Service decided that we ought to busy ourselves in the springtime by banding nestling doves. We got orders to work at dove banding. We also got orders to hold travel mileage down to a bare minimum (which was par for the course in federal law enforcement).

To attain both objectives, I put a notice in the local paper, courtesy of Irwin Sias's well-read column "Siouxland Sports Afield," asking people to call my home telephone number and report dove nests with fledglings in the nest. I should have known better, for the mourning dove is the sixth most numerous bird in America, and we were in prime dove country. That was a tactical mistake, for it seemed that there was a dove nest in every tree, and the people of Iowa, and Nebraska across the river, were anxious to tell me about every one of them. Several high school boys volunteered to help carry stepladders and to climb tall trees for me. We banded doves all day long, and my home telephone rang all day long. That experience gave me a good idea of the reproductive potential of the little mourning dove.

Courtship begins very early, triggered by the first few warm days. The male puts on a lot of different aerial displays, designed to show off what a fine catch he

is. Approaching the female on the ground or on a tree branch, he puffs out his throat, fans his tail, and makes a series of "trial rushes" at the female. The female is trying to look nonchalant, preening her feathers as if this was the most important thing in the world. In between the rushes toward the female, the male lifts his head as if surprised that she has not yet capitulated to his charms, then bows sharply, head almost to the ground, and immediately begins another rush. Once he has selected his lady love, the male becomes extremely aggressive toward other males and will do a good job of beating up on a competitor, with the damaging blows being delivered—domestic pigeon fashion—with the leading edge of the wing.

When the female accepts the ardent suitor, she signifies her willingness by placing her beak trustingly in his. With beaks locked together, they perform a few ceremonial bows, and that plights their troth. Most of this courtship ritual goes unnoticed by humans, but another part of the mourning doves' annual romance is overheard by many. The male bird starts singing early in the spring. His call can best be described as a series which goes: "Coooo, cooooahhh, coo, coo!" That sequence, which some people describe as being ineffably sad, may be continued monotonously. The most often used sequence, however, is the repetition of the cooing sequence only twice in a minute. Dove researchers have made use of this spring singing of the male birds to ascertain population trends. Observers follow preset routes, driving the car one mile, stopping, turning off the engine, getting out of the car, and then listening for exactly three minutes by the watch. It is easy to locate the different male birds and to get a good idea of the number of songs heard per stop. Comparing the number of songs heard per stop this year with the songs heard at the same stops on the same date last year will give a good indication of whether the population trend is up or down. These dove counts required an early departure from the comfortable bed, but it brought the wildlife observer out at the most enjoyable time of the morning. The call counts were started in 1953 and are continued to this day, giving a reliable indication of the population trends, although they cannot ever give a population estimate. Today, 1,000 such dove-call-counts routes are run on the same schedule each spring.

The nest is clumsily built, an invitation to disaster when the wind blows. And a strong wind can be a disaster to nesting mourning doves, for thousands of them are blown out of the flimsy nests, or the whole nest blows away. Let's describe their nest-building ability, or lack of it. Usually the male selects the nest site and begins the nest building. He lays a 4- or 5-inch twig across a pair of branches, or in a flat place on a tree or stump. Dove nests are usually in low trees, but not always. A high percentage of nests are on the ground, atop stumps, even atop buildings, anywhere that the dove can find a place to position his first one or two twigs. At times they have built nests out of metal shavings from a lathe, out of pebbles on the ground, even laid their eggs on the bare sand. But a twig nest in a tree or bush is the norm. The female, amazed at her mate's twig-placing skill, lands on top of the twig and perches there. Then the male brings more and more branches to her. He lands on her back each time and delivers the twig; she places the twig rather haphazardly under her breast feathers. He goes back for another twig. Sometimes both birds bring twigs.

Nesting activity is triggered by a change to springlike temperatures. Most researchers feel that a week of nice days—characterized by nighttime temperatures not below the 38° mark—will start the mourning doves off on their mad race to see how many descendants they can leave before freezeup. Obviously, there are times when the doves get fooled, when a warm week gives way to renewed winter. Doves will heroically attempt to stay with their nesting attempt, even when everything is covered with snow again and temperatures plummet.

By the time the nest has been built, breeding has taken place, and the female is anxious to lay her first egg. Sometimes she deposits that egg on a nest so flimsy that you can see eggshell—pearly white—showing through the latticework of twigs upon which she has laid the egg. Second eggs are laid the second day, and incubation begins with the first one laid. The male shares the incubation duties, almost always working the day shift, with the female having the all-night duty. When she is on the nest, the male is often very close by, sitting quietly. At this time, he is apt to continue his courtship "cooing" as he did before the mating took place. After all, he intends to keep right on mating—with a single-minded devotion to reproduction that is remarkable—until the neighborhood freezes over.

After fourteen days the eggs hatch, and the completely helpless birds (altricial is the right word) are covered with white down, which quickly gives way to feathers. For the first nine days of their lives, the fledglings are fed a particularly nourishing concoction called "pigeon's milk." It is fed to the youngsters by both male and female. The young stick their beaks inside the parent's beak, and the white, thick gruellike substance is regurgitated by the adult. It is obviously a very good food, for the young develop so rapidly that it seems that they grow before your very eyes.

Male doves provide more "pigeon's milk" than do females. Doves and pigeons are the only males that produce food by lactation. The lining of the crop thickens and begins to secrete an oily, thick viscous substance, which is very high in calcium and vitamins. It is so rich that it enables the baby dove to increase its weight thirty times in less than two weeks! A two-week-old squab may actually weigh more than its father. The supply of pigeon's milk is usually shut off on the ninth day after hatching, so the growth is even more remarkable.

Fledglings fly quite well when fourteen days old, and that is a good thing, because mother is busy tending a second nest full of eggs and has little time for the older young.

Is this dove fecundity keeping pace with the demand for feathered targets? Less facetiously, is the dove population able to hold its own, considering the mortality factors (including hunting) that affect that population?

Doves are hunted in thirty-four of the forty-eight conterminous states. The fourteen states not hunting doves are Montana, Minnesota, Iowa, Michigan, Indiana, Ohio, New York, New Hampshire, Vermont, Maine, Massachusetts, Connecticut, Rhode Island, and New Jersey. Interestingly, the states that do allow dove hunting are home to about 86 percent of the breeding dove population of this nation.

North Dakota, South Dakota, Nebraska, and Kansas have the greatest density of breeding dove pairs in the annual counts. These four states and the distant state of South Carolina all re-

corded more than forty calling mourning doves per route in the spring counts in 1983.

Note that the Dakotas have a fairly recent history of dove hunting, with North Dakotans starting to hunt doves in 1979 and South Dakotans in 1981. It will be interesting to see if this change in treatment of Dakota mourning doves has any effect upon the overall breeding population in those states.

Research has pretty much convinced most biologists that one heavy wind and rainstorm in prime dove nesting country will kill more birds than the hunter does in that same area. However, the hunter's mortality is taken from the portion of the population that has already reached maturity. Most dove mortality is—obviously—on eggs and young fledglings. Eggs and nestlings lost may be replaced by later renesting. Loss to hunters will just as obviously not be replaced by later renesting. Hunting mortality, to a small degree at least, will reduce the breeding population. However, remember that word *fecundity*. A depressed mourning dove population can rebound dramatically when nesting conditions are right.

Mourning dove breeding populations increase and decrease in hunting and nonhunting states at almost the same time and to the same degree. This is not surprising, for the dove is migratory, and birds hatched in a nonhunting state like Ohio are killed in a hunting state like Alabama. When North Dakota was a nonhunting state as far as doves were concerned, 15,000 mourning doves were leg-banded in that state, and 121 leg bands were recovered from that 15,000 sample. Of those band returns, 41 percent came from Texas, where dove hunting is a favored sport. Mexico provided 27 percent of the band returns, pointing up both the migratory nature of the dove and the importance of Mexico as a mortality factor. Much of the dove kill in Mexico is traced to *Norteamericanos,* who do much of the bird hunting in the land below the border.

Some doves do not migrate at all, and a surprisingly large number winter in the land of ice and snow. Given winter grain food, or another source of their beloved seed diet, they'll do quite well.

How well have they done? Well, the changes that man made in the face of this continent have mostly been beneficial to the mourning dove, which undoubtedly exists in far greater numbers today than it did in 1492. Elimination of the dark, mature forest and the creation of a million times more "edge" has undoubtedly benefited the mourning dove. As the dove is primarily a seed eater, it took readily to the seeds that man likes to raise, especially wheat and sorghum. The fact that man used mechanical harvesters, which left immense quantities of "waste" grain, was just another plus to the adaptable dove.

Dove numbers got their biggest boost from the Soil Conservation Service in the "Dirty Thirties." Shelterbelts and "tree claims" began to spring up all across the upper midwest as a valuable buffer against wind erosion. These shelterbelts provided better nesting habitat than the dove had ever found in that area before, along with a great increase in the variety of his seed menu. Dove populations in the Dakotas, Nebraska, Kansas, Oklahoma, and Texas reacted favorably, and these states still are the top production areas in the nation for mourning doves.

But there came a day of reckoning, and we are now about to face it. The shelterbelts have reached their maturity and are dying out. Dead trees are being cut down for firewood across much of the plains, and they are not being replaced. In addition, high grain prices and high production costs have squeezed the farmer into a cost bind, where he is tempted to remove the shelterbelt and plant another acre or two in productive grain crops. It is hard to blame the farmer who is fighting for his financial survival, but the shortsightedness of this practice should be immediately apparent. The shelterbelts did a great job of minimizing soil erosion. Their removal will set agriculture back two human generations, and dove populations will suffer incidentally. More than 200 million seedling trees were planted on 30,000 farms in six states during the shelterbelt program, and the dove was a direct beneficiary, along with the ring-necked pheasant, the white-tailed deer, the cottontail rabbit, and the prairie grouse. We can ill afford to lose the shelterbelts, but we are in the process of losing them.

In the mid-1980s, the total estimate for North America's mourning dove population runs to approximately 476,000,000 birds in the fall of each year. Federal estimates for the annual kill of mourning doves have risen from the eleven million taken in 1942 to the forty-nine million taken each year in 1983 and 1984. This points out the obvious fact that more mourning doves are killed by hunters each year than any other species of game bird.

What Do Doves Eat?

The simple answer is seeds, nothing but seeds. A Missouri study showed that 2,000 mourning dove crops contained corn, wheat, foxtail grasses, beans, croton, ragweed, hogwort, cane, and spurge. Other seeds used regularly include:

switchgrass, amaranth, birdeye, Sudan grass, sunflower, canary grass, Texas millet, blue panicum, California poppy, browntop millet, ragweed, rape, and Japanese millet.

A word about sunflowers, which are now found almost everywhere that doves are found. The cultivated variety with the tall stalks and huge heads draws doves from great distances. However, it is a poor winter food, as the seeds rot quickly. Fallen seeds germinate quickly, making them unavailable to doves. Wild sunflowers, which are found in and around the edges of man's cultivated fields, seem to fare a little better, but are still not a dependable winter food.

The dove finds his seeds on the ground for the most part. His small feet are poorly adapted to hanging on while he tries to feed on the seeds of trees or bushes. He does not scratch in the litter, chickenlike, and is poorly suited to prying loose anything that is not readily available. Doves will starve to death in the presence of frozen ears of corn, for their weak beaks are not powerful enough to pry loose one of the life-giving kernels of corn. However, food is seldom a problem for the dove, as seeds of many kinds are available all year around in all climates.

of its range. It adapts well to humanity and often nests in very close proximity to occupied houses. One dove built a nest atop the mailbox, which was fastened to the house, 2 feet away from the front door that was used fifty times a day by a brood of healthy young humans. I'm happy to report that the dove brought off two broods of healthy young mourners from that unlikely nest location.

If mourning doves winter in your area—and some doves winter almost everywhere, including Minnesota and Michigan—take a good look at their winter food supply. A few ears of corn, with the kernels scraped off the cob, please, will tide over a pair of doves in the worst winter snowstorm. It is well to provide such winter food early in the winter and make sure that the doves find it and use it before the need arises.

If a small patch of brush is used heavily as nesting cover, you can increase nesting success by fencing cattle out of the brushy spot, or at least out of part of it.

In the wild, it is an exceptional mourning dove that lives more than four years. Death awaits the dove at every turn of its life, but the dove has the answer. It's love, sweet love, which overcomes all. Fecundity, thy name is mourning dove!

Management for Mourning Doves

Preservation of trees and shrubs for nesting cover is perhaps the most important part of dove management in the areas of greatest production, the central plains states from North Dakota down to Texas. This is not a problem over the eastern part of the mourning doves' range, of course. However, the dove doesn't seem to be having any problems over most

White-winged Doves

The whitewing resembles the mourning dove in almost all things. His most evident difference in appearance is the white feathers on the shoulder of the wing, which flash brilliantly in flight and which give this bigger bird his name.

In addition to the white wing feathers, the whitewing has a shorter, more rounded tail. His flight is strong and more direct than that of the mourning dove. He is less given to "juking" about when reducing speed prior to landing.

The whitewing is primarily a Mexican and Central and South American species, but the northern edge of his range laps over into Arizona and Texas, and to a lesser degree into New Mexico.

I first met the whitewing in southern Texas' Rio Grande Valley. There, fifty years ago, the whitewing was a common colony nester over all the counties bordering on Mexico, northward to the New Mexico border. The mesquite scrub, which was its favored nesting spot, was a loud place during the courtship period, for the sound of whitewings—similar to that of mourning doves, but stronger, more assertive in sound—was like the roaring of distant surf. Fall flights numbered in the millions in 1930, but dropped to approximately 200,000 in 1940 as the result of drouth and food shortages.

These birds, far more gregarious than the mourning dove, tolerated another nesting pair in the same bush or tree with their own nest. At times, as many as twenty-six nests will be found in a single tree. They reared multiple broods, like the mourning dove, but had a far greater success ratio, simply because their southerly habitat did not often suffer the late spring snows or early fall snows that were the cause of extensive mortality in mourning-dove land. Their favored nesting tree was the Texas ebony, especially those that had grown to a height of 20 feet or more and formed an excellent canopy. They did not choose the mesquite tree for nesting very often. However, Texans have a habit of referring to all brushy habitat as "mesquite," even though it be composed of dozens of other shrubs and trees. This explains why early

observers said that it was nesting in the "mesquite" when actually *the* mesquite tree was not a favored nest site.

These Texas birds were definitely "wetbacks," as they crossed the Rio Grande into Mexico and back without benefit of passport. It was a two-way passage, and thousands of birds hatched in Mexico made the fatal mistake of flying north into the cultivated fields of Texas when they had exhausted preferred grain foodstocks below the border. In 1960 the hunting season on whitewings in the Rio Grande section of Texas was short but noisy. It was a free-for-all type of hunt. Hunters brought four or five boxes of shotgun shells with them and carried stepladders to sit upon. Spaced at regular intervals along the edge of a grainfield, they all faced Mexico and waited for the incoming thousands. When the birds came, they did not turn aside at the sight of hunters at work, rather they picked up the airspeed a few knots and dared the hunters to hit them. In some areas, where the shotgunners were expert, the carnage was terrific, but the great majority of birds successfully ran the gauntlet and disappeared into the feeding grounds. Later that day, of course, most of them would head back, and the shooting would again be continuous.

Today, the brush nesting grounds on our side of the Rio Grande have been displaced by citrus groves. Ruby Red grapefruit is now the crop, rather than whitewings. True, the whitewing still nests there, but in such greatly reduced numbers that it is disheartening to make the comparison with three decades ago.

However, in mid-1984 I made an extensive trip down into the Mexican states of Nuevo Leon, Tamaulipas, Coahuila, Zacatecas, Durango, Sinaloa, and Sonora. Great parts of this huge area are a combination of irrigated farming and undisturbed native brushland. We drove for days without being out of sight of white-winged doves. They flushed from the roadsides, where they were probably picking up their day's supply of grit, and from the water's edge at each pond or irrigation return flow. The whitewing is still in good shape in Mexico, although his total numbers have probably been reduced by more than half in the last forty years. What has caused this catastrophic decline in both nations?

In most cases, elimination of optimum nesting habitat and its replacement by row-crop farming and irrigation systems has been the biggest culprit. The whitewing is definitely not as adaptable to changing land-use practices as is the mourning dove. A further complication is the fact that the whitewing is not an aggressive "colonizer." They do not readily start new colonies, even when conditions and whitewing numbers are optimum for doing so.

The Arizona Game and Fish Department cites loss of habitat to land clearing, to irrigation, and to conversion from grain to cotton as a cash crop for the loss of a great portion of their whitewings. In an attempt to stem this trend, that state has withdrawn from farming use some areas of nesting habitat and is holding them for whitewings. They are also recommending planting of whitewing food crops close to the colony nesting sites in order to lure the birds into staying in the colony. In addition, they have tried to stop the removal of salt cedars and other phreatophytes along the irrigation canals. This misguided removal program is ostensibly to save precious water. According to the Bureau of Reclamation theorists, salt cedars and other emergent vegetation si-

phon up great quantities of water and lose it into the air by transpiration. They want to save water by removing the trees. It is strange that the water cycle has successfully gone on its way for millions of years without any phreatophyte control. To my mind, there is no evidence that water is actually saved by removing green growth and leaving the land a flat, plowed landscape, devoid of wildlife. The big saguaro cactus, a source of food and a preferred nesting site in Arizona, is important to the whitewing, and it, too, is threatened by cactus rustlers who steal the huge pincushions for use as subdivision decorations.

Not all whitewings are colonial nesters, happily, and there are enough birds distributed widely over less-than-optimum nesting habitat to give the whitewing a secure future in Arizona. The same thing cannot be said of the remnant population in New Mexico, which was probably never prime habitat for the birds, nor in Texas where loss of habitat continues at a fearful pace—a pace destined to make the whitewing only an occasional visitor to the Lone Star State.

Whitewings raise multiple broods of two every year, as the mourning dove does. The second egg is usually laid thirty-six hours after the first one, and incubation begins with the first egg. Like the mourning dove, the whitewing is a lousy nest builder but a determined reproducer, and his potential for population growth is excellent when conditions are right. The whitewing has learned to put his nest, most of the time, in a shady place—a sensible adaptation in the land of searing sun. The male helps incubate, taking the day shift—which is the harder part in the heat of the Southwestern deserts.

Nestling mortality, caused by wind and

rain, grackles, snakes, crows, hawks, and owls, is substantial. Adult birds fall prey to Cooper's hawks, goshawks and sharp-shinned hawks, as well as to the shotgunner.

When the shooting starts, it is often hot and heavy in the whitewinged-dove flyways.

Grackles have proved to be the biggest threat to whitewing production in the Rio Grande valley of Texas. Intensive grackle control (by shooting) in the preferred ebony-anacua brush resulted in killing 2,824 grackles in 1964 and another 1,398 grackles off the same small 15½-acre patch in 1965. At the height of the breeding season in 1965, the 15½ acres held 16,000 whitewings at the density of 529 pairs per acre. The dense nesting colony succeeded in fledging 93 percent of all the eggs that hatched, far better than they could have done with the usual loss to grackles. In this same south Texas habitat, the green jay is also a bad predator on whitewing eggs and young, but is not present in great numbers, or over a great area. In fact, if you want to see a green jay in Texas, you'd better confine your search to the Santa Ana refuge. The beautiful indigo snake, a wonderful ratter, is not above making a few big meals from a whitewing colony, specializing in both eggs and young birds. If the young birds do escape predation, their growth, fueled by the nutritious pigeon milk, is phenomenal. Their weights, on average, will increase from 7.6 grams on the first day after hatching to 38.8 grams on the fourth day and to 76.7 grams on the tenth day after hatching.

The hunting mortality can be controlled, and the species is no longer being overhunted in the United States. Its food needs are well met everywhere within its range. In fact, it has become so much of a small grain eater in many parts of Mexico that hunters are welcomed on most of the large landholdings—for one purpose, to minimize loss of grain in the field. I know one man who has found his own personal scatter-gunners' heaven. He comes to Los Mochis each fall, along with all the lead shot and gunpowder and primers he can carry. He shoots great numbers of whitewings, legally, almost every day. Then he reloads those shotgun shells and does it again tomorrow. By spending the winter on the whitewing ranges of Sinaloa, he shoots more sporty targets per month than most of us will see in a lifetime. Incidentally, none of the birds are wasted. I've eaten some of them to help him out, but all of his bag is used by a protein-hungry Mexico.

It is hard to criticize the whitewing for its depredations on mankind's cultivated fields. After all, he was there first, eating seeds and doing very well indeed. Along came mankind growing delicious new kinds of seeds on the same area and taking away the whitewings' nesting habitat at the same time. The dove simply continued doing what came naturally, which was eating seeds. In fact, when dove-weed seeds become available, the whitewings will often leave their grainfield dining tables to go to the preferred wild food. Whitewings eat a more varied diet than does the mourning dove. Preferred foods are doveweed, leatherweed, oak mast, legumes, cactus fruits, colima, coma, black-eyed peas in Texas, and even the mast from prickly pear cactus. They will fly to mature sorghum stands by the thousands and perch on the heads, eating them from the top down. A big flight of whitewings can reduce a sorghum field in short order, as many Texas Rio Grande farmers have found out.

Management for White-winged Doves

Preservation of habitat is of prime importance. As long as we continue such foolish and unproven practices as phreatophyte control, we will continue to lose our whitewings. Good-sized pieces of habitat are needed to preserve the colony nesting doves, while the "noncolonials" seem to be doing all right in their widely scattered nesting places. Perhaps it is a part of evolution that more and more whitewings are now nesting away from colonies?

But the state of Arizona feels that the future of the whitewing is wrapped up with the preservation of colonial nesting sites. They are advocating the growing of small grains and safflowers close to state-owned colonial nesting sites, in the hopes of preserving the colony. In Texas, a few good colony nesting sites are being preserved because the rancher has learned that he can sell the hunting privileges to his whitewings for more money than he can make with another crop—such as citrus. As one Texan told me, "Whitewings are a dependable crop, they've never been froze out on me, like my citrus has about

every eight or nine years." Whitewings will nest in citrus trees, but the total reproduction there is always lower than in their beloved brush type (ebony preferred) habitat.

Preservation of habitat is obviously the key to whitewing survival and prosperity throughout their range, whether it be saguaro preservation in Arizona, brush preservation in south Texas, or mesquite-huisache-lantana habitat in central Mexico. Providing water in otherwise completely dry areas is another form of habitat preservation, for it spreads the nesting flocks out, rather than concentrating them within flying distance of water. I well remember sitting beside the Charlie Bell Well, far out on the desert, part of the Cabeza Prieta Wildlife Range in Arizona, and watching whitewing doves come to this windmill-pumped water. Literally thousands of birds came each morning and afternoon, flying directly to the water, drinking deeply and then flying arrow-straight back to their nests—which were as distant as four miles from the well. Water is life in the desert, and the whitewing needs water. Yet this is a problem too large for the individual landowner to handle all by himself. It would help greatly if states would enact legislation that would make it financially profitable to preserve habitat, such as the Minnesota Wetlands Tax Credit Law or the Natural Streambed and Land Preservation Act passed in 1975 in Montana. Enactment of such legislation to provide habitat for whitewing doves would simply recognize that the bird has an economic value to the state—a value that is well worth perpetuating.

Lacking such legislation statewide, the only hope for managing the whitewing remnant flocks is the landowner.

"Woodsman, spare that tree whenever possible" should be the fervent plea of the wildlifer in the desert Southwest.

Cooking Doves

Doves are easily picked, so it would be a crime to skin them. There is very little meat on the legs, but it is delicious. Pick your doves in the field, if you can, for this sure avoids a mess in the backyard or garage, and it helps to cool the birds out quickly. I pick and draw my birds in the field and never carry them in a plastic pouch or in a hot game pocket. To do so is to ask for strong-tasting meat. Try a few of these recipes:

Delightful Dozen

> *1 dozen doves, whole*
>   *flour*
>   *cooking oil*
> *2 cans beef consomme*
> *2 large carrots, diced*
> *3 stalks celery, chopped*
> *1 large onion, chopped*
> *½ cup cooking sherry*

Coat the doves with flour and brown in hot cooking oil. Drain well. Pour consomme into 2-quart casserole. Add carrots, celery, onion, and sherry. Use enough flour to thicken to consistency of gravy—slightly on the thin side. Add doves to this casserole, cover, and simmer for 1 hour at 325°F in preheated oven.

Terrific Ten

> *10 strips bacon*
> *10 dressed doves, whole*
> *1 small jar chipped beef*
> *1 can cream of mushroom soup*
> *1 cup sour cream*

Wrap a strip of bacon around each bird. Spread out the chipped beef in the bottom of the casserole. Arrange doves on top. Pour soup and cream over the doves. Bake at 350°F until done.

Eminently Edible Eight

> *8 doves, cleaned*
> *3 tbsp. flour*
> *½ tsp. salt*
> *¼ tsp. pepper*
> *½ cup olive oil*
> *2 garlic cloves*
> *1 cup red dinner wine*

Coat the doves with flour, salt, and pepper mixture. Heat oil, with garlic, in a cast-iron skillet. Brown doves in skillet. Remove garlic and discard. Add the wine and barely enough water to submerge the birds. Simmer slowly for about 1½ hours. Thicken pan juices with a bit of flour, and you have both tender doves and tasty gravy.

Fried Doves

You can, of course, simply fry well-cleaned doves. Flouring them and frying them in hot olive oil works wonders. Add a bit of chopped onion to the doves while browning. After browning, add a bit of water to the pan and braise on low heat. Thirty minutes will do for young birds (most of them are young birds), but it will take about 45 minutes for last year's birds.

Doves Italienne

> *4 doves*
>   *garlic salt, pepper, and flour*
> *¼ cup olive oil*
> *1 8-ounce can tomato sauce*

½ can beer
4 medium onions, sliced
½ tsp. crushed oregano
3 tbsp. chopped parsley

Sprinkle doves inside and out with salt, pepper, and flour. Heat olive oil in skillet, add doves, and brown on all sides. Add tomato sauce, beer, onions, and oregano. Bring to boil. Cover and cook over low heat until tender. Add parsley and stir. Goes good with spaghetti.

This recipe was used by permission of the South Dakota Department of Game, Fish and Parks. It's true that it goes well with spaghetti. However, we used eight doves instead of four, didn't change any of the other ingredients, and enjoyed it without the pasta.

Recipe for Twenty or More Doves

So when you really get into the doves and when you combine your two-day limits for a big blowout, try this one. Simply remove all of the breasts (only) from the doves. Marinate overnight in a spicy salad dressing. We used Spicy Italian, and have also used a vinegar and oil salad dressing, going easy on the vinegar. Then broil the little breasts over a very hot heat, sprinkling a dollop of butter on each one when almost done. Yummm!

Sauerkraut Dove

It doesn't sound good, but it works out well. Stuff the doves with sauerkraut and roast for about 30 minutes in a 400°F oven.

Classic Mourning Doves

12 doves, whole
½ cup onion, chopped
1 cup mushrooms, sliced

1 cup chopped celery
½ cup butter
pinch each basil and oregano
2 tablespoons soy sauce
1½ cup cream
parsley, for appearance's sake

Put doves, whole, in shallow baking dish. In a frying pan, sauté the onion, mushrooms, and celery in butter for about 10 minutes, over low heat. Add seasonings, soy sauce, and cream, and bring to nearly boiling. Pour the whole works over the doves and pop them, *covered,* into a 350°F oven for an hour. Turn the birds a couple of times during the cooking.

BAND-TAILED PIGEONS

Band-tailed pigeons are native to a very large area of mountain country, extending from southern British Columbia down to the Baja peninsula's northern mountains in Old Mexico. They are found in all of the mountain states east to a line extending roughly from Santa Fe, New Mexico, to Denver, Colorado, to Billings, Montana.

Historically, this bigger-than-a-barn-pigeon bird wintered in Mexico's mountains all the way south to Nicaragua. However, it has become exceedingly scarce on Mexican wintering grounds in the last twenty years, which makes me worry for its future.

About 15 inches long, this handsome pigeon is named by the dark band of black across its gray-brown tail. A narrow stripe of white across the back of the neck, just below the head and just above a hard-to-see patch of green iridescent feathers, is the most important identifying mark.

This bird feeds on seeds and mast found in the high country and makes long flights to dine on waste grain in the flatland below its chosen mountains. A very strong flier, it thinks nothing of flying five or ten miles to feed, then hurrying back up to the clean air of the mountains.

Like other pigeons, it produces only 2 eggs at a time and sometimes has multiple broods in one year. However, its reproductive potential must not be as great as that of the smaller white-winged and mourning doves, for it has not maintained its numbers in recent years. The biggest danger to the bandtail is probably increased human disturbance of its nesting grounds. It nests in trees, usually at considerable distance above the ground, and it would seem that its nests would be quite safe, but such is not the case.

Bandtails cover great distances in fall and spring migrations, often traveling in groups of twenty-five or thirty. Highly gregarious, they are almost never found alone. Migrations are triggered by the onset of wintry weather, but the flocks may travel great distances in search of either food or water, if one of these essentials is missing.

Their flight is deceptively fast, as many a shotgunner has had impressed upon him by an inexplicable series of misses on what seemed like easy shots. When flushed from the ground, the bird offers the easiest shot you will get at bandtails, but when flushed from a high tree, the bandtail launches itself out and down in a swoop that builds up flying speed almost instantly. Look for bandtails near good supplies of acorns, pine nuts, pinyons, madrone, and all wild berries. If you know of a mineralized seep in the mountains, that is another good place to search for the "here today, gone tomorrow" bandtails.

Like all members of the dove family, the bandtail is a tempting meal to almost all carnivores, but suffers its greatest losses to the goshawk and peregrine falcon. These raptors are able to catch the bandtail in flight—although it takes some doing, even for the peregrine.

Outside of reducing human intrusion into nesting areas, I know of no measures available to the landowner that I can honestly say will better the lot of the bandtail.

4

Migratory Waterfowl

Probably the greatest wildlife treasure in North America when the first Europeans arrived was the migratory waterfowl. This was not immediately apparent, for settlement started in the east, of course, and our greatest wealth of waterfowl lay on the central flyway's limitless expanse of potholes and sloughs, production factories for mallards, gadwalls, pintails, scaup, canvasbacks, redheads, blue-winged teal, green-winged teal, cinnamon teal, goldeneyes, buffleheads, Canada geese (varying from little 2½-pounders up to the lordly Giant Canada, which weighed in at 20 pounds upon occasion), greater and lesser snow geese—with the blue phase of lesser snow geese not in sight yet, white-fronted geese, and the tiny white Ross' goose (which had not been identified yet).

Man rapidly usurped the home space of all species of migratory waterfowl, crowding the birds out of ancestral homes, paving over potholes, making shopping centers out of swamps. Worst of all, we drained their potholes and sloughs, thus removing the nursery areas upon which entire species of waterfowl depended. By 1932, waterfowl were in dire straits, reeling and ready for the knockout blow that the Dust Bowl years signified. Populations that once darkened the sun were reduced to pitiful remnants. One of the giants of the conservation movement, Jay "Ding" Darling, an Iowa cartoonist and lifelong battler for the rights of wildlife, came to the fore at this time, arousing the conscience of a nation, pointing out the excesses we were committing that endangered the future of the birds. At the same time, Hugh Bennett became the chief of the U.S. Soil Conservation Service.

Black duck with patagial marker, part of a migration study. *U.S. Fish & Wildlife photo.*

Newly elected Franklin Delano Roosevelt used the power of the presidency to give these two men top jobs and to give them almost a free hand with the management of our soils and our waterfowl.

Scientific management of waterfowl began. Spring shooting was slowed, then stopped, although stubborn pockets of resistance to the end of spring shooting remained well into the early 1950s.

In the northwest corner of Missouri, early in that decade, I approached a gentleman of about eighty years who was toting an ancient double barrel into a cornfield one snowy, windy day in March. After advising him that I was a federal game-law enforcement officer, I cautioned, "Dad, this is not a good time for you to shoot a goose!"

With a quizzical smile, the oldster retorted, "Sonny, the time to shoot a goose is when he's in range!"

The bulldozer was slowed in its relentless effort to drain every drop of water from the prairie pothole region. Farmers who had watched their topsoil blow away

were anxious to cooperate with the Soil Conservation Service in preventing wind erosion. They gladly took to any program that saved scarce water and that stopped the loss of valuable topsoil from their lands. The Migratory Bird Conservation Stamp was born, and sportsmen thus taxed themselves to ensure the future of hunting and the future of waterfowl. For waterfowl, the headlong slide to oblivion was checked, then slow progress began. But it was terribly slow, because that intangible thing that man calls progress is definitely not progress for migratory waterfowl. Wetlands were still being drained at a catastrophic rate, and that drainage still continues into the mid-1980s.

The Pittman-Robertson Act was passed by Congress and signed into law, thus earmarking the monies collected through an excise tax on sporting arms and ammunition for use in wildlife restoration work. These funds, which reimbursed the impecunious state game and fish departments for 75 percent of the cost of wildlife research and other costly wildlife management practices, were a godsend during the Depression years. Organized hunters provided the lobbying push that got this tax through the Congress, showing again the willingness of the hunter to pay for the good of his sport and pay any price to prevent the loss of migratory waterfowl for the future.

We began to see some results by the end of the thirties; the forties were even better; and there has been very slow— but steady—progress through the decades of the fifties, sixties, and seventies. The game-law enforcement effort has been beefed up, and public compliance has improved along with public understanding of the issues involved.

The reaction of waterfowl species to management measures designed to help them has been varied and complex. For example, Canada geese have greatly increased their numbers, demonstrating that they react to improved management to a greater degree than perhaps any other species of wildlife.

Too many geese in some areas is now the welcome problem. Depredations ascribed to "too many" geese on the wintering grounds has become commonplace. State and federal refuges have done perhaps too good a job of providing shelter and food for the birds on their southward migration in the fall, and this has "piled up" goose populations and made them too vulnerable to extremely localized hunting. This has even resulted in changing the ancestral migration patterns of Canada geese. They no longer go as far south as they used to go; this is called shortstopping. It arouses the ire of those at the southern end of the flyway and puts big smiles on the faces of hunters at midway points in the migration path.

The U.S. Fish and Wildlife Service now assigns "kill quotas" to some goose ref-

uge concentration points. When this kill has been reached, the season is closed. This arouses the ire of hunters who have scheduled their hunts too late in the season and angers those who rent out pits on their land to be used by goose hunters. In addition, the concentration of geese, relieved of hunting pressure, is free to feed very heavily on farm fields. Planes and carbide exploders have been used to haze the birds away from these spots and try to get them started south again. But when a goose learns the whereabouts of a certain supply of yellow corn, he is very hard to convince that he needs to fly farther south. Already in goose heaven, he does not go in search of paradise. While Canada goose numbers still are far below those found by the first explorers in the midsection of America, we now have about as many free-flying wild Canada geese as we can accommodate. It is now not a matter of numbers, but of distribution.

On the far end of the spectrum, diving ducks have not responded at all to the efforts expended in their behalf. Canvasbacks and redheads are "over water" nesters, building floating nests or nests tied to emergent vegetation. They need more water than do the dabblers. Divers get their name by their habit of diving to the bottom to feed on tender, submerged vegetation. Wild celery and other such foods growing in deeper water are the canvasbacks' delight. In addition, the diving ducks are strongly territorial. They will not usually tolerate another nesting pair in the same small pothole or slough that they have chosen to raise a brood. This "dog in the manger" attitude on the part of the divers greatly reduces nesting opportunities for the species concerned. When the rains do not come to the prairies, some water areas dry up. Others are

Nest of canvasback duck, carefully built over water, illustrates importance of pothole nesting cover for this prized species. *U.S. Fish & Wildlife photo.*

greatly reduced in size, which reduces their ability to support canvasback breeders—usually limiting it to one pair. In other water areas, the water is simply not deep enough to provide for the needs of the redhead or canvasback.

Drouth has hit in the wrong years lately. Just when the divers seemed to be making a comeback, exceptionally dry seasons reduced production of young, and the trend continues downward. We cannot escape the conclusion that divers simply do not respond to management. However, when we close the season entirely, as we have done in the past, we are taught anew the old lesson that you cannot stockpile game species.

In between the easily managed Canada goose and the hard-to-manage diving ducks, we encounter a most important group of ducks—the dabblers. They respond better to management than do the divers, but at their best, they are not as responsive as the geese. We call them dabblers because they feed by dabbling in the bottom muck, searching for the

aquatic seeds and plant and animal life they feed upon. Some dabblers, such as the mallards, love agricultural grain crops and cause significant loss to swathed grains when conditions are right. Others, such as the teal, never feed on farm grains, at least not enough to be noticed by anyone. Other dabblers include the pintail, gadwall, and widgeon, all three of which are important in the hunter's bag each fall.

Management of migratory waterfowl lies almost entirely in the hands of federal authorities. The federal government sets the season regulations. The states can be more restrictive—and often have—but they cannot be more generous. The "feds" have adopted the theory that "as mallards go, so go all other species of dabbling ducks." Each year, state and federal wildlifers cooperate in a series of population counts, or trend studies, all destined to show them if the hunting pressure on the mallard (and, by definition, all other dabblers) should be decreased or increased. They count broods seen on transects surveyed from low-flying aircraft on the same routes year after year. They tally the kill by species, with information derived from a nationwide collection of wing feathers from ducks taken during the season. They actually count birds on the wintering areas, again using low-flying aircraft on transects that are familiar from many decades of observation. More than any other species, they study the mallard.

For forty years, duck management has meant mallard management. Because of this emphasis on the most wanted duck— the mallard—management experts really do not know how the lesser species have fared. Their best indication of the status of widgeon, for example, comes from the kill figures. That is rather late to offset reduced production that spring by a re-

Mallards don't mind cold weather. As long as open weather and food are available, mallards stay around. These are on Amchitka Island. *U.S. Fish & Wildlife photo.*

duced hunting opportunity, for example . . . after the season is over. However, species-specific management of migratory waterfowl is almost impossible. The reason is that the average hunter cannot tell one species of duck from another, especially the dabblers, and especially in the poor light half an hour before sunrise, when most ducks are shot. A quarter of a century ago, wildlife artist Bob Hines, then an employee of the Fish and Wildlife Service, produced a tiny, pocket-sized pamphlet called *Ducks at a Distance,* which was, and is, the very best guide to North American duck identification under hunting conditions. It has been printed over and over and has done much to enable the American hunter to take the first few, faltering steps into species-specific duck management. This type of management must, obviously, be based upon the ability to recognize the different species. The average hunter cannot do this at the present time.

Canada geese are well suited to benefit from improved management practices. Diving ducks seem to be a law unto themselves, not reacting to anything we do. The dabbler ducks seem to be somewhere in between these two extremes. But there is still another kind of waterfowl, which is in a class by itself. This is the wood duck, a beautiful, good-tasting, sporting duck that does lots of strange things—such as nesting high in a hollow tree, in a very unducklike manner. Management of this species has been a very bright spot in the past few years. Woody has made a great comeback in numbers and bids fair to be as great a success story as the Canada goose.

THE CANADA GOOSE

To my mind, the Canada goose is the finest bird that ever lived, the final perfection achieved by evolutionary processes. After more than fifty years of hunting them, I have learned to admire their intelligence, their innate wariness.

But I have also learned that they have a few chinks in their armor, a few "Achilles' tendons" that render them vulnerable.

Canadas vary greatly in size and weight. I have weighed healthy adult Canadas that just barely topped 2 pounds. I've seen Canada geese dwarfed by oversized mallard ducks! Yet there are records of the Giant Canada weighing as much as 20 pounds. This giant strain was thought to be extinct for several decades. Then we noticed that a few of them were still around, and they were given special protection on some wintering places in southern Minnesota and in Missouri. They have staged quite a comeback. Brood stock from this giant strain was used by Missouri in reestablishing breeding flocks of Canadas, and they have prospered.

Conspicuous identifying marks are the white cheek patches and the solid black neck. There's another solid black band across the top of the tail when the goose is in flight. Outside of that, the Canada is a series of gray and black shades, lighter on the belly than on the back. Separate races of Canadas have been established by centuries of line inbreeding, and, of course, the size and habits of these separate races have been greatly influenced by the strikingly different habitat niches they call home. For example, one of the smallest Canadas lives in the Aleutian Islands. Living in the fog-bound, wet cold of the Aleutians, this race prospered until man, in his greed for quick fur riches, released foxes on the breeding islands of the Aleutian Canada. Results were catastrophic. Heredity had not taught the Aleutian goose that he need fear mammalian predators. The goose nested in the open, without any attempt to hide the nest. Foxes not only ate the eggs and young, but often were able to catch the adult birds on the nesting ground. The Aleutian goose almost disappeared. It was listed as one of the endangered species. Poisoning of the foxes to the point of exterminating them from entire islands was begun. As fast as an island was cleared of foxes—foxes that were never native there—the Aleutian goose was restocked, using birds reared at the Patuxent Migratory Bird Center in Maryland.

The Aleutian is now on his way back. Although he nests in the snows and cold of the fog-shrouded Aleutians, he winters in sunny California.

Canada geese are practical birds. Their migration flights are straight and direct and no longer than necessary. Winter holds no fears for these strong and hardy birds. They go only far enough south to find abundant food, along with a little (sometimes very little) open water. If these necessities of life are found well north on the migration path, the Canada will stop there and not go farther south.

In their efforts to make life better for

Canada goose with young. Bear River, Utah.

Canada geese at rest. These are at Monte Vista National Wildlife Refuge, Colorado.

Canada geese, the U.S. Fish and Wildlife Service developed goose heavens on the migration routes. These goose heavens consisted of national wildlife refuges strategically located in farming country, with the required amount of open water in winter. Then, to improve on paradise, the Fish and Wildlife Service went into corn farming in a big way. Farming was usually done by neighboring farmers on a share basis, with Uncle Sam's share of the corn left in the field for the geese. Crab Orchard, Horicon, Horseshoe Bend, Necedah, Brigantine, Bombay Hook, Squaw Creek, Sand Lake, and a dozen others were serving the geese well, and the goose population responded. Large flocks of Canadas stayed at these refuges as long as there was food available on the refuge and in the surrounding area. This "shortstopped" the geese, delaying or eliminating entirely their habitual flight to the southern end of their flyway.

At the same time, other forces were at work that intensified the trend toward wintering farther north. The development of local nesting flocks in states along the flyway provided a nucleus of wintering birds that did not see any reason to move farther south. Most successful example is the Foothills flock of local nesters in Colorado. By protecting pinioned nesting birds, Colorado authorities were able to establish flocks of nonmigrating geese in and around the Denver area. Semi-tame Canadas are now a familiar hazard on many of the golf courses in Denver, as the birds help the greens keepers mow the short, tender green grass. There was an unexpected dividend from this local nesting flock program. Conditions were made so attractive in the Denver area that geese coming from farther north find what they want and spend the winter in the area, instead of following ancestral habits and wintering in the lower Rio Grande Valley of New Mexico. While Colorado has greatly increased its population of wintering Canadas, New Mexico's wintering Canadas are down to a few thousand.

Farther east, the same thing hurt Louisiana's Canada winter populations. Shortstopping kept the birds in Illinois

Leg-banding Canada goose as an aid to tracing migration paths. *U.S. Fish & Wildlife photo.*

and in Missouri, reducing the number of birds that went on down to the Sportsmen's Paradise in Louisiana. At the same time, intelligent management was dictating that the birds be hunted only on two or three days out of each week, which eliminated the former result of hunting, which was to drive the birds out of the area.

The most successful example of Canada goose management is the Eastern Shore wintering flock of Canadas, which piles geese up to the 600,000 population mark in Maryland. Here, commercial operations furnish goose-hunting opportunities from pit blinds for a price. Goose

hunting here is most rewarding in numbers of birds killed per hunter day. Many of the "pay to hunt" operations provide expert goose callers who greatly increase the chances of getting a close-in shot. They also furnish large spreads of correctly placed decoys—an important part of shooting geese the right way.

What do we know about Canada geese?

They are monogamous, mating with only one mate per season. Usually, the mated pair will remain together until one or the other is killed. Then the survivor promptly seeks a mate for the next season. They usually lay only 4 to 6 creamy-white eggs, but they do a very efficient

Family group of Canada geese. *Frank Martin, U.S. Fish & Wildlife photo.*

platforms can be constructed by setting two straw bales atop a platform 8 or 10 feet high. If the legs are shrouded with metal circles to prevent mammalian predators from climbing up, the hatching success rate will be very high.

Both birds share the parental duties, and the gander can be very belligerent in defense of his goslings. He will often drive off a human by a direct frontal attack, wings extended, head held low in front of him, hissing as he comes. Once within range, he can deal out a lot of damage with repeated blows of those powerful wings.

The family ties are very strong, and the family group stays together on the flight south and until time for the return flight the next spring. Because the young stay with their "older and wiser" parents through the hunting season, they learn to avoid the hunter from an expert teacher.

Goslings feed heavily on insects when

job of incubating and rearing the young. The top of a muskrat house is a preferred nesting place, and islands are often chosen because they offer protection from land-based predators. Artificial nesting

Neck-banded Canada goose, in typical threatening posture, protecting nest. *U.S. Fish & Wildlife photo.*

Young of the Canada goose, still in the nest. *U.S. Fish & Wildlife photo.*

they are newly hatched, then switch to green grass, which makes up a large part of the diet during the summer months, and to seeds as the season goes along. By fall, they have learned that the seeds that man produces on his grainfields are bigger, tastier, and easier to find than natural seeds, so they head for the combined wheat fields and the cornfields, which offer lots of waste grain after the harvest is over.

To make your land more attractive to migrating flocks of Canada geese, you can employ fire at the right time in late summer, so that new greenery will spring up to lure the migrating birds. The time of burning must be carefully chosen so as to minimize losses of habitat to other species such as upland game birds and cot-

tontail rabbits. Geese will do a good job of finding waste grain in the fields, especially if there is an undisturbed resting area on a lake or slough nearby. That word *undisturbed* is very important here. Geese will quickly locate an area where they are not going to be disturbed and will use it in succeeding years if the situation doesn't change.

If your land is within the traditional breeding areas of the Canada, you may establish a breeding flock by purchasing paired adults from one of the many game farms that offer them. Pinioned birds, unable to fly, will take advantage of the water area you provide, use the safe nesting spots you provide, dine on the foods you provide, and produce healthy young that, of course, may fly away and never return.

Canada geese form a tight family grouping, which endures until next spring's northward flight. *U.S. Fish & Wildlife photo.*

However, the chances are good that the offspring will "imprint" on the area where their life began, and will either stay over winter with their parents or will return to the home place after migrating south and back. Remember that your breeding adults are handicapped by not being able to fly. Provide them with a safe nesting spot, preferably on an island in the center of your water area. Keep a sharp watch-out for predators at the beginning. You paid for those geese and you didn't intend them to be dog food or a sacrifice to a fox or coyote.

Creation of a local breeding flock can be a very rewarding project. But it can also be a heartbreaking proposition. You may raise a big brood of youngsters and proudly watch them learn to fly. Then you may see them all shot on the opening day of the hunting season. If your goose-rearing project is in the center of a large land holding, it has a better chance of success, of course. Liberal handouts of yellow corn will do more to keep the birds in your small area than will anything else.

Because the Canada goose is very in-telligent, he is easily tamed—which only shows that he recognizes friends. But that tendency to domestication has proved frustrating at times. For example, Missouri has many local breeding flocks of very large Canadas that have become pampered pets, pets that approach people seeking a handout, pets that are better suited to grazing on ornamental lawns and golf courses than to making a living in the wild.

Canada geese are strong fliers. They often form vee-shaped formations when migrating, each bird benefiting by flying in undisturbed air, rather than following their brood mate's path. They migrate northward in the spring, following the 35°F mark. As it comes up to 35° in an area, the Canadas appear. Of course, they often guess wrong and have to wait it out while the 35° line retreats temporarily.

Their breeding ground in the wild may be on lakes or along rivers, and they take to wooded areas more readily than do the duck species we call divers or dabblers. Bear River Migratory Bird Refuge near Brigham City, Utah, is a fine place to observe geese nesting and to watch the young birds learn the facts of life from their solicitous parents.

Cooking the Goose

A wild goose is a lean, trim, hard-bodied athlete, completely different from the fat, lazy, domestic goose. The most basic difference is that the wild goose is not full of lard. For this reason, you must sauté everything you intend to place inside a wild goose to be roasted. It will *not* cook itself in the goose grease—there isn't any grease on this healthy bird's body.

The second basic difference is that you must baste more often or cover the carcass completely with foil to prevent it drying out. Outside of those two differences, it is routine to cook a wild goose . . . the flavor on the table is strictly not routine.

Roast Young Goose

For tender young geese, you'll need:

> *1 lemon*
> *1 apple-sized onion, chopped to ¹/₂-inch pieces*
> *¹/₂ cup margarine (not diet margarine, which burns instead of melting)*
> *1 cup chopped apple, green or ripe*
> *1 cup chopped, dried apricots*
> *2 handfuls of croutons (not sage or garlic, just plain croutons) salt and pepper to taste*
> *4 slices bacon*

Quarter the lemon, and use it to rub the bird inside and out. Squeeze it to get out the remaining juice and put that juice in the body cavity. Sauté the onion in margarine till soft. Mix together the apples, apricots, and croutons, and add to the onion. Salt and pepper to taste. Stuff the bird with the mixture, and sew the opening shut. Skewer the strips of bacon to the outside of the breast. Place bird, breast side up, in a brown paper bag, and place in roasting pan. Bake at 325°F, allowing 30 minutes per pound of raw goose— weighed before you stuff it, of course.

A variation of this is:

Fruit Stuffed Goose

> *3¹/₂ cups soft bread cubes*
> *1¹/₂ cups diced apple*
> *2 oranges, sectioned*
> *¹/₂ cup raisins*
> *³/₄ cup chopped onion*
> *1 cup grapes, halved*
> *1 cup melted butter or margarine*

Mix the whole works thoroughly and stuff the bird with it. Sew shut and skewer bacon strips on outside of breast. Place bird, breast side up, in a brown paper bag, and place in roasting pan. Bake at 325°F, allowing 30 minutes per pound of unstuffed goose.

Twice-Stuffed Goose

This is my personal favorite. It works equally well with young or adult geese. Get all the pinfeathers and fuzz off (try singeing them off with a fire built of rolled-up newspaper, but do it outside!). Then soak goose at least 4 hours in a bath of lightly salted cold water to draw out dried or clotted blood. Rinse the bird thoroughly under running cold water to remove excess salt.

> *3 fist-sized onions*
> *2 cans mushroom bits and pieces*

> 2 cups ripe olives, pitted
> 2 packages "brown and long-
> grained" rice
> 3 cans cream of mushroom soup
> 1 small can diced pimentoes

Sauté the onions in butter. When soft, add mushrooms and olives. Simmer all together. Next boil the rice, including the flavoring package that comes with it. Boil almost all of the water away and set it aside to cool.

Next, spoon all of the sautéed ingredients into the wild rice, stirring well. Pack mixture into the body cavity of the goose, and lay the excess around and on top of the goose.

Roast your goose in a preheated oven at 350°F for 1 hour. Then turn the oven down to 300°F and let it cook slowly for several hours. When a fork slides in easily, remove the bird from oven and scoop out all the body cavity stuffing. Mix it thoroughly with the excess that lies in the bottom of the roasting pan. Stir well. Now comes the different part.

Mix the stuffing material with the cream of mushroom soup. Do not dilute the soup; it should be thick and gooey. Pile this mixture 1 inch thick atop the goose's breast. Return the goose to the oven, uncovered, and cook till very tender. Distribute the pimento on top of the goose for visual appeal.

The dressing so created is almost as good as the goose. There's no gravy—but you won't mind.

White-Fronted Goose Special

A young whitefront is the finest eating there is. To prove it, you'll need a goose, plus:

> 1/2 lemon
> 1 large onion, chopped

> 1/2 cup peach marmalade
> chopped ginger
> 3 cups ginger preserves
> 3 tbsp. cooking sherry
> 1/2 cup honey
> 6 strips bacon

Rub the lemon all over the goose, putting excess juice inside. Then sprinkle the chopped onion inside the young whitefront. Mix together remaining ingredients, except the bacon, to make a glaze. Baste the outside of the goose carefully with the glaze mixture, making sure it is well covered. Pop it into a broiler for 15 minutes to set the glaze. Then baste it again, very carefully. Drape the bacon strips over the breast and put it back in a 325°F oven until tender to the fork test. Baste occasionally with the remaining glaze. Serve it hot and smile!

How to Soften Up a Tough Old Goose

This time I want you to skin the goose. I hate to say that, but this time we are doing radical things to save a tough old goose for the epicure's table. Put the naked carcass to soak in lightly salted cold water. Then get together the following:

> 1 clove of garlic, sliced in half
> 1 big onion, diced
> 3 big sprigs fresh parsley
> 1 cup port, burgundy, or sherry,
> or other red wine
> 1 teaspoon Worcestershire sauce
> 1 can whole mushrooms,
> drained
> 2 cans cream of mushroom soup
> 1 1/2 cups sour cream
> lots of melted butter

Drain and dry the goose; rub inside and out with the garlic clove. Toss out the garlic. Put the bird in slow cooker; sprinkle onion and parsley over its breast. Pour on the wine and Worcestershire. Cover it with the mushrooms and mushroom soup and stir well. Cover and slow-cook for 8 hours. Now you have a goose that falls off its bones. Good! Remove the boneless goose to a bowl and carefully and slowly add the sour cream to the fluid mixture, being careful not to let the sour cream form chunks.

Put goose meat in an individual serving bowl. Pour the sour cream mixture over the top, add the melted butter on top of everything, and put it on the table.

Leftovers?

We usually don't leave anything the first time, but if you have leftover goose, it makes up into excellent goose soup or goose salad. Chunk the cold goose meat and add it to any fresh vegetable or fresh fruit salad, with your favorite dressing. Try it!

WILD DUCKS

All Dabblers Follow the Mallards

As we have said before, the management of dabbling ducks is really the management of mallards, insofar as the regulating agency is concerned. Dabbling ducks, once again, are ducks which feed on the bottom, tipping up and stretching their necks down to get the food, not diving. The regulatory agency is the United States Fish and Wildlife Service, and for the last fifty years, management of mallards has consisted merely of surveying the breeding ground success or failure, then adjusting the hunting regulations to fit. In other words, the Service went into

a long arithmetic process that attempted to predict how many mallards would be available over and above the numbers predicated as being necessary for next year's breeding population.

No attempt has been made to survey the breeding ground success of the other dabblers—all of our hopes were riding on the assumption that "as the mallard goes, so go all dabblers." This is a reasonable hypothesis, and no one really knows if our other dabblers are in need of help or not. Let's take a look at how this mallard hypothesis has worked.

Way back when, mallard seasons and bag limits were set by the Director of the U.S. Fish and Wildlife Service. According to the law, he merely recommended to his boss, the Secretary of the Interior, and that worthy decided upon the regulations. With rare exceptions, the politically appointed Secretaries of the Interior have known almost nothing about waterfowl, so the recommendation of the Service was usually accepted without change. Exceptions to that rule were not based on waterfowl mathematics but rather on political considerations. We should admit that this type of management has been surprisingly free of political considerations.

Then a great day dawned. The Service decided to try to find out how well the birds were doing on their nesting grounds *this year* before announcing this year's regulations. The late Charlie Gillham, a legendary figure of the early days of the Fish and Wildlife Service, once told me that he was instructed to take a canoe and tour a big circle of Canada, where most of our ducks are hatched, and get to a telephone and report on what he saw.

An excellent outdoorsman, Charlie Gillham hired Indians to man the other paddle as he went, and he toured a big chunk of Canada. "Not," as Charlie told me, "the best part of the breeding ground, for that is prairie potholes and not accessible by canoes." He came out of the bush in mid-August and placed his phone call to give them the data upon which to base the fall hunting regulations. Only one problem—the regulations had already been announced. "They had to meet the printer's timetable for printing the regulations, and that was more important than knowing how many ducks would be flying south," said Charlie.

This and a hundred other anecdotes came from Charlie Gillham's lips one memorable evening at the Outdoor Writers Association of America meeting in Escanaba, Michigan, in 1951. No one left while Charlie was telling stories, I can guarantee.

But this first attempt at scientific data-gathering on the breeding grounds continued and was refined. Airplane transect surveys were added, and their accuracy checked by ground crews covering parts of the same transects to see how accurate the aerial observers were. A greatly expanded leg-banding effort was directed at—you guessed it—the mallard. The purpose was to band a stated number in each breeding area. Purpose was to determine which ducks went where to winter.

If all the mallard ducks raised in southern Manitoba went directly south to Texas, then an increase in Manitoba production of mallards would be reflected in liberalized regulations all the way down the central flyway. However, if they found that the banded mallards from southern Manitoba fanned out as they went southward and wintered in the southern end of the Mississippi flyway, that would shape a different sort of regulation. Because flightless broods of mallards head for the grass—out of the water—and hide when a human approaches, the job of banding mallard young was greatly simplified by a corps of retriever dogs, most of them loaned to the Service for summer-banding use.

I had the pleasure of working with a banding crew using dogs in 1955. When

Mallard duckling. *U.S. Fish & Wildlife photo.*

we approached the water area, we tried to see which direction the young ducks took as they followed their mother into the tall grass. We sent the dogs to work, guided by whistle and hand signals into the general area in which the ducks had hidden. Then the dogs' superior noses took over. They would carefully pick up the hidden duckling and bring it to their human partner in the operation. When we had sacked up all the ducks we could find with the help of the dogs, we leg-banded them and released them into the same cover we had taken them from. I wondered what went through the minds of the dogs as they watched us liberate the ducklings they had worked so hard to find. Not every proficient retriever could qualify for this work, in which a soft mouth was of overriding importance. A lot of very valuable information was gained through the leg-banding program. In other parts of the duck factories of prairie Canada, drive trap crews hazed flightless ducklings (and occasionally their de-

voted mothers) across shallow water areas and into wing walls, which guided them into a vee trap. Once in the trap, the ducklings were leg-banded and released. While the emphasis was on mallards, a great number of blue-winged teal were banded by early season drive banders, and a good number of gadwall and baldpate by mid-season banding crews.

During this change period, the work of the various flyway councils was greatly expanded. These were groupings of technical waterfowl biologists from each state in the flyway, along with an administrator from each state. The technical councils came up with recommendations to the flyway council as a whole. If the administrators agreed, the recommendations were made to the national flyway council and either accepted or rejected. A word about the arbitrary designation of the flyways. From east to west, they were named Atlantic, Mississippi, Central, and Pacific. Although many birds crossed imaginary flyway boundaries on their migra-

Mallard hen with brood of young. *Hans Stuart, U.S. Fish & Wildlife photo.*

tions, the concept was valid for waterfowl management purposes. However, it aroused no little animosity when the season was liberalized, for example, in the Pacific flyway, giving them a daily bag limit of eight mallards, while at the same time the Mississippi flyway bag limit was being cut down from four to three mallards per day. That variance in hunter's bags was dictated by the facts, but that didn't make it any more palatable to administrators in the states having their hunting privilege curtailed. On the other hand, there were times when the federal authorities authorized a liberal season in defiance of the data presented to the councils. When this happened, Minnesota, to its everlasting credit, further restricted the bag limits of its hunters. That's hard to do, to deprive your hunters of privileges given them by the feds. But it surely showed that the state people were motivated by concern for the resource and less motivated by political considerations in at least one case. The flyway system was effective in gathering data, in eliminating research duplication, in coordinating research across state lines, and in helping gather the information needed to manage intelligently a resource that never holds still to be counted.

The importance of learning which production area fed which flyway is emphasized by the results obtained on one pothole near Morden, Manitoba. On the same day, we banded eleven canvasbacks and nineteen mallards on that same pothole. Six of the canvasbacks were shot on Chesapeake Bay. Three of the mallard bands were returned from Texas and one from Mexico.

By the early 1960s, waterfowl biologists were beginning to say that they could forecast the fall flight with a high degree of accuracy. Their faith in themselves was not shared by all of the members of the flyway councils. In fact, when the data were presented in a meeting in Washington, and the representatives of the various state agencies were there to listen and to ratify the decisions of the feds, there was a clear demarcation between biologists on one side and administrators on the other side. Some administrators were scientific. Others tried hard to represent the wishes of the hunters in their home state and paid no attention to the data about forecasting the fall flight. They obviously did not believe that the fall flight could be forecast with any degree of certainty. Of all the waterfowl minds assembled, Walter Crissey of the U.S. Fish and Wildlife Service and his mathematical genius sidekick, Aelreid Geis, surely carried the most weight. This caused considerable rancor on the part of some of the more politically oriented attendees. As Walter Crissey arose to present the mathematical model of the fall flight prediction for the mallard, one of the administrators of a western state said in a stage whisper, "Now we will hear the gospel according to Saint Walter!"

In the middle and late seventies, biologists came to the mind-boggling conclusion that regulations might not make any difference at all. Hunter mortality was much less important in the overall scheme of things than had been thought. Today there is considerably less than unanimous opinion that we humans have as much to do with the duck flights as we once thought we did. It is possible that a delayed spring blizzard can reduce the total continental population of ducks more than can the licensed hunters of the forty-nine states that shoot the continent's waterfowl.

Management for Dabblers and Mallards

Management practices, some within our ability to control and others outside our ability to control, seem to have a great impact on the continent's duck population. During the twenties and thirties, when drainage reached its most damaging peak, it is doubtful that any change in waterfowl regulations would have saved as many ducks as were lost by pothole drainage. Perhaps the weather on opening day in the Dakotas and Minnesota has more to do with the harvest total (number of ducks killed by hunters) than our regulations have.

But let's get down to the wildlife management on your land. If you are within the breeding range of dabbling ducks, there is much you can do that will affect the dabbler population. First and foremost, if it is not too late, you can preserve water areas on your land. Water is the first half of their name and without water we do not have waterfowl. Even if it is only an intermittent waterway or a slough that dries up in mid-summer, it is better than dry land as far as a duck is concerned.

Mallards, our bellwether species, nest in tall grass at varying distances from the water's edge. This distance to water may be as great as half a mile upon occasion, but I think it averages closer to 100–200 yards. The hen does all of the incubating, the drake spending his time loafing with his fellow males on the water or very near to it. He takes no part in the incubation. The camouflaged hen is a very good mother and hatches a high percentage of her eggs when conditions are good. Ground predators find a high percentage of the nests when our mowing machines narrow down the area they must search to locate a duck egg dinner. Skunks, badgers, foxes, coyotes, raccoons—all take a lot of eggs, but the duck got along just wonderfully with these predators until man came upon the scene with equipment that changed the face of the land.

As soon as the ducklings hatch out, the hen leads them directly to water. If the pond she seeks has dried up in the meantime, that brood is in trouble, for it has no place to hide during the long weeks before the young can take wing. However, even when she finds her favorite pond dried up, the mother duck is resourceful enough to start out on the long trek to another water area—if there *is* another water area. Overland treks are very dangerous, however, and the brood that survives is a rarity.

Overland trek or shallow pond, the young ducklings always seem to find lots of small insects to furnish the high protein diet that allows them to grow rapidly and to develop feathers—especially the flight feathers that mean the difference between life and death when winter is nearing. But before they are fully grown, they are already switching to become seed eaters—and seed eaters they will be until they die. Now, I know that minnows have been found in duck gizzards, and I've seen the aristocratic mallard squabbling with seagulls for decaying salmon bodies alongside far northern streams. But their favorite foods are corn, wheat, smartweed, tame and wild millets, acorns, chufa, bullrushes, cutgrass, pondweeds of several kinds, and spike rushes. They will consume green grass, à la the Canada goose, but will not feed on grass regularly.

To set the table properly for dabbling ducks, you must make these foods available in 3 to 6 inches of water. From a duck's point of view, the entire world should be under half a foot of water—it makes food much more readily available and it is so much easier to get around. Smartweed is perhaps the perfect food for the shoveler, or spoonbill (*Spatula clypeata*) duck, but he will almost never venture onto dry land to eat smartweed seeds, no matter how abundant they are. Put an inch or two of water over that same area and the spoonbill will greedily eat up all of the smartweed seeds.

Acorns are a preferred food of the mallard, but only when the pin-oak flats are flooded will they be an important part of his diet.

A dry cornfield that has been picked will be used by mallards and pintails for the sake of the corn that is there. But it is occasionally visited by the green-winged teal, which feeds on the foxtail, pigweed, millet, and smartweeds that are available there. If it is possible to flood that cornfield, these same species will all visit in greater numbers, and they will be joined by the shovelers, the widgeon, black ducks, and gadwalls. The same is true of a maize field, a soybean field, or an oats field.

Occasional flooding encourages the growth of chufa, which is a prime duck food.

Management of dabbling ducks in the breeding ground area consists of providing two things: water areas that do not go dry before the birds are on the wing, and tall grass nesting cover. It helps if the area of tall grass is large enough to make it hard for predators to find the nests.

Those are the necessities. The luxuries, from a duck's point of view, are flooded feeding areas, where the duck broods are much safer from predators and flooded grainfields after harvest. (This is admittedly hard to provide in the areas where most of our dabbling ducks are produced.) A very high percentage of our dabbling ducks are produced in the great duck factory—part of Nebraska and part of Minnesota and Iowa, all of the Dakotas, all of Alberta, Saskatchewan, and the southern half of Manitoba. The ability of this prairie pothole region to produce millions of ducks has been severely curtailed by drainage. When the farmer is faced with a choice between draining a pothole (usually with misguided help from federal subsidies) and thus enlarging his production base for grain crops, or leaving the pothole to produce one or two broods of ducks, which then fly off and get shot down south, the choice is almost always in favor of the drainage and the increased number of bushels of wheat or corn.

For fifteen years, the Department of Agriculture paid the farmer for draining sloughs, and the Department of the Interior paid them for not draining potholes. Today, there is an intelligent wetlands easement program in operation, which has saved many small water areas, which are great producers of ducks.

If your land is located south of the great dabbling duck production region, your problem is one of attracting and holding ducks in your area. But the solution is basically the same as the solution to attracting nesting ducks. Now the emphasis is on food and security. Make food available by flooding whenever possible. Space the hunting days well apart, so that ducks are not "shot out" of an area. Once these surface-feeding ducks have become accustomed to going into a rich food area twice a day, they are remarkably stupid as far as running the gauntlet of shotgunners to get into that rich food area. Years ago, as a Game Management Agent working in the Lake Erie marshes, I watched mallards and black ducks, woodies and the occasional teal as they dropped into an illegally baited water area, despite the fact that four hunters stood in plain sight and shot down limits of the incoming ducks. Those ducks were rushing to the dinner table, and they ended up upon that table instead of at it. The hungry gluttons paid no attention to the sound of shotguns or the death of their brethren. This was on a water area 1 to 3 feet deep, and the bottom was liberally covered with illegal buckwheat.

Some trees die if made to stand in water for an extended period of time, but if the trees are dormant—leaves gone or almost gone and the sap not flowing, they can be flooded for as long as three months without loss of the trees. This makes a good deal for the ducks and the duck hunter when willow or pin-oak can be flooded just a week ahead of opening day. A week's time will let the greedy mallards, who seek acorns, and the greedy wood ducks, who seek weed seeds and an occasional acorn, get used to dining at that table. Then when it is legal, they will come readily to the same spot and furnish fine sport.

Flooding must be done with care. You must avoid flooding trees at the wrong time. Remember that dabblers seldom feed on the bottom in more than 18 inches of water, so flooding deeper than 15 inches is a waste of water and pumping time.

When the hunting season is over, you should try to dry out the flooded areas as soon as possible to reduce the attractiveness of round, hard black seeds, which turn out to be lethal pellets of lead. If you can dry out a flooded grainfield, and then cultivate it, you will eliminate the dangers of lead poisoning.

Flooding, used intelligently, can produce good stands of millets and smart-weeds, especially if you can control the time of flooding and of drying out. Check with your county agricultural agent about the possibilities of flooding cropland, or pin-oak land, to produce better conditions for wintering, or migrating, waterfowl. Remember that the same conditions that help the ducks also make for good hunting.

It is usually not cost-effective to fertilize marshes to increase their food production for ducks.

It is also contra-indicated to use herbicides to eliminate broad-leaved plants, for that same herbicide will also eliminate some good duck foods.

The greatest single limiting factor in dabbling duck production is the availability of suitable water areas with good cover nearby. That is the only thing the dabblers lack. Given that—and sadly, we admit that they will not be given that—the dabblers would make a wonderful recovery in numbers.

For that reason, we salute the work of Ducks Unlimited, which has done more than any other single entity to perpetuate the flights of dabblers in North America, and we shout hurray for the pitifully small federal program that seeks to preserve nesting habitat. Habitat improvement is the number one objective if we want more ducks.

There is a shortage of good resting spots on the migration routes, but this is not a limiting factor.

Wintering habitat could be improved, but this would only reduce the hunter's bag, not help the ducks. For, again, this is not a limiting factor. Boiled down to the simplest statement, Ducks Need Watery Homes. If they are well housed when in the egg and for the first two months after hatching, we will have lots of dabblers.

Cooking Wild Ducks

If possible, bleed all waterfowl as soon as you kill them. This can best be done by cutting through the windpipe and the blood vessels of the neck and hanging the bird head down until bleeding stops. Next, if you want tasty food, draw the entrails as soon as possible. Cool the carcass; do *not* store it in a closed container for the rest of the day's hunting.

Please pick the duck, do not skin it. The fine taste comes from the self-basting service performed by the skin and the layer of fat immediately under it. Pick birds by hand; it is easy once you get the hang of it. Pour melted paraffin over the picked carcass, let it harden, and then remove it by hand, taking all of the pinfeathers with the wax. Lacking paraffin, singe off the pinfeathers and down by holding the carcass over a flame formed by lighting some loosely rolled newspaper.

Always soak the duck carcass in lightly salted cold water at least three hours, overnight if possible. Then you are ready to start cooking.

When I worked as U.S. Game Management Agent in Iowa, I had a friend named Frankie Heidelbauer. Frank has many talents—he twice won the world's goose-calling championship, he is a mean man with a flyrod (or any fishing gear, for that matter), he has called red foxes so close to the muzzle of his gun that he measured it in inches instead of feet, he is a gourmet cook—and, well, Frank is an outdoorsman's outdoorsman. He also knows how to cook mallards—especially corn-fed ones:

Baked Stuffed Mallard

"For each bird, crumble a quart of dried bread for dressing. Dice gizzards and hearts into quarter-inch cubes and add salt and half a teaspoon of sage. Add one heaping teaspoon of butter and boil for ten minutes. Pour over crumbled bread and add a small can of mushroom chunks and juice. (Frank may also add water chestnuts, wild rice, or a dash of "liquid smoke" to his dressing.) Rub birds inside and out with salt or poultry seasoning, stuff with dressing, and lay the birds on a large sheet of aluminum foil. Wrap in the foil, crimping all of the edges. Place birds in a shallow pan and put in preheated oven at 400°F. After about ten minutes (when birds begin to sizzle) reduce heat to 350°. One hour and 45 minutes should be sufficient. Do not unwrap birds to brown them, as this will dry the meat."

For the real connoisseur of the wild duck taste, Frankie provides a small cup of the rich, clear juice—oh, call it not fat—that is rendered out of the cooking duck. Placed beside the dinner plate, this cupful of duck taste is used to dip the slices of breast meat. Gourmet cook John Madson, who has been the recipient of this largesse from the kitchen of Frank Heidelbauer, recommends a bottle of Chianti to accompany this wonderful meal.

Duck Burgundy

After cleaning and washing the duck, split it lengthwise along the breastbone. Place the two parts, breast-side down, in a marinating dish, and add a quart of Burgundy cooking wine to the dish. Let it marinate overnight. Then place the duck breast-side down in a dutch oven or heavy cooking pot. Lay in enough thinly sliced apples (or applesauce) to cover half of the body cavity. Pour in the marinating wine to the level of the highest part of the duck. Cook in a 400°F oven until well done, being sure to baste occasionally to prevent the upper portion from drying out.

Oven-Fried Duck

Carve off the breasts only. Dredge in flour with salt and pepper to taste. Brown lightly in a cast-iron frying pan—is there any other kind? Add half a cup of cooking wine of your choice and a can of beef consomme. Put this into a covered dish in a 325°F oven for about an hour. Check regularly to make sure it does not boil dry. When tender to the fork, add flour and your usual thickening to the juices to make a good gravy.

Sweet and Sour Duck

Quarter three ducks (this is a big meal, so invite friends you really are fond of) and place the pieces in a shallow baking pan. Then combine a 12-ounce jar of apricot, orange, or other marmalade of your choice, ¼ cup of vinegar, 1 sliced lemon, 1 teaspoon of salt, a dash of black pepper, and ¼ teaspoon of dry mustard. Spread this mixture over the duck pieces. Bake at 325°F for an hour in a covered pan. Remove cover and bake until tender, basting with drippings as necessary to avoid drying out.

Barbecue Grill Duck

Separate only the breasts of your ducks, marinate them overnight in your own special marinade, and cook them quickly on an open grill over a good hot fire that has long since lost its flames and is now only glowing, gray-covered coals. I like them best when still oozing a bit of red juice in the very center.

Woodies—The Different Ducks

This species takes my vote as being the most beautiful of all ducks, although a dandy drake mallard is a close second. The wood duck is very different from other ducks, in so many ways. The male has a crest of feathers on the top and back of its head, which gives it a sort of "mallet-headed" look. This is heightened by the fact that both male and female hold the head up rather than stretched out in front while they are flying, with the bill pointed almost straight down. The male shows white lines on the side of the face. Both sexes show a long, square-tipped, rather dark tail in flight.

The gaudy male shows a red eye, a rich chestnut-brown breast stippled with white dots, and a white belly with soft tan flanks leading to another chestnut patch under the tail. In eclipse plumage, however, the male is much more subdued in color, almost like the female. The female shows a white spectacle around each eye.

Woodies are different. They don't quack, but they do whistle.

They don't nest in the grass or in the cattails. They do nest in hollow trees, or in artificial nest boxes provided by humans to take the place of den trees destroyed by humans.

Woodies are different. The young will fearlessly jump out of the entrance hole into the nest cavity, fall as far as 50 feet to the ground, bounce like ping-pong balls, and walk away unhurt! If the nest *happens* to be built over water, the hurtling youngsters land in the water with a splash, right themselves, and swim confidently away, following their mother.

Woodies are different. Instead of choosing the prairie pothole country or the nation's marshlands as their habitat,

Wood-duck hen with brood. *U.S. Fish & Wildlife photo.*

the woodies love timbered areas. Any place there is clean water and trees to nest in is woody country, although their range is confined to that part of Canada between Nova Scotia and southern Manitoba, southward to Louisiana and Texas. There is a second, smaller breeding population on the West Coast, which summers in British Columbia and winters south all the way to Mexico.

As the forests disappeared in front of the wave of European colonization, the woodies declined in numbers as their nesting habitat disappeared at the same time. This is probably what inspired famed ornithologist Richard H. Pough to write, rather petulantly, in a 1951 edition of the Audubon Society's *Water Bird Guide,* "Unfortunately, the 2 million or so of our citizens who hunt ducks have not been willing to exempt from hunting even this one rather small species so that the 150 million of us who do not hunt can have it around in abundance where we can enjoy its beauty." Two comments are in order.

One, this rather small duck weighs in at 1½ pounds.

Two, if it were not for the efforts of organized sportsmen, there would be considerably fewer wood ducks in the world than there are today. Organized sportsmen pushed through the Pittman-Robertson wildlife legislation, which taxed the sportsmen for sporting arms and ammunition and thus financed much of the wood duck restoration work that has been accomplished over the years since 1951. Organized sportsmen's clubs erected most of the wood duck nesting boxes on poles over water, which today make a very sizable contribution to the wood duck production every year.

What do we know about wood ducks, other than the obvious fact that they are maintaining their numbers in better shape than are most ducks these days?

They are almost 100 percent vegetarians, consuming only small amounts of aquatic insects when grown, about twice as many insects when very young. Floating plants, such as duckweed, make up a very large part of their diet when small. Adult birds relish acorns, especially the smaller nut varieties. They evidently have a very powerful gizzard, because even the biggest acorns are swallowed whole and ground up in that gizzard. Wild rice, which is now available only in a few places, is another preferred food.

Woodies are different in their flight, also. Agile dodgers, they flit in and around the branches of large trees with the grace and agility of a much smaller bird. They nest in a hollow of a dead tree, sometimes in an abandoned woodpecker nest. The preferred nest site is usually well within the woods, not at the edge. Whether or not it is over water seems to be of small importance to the nesting adults. They remember their own fall from the nest, and figure if it was good enough for them, it will do for their babies.

Usual clutch size is about 12 eggs, which makes the woody a prolific breeder—if nest sites are available. In the past two decades, artificial nest boxes have been provided over a large part of the woody's range, and this colorful duck has taken advantage of the *lebensraum* to rear their broods.

These nest boxes can be simple—a nail keg with a lid fastened on it and an entry hole bored in the lid is fine. The nail keg is then mounted horizontally, atop a pole sticking up 10 or 12 feet above the water. The woody will find it, nest in it, and rear a brood safely. If the support pole is wood, it should be protected from climbing predators by having circles of smooth sheet metal fastened around the pole to prevent the climber from coming up to dine on wood duck eggs or young. A length of 4-inch steel pipe makes an ideal support pole and will last for several seasons before the pole rusts through and falls. In some wood duck nest box projects, the sportsmen's clubs remove the nest boxes after the woodies have left them, clean them, and stack them safe from ice damage and rusting until time to erect them again next spring.

A more sophisticated nest box is made from a length of 12-inch-diameter furnace pipe. The ends are capped with circles of wood—completely closed on the end that points north and only a half-circle covering the bottom half of the pipe entrance on the southern exposure. That's the basic nest box. Refinements include painting the bright metal with a dull green paint to make it less conspicuous. If it is painted, scatter some sand or sawdust on the paint when it is tacky (on the top side only) to provide better footing for the female when she arrives to take a look at the new apartment.

The furnace-pipe nest box is mounted over the water by two bolts passing through one side and through a steel post driven into the pond bottom. Be sure that the bottom of the pond is solid enough to prevent the entire structure from slowly sinking down to water level. A cross piece bolted to the post at the approximate level where it will sit on the bottom will stop any further sinking.

Another necessary refinement is a series of small holes bored through the bottom of the nest box to allow for drainage if a rainstorm blows water into the box.

Want to improve the stovepipe box even more? Use a 4-inch-diameter length of stovepipe, about 3 feet long, placed around the support pole. Attach it with one long bolt through the support pole and both sides of the 4-inch stovepipe. The attachment bolt should be placed at the top; nothing is needed at the bottom. This piece of stovepipe will stop the hungry raccoon from climbing up the pole to dine on wood duck.

Wooden nest boxes of more complicated structure can be built. They should feature an inside measurement of 10 inches by 10 inches on the floor, and be about

SPECIFICATIONS FOR WOOD DUCK NESTING BOX

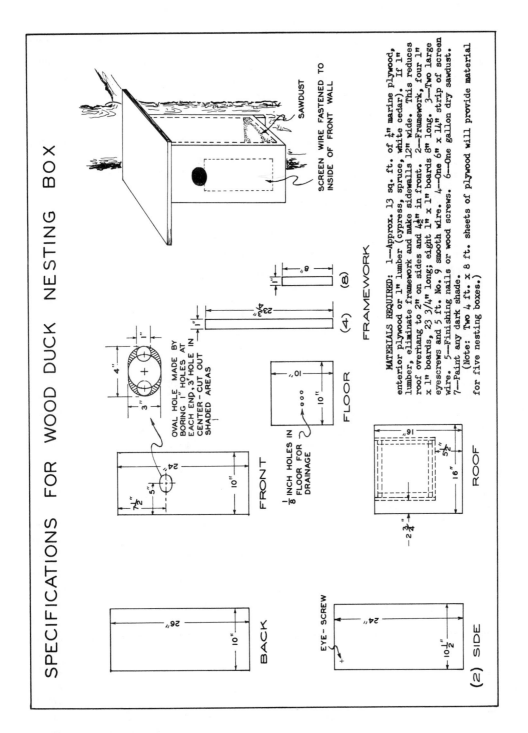

A wood-duck nesting box can be easily built by following these plans.

25 inches high at the back and a couple of inches lower at the front, which provides for a sloping roof to let water run off more efficiently. The entry hole, located near the top of the front panel and protected by the overhanging roof, should measure 3½ inches in diameter. The perfect entrance hole would be 3 inches high and 4 inches wide, bored in sort of an oval shape. A piece of screen wire fastened to the inside of the front panel will make it easier for the young birds to climb up to the entry hole and make their "Geronimo!" leap out of the box. Remember to mount this box in such a way that it is impossible for climbing predators to enter.

After the nest box has been mounted, it is a good idea to place 3 inches of dry sawdust in the nest box. The hen usually lays an egg a day, covering the newly laid eggs with sawdust and with feathers plucked from her own breast. Incubation takes a month—counting from date of first egg laid. Serious incubation lasts twenty-three or twenty-four days, and all the eggs hatch within one twenty-four-hour period.

After the young birds do their fearless high dive out of the box, they are tended closely by the attentive mother, yet mortality is great at this period of their young lives. They are fed upon by raccoons, hawks, owls, water snakes, snapping turtles, even northern pike. It is doubtful that half of them live to the age when they can fly.

As the youngsters mature, they often combine with other broods to form quite large social gatherings.

Management for Wood Ducks

Management of wood ducks consists of really only one practical step—pro-vision of nesting boxes. If you have woodies using your area in the summertime, you can increase their numbers and help assure their survival by providing nest boxes. If they are not present, putting up nest boxes will do no good, of course. Don't worry about food for woodies; they are very adaptable and able to find a meal almost anywhere.

HABITS AND PROBLEMS OF WATERFOWL

Migration of Birds

We know so very little about the whys and hows of migration that even after a century of leg-banding and other research into migration paths, we still cannot predict with any degree of certainty which wintering ground will receive which breeding ground's birds. Witness . . .

A Manitoba pond produces two broods—one of mallards, one of canvasbacks. Both broods survive the rigors of growing up and live to fly south. The mallards fly to Texas where two of them are shot near San Antonio. The canvasbacks fly across Lake Erie, where one of them is shot, and winter in Chesapeake Bay, where another bird surrenders its tell-tale leg band to another hunter. Why? We can only guess that the canvasbacks, being deep water birds, chose the route that brought them to deep water, while the mallards, being corn lovers, headed down the center of the country where corn is king.

Near Moose Jaw, Saskatchewan, three broods of widgeons were banded on the same day. Some of them spent the winter on the Bosque del Apache National Wildlife Refuge near Albuquerque, New Mexico. Others—same species, same age—

Canvasback hen on nest. She is very protective during critical period when eggs are hatching. *U.S. Fish & Wildlife photo.*

spent the winter 500 miles east, deep in the lower end of the Mississippi Flyway. Why? I don't even have a guess.

Pintails are impatient to go north in the spring and often fly north faster than the melting line moves north. They are often caught in late spring blizzards. Obviously, birds want to go north and are loathe to go south, right? Then why do blue-winged teal head south while it is still sweltering in August heat? And why do green-winged teal often hang on up north until there is no sign of insect life available for them to feed upon?

Mallards are among the strongest fliers in all the world of migratory waterfowl, yet they seldom cross the border into Mexico. Blue-winged teal, miniature buzz bombs of duck flight, travel far down into Central America, some of them to South America—why?

Blue geese and snow geese are simply different color phases of the same bird. Yet the blues do not migrate as far south as the snows do. Is it because the darker colored bird absorbs more heat from the winter sun? No one knows, but when the great flights of mixed blues and snows pass through the Dakotas, they are now nearly half and half. When they arrive at the southern terminus of their flight, in northern Mexico, the blue is so uncommon that it makes up less than 1 percent of the flock. Why?

Speaking of blues and snows, why do they dawdle along going northward and often make jumps of more than a thousand miles nonstop when heading south?

Snow geese leaving Forney Lake in southwest Iowa in flocks of 80,000 to 100,000 birds turned back when jet aircraft roared across in front of them, coming from Offutt Air Force Base in Nebraska. Three days in a row this happened, and the birds milled around uncertainly, some of them even flying back a hundred miles farther south to the vicinity of Squaw Creek Refuge, as if seeking reassurance

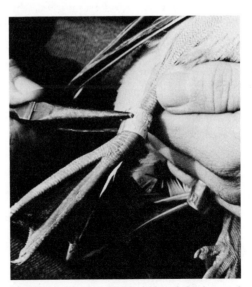

Metal leg bands placed on ducks have helped unravel the mysteries of migration. *U.S. Fish & Wildlife photo.*

that they were on the right path. The fourth morning, I followed them again, and watched them ignore the screeching jets and plod steadily northward all the way to Elk Point, South Dakota, before any of them let down for a rest and a meal on the corn that survived the winter on a "hogged over" field. During the same week, smaller flocks of Canada geese migrated northward almost daily, ignoring the jets, not even turning aside, but continuing northward under the roaring planes. Are Canadas more intelligent? Is their migration urge stronger?

Or is there such a thing as a migration urge at all? If the ancestral habit of going south for the winter is so strong, why did half a million mallards suddenly change their habits and winter on the broad expanses of open water provided by the newly impounded reservoirs on the main stem of the Missouri River, way up in the icy Dakotas? Maybe they only go far enough south to have open water year around? Then why do the teal go all the way to South America?

Coots are strong fliers, although they surely don't look like it as they patter across the surface of the water in clumsy take-off. They usually travel at night. In fact, the only time I've ever seen migrating flocks of coots was one dawn at Lower Souris Wildlife Refuge in North Dakota. There had been a strong headwind from the south all night long, which may have put the coot flocks behind schedule. There were at least 3,000 of them, all arriving at once, spiralling down from about 5,000 feet, splashing happily into the familiar waters of the refuge, which they had probably visited on their northward flight. With that one notable exception, I've never seen migrating coots.

Of course, many waterfowl fly at night with great pleasure. One of the most welcome harbingers of spring on the Great Plains is the mellifluous sound of Canada geese honking overhead on a warm spring midnight. People in the small towns go outside and cock an ear toward the heavens and smile with pleasure when they hear the flight talk of the great birds overhead. On a very black night, what guides the geese? How do they know which way is north?

Night-flying birds do make mistakes, as witness the slaughter of birds under a radio or radar tower when conditions are wrong for the birds' flight. Night-flying birds sometimes try to land on rain-swept blacktop, mistaking the shiny pavement for shiny water surface.

Many theories have been advanced, stating that the birds can assess the gravitational pull of the earth, that they home on magnetic impulses, that they are following a gyro compass in their heads that enables them to home in on a tiny island in a vast wilderness, despite the off-setting forces of winds and rains. Research has shown that some migrating birds can continue heading northward even when blindfolded, but this is rare. Most birds react to a blindfold by sitting down and not moving.

Can a goose read the stars and plot his course from their position? No, that's not it, for they fly equally true under a complete overcast that hides all astronomical bodies.

What triggers the southward flight, other than a need for open water and food? Sometimes a coming change in weather will start the ball rolling in amazing style. Such a flight was accurately reported in 1955.

It was the last day of October when

they left the wheat lands and sloughs of southern Alberta and southern Saskatchewan, more than 10,000 mallards in one flight, other, smaller flights on both sides of that group. As a Game Management Agent in Iowa, I had been disappointed at the slowness of the southbound migration that fall, which had provided very little hunting for Iowans. On the morning of the first day of November, I got a call from my fellow agent in South Dakota, stating that huge flocks of ducks were headed south over Aberdeen. By noon, I saw those same birds, and I was in the vicinity of Ruthven, Iowa. Binoculars told me that they were almost entirely mallards, flying at heights of up to 1,500 feet. No dilly-dallying, these birds were headed south and east and they knew where they were going.

Early the next morning these same flocks were passing Reelfoot Lake in Tennessee, and others were noted in western Arkansas. That night they plopped down in Louisiana. They had flown about 2,000 miles in forty hours, according to my figures. That figures out to fifty miles per hour, for nearly two days of nonstop flight. That hardly seems possible, but the evidence was there if you would only believe the reports coming in from credible wildlife observers. But even if we go on the ultraconservative side, we would have to say that the birds flew at least 1,800 miles, and that they took less than forty-eight hours to accomplish that feat. That would figure out to 37.5 miles per hour for two nonstop days. That's a Herculean achievement, which one driver can not match in a modern car with safety.

But other birds also perform amazing feats of annual migration. Arctic plovers travel from the Arctic to the Antarctic circles, a round trip of 18,000 miles, and some of them do it at the tender age of three months.

Kirtland's warblers, an endangered species, summer in the jack pines of Michigan. They winter on the Caribbean Islands, which involves a long over-water flight for such a tiny bird.

When small insect-eating birds ingest DDT along with the insects they feed upon, that DDT is ofttimes stored in the body fat and is harmless when so stored. However, when the birds consume that body fat to fuel their long migration flights, they assimilate the DDT and die—many of them perhaps drop into the ocean unseen, their lives snuffed out by a chemical they ate six months earlier.

Once we assumed that all migration was straight north and south, but such is definitely not the case. In addition to the case of the canvasbacks that migrate southeastward each fall, from Manitoba to Chesapeake Bay, we can point to the interesting circular migration route of the pintail. It flies north in the spring over the shortest path that will lead it back to the breeding grounds of its ancestors. But when it is time to head south, the pintail usually decides to see new country and flies in a counterclockwise circle, northward for a bit, then westward, and then south on a path that may be 500 miles west of his northbound trip. Why? Not being able to psychoanalyze a pintail, we cannot even hazard a guess.

No, we do not understand migration, nor even know why birds migrate north and south. But for purposes of management of the continent's migratory waterfowl, we assume arbitrary divisions between major migration paths of waterfowl. In an oversimplification, we named them Atlantic, Mississippi, Central, and Pacific flyways, and the division has served us well for purposes of setting hunting regulations and for predicting fall flights. We know that the pintail circles to upset our plans, and that the canvasback goes on the bias, and that redheads from a canvasback slough will generally go straight south, but all in all, the system works as well as any that could be devised without consulting the ducks and geese.

Using the flyway boundaries as parameters, the U.S. Fish and Wildlife Service sets a framework within which the individual states can select their own season dates. The bag limits are set by the feds and the states have the authority to make them more but not less restrictive. For example, the federal authorities can say, "You have a seventy-five-day duck season and a ninety-day goose season." And the states then decide which seventy-five days they want to hunt ducks and which ninety days they wish to hunt geese. Many considerations go into the decision. For example, the opening day cannot be earlier than October 1. However, winter weather will usually close the season— for all intents and purposes—in North Dakota—before those hunters can get in seventy-five days measured from a starting day of October 1. North Dakotans would like a September 15 opening date, but the federal government has felt that this would open the season before the late broods are strong on the wing.

The bag limit—the number of birds which may be killed in any one day—and the possession limit—the number of day's bags that are allowed in possession—are set by the federal authorities. Sometimes the framework allows the states to choose split seasons. They do this to allow their hunters a crack at early migrating species

during the first half of the season, and then close it, to reopen again later on when the late migrating species are available. In some states there is a very great difference between peak migration periods at the north end of the state and peak migration dates at the southern end of the state.

This type of split season is perhaps most popular in the case of setting the seasons on migrating mourning doves. The early season catches the locally produced birds, before they head south, and the second half of the split season takes place at the time of peak migration into the state of birds reared farther north.

We know very little about migrations of birds. Most of what we know has been learned through the leg-banding program. We know the point where the bird was banded. If we then learn the place where the bird was killed, or recovered, we can draw a straight line between those two points. When the straight lines for many specimens of the same species are plotted on a map, we know where the

Leg-banding an immature least tern. *U.S. Fish & Wildlife photo.*

birds went on their migration. We do not know much about the whys or the whens of migration, but this will come as man broadens his knowledge of wildlife through continued research.

And don't forget, most of that research is financed by the hunter through the Pittman-Robertson excise tax on sporting arms and ammunition.

Feeding versus Baiting

Feeding migratory birds—waterfowl or doves—can be a humanitarian practice, aimed at helping the birds. Baiting those same birds within gun range with those same grains can be an illegal act, resulting in unsportsmanlike butchering of countless birds.

How can we make sure that what we are doing is accepted as feeding and is not culpable in the courts as baiting?

This is a very difficult question to answer, because the federal regulations have changed so often and so markedly over the past thirty-five years. However, fools rush in where angels fear to tread, so let me try to explain what you can do and what you cannot do legally in making food available to migratory fowl.

First of all, there is never any violation of the law if you do not shoot over the exposed food, nor allow anyone else to shoot over the exposed food. Let me qualify that—the law states that you cannot shoot on or over bait, nor can you shoot birds that are coming to the attraction of the bait. In some cases, the courts have construed this to mean that bait was luring the birds to the gun, even though the actual bait was more than a mile away from the shooting of the birds. Other court cases have put an even wider construction on the words. They have

gone so far as to say that the birds flew within range of a shotgunner because there *had been* bait placed there, even though all of the bait was gone two weeks before the shooting occurred!

Why does anyone worry about baiting being a violation of the law? Why can't we say that the regulations permit bagging five ducks per day, or fifteen doves, and not worry about why they came within range? Well, ducks and doves do not behave rationally when they are lured by grain (or salt) handouts. They ignore their native caution in their gluttonous haste to reach the buckwheat or cracked corn or whatever else is used as bait. This means that more than an average number of hunters will then shoot limits of birds, which upsets all of the fine arithmetic that went into setting the regulations to achieve a particular harvest kill figure.

The feds know that only a small percentage of hunter days will result in limit bags. If that average bag-per-hunter-day is suddenly greatly increased—which happens when baiting is practiced—then the total continental kill will be greatly increased and fewer than desired numbers of breeders will return to the northern potholes the next spring.

Is baiting really that effective? From personal experience I can assure you that it is fiendishly effective. Examples are easy to remember: A day in a commercial hunting club marsh on the shores of Lake Erie, when we watched relays of hunters, five to a gang, shoot limits of black ducks (normally one of the wariest of the ducks) and wood ducks as they funneled into an opening in the flooded timber. Hunters waded about in plain sight, picking up their dead birds, and still more black and woodies came dropping in to alight within 50 feet of the hunters! The lure was buckwheat, a ton of it, spread over the bottom of that 2-foot-deep flooded space in the timber. I watched through glasses and made copious notebook entries to guide my memory in case any of the violators pleaded not guilty. As each relay of shooters—oh, call them not hunters—left the baited area, another relay took their place. And as each departing group went out through the gates of the hunt club, another set of game law enforcement officers took them into custody and charged them with hunting over bait. In a surprisingly large percentage of the cases, the easy shooting had also increased their greed and they had overlimit bags of ducks. Baiting is too effective to be allowed given present-day populations of ducks.

Does this mean that you cannot provide food? No!

You may put out all the bait you want to put out, as long as no one hunts birds attracted to it. It has happened that courts have convicted innocent hunters who did not know that they were hunting birds attracted to bait. In effect, the judge ruled that ignorance of the existence of the bait was not an excuse. This can work a very real hardship on law-abiding hunters, but it also prevents scoundrels from getting off by reason of a plea which said, "But judge, I didn't put any bait out! I didn't know it was there!" Judges get cynical after years of listening to game law cases. They are very apt to believe the worst of an apprehended hunter, rather than giving him the benefit of a reasonable doubt.

To repeat, if there is no hunting involved, there cannot be a baiting violation of the law.

Second, if grains are made available to the ducks through *normal agricultural practices,* it is perfectly legal. This, again,

is a fine distinction. If you go out into a field of standing corn and break off a few cobs and shell them out on the ground, and then shoot over that corn, you are breaking the baiting regulations. However, if your corn-harvesting practices scatter corn, shelled and unshelled, all over 1,500 acres, you can shoot over that acreage, because it was a normal agricultural practice that made the grain available. Thus, the mechanical corn picker must be recognized as one of the best friends the waterfowl ever had, for it wastes hundreds of bushels of corn, and wastes them in a legal manner to allow hunters their sporting opportunity.

To improve hunting opportunity on your land, and do it legally, you might consider "progressive" corn picking, which picks a percentage of the field and then leaves the rest . . . for a while. After the ducks have picked the harvested portion of the fields clean, and you've had all the hunting you are going to get on that picked-over portion of the field, you simply corn-pick another portion of the field and do it all over again. However, if you go out and "roll down" the corn, simply knocking it over to make it available for the ducks, you are violating the law if you shoot over this field. Why? Because rolling down the corn is not a normal agricultural practice.

Want to be sure about the baiting regulations for the upcoming year? Contact your state game warden, or better yet, contact the U.S. Game Management Agent, listed under Fish and Wildlife Service in the telephone book. He's usually in the capital city of your state and may or may not have assistants in other cities around the state. Your local game warden definitely will know him and can furnish his address.

To sum up, baiting is a violation of the law and unethical conduct for anyone who calls himself a sportsman. Feeding migratory waterfowl is a humane practice and a good idea if you want to have good hunting. But it is of prime importance that you know the difference between feeding and baiting. It is up to you, the landowner, to be informed.

Lethal Lead

The shotgun pellets that miss a flying bird can still kill another bird. Unfortunately, they not only *can* but often do. Many birds ingest the lead shot, thinking it is an edible seed. This is especially true of dabbling ducks, which find the pellets underwater and greedily take them in along with their food. The lead pellets are stopped in the gizzard, of course, and there they remain, slowly being ground up by the churning action of the big gizzard muscle. The ground-off lead is absorbed by the digestive system of the duck, and the duck falls victim to lead poisoning.

Lead poisoning makes it impossible for the duck to digest its normal food. The affected bird loses weight at a drastic pace, its breastbone sticks out like a razor-sharp edge, with severely atrophied breast muscles on either side of that sternum. Unable to fly, and unable to digest normal food, the duck develops a severe diarrhea, with a characteristic green color to the stool and quickly dies. Because it is normal for a sick duck to hide itself from possible enemies, the lead-poisoned duck is seldom found.

Ducks and geese are not the only victims. Quail find the pellets on dry land and ingest them along with weed seeds. The quail that dies from lead poisoning is often eaten by a raptor—hawk or eagle. If the eagle eats enough internal organs, swallows enough gizzards, that eagle goes the way of the first casualty. This secondary poisoning is mercifully rare in wildlife, but it does occur.

My acquaintance with lead poisoning began in the early 1950s when, as a Federal Game Management Agent, I was instructed to gather up any lead-poisoned waterfowl I found and send them to Frank Bellrose, of the Illinois Natural History Survey. Mr. Bellrose is still our number-one authority on lead poisoning. From my headquarters in Sioux City, Iowa, I searched parts of South Dakota, Nebraska, and Iowa for lead-poisoned birds. Unfortunately, I found them. Lots of them. Wading a slough with chest waders on, I found them hidden away under the vegetation, where they had crawled in to die. Some of them were alive and I took them along home and tried my hand at doctoring a few of them. If the duck still had enough life left in it to sit up and take nourishment, I fed it shelled yellow corn. Those ducks lived. Most died.

No one knows the exact impact of lead poisoning on today's continental populations of waterfowl, but knowledgeable authorities admit that it must be very damaging. The most common estimate of numbers of waterfowl lost each and every year runs between two and three million birds.

The U.S. Fish and Wildlife Service, custodian of the nation's migratory waterfowl resource, had completed research into this problem and was embarking on a very forward-looking program of trying to get the nation's hunters switched over from lead shot to nontoxic steel shot. The U.S. Fish and Wildlife Service was requiring steel shot only on special hunts that took place on the national wildlife refuges. This program was proceeding normally up until the Reagan Administration took over the reins in the 1980 election.

That administration stopped all action on the steel shot program, quashed a "paid-for" educational movie on steel shot, and refused to admit that there was a big enough problem to worry about. The reason for this turnabout is not known to me.

I have personally used steel shot, off and on, ever since I was introduced to it at Remington Farms on the Eastern Shore of Maryland. There, its use encouraged by the munitions maker, I found that it would kill geese equally as well as lead shot—if I did not stretch the barrel trying exceedingly long shots. But every waterfowl hunter knows that the very long range shot is an "iffy" proposition, at best, even when using lead shot.

The munitions companies recognize the fact that steel shot will be the only shot used in a few years. They are not dragging their heels in making it available and are not fighting implementation of steel shot regulations. Hunters grudgingly agree that it is better to use steel shot and stop lead poisoning of waterfowl. State conservation agencies have led the way in establishing steel shot zones in heavily hunted waterfowl areas.

As soon as the federal government wakes up to the self-evident danger, it is certain that lead shot will be outlawed.

Plowing or disking land areas that have been heavily shot over will usually eliminate most of the lead shot danger, for it allows the heavier lead shot to move down through the soil and become unavailable to feeding birds.

If water areas go dry, or can be drained, it is a good idea to plow or disk those areas, also, to eliminate the ever-present danger of lead-shot poisoning. If you switch to steel shot on the lands you control, you can be sure that 99 percent of your problem will be gone in two years, for the lead shot moves of its own weight down through the soil and out of the danger zone.

It is not a case of *if* lead shot is banned. It is only a question of *when*.

Botulism

For many years, we called it western duck sickness, but scientific research finally found the cause, which was an anaerobic bacteria with the scientific name of *Botulinus clostridium*. We now know this dread duck disease as botulism.

There have been years when hundreds of thousands of ducks have died of botulism, but we must remember that botulism poses no threat to humans at all. Cooking destroys the toxins which are produced during the life of this bacterium.

Botulinus clostridium is harmless enough as it lives out its life in the bottom ooze of many of our western duck waters, especially the shallower ponds and sloughs favored by dabbling ducks. It gets by in waters containing very little oxygen, but it produces a toxin that is deadly to many forms of life in and around the water. Once the deadly toxin is ingested by the feeding duck, or simply obtained by preening its feathers with its bill, death comes within four or five hours. Then the dead carcass becomes a real "Typhoid Mary" type of death trap. Gulls and hawks feeding on the botulism-killed ducks will in turn die. Maggots and other worm larvae developing in the rotting flesh of the dead bird will become highly toxic to birds that feed on them. Most surface-feeding ducks relish a meal of larvae.

Botulism seems to be restricted to

shallower waters rather than deeper, for the simple reason that the shallower waters are more apt to be alkaline and *Botulinus* requires alkaline waters to survive. The slightly acid waters of lakes and rivers will not produce botulism toxins.

There is no way to eradicate the bacterium, of course, so there are only a few ways in which we can combat an outbreak of botulism. If possible, the pond area should be drained completely and sun-dried to make it unattractive to waterfowl, which will reduce the degree of exposure. In addition, the parching under the sun's rays will do much to reduce the actual number of bacteria because those bacteria are anaerobic, and oxygen will deplete their numbers.

Whether or not you can drain the water area, it is important to pick up and bury the dead and dying organisms in the pond. A snapping turtle that succumbed to botulism can be a source of the dread toxins for more than a month. Use rubber gloves when handling any of the dead organisms in the water, and avoid contact of the bare skin with the water. As we said before, botulism toxins are destroyed by cooking, but it is better not to take any chances.

If it is possible to direct a strong current of fresh water into and through a botulism-infected pond, this may help slow the production of the toxin *in that pond,* but you have to remember that downstream areas will receive the toxins and the bacteria from your pond if you follow this procedure.

In most cases of botulism, it is best simply to bury all victims and try to keep waterfowl out of the area by scare tactics—which is much harder to accomplish than to describe. The last word on botulism is the best word of all—there is no record that *Botulinus clostridium* has ever been transmitted to humans.

5

Small Game Animals

SQUIRRELS

Fox and Gray Squirrels

The squirrel family is a large group, with many interesting species. For our purposes, there are only two species big enough to eat that arouse our interest. These are the fox squirrel and the gray squirrel. Although they have many differences, they are more alike than they are different, so we will consider them more or less together.

Larger of the two, the fox squirrel may weigh as much as 3 pounds, with 2¼ pounds being more nearly the average. A chunky, meaty animal, the fox squirrel measures about 25 inches in total length with half of that length being made up of tail, the fox squirrel's pride and joy.

That tail, like his underparts, is a dull yellow-orange; his upper parts are a salt

and pepper gray-brown. This color combination has many variables, and fox squirrels are found in almost every shade from the very rare albino's pure white to the almost as rare melanistic solid black. Only one fox squirrel in more than 10,000, however, will vary from the uniform yellow-orange underparts and fringed tail with salt and pepper gray and buff upper parts.

The gray squirrel is much smaller, seldom measuring more than 22 inches in overall length. Adult males weigh slightly more than 1 pound on the average, with heavyweights bending the beam at about 1½ pounds. Color schemes for the gray squirrel vary to a far greater degree than they do for the fox squirrel. However, all grays seem to have white underparts, which separates them from the "orange bellies" of the fox squirrel clan. Gray squirrels are found in colors ranging from

Gray squirrel. *U.S. Fish & Wildlife photo.*

Mother fox squirrel carrying young in mouth. This scene is in Alberta, Canada.

albino to solid black, and the darker shades are much more common than in the fox squirrel family. The farther north we go into the range of the gray squirrel, the more dark individuals we find, until parts of eastern Canada show us gray squirrels

A dark-phase fox squirrel with its head poked into den tree.

that are almost uniformly black. This shifting of darker color strains into the limelight as we go north is nothing new in wildlife, of course. Witness the blue variation of the lesser snow goose. It winters farther to the north than does the white strain of the same species.

Both fox and gray squirrels tend to be larger in the northern part and smaller in the southern part of their range. This is probably a question of conservation of body heat; in the deep South the animal has more skin area per unit of mass and thus can cool the body better than its chunkier northern cousin.

When the first Europeans came to this continent, they found the gray species present in untold millions. Ernest Thompson, famed wildlife observer, estimated that their total must run to a billion squirrels. A lover of unbroken hardwood forests, the gray ranged from the Atlantic Coast all the way west to western Minnesota and south along the line of demarcation between woodlands and open prairie. This "gray" species was almost entirely black in northern Michigan. The gray's home range is coincident with the range of the eastern hardwoods, notably oak, hickory, and chestnut in the early days.

Not as numerous as the gray, the fox squirrel occupied much the same overall range but with a notable difference. Where the gray loved the unbroken forest, the fox squirrel preferred openings in his forest, and was found where there were trees bordering open areas. For this reason, the fox extended its range slightly farther to the west than did the gray squirrel. He did this by using the tree cover along rivers that drained the prairies. The same thing happened during the period of the early thirties in the Great Plains areas of the Dakotas and Nebraska. Here the shelterbelt program encouraged tree plantings on what had been treeless prairies. The fox squirrel gladly took to these new "tree fringe" areas and many prairie folks saw their first squirrels in their trees shortly after the plantings rose to 10-foot height. Wherever he found food in proximity to trees, the fox squirrel flourished. On the other hand, the gray prospered where there was a lot of food in an unbroken forest cover.

Although they occupied the same territory, there is no evidence of hybridization between the two species. Color variations are so common that it is often impossible to tell the two species apart by appearance alone. There are a few tests, however, to settle baffling cases. The gray squirrel has tiny teeth located in the upper jaw in front of the premolars; the fox squirrel does not. Squirrel expert John Madson reports that you can finally solve the dilemma by eating the squirrel in question. The bones of the gray squirrel are always white; fox squirrel bones are always pinkish-orange.

When European colonization began to change the face of North America, the unbroken forests began to disappear and both species of squirrel benefited for a while. Then as the deforestation continued, large areas of the country were no longer attractive to the gray squirrel and his range shrank alarmingly. While the settler created more edge and opened up the forest, he made it into exactly what the fox squirrel wanted, and the fox took over large areas that had formerly been exclusively the territory of the gray squirrel.

Clarification of habitat requirements might be helpful here. Generally speaking, if your trees are of the low variety, broken by openings, the fox will move in—not the gray. If the land is swampy with lots of "wet" type vegetation, the fox will take it. If the forest cover is solid with hardly any openings, the gray will prefer it. If corn is available, the fox will surely move in—the gray just might come also.

Both species have a high reproductive potential, with litters averaging from three to five in the fox, two to six in the case of the gray. Given an average of three young per litter and a history of raising two litters per year when food is plentiful, the two squirrels can do an excellent job of perpetuating their species in the face of high hunting mortality.

The squirrels are about the only rodent that does not suffer a high annual mortality due to predation by meat-eating birds and animals. They are very alert and incredibly agile in avoiding the rush of a hungry predator. The great horned owl is one of the most efficient of all predators, but he operates at night when the squirrel is safe inside his hollow tree or hidden inside his leaf nest. The pine marten, which can run down and catch squirrels in their arboreal haunts, has disappeared from most of the squirrel range.

Although your domestic dog or cat may spend endless hours harassing the squirrels in your neighborhood, the chances that one will actually be caught are about equal to the chances of one being struck by lightning.

Unlike most rodents, the squirrels are remarkably free from internal and external parasites. True, tree dens are usually infested with fleas, which may account for the squirrels' summertime preference for leafy nests even when den holes are available. A "warble" (actually the larvae of the botfly) infestation is found in squirrel populations in the southern half of their range, but this unsightly parasitism doesn't seem to cause the squirrel any harm.

Mating and Reproduction

Fox squirrels pair off during the breeding season, and there is a pair bond that remains until near the time for birth. Then the female chases the male away, and with good reason. Adult males have been known to kill and even to eat the young if they get the chance.

Gray squirrels, on the other hand, mate indiscriminately, with no apparent pair bond lasting for more than a couple of days. No males of either species have anything to do with rearing the young they have sired.

After a forty-four-day period of gestation, the young are born naked, blind, and completely dependent upon their mother's milk for the first seven weeks of their life. The females of both species make excellent mothers and the survival rate is very high. This is proved by the fact that small litters can maintain a population with ease.

When food supplies are good, most adult females will produce two litters per year.

This holds true for older females, but not for "virgins," who usually produce only one litter their first year. Second-litter females of one year will usually produce only one litter the following year. First-litter females, on the other hand, will often produce two litters if conditions are right. Research has often shown that in a poor mast year, litters are few and their average size is less. However, this drastic drop in the overall population can be quickly remedied the next year if the mast crop is good. Then two litters will be the rule and the average litter size will be greater, quickly restoring the population to its optimum number.

Home Range

Most squirrels spend their entire lives within a half-mile of where they came into this world. A home range encompassing more than forty acres would be a very large one. During the mating seasons, young males may do some gadding about, but they seldom venture very far from their home den.

In recorded history, however, this was not always the case with the gray squirrel hordes of early colonial days. Then, for reasons we do not understand, tremendous throngs of gray squirrels traveled—lemming-like—for great distances, going through areas of good food supply for no apparent reason except to spread out their numbers. During those migrations, they were exposed to predation at a far greater rate than normal, resulting in a lessening of population pressure by reason of dispersal and attrition in numbers due to predation. The last recorded migration of grays was reported more than a century ago, however, which probably reflects the fact that grays have not reached saturation population levels anywhere in their range for at least a century.

Other Differences

The gray is faster in movements, quicker to make up his mind, quicker to take to the trees than is the fox squirrel. He is also a loudmouth compared to his heavier, more stolid cousin. Almost never still, the gray is perpetual motion until he decides to flatten out along a limb to avoid detection. Even then, he sometimes cannot resist flipping his tail and thus giving away his position. The fox squirrel may run a long distance on the ground to avoid a predator; the gray will almost always tree first, then do his running through the tall tops of the trees where he is a much more agile acrobat than the fox.

Foods

Nuts are the staff of life to squirrels. A gray needs about 0.2 of a pound of nutritious food daily; the fox is larger and needs slightly more food. Having said that, we can begin to list the things that both species eat—for nuts are not available throughout the year.

If you want to prepare an epicurean banquet for either species, you'll start with the hickory nut, for it is preferred above all other foods. The peanut is the food of squirrels only in Central Park and similar habitats. Squirrels fed on peanuts exclusively will lose weight and finally die, for the goober lacks something in nutritional value for squirrels.

After hickory nuts, the squirrels turn to the acorns of white oak. If they run out of the preferred white oaks, they'll eat the mast crop from scarlet, black, and pin oak. In tough winters, the squirrels

will even eat the bitter acorns of the red oak. Because they develop their mast crop in differing sequence, it is wise to have both white and black oak available in the perfect squirrel habitat. When acorns and nuts are not available, squirrels feed heavily on buds, especially those of maple and elm trees. When life is even tougher, squirrels will browse on the tender ends of twigs and eat leaves, but they must be starved to this diet.

When fruits and berries become available in summer, they are heavily used by squirrels. But don't think the squirrel is strictly a vegetarian. He is not and often spends a lot of time hunting grubs under the tree bark and dining on "winter-sleeping" insects. He is also not above eating solid red meat from a road-killed carcass, even the carcass of a relative. Red meat provides only a tiny portion of his food, however, and is not statistically significant.

The diet must contain vitamin A if the males are to be sexually active and for the proper development of embryos. Corn is a good source of this vitamin and is also the best possible food source for emergency winter feeding in the rare cases when such feeding is necessary.

Everyone is familiar with the squirrels' habit of caching nuts by burying them several inches deep when they are plentiful and digging them up again when food is scarce during the long winter months. Remember that squirrels do not hibernate, but simply reduce their level of activity in winter. True, they may stay in their dens for several days to wait out a storm or an unusually bad cold snap, but they do not hibernate. This means that their cached nut supply must carry them through the winter. Does the squirrel remember where he cached each nut?

Hardly, but his excellent nose will tell him where the buried nuts are and he unerringly digs them up—both his and those stored by another squirrel—when he is hungry. They can find and retrieve the buried nuts under 6 inches of snow. Very rarely, a squirrel will cache a large number of nuts in one place, but the usual pattern is to store them individually, one at a time, a few feet from where the nut was first found. The squirrel digs a small hole with his front paws, then pushes the nut into the hole with his head, scratches dirt over the buried nut, and tamps it down with his paws and with ''butting'' motions of his head.

Cooking Fox or Gray Squirrels

When we lived in Iowa, we enjoyed lots of squirrel meals, big, fat fox squirrels that had fed on black walnuts, sweet corn, acorns, and wild plums to their hearts' content. Squirrels have a distinctive taste, one not easily mistaken for anything else. It is a flavor not easily overcome by strong flavorings and spices, so you can use your imagination in dreaming up new and savory ways of presenting the squirrel to the diners. There are as many ways to cook squirrel as there are squirrels running around the hardwood forests of America, and most of them are good.

Fried Squirrel

This is perhaps the most common way of preparing the tasty tree-toppers. Clean and wash the squirrel, soaking for several hours in cold salted water if the meat has been shot up at all. Dredge the squirrel pieces in flour, and fry them in hot bacon fat. When lightly browned, add chopped onion to taste. Remove from skillet and sprinkle with garlic salt and lemon pepper. Put in covered casserole dish with one apple, cut up in small pieces (use two apples if you are doing a generous dish). Bake in covered dish at 300°F for 2 hours, or until tender.

Just Like Chicken

You can simmer, stew, fry, braise, or broil squirrel exactly as you would a small chicken, being slightly more careful to prevent overcooking.

Squirrel Stew

> 3 squirrels, cut into serving
>   pieces
> 3 quarts water
> 1/4 cup diced bacon
> 1/4 tsp. cayenne
> 2 tsp. salt
> 1/4 tsp. black pepper
> 1 cup chopped onion
> 2 large cans tomatoes, drained
> 2 cups diced potatoes
> 1 pkg. frozen lima beans
> 1 pkg. frozen corn

Put squirrel and water in large pot and bring slowly to boil, and simmer for 1½ hours or until meat is tender. Skim fat off surface once or twice. Remove meat from bones and return meat to pot. Add all other ingredients and cook for 1 hour. Thicken with flour if desired. Spoon into soup bowls and have at it.

Squirrel Cakes

Boil squirrels until meat is easily removed from bones. Then run meat through fine grinder. Mix with corn meal, chopped onion, and a can of undiluted cream of mushroom soup. Form into 3-inch-diameter cakes—adding corn meal if too soupy, adding milk if too thick. Fry in hot butter until crisp—serve with ½ teaspoon of mayonnaise on each cake.

Red Squirrels

The red squirrel measures just under a foot in length, tail and all. What he lacks in size, he makes up for in noise, for this is perhaps the noisiest of all North American squirrels. A bundle of nervous energy, the red squirrel scolds everything that moves in his woods. His feeding preferences are similar to those of the larger huntable species, with one notable exception. He prefers pine seeds and, in fact, the seeds of all conifers. He also seems to prefer coniferous tree stands to hardwoods for nesting, although he will use hollows in hardwoods and leaf nests, just as the larger ones do. His coloring changes with the seasons, being more reddish in summer, more grayish in winter pelage. The red is most pronounced on the back, while the underbelly is a dirty white. In wintertime gray, the red still carries a dorsal streak of bright red to keep his right to the name of red squirrel.

Pine seeds, acorns, nuts of all kinds, plus mushrooms, insects, fruits, and berries, and even an occasional young bird or bird egg—this is the diet of the red squirrel, a perky, noisy, attractive member of the wildlife community.

Reds are found in pine forests throughout the northern part of the continent, wherever it can find the conifers that supply its favorite food. Its range extends all the way up to Alaska and down along the Rocky Mountain states from western

Red squirrel in a rare moment of quiet. *U.S. Fish & Wildlife photo.*

Montana through the mountainous areas of Wyoming.

Flying Squirrels

We have two kinds of flying squirrels, the northern (*Glaucomys sabrinus*) and the southern (*Glaucomys volans*). As usual, the northern variety is slightly larger, but neither is a heavyweight—as befits an animal that glides long distances through the air. They are 10 inches or less in length, and that includes 4 inches of tail. Both subspecies have loose flaps of skin stretching from front leg to back leg. When the legs are extended, this flap of skin becomes a wing that enables the animal to launch itself from a high spot and glide long distances to alight with a "whump" at some lower spot. Seldom seen, as they are completely nocturnal, the flying squirrels are among our most interesting mammals. They have very large eyes as befits a nighttime feeder.

These small squirrels customarily den in abandoned woodpecker nests, tunnels into dead trees. Their food habits are very similar to those of the gray squirrel, with perhaps a greater dependence upon fruits and berries than is exhibited by the gray.

Kaibab Squirrels

A beautiful, very large squirrel that was once on the endangered species list, the Kaibab is named for its home range, the Kaibab Plateau of Arizona. This squirrel, larger on average than the fox squirrel, has tasseled ears, a pure white tail, and a black belly. Unless you live in Arizona or southwestern New Mexico, chances are that you'll not have any on your land. Given full protection from hunting in their original home range, they are doing well now in their fight against what once seemed certain extinction. Outside of their home range, they have been transplanted into similar habitat and are doing extremely well in their new homes. In fact, the transplanted population now supports a hunting season without loss of its numbers.

Tassel-Eared Squirrels

Tassel-eared squirrels are the most common members of their subspecies and closely related to the Kaibab. They sport dark, gray-black backs, with bellies that are usually white. The tail—surprisingly—is black on the top and white underneath. Colorado, Arizona, New Mexico, and Utah all have huntable populations of this large, very sporty squirrel. They seem to prefer a mixed ponderosa pine-oak habitat, although they nest almost exclusively in ponderosa pines. Because they are wary and prefer isolated country far from man's roads and homes, they seem to be holding their own

in numbers in my home state of New Mexico and across the border in Arizona.

Management for Squirrels

Basically, all a squirrel needs is food throughout the year, denning sites, and water. Water seems to be the least important of these three elements, yet we know that all species must have water in some form. There is water available in most of the foods eaten by squirrels, but they use free water when it is available. In fact, during drought conditions, you may find all of the squirrel population concentrated around the only source of free water.

The two most important trees to a Missouri squirrel are the white and black oak. In Pennsylvania, squirrel managers put their faith in the red oak. All species of oak provide food; most provide den sites. Remember that the trees you plant will not have any effect upon your squirrel populations until they become mast-producers, which means that three decades will pass between planting trees and reaping a crop of squirrels. Long-range planning, then, is essential for squirrel habitat improvement.

The Missouri Conservation Department is the source for some of the best information about squirrel management. They feel that a minimum of fifty to seventy-five mast-producing trees, such as oaks, hickories, walnuts, elms, maples, and mulberry, is a potential squirrel producer. Let's go through the year with a typical Missouri squirrel to discover what he eats at various times.

When the first litters arrive in late winter and early spring, the parent squirrels are feeding on buds and flowers of hardwoods, especially elms, maple, oaks, and sweetgum. Some springs may find a few acorns left over, but this would be unusual, for the winter-hungry squirrels have searched out every cached nut in the average year.

As spring progresses, the Missouri squirrel switches to mushrooms and mulberries, then to the mid-summer crops of wild berries and cherries, wild strawberries, wild plums, and wild grapes.

Late summer finds corn in the milk stage heavily utilized, especially by the fox squirrels. Crop damage at this time can be extensive. Squirrels are also feeding on fungi and some leafy plants. About the middle of August life starts turning beautiful for the squirrels as the first cutting of mast crops becomes available . . . hickory nuts and the first of the acorn crop, their perennial staple food. Fruits of sugar maple and honey locust are also on the menu, along with walnut, pecans, beechwood, pokeberries, and ripe corn.

In late October the squirrels like seeds of cypress and Tupelo gum as well as pine.

After that, it is the cached food, the stored-up nuts and acorns, that must carry the squirrel through until the first green-up of spring. Unless, of course, the adaptable fox squirrel supplements his slim winter pickings with corn, soybeans, wheat, oats, and apples from the farmsteads. The less-adaptable gray squirrel will make do with stored foods to a greater degree than the fox.

Which of these crops are available on your land? Which ones can you provide? These are the two most important questions facing the landowner who wants a bigger population of squirrels.

But there is another question that must be faced. Where are the den sites?

Leaf nests are second choice for all squirrels during the winter and into the time when they have young in the nest. When forced to bring a litter into the world with only the leaf nest for protection, the chances of heavy losses due to high winds are very great. At the same time, there should be no loss in dens inside the hollow of a tree. Most den sites are hollows in the side of a hardwood tree.

As the tree matures and grows a heavy crown, it shuts off sunlight from the lower branches. These branches die and wind breaks them off at the junction with the healthy trunk. Where the branch once grew is the spot where a hollow is formed as the wood decays into the inner part of the trunk. A perfect den site has an opening of 3 to 4 inches in diameter into a hollow measuring 6 to 8 inches across and 20 inches deep. It takes years for such a cavity to form naturally, and den trees are very important to squirrel management. If the nest of a big woodpecker is used by the squirrels, it is usually in a dead tree. Do not cut down dead trees if they contain dens, for they may remain useful for many years. If it is necessary to kill a large hardwood tree for purposes of forest management, it is best—from the squirrels' standpoint—to leave the dead tree standing, for it provides den sites that are invaluable.

But if your woodlot lacks the necessary oaks, ash, elms, sweet gum, and Tupelo gum that provide den sites, there is another route you can take to good denning situations. Provide nesting boxes!

Nesting boxes should be made of 1-inch lumber, not sanded smooth, and should have a 3-inch opening, preferably situated close to a branch or stub, which will make it easier for the squirrel to get into the safety of his den box in a hurry. It should have a hinged lid to allow for periodic cleaning. Inside dimensions of 6 inches by 6 inches and 20 inches in depth will make the best den. The hinged lid should extend out over the entry hole to keep rain out. The wood should be painted, unless it is cypress, which is rot-resistant. There should be a small (½-inch diameter) hole in the lowest part of the floor of the box to allow for drainage of any water that does get in. The entry hole should face south, for protection from the elements.

Each pair of squirrels really requires three dens. They will share a den until near birth time, then the male is kicked out and hunts up a second home. After the young are weaned, they may occupy still a third den, while mother and dad live solo.

Placement of den boxes is important. For fox squirrels, a location at the very edge of forest cover is ideal, while the grays will prefer a home 50 yards or more into the dense forest.

To Improve Your Squirrel Woods

1. Let your hardwood trees mature, even though it takes thirty to forty years to do that.

2. Preserve den trees at all costs, or provide denning boxes.

3. Preserve and provide food plants, especially the oaks of different species, so as not to put all your eggs in one basket.

4. Provide winter food, such as corn, in cases where your overwintering supplies of natural crops are not sufficient.

5. Protect your squirrel woods from overgrazing, which denudes the land and packs the soil, and protect it from burning, which destroys many things that the squirrels need.

6. Make sure that free water is available through the year.

Optimum Populations

Count up your acres of good squirrel habitat and multiply that number of acres by three squirrels per acre, which is a good population. You can then plan on hunting mortality as high as one half of the existing population each year and still keep a healthy population on your land. Grays live longer than fox squirrels, which is surprising when you consider the frantic pace of a gray's life as compared to the more stolid fox squirrel.

Wise woodlot management is usually wise squirrel management. The essentials are mast-producing trees, den sites, and water. Given these three essentials, you should have squirrels. Provide more of the essentials and you should have more squirrels.

Cottontail Rabbits

What game animal is sought by more North American hunters than any other? What game animal is bagged in greatest numbers each and every year? What game animal can boast of being shot at more times each year than any other species?

If you answered "Cottontails!" to each of those three questions, you can go to the head of the class. Easily the most important game animal in the United States, the cottontail rabbit is found from timberline down to sea level (and below sea level in the Salton Sea country of California and other similar sinks). Tax-onomists recognize as many as seventy separate subspecies, which vary greatly in size, shape of ears, coloration, and habits. But in all cases, we are talking about the rabbit that has much shorter ears than the jacks and much lighter bodies than the snowshoes and is just generally the most numerous of all rabbits—King Cottontail. His much-sought-after body weighs in at anywhere from 2 to 3½ for adult females, with males slightly smaller. It is a big cottontail that measures more than 19 inches from tip of nose to tip of that ridiculous cotton puff tail. The smallest subspecies measure as little as 14 inches from tip to tip.

My Dad hunted for meat—as you would if you had eleven kids to feed. He was an excellent wing shot and did wonders with a venerable Model 12. But there were days when even Dad had such poor luck on the North Dakota prairie that he didn't bag enough for even one meal of wild game. Perhaps it was a bluebird day and only a few ducks were flying, or maybe we were after sharp-tailed grouse and it was so windy that the edgy birds flushed wildly. Anyway, when Dad felt the need to "flesh out" the day's bag, he turned to the one never-failing source of protein—the rabbits of the Red Willow Swamp.

I never knew if it had another name, but that is the place where Dad took his stance atop a muskrat house in the center of the swampy area, and brother Ken and I, too young to hunt then, took the place of beagles as we tromped the dry land and sloshed through the swampy land to start the cottontails moving. Reluctant to leave his well-learned home range, the cottontail always circles around when chased by boys or beagles, and that gives the stationary gunner a real advantage. From his clear vision post atop the 'skrat house, Dad wielded the full-choke 12 with deadly effect. Six shots and we had six

bunnies to retrieve. "That's enough, boys," Dad would yell, and we'd happily gather the bag and carry them to the Model T where Dad was rolling up his sleeves.

He dressed cottontails with his big, thick thumbnail. Slitting the tender belly skin, he peeled it both ways, up over the head and back over the hind legs. Then he used the same stiletto thumbnail to pierce the abdominal wall. Tearing open that area, he grasped the rabbit by the head with his left hand, by the hind legs with his right hand. Giving a sudden downward snap, which ended with a motion spreading the hands apart, he dumped the "innards" out on the snow.

The skin still wrapped the head as Dad twisted it off and dropped it. Then he put the rabbits on a clean burlap sack in the back seat and we headed for home. Cut into small pieces, dredged in flour, and cooked with a mess of sautéed onions, those six rabbits did yeoman work in padding out a feed of duck or grouse.

I became a real cottontail addict when I moved to Sioux City, Iowa, to live. Iowa in the early fifties had more good cottontail habitat in any one country than I had ever seen in my lifetime on the prairies. Brush piles were everywhere, and no one burned them in those days. Each brush pile held a breeding pair, or so it seemed. Our hunting method was to climb atop the brush pile—usually 6 to 8 feet high, and bounce it. Once we created enough panic in the mind of the hiding cottontail, we would see a flash of soft brown against the snow as the cottontail got out of there—but fast. It was fast, sporty shooting and I will not brag about my shooting percentage.

If you wanted the high percentage shooting, you took a .22 rifle afield the first bright, sunny day after a couple days

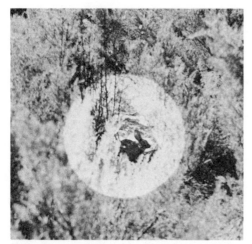

Naturally camouflaged, the cottontail rabbit is hard to see until he moves.

of bad weather. The rabbits seemed to love to come out and sun themselves and hunting was good all day long, not just the usual two hours in the morning and two hours in the late afternoon offered by this (mostly) nocturnal feeder. We looked for the rabbit to be sitting under the overhang of a cutbank, or just at the edge of the sweet clover patch, anyplace where he could soak up the sun without exposing himself too far from the safety of the brier patch.

When you were a real expert at this type of hunting, you looked for the liquid brown eye of the cottontail and shot at that target. You spoiled little meat and, if you knew your way around with the .22, your average ran near 100 percent.

In one year, Missouri cottontail hunters shot more than three million cottontails! For many years, Missouri exported hundreds of thousands of cottontails to other states that were envious of the great rabbit hunting in the Show Me State. Yet these importing states ignored the plain evidence. That evidence said that when

conditions for reproduction were right, as they obviously were in Missouri, you could not reduce the population by shooting as many as three million a year and exporting another hundred thousand trapped rabbits. In their own states, they ignored the other part of the evidence—when conditions are *not* right (and they must not have been, for the rabbits did not increase) you cannot increase the population by stocking. Doesn't work!

The cottontail rabbit is the main source of food for: coyotes, foxes, bobcats, weasels, great horned owls, many hawks, eagles, and assorted other meat eaters. When his numbers are high, he is the preferred item of diet. When he becomes scarce, mice take over his place as the top food item for most carnivores. Yet predators never control the numbers of cottontail rabbits. The opposite is true. When cottontails are numerous, predators increase and multiply. When cottontail numbers go down, predators move out of the area. I cannot cite a single

Only the bright eye gives away this cottontail rabbit in New Mexico.

instance in which predators lowered the numbers of a cottontail population.

The cottontail is high on the menu of almost all meat-eating species. The bobcat is perhaps the most efficient cottontail eater, but is nowhere numerous enough to balance the numbers eaten by foxes and/or coyotes. Even armed with a 12-gauge shotgun and a pack of beagles, man is a very inefficient killer of cottontails. Maybe you get twelve bunnies with twelve shots—but you are the exception if you do. Also, man hunts but a short period of time during the yearly cycle of the cottontail, and when man takes to the field, most of the rabbit mortality has already occurred. We hunt the survivors of the more deadly months between birth and six months of age—the time when 80 percent of all young cottontails die.

How does the cottontail survive in this world of fang and claw, with everything against him? He certainly is not a fighter, for he is poorly equipped to tackle a fox or a coyote. He is not a fighter, but he surely is a lover and in his tremendous reproductive potential lies the key to his survival.

How great is his reproductive potential? Well, if you start with a young breeding pair and all of their offspring survive to breeding age and reproduce themselves, in five years, your original pair will number 350,000 rabbits. That is, without the usual mortality. Obviously, it is a good thing that all carnivores eat rabbits or we would simply be up to our hip pockets in rabbits.

We used to think that cottontails raised two, or at most three, litters of young per year. Now, research has shown that northern states cottontails will rear four—and occasionally five—litters per year. Southern states, where the living is easy,

find that cottontails *normally* raise five or six, and occasionally seven litters per year. This takes a little doing, but the female cottontail seldom wastes gestation time. It is usual and normal for the female to go hunting for a male the same day that she gives birth to her young. That way, it is true that she is *always* pregnant.

We have also found that a young female may mature, breed, and give birth all in her first year of life. This is good, because the great majority of cottontails never live to see their second birthday roll around.

The breeding season ends in September in the northern climes, October in southern areas. However, May, June, and July are the peak months for cottontail production. Obviously the cottontail population is at its peak at the end of the breeding season. Unfortunately, this is one or two months ahead of the opening day of our rabbit-hunting season—for humans, that is! Other hunters know no closed season on the toothsome rabbit with the cotton puff tail.

The period of gestation is approximately thirty days, and that is a mighty short time to turn out a finished product. The newborn cottontails, scarcely 4 inches long, are pink, naked, and blind—absolutely helpless. Surely they do not look like a finished product. The female goes off in search of a male, breeds back, and then starts to take care of her newborn young. She is a good and devoted mother. However, there can be times when the cottontail doe actually will eat her own young. This is not to relieve herself of the onerous chores of motherhood but is a reaction to bad conditions or extreme nervousness. It happens most often when a cottontail gives birth to her young in captivity. Contrary to popular belief, the cottontail seldom uses a burrow for a nursery. Instead the mother rabbit digs out a shallow "form" about 4 or 5 inches deep, using her front paws to excavate. Then she lines the cavity with dried grass, leaves, and the soft, downy fur pulled from her own breast. The birthing process is evidently quick and painless. Sometimes the female is caught by surprise and gives birth away from her well-prepared nursery. When this happens, she licks the newborn infants dry and then carries them, one at a time, in her teeth to deposit them in the nursery.

The nursery is completely covered by the same mixture of dried grass and rabbit fur. When the female comes to the nest, she stretches out over the nursery and the young nurse quickly and greedily. Nursing completed, the mother goes about her business of feeding—for she must eat for the four, five, or six young in the nest who live entirely on her milk, and she must also eat for the next production—another four to eight embryos growing within her body.

Eating is usually a simple task for the cottontail, for they eat almost everything green, as well as mushrooms, berries, fruits of many kinds (apples being a prized delicacy), the bark of many trees, the buds and tender tips of branches, sweet corn when they can get it (which is seldom), almost all garden crops (they do not prefer carrots above all else, Bugs Bunny to the contrary), nuts when they can handle the shells; acorns are a prized item.

This catholicity of diet gets the small rabbits in trouble at several times of the year. When farm and suburban gardens are at their tender and juiciest best—before humans start to crop them, the rabbit does a lot of damage to emerging crops of lettuce, carrots, peas, beans, and other

table delicacies. The worst damage, however, is when the winter snows cover all of his regular foods, forcing the cottontails to switch to bark. At this time, they girdle—and thus kill—many fruit and ornamental trees and shrubs, which doesn't add to their circle of admirers.

The strangest item in the cottontail's diet, however, is its own excrement. At some times of the year, the cottontail excretes two different kinds of pellets. One is the normal brownish-black pellet, product of normal digestion and metabolism. The other pellet, similar except in color, is a bright green. It is partly digested food. Unlike the cow which can bring up its food several times to chew the cud and extract all of the nutrients, the rabbit does not have a cud-chewing system. The only way it can get full value out of its food is to pass it through twice. I do not know of any instances wherein the cottontail made a mistake and re-ate the brown pellets. But "copraphagy," the second chewing of the bright green pellets, is quite common at certain times during the year. Some biologists claim that it is an attempt to save the vitamins manufactured in the lower digestive tract, but no one has the final answer on this yet.

Management for Rabbits

Like every other living thing, cottontails need food, water, and a place to live. But the cottontails' prosperity depends upon escape cover to a greater extent than most species. He can eat almost anything, and his "free" water requirements are very little. He seems to be able to draw sufficient moisture from the driest of diets. But he is a lover, not a fighter, and his only means of defending himself is by flight. His preferred flight routes lead into impenetrable woody cover, where the larger predator cannot follow. Because the cottontail lives in such a very small home range, he knows every centimeter of that home range like the back of his front paw, and can dodge, twist, and turn through his favorite brush pile at a remarkable rate of speed.

Because his knowledge of his home range gives him an advantage over a pursuing predator, the cottontail is understandably reluctant to leave his known territory. In fact, even when hotly pursued by a pack of beagles, the cottontail will still refuse to allow himself to be driven out of home territory. He will circle around to stay within his preferred and well-known range, and will even double back right under the noses of the dogs to stay at home.

To provide the things that a cottontail needs, we must have a habitat where small bits of escape cover—such as thick, sweet clover stands, brush piles, even old car bodies and other abandoned machinery overgrown with vines and weeds—are interspersed with patches of dependable food supply in winter. The most perfect rabbit food supply will go uneaten if it is located in the center of a plowed field. The cottontail has learned through millennia of dodging predators that he cannot cross open fields and expect to stay alive.

Cottontails graze on new young grass, but they will not venture out into the middle of that new lawn to eat . . . they will confine themselves to the edges, where they can reach cover in one quick bound of those powerful hind legs. Naturally, the cottontail becomes more daring under cover of darkness, but he still remembers that rabbit eaters are watching him every step of the way. The great horned owl takes the place of a daytime hunter; the bobcat is most active at night when almost all other meat eaters are on the prowl. The protective mantle of darkness hides the rabbit, but it also cloaks his enemies in a covering of reduced visibility.

Improving Rabbit Habitat

You can provide the required escape cover in many ways. One of the best is by providing brush piles. Best way is to use something solid and strong, something that won't rot away quickly as a basis for the new brush pile. A log is a good beginning. Then pile and stack brush criss-cross over the base log, spreading it to a shape of about 6 feet high and 20 feet across. Smaller brush piles provide less escape cover, but serve many useful purposes for the rabbit. Don't place this brush pile out in the middle of a field, for rabbits find it too dangerous to go out there and explore. Place it at the edge of the rabbit's food plot, or at the edge of his forest home, somewhere where he can reach food in a few short hops, and where he can travel to food and cover without exposing his tender haunches to the hungry.

Gullies can be made into excellent cover for cottontails, at the same time stopping the gully erosion that is destroying the land. Use old car bodies, old junk machinery of any kind, piles of brush interspersed with old fence wiring (either barbed or woven wire fence is good). Almost anything thrown into that gully will help stem the rushing water that is eating into the land, and, at the same time, provide a home for the furtive cottontail. Again, remember that the gully home must be reachable without traveling over a large expanse of open ground.

Clean farming can be the cottontail's worst enemy. With high grain prices we often see the land plowed up to the barbed wire on one side, then plowed up to the barbed wire on the other side, and then the barbed wire is lifted so that we can plow underneath that wire. There is no place for the rabbit in this type of agriculture. A weedy fence row, preferably one where the fencing job is done by multiflora rose, or similar thick cover, is both a home and a travel lane for the cottontail. He doesn't need large areas of such cover, in fact one-tenth of an acre is plenty, if there are enough of these escape and travel lanes scattered around the farm.

The average farmer finds it difficult to get into fence corners with machinery. There is an easy way to provide rabbit cover and ease the farming machinery job. Just make a wide circle turn at each fence corner and let the undisturbed land grow up into rabbit cover. Better yet, plant rabbit cover—such as lespedeza, multiflora rose, and many others. Because different parts of our great nation have different plant successions, it is best to contact your County Agricultural Extension Agent for good advice as to which plants to place your bets upon. Remember, too, that fertilizers will grow more lush vegetation, thus growing a better crop of rabbits.

Obviously, burning is an enemy to the cottontail rabbit. Not only will the grass fire destroy the newborn young in their well-hidden nests, but the fire strips bare the land, leaving no escape or travel cover. Without that cover the rabbits cannot exist. Perfect cover conditions for cottontails would probably be 10-foot-wide stretches of good cover, such as multiflora rose, between 10-foot-wide patches of food, such as alfalfa, sweet clover, or just plain grass. At 100-yard intervals in the cover and travel lanes, we would have big sturdy brush piles as perfect barriers against fox, coyote, hawk, and eagle.

We place all of our "rabbit improvement" hopes on "habitat improvement," for past experience has shown us that nothing else is needed. If you have even one pair of cottontails, and good habitat, your troubles will soon be over, for the fertile female of the cottontail clan never says "no," and she can produce as many as forty-five young per year when conditions are right.

Predator Control?

Thank you just the same, but cottontails do not need any help in their never-ending battle with the meat eaters. After all, predators have been eating cottontails for many millions of years and they have never succeeded in "wiping out" the cottontail. If escape cover is present, the cottontail holds his own nicely. If it is not present, controlling predators won't help, for the rabbits will not be there to protect.

In other words, by providing effective travel and escape cover, you *are* controlling the effectiveness of predators, and that is all the predator control you'll need. A 20 by 40-foot patch of sumac or blackberry will do more to help your rabbit population than all the steel traps or poisons you could ever hope to use.

Restocking Rabbits?

Restocking rabbits simply does not work. Between 1915 and 1951, the great hunting state of Pennsylvania released

1,427,317 adult rabbits. Pennsylvania raised them on game farms, bought them from other states, and live-trapped them in Pennsylvania coverts. There is no evidence that the rabbit population of Pennsylvania was increased by even one rabbit as a result of all this expenditure of time and money. Missouri, perhaps our top rabbit state, exported several millions of rabbits during that same period. In Missouri, the rabbit population went up—despite the removal of millions. In other states, the population went down, despite the addition of millions of transplanted rabbits.

Need we say more?

If the habitat is good, you will have rabbits. If it is not good, you will not have rabbits. It is that simple.

Tularemia

Cottontail rabbit numbers fluctuate wildly, following cycles that we have not succeeded in charting yet. There can be a very high population of rabbits one year and very few the next year in the same habitat. These cyclic fluctuations are dampened in areas of good habitat, most noticeable in areas of marginal habitat. Disease and parasitism play a part in these cycles, but we do not have evidence to prove or disprove this.

The only rabbit disease of importance to man is tularemia. Named for Tulare County, California, where it was first discovered, tularemia is a disease that can be transmitted to man. Transmission can be accomplished by handling the rabbit in preparing it for the table, in washing the carcass, in many ways. The bacteria *Pasteurella tularensis* is one of the smallest of all bacteria and can enter the human body through the unbroken skin.

Since the discovery of the wonder-drug antibiotics, tularemia is seldom dangerous to humans. Streptomycin and others of its immediate family lessen the fever and aches of tularemia in humans. However, there are no antibiotics available to cottontail rabbits, and tularemia is invariably fatal to them. It usually appears as an epizootic when rabbit populations are too high, and no rabbit lives through a case of tularemia. This is just another example of the ruthless way in which Mother Nature takes care of an overpopulation situation. Wouldn't it be much kinder to use the shotgun to hold the population down to the level where tularemia is not so apt to rear its ugly head?

Tularemia is most dangerous in hot months, seems to ebb in cold months. A good rule of thumb is not to handle rabbits or eat them until after at least two weeks of cold weather. In the north, you will probably have plenty of snow and cold weather in December. If you wait until the New Year to start your rabbit hunting, you will not have tularemia worries. It's a lot harder to know when you are safe from tularemia in the Southland.

However, you can be perfectly safe if you wear long rubber gloves while dressing out rabbits, if you avoid contact between bare hand and rabbit blood, if you thoroughly cook all rabbit meat before eating. In addition, if a rabbit seems slow or sluggish, shoot it and leave it lie. Don't let your dogs touch it if you can help it. That rabbit might have tularemia, and it isn't worth taking a chance. Tularemia is only something to be aware of, it is not a reason to pass up rabbit hunting or rabbit eating.

In warm weather, cottontails are often afflicted with warbles. These are swellings with a tiny opening in the rabbit's outer skin. They are caused by fly larvae that burrow through the skin and live off the body fluids of the rabbit while completing their larval stage. Then they drop out of the rabbit and the tiny sore quickly heals. They do not seem to cause any harm to the rabbit host, and are of no concern to the human who finds them. They are usually all gone by the time cold weather rolls around, and the hunter seldom sees them.

Cooking Rabbits

When we lived in Bethesda, Maryland, we often enjoyed the haute cuisine of a tiny French restaurant named Michels. One of our favorite dishes, out of that wealth of choices, was the rabbit. I don't remember the name they gave it on the menu . . . *"lapin de something or another,"* but it was excellent.

Strange thing about rabbit, wild rabbit, that is—any culinary scoundrel can prepare a half-way decent dish from this tender, very bland meat. But it takes a really good cook to come up with something out of the ordinary. Remember that the meat is almost without fat, that it is bland, and that it cannot handle a big load of seasonings, and you'll do all right. Here are a few ways to put rabbit on the table and get compliments on your work.

Fried Rabbit

> 2 dressed rabbits in serving-size
>   pieces
> 1½ cup flour
>   1 tsp. salt
>   ½ tsp. pepper
>   3 tbsp. salad oil
>   2 tbsp. butter
>   2 chicken bouillon cubes
>   1 cup hot water

Dredge rabbit pieces in flour, salt, and pepper until well coated. Brown on all sides in a mixture of the salad oil and butter in a skillet. Dissolve bouillon in the hot water and pour over the meat. Cover and cook for 45 minutes over low heat, or until fork tender.

Hassenpfeffer

> 1 dressed rabbit
> 1 cup cider vinegar
> 1½ cup water
> 2 tsp. salt
> ¼ tsp. pepper
> 1 tsp. whole cloves
> 2 tsp. sugar
> 6 bay leaves
> 1 cup sliced onion
> 6 tbsp. flour
>   oil for frying

Place rabbit in enamel or glass bowl. Mix vinegar, water, salt, pepper, cloves, sugar, bay leaves, and onions, and pour over rabbit. Cover and let stand in refrigerator overnight. Remove rabbit and pat dry with paper towel. Dredge in flour and fry in ⅛-inch hot fat. Add the marinade in which the rabbit spent the night, cover tightly, and simmer for 1 hour or until rabbit is tender.

Fried Rabbit

> 1 rabbit, cut in frying pieces
> 1 cup flour
> 1 tsp. salt
> ¼ tsp. pepper
> 2 tbsp. salad oil
> 1 tbsp. butter
> 1 chicken bouillon cube
> ½ cup hot water

Dredge pieces of rabbit in flour, salt, and pepper to cover well, then brown on all sides in skillet with salad oil and butter. Dissolve bouillon in the hot water and pour over the well-browned meat. Cover and cook for 45 minutes over low heat, or until tender.

Rabbit Pie

> 1 rabbit, cut into serving pieces
> vinegar
> water
> salt
> pepper
> flour
> 2 onions, sliced
> 2 carrots, diced
> 3 potatoes, diced
> flour
> rich biscuit dough

Marinate rabbit overnight in equal parts of vinegar and water. Dry. Sprinkle with salt and pepper and dredge in flour. Sear quickly in frying pan, add water to cover, and simmer slowly for 1½ hours in covered pot. Add vegetables, and cook until they are done. Thicken stew with flour. Put in greased baking dish and cover with rich biscuit dough crust. Return to oven and bake at 400°F until crust is done.

Rabbit Sesame

> 1 rabbit, cut into serving pieces
> 1 egg, beaten
> salt
> pepper
> 1 tsp. seasoning salt
> ¼ cup sesame seeds
> ¼ cup cooking oil
> ¼ cup butter
> ¾ cup chopped celery
> 1 onion, sliced
> 1 bell pepper, chopped

> 1 small can mushroom bits and
> pieces
> 1 tbsp. Worcestershire sauce
> 16-ounce can stewed tomatoes
> ½ cup cold water

Dip rabbit pieces in beaten egg, then into a bowl with the salt, pepper, seasoning salt, and sesame seeds. Then pop the rabbit pieces into a hot skillet, with the cooking oil, for 20 minutes over medium flame. Remove the rabbit. Add butter to oil and sauté celery, onions, and green bell pepper until tender. Put the rabbit back in, and add the tomatoes and mushrooms with their juices. Add water and Worcestershire sauce. Cover and cook until rabbit is tender. Serve over buttered noodles with Parmesan cheese sprinkled on top.

Rabbit in Cream

> 2 rabbits, cut up
> 3 tbsp. flour
> 1 tsp. salt
> dash black pepper
> ¼ cup salad oil
> ½ cup milk
> 1 cup sour cream
> 1 cup sliced onions
> 1 minced garlic clove
> 1 tsp. salt
> 1 tbsp. flour
> 2 tbsp. cold water

Preheat oven to 350°F. Roll rabbit in 3 tbsp. flour combined with salt and pepper. Brown in hot oil in Dutch oven, add milk, sour cream, onions, garlic, and salt. Bake covered until tender (about 75 minutes). Arrange on hot platter. Blend 1 tbsp. flour with cold water, and stir this into sauce. Cook until thickened, then pour over rabbit.

Barbecued Rabbit

Dust pieces with flour and seasoning salt, then brown in cooking oil. Pour your barbecue sauce over the rabbit and cook for an hour at low heat. Goes great with beer. If you haven't got a favorite barbecue sauce, try this one:

> 3 *tbsp. meat stock*
> 3 *tbsp. chili sauce*
> 1 *tbsp. Worcestershire sauce*
> ½ *cup catsup*
> 2 *tbsp. vinegar*
> 1¼ *tsp. salt*
> ¼ *tsp. black pepper*
> 1 *small onion, minced finely*
> 2 *tbsp. brown sugar*
> 1 *tsp. monosodium glutamate (Accent).*

Stir together all ingredients and pour over browned meat. Baste occasionally if all of the meat is not covered by the barbecue sauce.

Rabbit Casserole

> 2 *rabbits, cut up*
> *flour*
> *salt*
> *pepper*
> ½ *cup cooking oil*
> 1 *pinch rosemary leaves*
> 1 *clove garlic, pressed*
> ½ *cup white wine*
> ½ *cup meat broth*
> 1 *tbsp. wine vinegar*

Dredge rabbit in flour, salt, and pepper. Put oil, rosemary, and garlic in skillet and brown the meat in the mixture. Remove rabbit to a glass casserole. Add wine, broth, and vinegar to skillet, and bring the mixture to a boil. Scrape the pan thor-

oughly and pour it all over the rabbit. Cover and bake at 350°F until meat is tender. The juice makes good gravy, so serve it over pasta if you like.

RACCOONS

Procyon lotor is the scientific name for one of the most interesting animals on your land. Chances are good that he *is* on your land, for the raccoon is now found in all forty-eight conterminous states. It is hard to classify the 'coon, for he is at once fur-bearer, predator, game animal, and nuisance. Wonderfully adapted to life in close proximity to man, the raccoon has increased greatly in numbers during the past two centuries, while the largest predators were becoming very scarce indeed. Got time for a few stories about raccoons?

At my former home in the center of Bethesda, Maryland, just outside of our nation's capital and in the big middle of some ten million human beings, our garbage cans were tipped over and strewn around with disconcerting regularity. I never saw a dog or cat running loose in the vicinity and was really at a loss to know what was causing the mess.

I rigged a camera with a flash gun, prefocussed on the top of the garbage can. The camera was mounted just outside the window of the house where I could easily reach it to set the flash last thing before going to sleep. But it was only an hour after sunset when I saw the flashgun light up the yard. I went to the window and looked down at a big fat raccoon, perched atop the garbage can and looking at me with nonchalance written all over its masked face. Removing the camera from its fastenings, I wound the film, reset the flash, and took four or five pictures at 6-

foot range. The coon simply watched warily.

Two days later we saw the mother coon parade across our backyard, leading five young coons. Likable animals, but quite a nuisance. We had room in our hearts for the six raccoons and often wondered how they made ends meet in the big city. So much for the nuisance.

Working with a big game warden from Onawa, Iowa, named Jacobson, I helped him zero in on a mysterious jacklight moving slowly through the night-darkened woods about six miles from the Missouri River. We thought they might be night-lighting deer. When we caught up to them, we found three young men in their early twenties, with six tired-looking, rack-of-bones hound dawgs following along, carrying a tow sack containing the bodies of two raccoons. They were entirely within their rights, as they had trapping licenses to exhibit to Jake. Exasperated at having wasted a couple of hours, Jake asked, "How much do you get for a coon skin these days?

"Cain't hardly sell them anymore," the man answered.

"Do you eat coon?" persisted Jake.

"Lots of folks like 'em, but I don't. Too greasy fat," was the reply.

"If you don't eat them or sell 'em, what the hell are you doing out here in the night, banging around in the brush for?" Jake asked.

"We get our kicks out of listening to the hound music!" was the quick answer.

"Hell's bells," muttered Jake, "you'd get the same results by tying the hounds to a clothesline and whipping hell out of them."

But lots of people do enjoy following the hounds as they race a coon across a frozen cornfield and tree him high above. Then they either shoot him out of the tree, or simply yoke the dogs and drag them off to race again another day. An old boar coon can learn a lot of tricks when he is chased by hounds. Tricks such as taking to the river to leave no scent behind—such as leaping to a tree and back off again in another direction to make the dogs think he has been treed. And when the dogs do catch up with him, the flight may not be all one-sided. If the hounds make the mistake of going after a swimming coon, they may be drowned by the quick and strong animal, which has been known to get all four feet on top of the dog's head and to hang on with all its might until the dog drowns.

I must plead guilty to having been silly enough to follow hounds through briars and into foot-freezing bogs, to smashing head-first into oak trees, to being nearly decapitated by running into a wire strung at the right height to remove head from body, to pitching into water cold enough to form an icy crust when that was necessary to save a dog from a wise coon that was drowning my pup. I've thrilled to the savage yammer of the hounds as they follow a running coon across the level cornfield, listened to the dog music change as they put him up a tree—but that was long ago. As one matures, one is supposed to have more sense.

Where does the coon fit into your wildlife management program? Probably you regard him as an inveterate nest robber, a clever egg-sucking scamp, able to open henhouse doors despite the latch being flipped shut. Maybe you see him as the real reason why you are not having any luck rearing pheasant broods to the flight stage—or maybe you see him as a comical clown parading to and from your garbage can?

The most effective way of getting rid of raccoons is by trapping them. They are fairly easy to take in steel leg-hold traps, which should be run twice a day to shorten the period of suffering that the animal must endure. They can be taken in two kinds of traps that do not cause pain. The Havahart trap lures the animal into a box, then closes the door behind him. Trouble is that it is three times as hard to fool him into going inside as it is to take him by a leg trap . . . and you still have to kill him or move him many miles away to liberate him.

The other kind of trap that will not cause suffering is the Conibear. It kills upon being sprung! It is dangerous to set, however, and will kill a dog or house cat, or a small child caught in its grip.

A chicken egg, treated correctly with strychnine and placed where *only* a coon will find it, is a sure-fire way of eliminating the coon. But it is also dangerous, for other things also eat eggs.

If you have corn in the milk stage, chances are that you will lose some to coons. If the loss is too heavy to bear, might it not be a good idea to invite some hound dog man to run his hounds out your way? He might eliminate a few coons for you. But don't go along with the coon hunter; you might enjoy it and turn into a hound dog man yourself. That's an ever-present danger.

If you want to keep coons, be sure to keep den trees, for the raccoon loves nothing more than a hollow tree that gives him a snug, warm nest for the winter months and a secure place in which to raise a family. They also like to live under buildings with false foundations, in caves, back in jumbles of big rocks, and in ground burrows—upon rare occasion—that they have appropriated from a hard-working badger or other den-digging animal.

One last coon story. With Bob Wahlin, an Animal Damage Control expert work-

ing for the Fish and Wildlife Service up in Ipswich, South Dakota, I went to a corn farmer's field to see if we could stop the sizable loss of milk-stage corn. The farm was owned by two brothers, both stone deaf and in their late seventies or early eighties. Bob used six hounds of his own breeding, with lots of Plott hound and lots of bloodhound thrown in. The dogs ran an adult coon and six three-quarter-grown young coons into a hole in the stone foundation of an old granary. With their noses full of hot coon smell, the dogs were going crazy trying to force their way into the narrow hole that led underneath the empty granary.

The farmers were hot with the passion of the chase and they quickly unlocked the door into the granary and yelled that we should "stomp a hole in the floor" of the old building to get at the coons. Being the heaviest one, I did the stomping. Just as I got a hole through the floor big enough to let an animal come up through it, the dogs forced a big stone out of their way and shouldered themselves into the crawl space under the granary. One of the farmers shut the door just as the seven terrified raccoons came up into our room, the six big hounds hurtling after them. Each one of the coons tried to escape the dogs by climbing as high as they could—on the backs of the four men inside the tiny granary. Somebody kicked the lantern over and broke the mantle, leaving us in total darkness. It was a darkness split with screaming coons; howling, barking dogs; cursing men; and two old farmers who yelled in great glee at all the excitement—excitement loud enough for even them to hear.

Then it was quiet. Six coons lay dead, the survivor being a youngster that had succeeded in squeezing itself into a high corner out of reach of the dogs. Six dogs stood around, idly sniffing the dead coons. Wahlin and I had some nasty long scratches on our necks, where the heavy winter clothing had failed to protect us from the feet of coons climbing for their lives. After we got the lantern going again, Wahlin pulled the surviving coon out of its perch and the dogs killed it instantly with one big snap.

"That ought to save some of your corn," Wahlin yelled at the oldest brother.

"Yup, you are right," answered that worthy, "More fun than I ever had, too."

Coons can be a nuisance, but they sure can be fun, too.

Raccoons eat frogs, crawfish, minnows, small birds, bird's eggs of any size, mice, corn, tomatoes, fruits and berries of all sizes and descriptions, skunk cabbage, wild asparagus—and your garbage. They especially like fish and will do almost anything to get at it. My friend Frank Bush caught six nice rainbow trout out of Charette Lake, New Mexico, one night and left them in the water on a stringer while he put his rod away. When he returned to clean his fish, he found six fish heads and the tracks of a very contented, well-fed raccoon.

Cooking Raccoons

Yes, raccoons are edible. They are not my first choice, but I would rank them ahead of beaver tail and moose nose, both of which I *have* sampled, thank you.

Older, larger coons are almost always butter-fat, and that fat does not cook up well. Small, young coons are not as fat, they are more tender, and they cook up better.

The best way to handle the fat problem on a large coon is to boil the whole carcass, after careful dressing, in water. The fat comes to the surface in the form of oil, which can be skimmed off or just dumped out. The remainder of the fat is visible, as it becomes milky white after boiling. Cut away all of the fat—every little bit if you want to have good eating.

Pour out the water in which you boiled the raccoon. Cut the coon into serving-size pieces, dredge in seasoned flour, and brown the pieces in hot bacon grease or cooking oil, whichever is handy. Then you have many options . . . the easiest being to cover the raccoon with your favorite barbecue sauce (use the one we told you about in "Cooking Rabbits," or use your own). It may be wise to increase the proportions of garlic, onion, and Worcestershire in your favorite barbecue sauce—we want to end up with a spicy product. Covered with the barbecue sauce, the coon should simmer for two hours, or until very tender. That is not half-bad eating.

South Dakota Chef's Special

The South Dakota boys simply soak the coon carcass overnight in salted water. Pat dry and cover with a red pepper paste, made with lots of red pepper and a bit of water. Put the coon on a rack to allow the fat to drip away, not into the meat. Bake at 350°F for 3 hours. Then remove from oven, and scrape off coating of red pepper. Salt and black-pepper the meat, cover it with lots of sliced onions, adding sliced onions inside the body cavity. Bake for another hour. Sounds good, and I'm going to try it.

Sweet and Sour Raccoon

Parboil the raccoon carcass and remove all possible fat. Then simply cut it into bite-size pieces and make your sweet and sour sauce, same as for pork. But remember that it will be fatter than pork, and treat accordingly. I'd double up on the gingersnaps you use and perhaps also double the brown sugar amount. This is raccoon, not pork. Otherwise, do everything just the same as with any other sweet and sour recipe.

6

Life in the Watery World

It is easier for humans to identify with the needs of air-breathing animals than it is to identify with the needs of fish. When it comes to putting ourselves into the picture of a fish's world, we are like a fish out of water. We do not have the same needs; we do not react as fish do. So it is a good idea to look at the fish's world, to realize its limitations, before we start talking about managing this watery resource.

The fish's world is a closed environment to a greater degree than our world. Most of its conditions for life are self-contained, not derived from outside. The fish that live in water are prisoners of their environment to a greater degree than are animals that live in the air-breathing world. A simple comparison will illustrate. If it gets too hot for us in one part of our environment, we move to a different part of our environment, and in so doing we may greatly change the temperature and greatly improve our own creature comfort. If a trout stream becomes too hot, the trout simply dies. There is no way for the trout to improve the situation.

If the air we breathe is full of dust, we go inside, where our window screens and air-conditioning filters remove the dust from the air. If silt chokes the water that a fish breathes, he may ease the situation a little bit by moving to a less agitated portion of his watery world, but he cannot entirely escape. He may choke on the silt, he may not get enough oxygen, he may die—a victim of a change in his environment.

When food becomes scarce for a mallard duck, he moves farther south, seeking new sources of food. When food becomes scarce for a fish, he starves.

When conditions for reproducing his species are bad in one locality, a bird moves to area that offers the things he needs. When conditions for reproduction are bad for a fish, reproduction does not occur.

When it is too cold for mammals, they speed up their metabolism, burn up more body fat and more food, to keep their body temperature at the right level. When it is too cold for fish, they cannot do this. They are what we call "cold-blooded," which means that their body temperature is the same as the temperature of the water that surrounds them. Some ocean-living fish are exceptions to this rule, having body temperatures slightly higher than the temperature of the ocean they swim in, but these are of no concern to us here.

This business of being a prisoner of the environment is not entirely bad. Because it takes a long time for a change in temperature to affect the great mass of a body of water, changes in water temperature are slow and very gradual for fishes. This is good, because they are not able to handle sharp changes in temperature. To a far greater degree than is true of warm-blooded animals, fishes live in a world of permanence, a world that changes but slowly.

As landowners we are concerned with the fish and wildlife that make their homes in our waters. These waters are of two kinds, moving water and still water. Slow- or fast-moving water is called a river. Nonmoving water is called a pond or lake. Both streams and ponds are extremely complicated ecosystems where life is prolific and the value of one unit of life

is seldom high, environments where life usually ends with one unit of life being eaten by a larger unit of life.

Food cycles are uncomplicated, however, because all of the links in the chain are contained in one relatively small area. Basically, the food cycle goes from plants that are eaten by insects and fish; to small fish that eat the insects and the plants; to larger fish that eat the small fish; through the death of the large fish, which returns nutrients to the floor of the water area. These nutrients are utilized directly by insects or indirectly by plants—and by minute, single-celled animals that provide food for insects. Which in turn are eaten—but you get the idea.

Occasionally, a larger organism interrupts this food cycle. This happens, for example, when man catches a fish and removes it from the pond. That opens a larger food cycle but does not alter the fact that nutrients are neither created nor destroyed but only change their shape as they proceed through the cycle. If a mink eats a fish in your pond, that mink inevitably dies and returns his body nutrients to the pond or to the soil that makes up the drainage of the pond. The cycle is never broken, only changed a bit in its routine operation.

Fish species are of two kinds, cold-water species and warm-water species. The trout and char family and the salmons are cold-water species, and water temperature limits their choice of homes. Largemouth black bass, catfish, and yellow perch are examples of warm-water species. In many cases, the range of warm- and cold-water species overlaps, and there are thousands of waters that contain both trout and bass, for example.

All of the fish we will discuss as being

amenable to management on our land are egg-layers. Their methods of providing for the hatching of their eggs vary with the species, however, and we shall describe them in some detail, because those differences affect management.

Because entire libraries have been written describing the entire world of fishes, we will content ourselves with descriptions of the species that we feel are amenable to our management. First, we will talk about the trout—brook, brown, cutthroat, and rainbow, which are the backbone of our cold-water fisheries. Second, we will talk about the largemouth black bass, the smallmouth black bass, the bluegill sunfish, and the channel catfish, backbones of pond fish production systems.

TROUT

There are three situations in which the landowner can be interested in the trout family. These are:

1. A trout stream flows through your land. You want to improve the trout fishing, either to charge a fee for fishing or simply to improve the fishing for yourself and your friends.
2. You have a cold, spring-fed lake that will hold trout. You want to improve the fishing, in order to charge a fee for access, or simply to provide better fishing for yourself and for your friends.
3. You are considering trout farming, which is another subject and another challenge entirely. Because trout farming is too big a subject to be covered by one chapter in a book, we will leave that subject to the experts. If you want information on trout farming, your first step should be to contact your County Agri-

cultural Extension Agent. Your second step should be to contact your state Department of Natural Resources, or State Game and Fish Department, or whatever it is called in your state. Your third step should be to subscribe to the publications of the Trout Farming Association.

But if you just have trout waters on your land, we have some information that should be of assistance to you. The best way to present this information will be to discuss, in turn, each of the four beautiful small trout species—rainbow, brook, brown, and cutthroat—and then make a passing reference to other members of this family, the lake trout . . . a much bigger, much more difficult to manage, fish.

Rainbow Trout

Salmo gairdnerii is the scientific name for this trout. It is the darling of the commercial trout-farming boys and also the preferred trout of the fish hatchery operations across the nation. Hardy and disease-resistant, the rainbow is a brightly colored fish. Further description is difficult because these fish change colors with the seasons, change colors in different waters, and change colors when they move to salt water, as some of the subspecies do. Suffice it to say that their bright silver bodies shade to olive or dark brown on the top side, almost pure white on the belly. There is almost always a red or pink band extending from gill cover to near the tail, along the lateral line. The pectoral, caudal, and anal fins are usually—but not always—colored with some shading of pink or red. In streams, these fish are usually heavily spotted along the top half of the body.

Some giant strains have been developed, such as the Kamloops, which grows to 52 pounds and which has been widely transplanted from its native waters in Idaho all the way to New Zealand—with wonderful results.

This most popular of trouts is native to the cooler waters of the western half of the United States, from northern Mexico to Alaska. It has been stocked into every state of the Union, however, and will be encountered almost everywhere on the North American continent where clean waters run cold.

Rainbow trout spawn at different times of the year in different waters. The male and female both assist in fanning out a nest or "redd" in the clean gravel and stones of a flowing stream. When the female is ready, she will squirt out large numbers of eggs, and some of them will fall into the prepared redd. At the same time, one or more males will squirt milt (fish semen) into the cloud of eggs as they fall to the redd. The current mixes eggs and milt, and fertilization takes place immediately. The eggs are allowed to fall to the bottom, and the trout do a rough job of covering them with fanning motions of the tail. Insofar as the parents are concerned, that's the end of it. If water temperatures are right, the eggs will hatch in days. Temperature affects hatching time greatly, with colder water making the process longer. Warmer waters speed up the process, but if the waters pass the optimum temperature, fungus and egg rotting occur, greatly diminishing the hatch.

When the young hatch, they are equipped with an egg sac, which feeds them until they continue their development to the free-swimming stage. At this time they are very tiny but are actively feeding on minute organisms in the water. As they grow, their diet changes to include large numbers of many kinds of aquatic insects. As they near the 3-inch stage, they begin taking insects that fall into the stream and also begin to utilize larger aquatic insects. Adult rainbows feed on minnows and small fish, including small rainbow trout. As the fish gets longer than 12 inches, it becomes something of a meat-eater, skipping over insects and aquatic organisms to demand larger "bite-size" meals of minnows and young fish. At this time they have been known to feed heavily on young frogs, although this is rare because trout like cold water and frogs like warmer water.

The newly hatched trout, free of the egg sac food supply, are called "fry." They are less than 1 inch long but are copies of the adult in movements. They remain in schools, seeking out aquatic vegetation for two reasons—to provide them with more food and to prevent them from becoming food for the many predators that relish a dish of trout. Many aquatic insects are large enough to capture and devour the fry; all small fish feed on them. Herons and other wading birds spear them out of the water; kingfishers and other birds dive into the water to capture them. As they get bigger, the cast of enemies grows, with the addition of mink, otter, water snakes, and mergansers, while all of the other birds stand ready to take their share. The mortality rate is very high and less than 1 percent of the fry live to attain 6-inch length.

If they can escape those that feed on them, the young rainbow trout feed almost entirely on insects until they reach the size that will enable them to take a whack at minnows or young fish. Then they become meat-eaters to a great degree and are not above cannibalizing their siblings.

The rainbow trout will not tolerate water temperatures above the 70°F reading, and will be off their feed at about 64°F. Water does not get too cold for them, and they will thrive in inflow creeks when the water temperature is way down at the 34°F marking. They do not feed well until the temperatures go up into the high forties, however. The rainbow trout is one of the most efficient feeders to be found in any species, having the ability to put on 1 pound of weight with a feeding of less than 2 pounds of high protein food! Commercially available foods are used to put on this rapid growth, and natural foods will give a much lower conversion rate.

If there is an existing rainbow trout population in your waters, you will be most interested in the following sections, which tell you how to improve a trout stream, lake, or pond for fish life.

If you do not have an existing trout population, but want one, your investigation starts with a thermometer. Record the water temperatures, at the surface and at 4-foot depths, every day for two weeks in mid-summer. Is the water temperature within the tolerance range of the rainbow trout in your latitude? Check with the fishery biologist of your state game and fish department.

Then take water samples from various parts of your water area, using a clean glass jar that has been thoroughly rinsed in hot water to remove any chemical residues that might affect the analysis of your water supply. Take about six different samples, of a cupful each. Send these to your state water analysis laboratory or to the state conservation agency that has jurisdiction over fish stocking. Rainbow trout cannot handle highly alkaline waters,

and the pH of your water is of great importance to your plans for trout.

There are two methods of introducing rainbow trout into your waters—by stocking fry or fingerlings, and by stocking "catchables." Because of the extremely heavy mortality experienced by the tiny fish, it is highly recommended that you stock with the 9- or 10-inchers— but remember that catchable-size trout are expensive. Make sure that the source of your trout is above criticism when it comes to disease and parasitism. Trout are susceptible to many diseases, and when one hits a small trout water, it kills all of the fish and removes all of your investment. If you intend to allow access to your land for purposes of fishing, and if that access is free, you may qualify for trout stocked by the State Conservation Agency. But this means that you will have to sign an agreement allowing the public access to your lands for fishing purposes for at least a three-year period.

Harvesting your rainbow trout can be a very pleasant task—the fish are excellent fighters on light tackle and usually put on a display of aerial acrobatics if the tackle is light enough to permit them to get airborne.

Naive rainbows will be more easily taken on artificial fliers and small spinners than on natural bait. Once they get the idea that something up there in the nonwatery world is trying to snatch them out of their world, however, they become fairly sophisticated. Like all trout, they will be more easily fooled in poor light and hardest to catch in bright sunlight. A small angleworm on a very small hook is a hard thing for a rainbow trout to resist. Crickets and grasshoppers are excellent baits for trophy-sized trout, as are minnows.

Rainbow trout will get along fine in a stream or lake where they are the only fish species. They will also do well where the only other species is small, big enough to be eaten, but not big enough to outgrow the mouth of a rainbow. They prosper where small threadfin shad are numerous, or any other food species, such as the fathead minnow, or golden shiner. However, they will not feed on minnows until they have reached at least the 9-inch size. If minnows are too numerous, the trout will be fat and contentedly burping away in his resting place—and no lure will entice him when his stomach is full, so your fishing luck will be poor.

Despite his great speed, the rainbow trout is not good at avoiding the larger toothed predators, such as the northern pike. I know of one lake in New Mexico—Springer Lake—that has a goodly population of both rainbows and northerns. The pike grow fat-bodied and big, with 20-pounders not exciting much notice around the lake. We caught six large pike on a recent fishing trip, and every one of them contained the partially digested (but easily recognizable) remains of a 10-inch rainbow trout. And that is expensive food for northern pike.

Brook Trout

Salvelinus fontinalis is perhaps the most beautiful of all trout. Strikingly colored in reds, corals, yellows, and dark green, the brookie positively flames at spawning time, and the bright dots on his sides seem to glow. Some of the spots are red, surrounded by silver, on a dark olive-green background. The fins of brookies are almost always brightly hued in reds and yellows. The end of the tail (the caudal fin) is only slightly indented, or forked.

For this reason they are often called "squaretails." The males have an undershot lower jaw when they are of breeding age, while the female keeps the typical trout mouth configuration.

Brook trout have been raised successfully in hatcheries ever since 1864, and that is both good news and bad news for the angler. The fish resulting from a hundred generations in the hatchery are domesticated and lack much of the wariness of the native, wild-reared brookie. This domesticated strain is easily raised and is fairly disease-resistant. The pure wild strain fish are harder than ever to find these days, and it is doubtful that brookies without domestic-strain blood in them can be found anywhere south of the Labrador and Manitoba big streams.

Brook trout are native to northeastern North America from Georgia north and west to Labrador and nearly to the Arctic Circle. The biggest fish are taken from Labrador, with many specimens reported to 11 pounds. The brookie has also been stocked into South America, where it grows to tremendous size in Argentina. But before you decide that the beautiful and tasty brook trout is just right for your stream—hear this: Brook trout grow big only in big waters. In small streams and lakes, the average size will surely be 7 inches or less. In addition, the brookie does not do well on commercial feed in a natural waterway. Even in fish hatcheries, where everything is controlled to the benefit of the fish, the brookie does not grow as rapidly (or as big) as the rainbow or brown trouts.

Although heavy fishing does not reduce their numbers, it does reduce the size of the brook trout on the top end of the scale. Generous limits and heavy fishing pressure will remove thousands of brookies from a stream or lake, but the average size of the fish will not usually go up, which seems to contradict what you learned in chapter 1 about the carrying capacity of a water for fish. In addition, hear this: The brook trout will not do well in any water that does not allow them to find a cool spot (65°F or cooler) when the summer sun bakes down. Be sure to read the section on improving a trout stream, which follows this section on trout.

Brookies are fast reproducers and will overpopulate almost any small water. This, of course, means that the overpopulation will be made up of stunted fish. In fact, this is the only trout that does well in waters with northern pike and walleyes. The individual brook trout might not think it such a good deal, but if enough brookies are eaten by the rapacious, toothy pike, the average size of the brookie will go up to the point where it is fun to fish for them.

Brook trout spawn in September up north and as late as December in more southerly waters. They are very choosy about their spawning place, needing cold, spring-fed water if possible. They will go up into tiny brooks in search of their choice conditions. In lakes they will spawn on almost any bottom, provided the water is clear, clean, and cold. Depending upon size, the brook trout female will produce from 100 to 1,200 eggs.

Mortality, as in all egg-laying fish species, is very high, but the main limiting factor for brook trout is water temperature. If the water temperatures rise to 75°F for more than an hour or so, you can say goodbye to this fish.

There are very few situations where the brookie would be your choice for stocking into the waters of your land. He's too finicky about upper temperature levels and about cold water for spawning and survival most of the year. In addition, it is doubtful that a small water area would ever produce a big brook trout.

But if you were picking your trout for beauty alone, the brookie would rate the top.

Brown Trout

Salmo trutta is not a native of these shores, having been imported from Germany and other European countries to provide a larger fish in the northeastern half of the country, where flyfishing was favored, where the brookies over 10 inches had almost all been caught out, and where the flycaster wanted a worthy opponent. He got it!

The brown trout is less tolerant of warm water than is the rainbow, but is much shrewder—more able to get along with native species already in a stream or lake. They grow to great size, especially those meat-eaters who live on minnows and small fish. Because they are harder to catch than rainbows and brookies, they live longer and thus they grow to larger size and then prey on smaller trout.

Today, the introduced brown trout has captured the hearts of fishermen all over the United States, wherever trout waters exist. He grows much larger than brookies, with trout over 10 pounds being taken in widely scattered habitats every year, and occasional lunkers going up to 40 pounds. Flaming Gorge Reservoir in Wyoming is now well known as the big brown capital of America, but there are many other prime waters.

Once seen, the brown trout is easily recognized. It is a golden brown color overall, with darker hues on top, lighter beneath. It is generously spotted with big brown or black spots on fins, back, and tail. Many of these black and red spots are surrounded by lighter-colored circles of silver, as if to underline the fact that this is a brown trout.

Like other members of the char family, the males become hook-jawed when adult, and this characteristic is especially noticeable when spawning excites the fish.

In spawning requirements, the brown trout approximates the brookie, although showing more tolerance for less than perfect stream beds. The female lays from 1,000 to 3,000 eggs, depending upon size—and remember that brown trout grow big. The fertilized eggs are covered with fine sand and coarse gravel on the stream bed and will lie there until the next spring before hatching. In hatcheries, the hatching period runs from forty-six to fifty-four days, depending upon water temperatures.

Research has shown that browns are notoriously harder to fool than brooks or rainbows. In fact, when equal numbers of rainbows and brown trout are stocked in the same water, it is not unusual for ten times as many bows to be caught as browns. If fishing at night is legal in your state, you'll find that it produces many more brown trout per hour than daylight fishing. On a three-day fishing trip on the Los Pinos River in northern New Mexico, we found it absolutely impossible to catch even one "overwintering" brown trout during daylight hours. However, when the shadows began to reach out across the clear, cold river, we could fool the browns on spoons, wet flies, and streamers that imitated minnows. Yes, the brown trout grows to a great size, but don't forget, the bigger he gets the harder he is to catch.

Unlike many other importations from Europe—carp, starling, house sparrow, for examples—the brown trout has proved to be a very welcome addition to our catalog of fishing pleasures. If your state game and fish department urges stocking of browns in your waters—rejoice, man, rejoice.

Cutthroat Trout

Salmo clarkii is the scientific name for this beautiful inhabitant of the western high country streams and lakes. Cutthroats take the place of brook trout in the western half of our continent and rate the name of "native" trout as much as the brookie does.

The name comes from the lengthwise bright red stripe below the jaw, on the edge of the gill cover, which looks as if the fish had suffered the indignity of having its throat cut. Olive-green backs shade across heavily spotted sides to light yellow or even orange bellies. Like brookies, the cutthroat does not grow to great size in small streams, but some of its race are huge indeed. The tail is forked more than that of the brookie, and it lacks the lateral line blushing red of the rainbow trout.

Cutthroats are not as acrobatic as brookies, or as determined fighters as the rainbow and brown. They are shy fish, and not as easily caught as the brookie, and they sure do taste good—a result of the beautiful, clean waters they come from.

Although one cutthroat from Pyramid Lake in Nevada actually weighed 41 pounds, it is a huge inland cutthroat that weighs in at 5 pounds. I say "inland" because some of these fish do go to sea, returning to their natal rivers to spawn. Those sea-run cutthroats grow much larger, proving again the old adage that big trout come from big waters.

Cutthroats do not put on weight as easily as do browns and rainbows. They are not recommended as a species to be stocked in the waters of your land. If those waters were suited to cutthroats, you'd probably already have them. If the species is not native to your land, you'll be better off with rainbows or browns.

Lake Trout

Salvelinus namaycush is the scientific name of the fish we call lake trout, laker, togue, mackinaw, or gray trout. The important thing to know about lakers is that they always inhabit deep, cold lakes. If you have a deep, cold lake, you might want to introduce the laker to act as your big predator. Big he certainly is, with specimens as heavy as 40 pounds being taken, and commercial operations occasionally turning up a 100-pounder. Native across North America from the Arctic Circle south to the Finger Lakes Region of New York, and in many western mountain lakes where it has been introduced, the laker is not suited to small lakes or to small streams.

Lake trout colors vary widely, from a steely blue-gray to a warm, rich brown. They are covered with a pattern that looks like small mesh wire netting. In some areas, the only time that they are caught is in early spring and late fall, just after ice-out and just before freeze-up. At those two times of the year, the lakers venture into shallow waters; at other times of the year they go several months without rising to within 100 feet of the surface.

An excellent food fish, the laker was the basis for commercial fisheries in the Great Lakes until the parasitic sea lam-

prey (and overfishing) put a stop to that fishery. Now, after the successful control of the lamprey, the lake trout is coming back and offers food and sport to many around the deep, cold Great Lakes.

Improving a Trout Stream

Basically, there are four ways in which to improve a trout stream:

1. Lower the water temperature;
2. Increase the depth;
3. Increase the dissolved oxygen content; and
4. Improve the water quality.

There are many variations, but all trout stream improvement boils down to these four objectives.

The simplest way to lower water temperature is to keep the sun's rays off the water. Naturally, we need some sunshine for proper growth of aquatic plants and the aquatic insects that live and feed upon those plants. However, every square foot of water we can shade will be cooler than the same square foot of water unshaded.

Planting trees to shade the water is of first importance. The trees should be planted as close to the water's edge as is possible. Remember that there will be more flow in the stream in the spring when the snow-melt occurs. Plan your plantings so that the spring flood will not uproot them. Use species that are water-tolerant, so that they will not be killed by a prolonged period of high water. Most members of the willow family are excellent for this duty, because they put out a spreading root system that helps to stabilize stream banks. If your ultimate aim is to have good trout fishing on your land, be sure to plan your planting so that there is room to get in and work a fly rod. Don't do too good a job, and bar yourself entirely from that shaded stretch of river. Check with your County Agent to see which species of tree will do the best job in your region. If purple osier will grow in your area, try it—it does a wonderful job of spreading out and increasing the cover.

Trout like deep shadows to stay in during the sunlit hours, and deep shadows are provided by logs dropped across a small stream or dropped into a larger stream. If you drop a tree into a stream, but the tree is not big enough to span the creek, be sure to anchor the upstream end of the tree very solidly, so that you will not lose that shade-producer when the spring runoff raises the water level. This can be done by chaining or cabling the root end to a solid tree, or by driving strong fence pole stakes alongside the downstream side of the log to hold it in place.

Undercut banks are good shade producers, but undercut banks are usually caused by ongoing bank erosion. If you have an undercut bank that seems to be stable, you can help keep it stable by fencing livestock away from it or by planting tall grass cover on the undercut bank.

Small trout streams will benefit by having artificial sunshades constructed over them. Four corner posts supporting grain doors or other sturdy flat surfaces (such as 4 by 8-foot sheets of cheap plywood) will provide large patches of shade on small streams. These patches of shade should be in water at least 4 feet deep for maximum effectiveness. I know of a pasture trout stream in New Mexico where I can almost always find a rainbow or two sheltering under an artificial shade,

watching the flow from upstream for food to come his way.

If you can replace a ford with a short bridge and make that bridge strong enough to support farm equipment, you will kill two birds with one stone. You will provide a shade spot, and you will remove a source of stream bed disturbance.

Basic to any trout stream improvement is the fencing of livestock away from most of the stream area. Leave a few spots for cattle to reach the stream, preferably on the downstream end of your property. Be sure your fencing is well positioned to keep the cattle from wading around it and going into the area you are trying to protect. Good planning will enable you to have cattle-watering places and good grassy banks shading the water in your trout stream.

Increasing water depth provides a margin of safety from winter-kill; provides more safe sheltering spots for trout; increases the oxygen-storing capacity of the moving stream; and, by reducing the surface area per acre foot of water, actually lowers the temperature of the stream. In fact, most of the problems of trout streams can be cured by adding a bit more depth.

First thought, obviously, is to build a dam that will stop the flow and pile up the stream to a greater depth. But dams that stop the entire flow of a trout stream are seldom good for the trout population. Beaver dams do a much better job because they (usually) provide deeper water without stopping the entire flow of the stream.

A detent dam, which piles up water to a higher level, then permits the usual flow to pass over it and does not impose an impassable barrier for fish travel, is a welcome addition to almost every stream. These detent dams can be made of large

This small log detent dam properly placed in trout stream increases depth above dam, cuts a deeper hole below dam. *USDA photo.*

stone, big enough not to be rolled by the spring runoff, strategically placed so as to provide deeper water on the upstream side and yet allow fish to come up over the dam without getting sunburned. The long riffle below such a detent dam is usually a good place to offer a lure to a feeding fish in the evening and early morning hours.

If the stream is fairly swift-flowing, you can pile up water in the middle every hundred feet or so by building side dams, structures that squeeze the river from both sides, forcing it to bulge upward in the middle. This speeds up the current for a short bit, causing it to scour clean the bottom directly below this structure. It also provides deeper water right in the damming structure itself.

In the preceding paragraph, we re-

A log structure such as this can deepen the water in a trout stream. *Bureau of Land Management photo.*

ferred to scouring clean a spot right below a structure, due to the increased "earth-moving" ability of the faster water. Controlled scouring, or bottom cleaning, is a good thing, as it provides spawning places for trout, cleaning the silt off likely looking places for trout to scoop out their redds. However, a scouring that moves sand and gravel as well as silt, leaving the stream bed denuded of redd-building material, is certainly not good for trout. No trout eggs will be hatched on a bare bottom.

How can we increase oxygen content of our trout waters? Anything that causes water to splash will increase aeration—simply a greater surface area of water exposed to a greater air supply, picking up more oxygen. If you have water flowing over a dam, large or small, it is usually possible to divert some or all of the flow into pipes that will drop at a slower rate than the surface of the stream drops. Then the water splashes out of the end of the pipe, back into the flowing creek. By its splashing effect, it increases aeration and multiplies oxygen content of the water.

If you are fortunate enough to have springs or seeps flowing into your trout stream, find a way to collect their flow above the stream level, pipe it to the stream, and let it splash out of the pipe onto a flat rock and then into the stream itself. This double-splash method of adding the spring's or seep's production to your trout stream will double the aeration. Remember that cooler water can hold more oxygen than warm water, so your stream-deepening and stream-shading structures have already helped to improve the oxygen content of the trout stream.

Stones and rocks can be piled up in the running stream to cause splashing diversions of the current. Making the current splash back and forth between rock formations will increase aeration.

So far, we have talked only about keeping the oxygen supply high during the summer months, but there is a lesser problem when ice and snow cover the trout stream. If the stream is fast-flowing, there usually will not be a problem in supplying enough oxygen. Remember that the fish's oxygen demand goes way down with reduced metabolism resulting from lowered water temperatures. However, if the stream is slow-moving, it is important to keep some of its surface exposed to wind and wave action, as a source of oxygen. In the section on pond management, we will discuss aeration devices that can be used to supply oxygen under the ice and prevent winter-kill due to oxygen depletion.

Water quality is a matter of ever-increasing concern in this day of chemical pollutants. But water pollution is not always the result of chemical plants. If the runoff from your cattle feedlot drains into the stream, you may so greatly increase the ammonia content that the stream will not support trout. If the stream flows slowly, the increased nutrients (fertilizer) washed into the stream may cause unwanted algal growth, speed up plant growth, and crowd out the trout. Runoff from feedlots can reach the stream by percolating through the soil, so simple barriers on the surface will not protect the stream's water quality. Planning is important, so that feedlots and other places that concentrate livestock waste will not be placed at higher elevations than the trout stream.

Trout are excellent bio-accumulators. This means that they will concentrate unwanted chemicals in their body tissues to a great degree. If there is one part per million of an unwanted chemical in the trout stream, the trout can be expected to contain three or four parts per million of that same unwanted chemical in their body tissues. Trout have concentrated mercury in this way as well as PCBs, the poly-chlorinated biphenyls that are thought to be carcinogenic.

Aerial spraying of pesticides and herbicides must be carefully planned and the amount of application carefully controlled. If the aerial spray actually falls on the surface of the trout stream, you may reasonably expect to lose all of your trout. If the chemical is applied in excess, or applied where it will be washed into the stream with the first rain, there is a good chance that your trout will disappear. This is primary poisoning, but a greater fear is that secondary poisoning will hit the trout. Insects killed by the poisons are washed along in the current of your trout stream, and they look very appetizing to the feeding trout. He ingests large quantities of these poisoned insects and "bio-accumulates" the poisonous chemical in his body tissues.

At times, such accumulations of chemicals are stored in the fatty tissue of the fish and seemingly have no short-term effect upon that fish. The chemicals may, however, be very harmful to the humans who eat those fish. At other times, ingestion of certain chemicals may cause the fish to die. More commonly, ingestion of these chemicals can have a long-term effect, such as making the fish's eggs infertile, or rendering the male fish impotent by reason of chemical impairment of his gonads. In such cases, we have caused the loss—not of the fish that ate the chemical-laden insect—but of his or her offspring. We can exterminate a race of fish from a water, and never see a dead one—because the species that cannot reproduce itself is the species that, for all practical purposes, is exterminated.

But there are other ways of improving the quality of water than simply preventing the addition of unwanted chemicals. Sheet erosion of farm land carries a load of silt into the trout stream, burying fish eggs and causing the loss of the entire year class of that fish. Silt from eroded fields fills up the area behind detent dams, an area that was supposed to store water, not dirt. In this way, the water temperature is raised, the water depth is reduced, and the stream is much less suitable for trout.

The only way to prevent erosion from cultivated fields is to make running water walk. This old slogan of the U.S. Soil Conservation Service is still true today. If water moves slowly, it does not rip off the topsoil and carry it along.

Level fields do not erode as badly as sloping fields, naturally. But even sloping fields can be terraced so as to make a series of small level fields instead of one big sloping field. To reduce soil erosion on your land, look and see what the U.S. Corps of Engineers does, and do the opposite. Where the Corps tries to solve flooding problems by channelization, straightening and scouring out a channel to get the water off of your land (and onto your downstream neighbor, of course) as fast as possible, you must do exactly the opposite. A curving, meandering stream slows water, whereas a straight-line stream speeds up flow.

Small earthen dams on the upper half of a coulee or arroyo will stop the erosion before it can start, and silt collecting behind such small dams will start its own terracing program. Reed canary grass or other good—strong rooted—grasses will anchor waterways, if the planting is allowed to mature before it gets its real test. The grassy cover will slow down the rushing water, making it do its job of percolating into the earth to replenish streams at lower elevations.

Anything that will slow or stop rushing water in an eroding gully is a good trout stream improvement measure. Brush piled in a gully will slow the water and slow the gullying. Even old car bodies can serve this purpose by slowing the water and stabilizing the banks.

Those measures will improve the quality of the water entering your trout stream. But how about the stream itself? Your trout stream can dig its own grave by eroding its banks, carrying a load of silt to the detent dam, and then reducing the water storage capacity. How to keep your own stream from eroding its banks? Rock structures that switch the river from side to side will slow its downhill velocity, but they may increase undercutting of the banks by direct assault with the full force of the trout stream's flow. Rock riprap will be effective if properly placed, giving

Wire gabion-type of detent dam can improve trout stream. *USDA photo.*

the stream something solid to impact instead of the vulnerable, undercut bank. In difficult situations, gabions (heavy fence wiring holding together a filling of football- or larger-sized rock) will resist the strongest current and prevent soil erosion. If you are fortunate enough to have a place where the water actually falls a foot or more, make sure that the falling water lands on solid rock. This will de-

Bank improvement on trout stream. Stone riprapping prevents bank undercutting. *North Carolina Tourism photo.*

crease soil erosion and scouring and will increase aeration.

To sum up, you can improve your trout stream by lowering the water temperature through shading or increased depth. You can improve your trout stream by "piling up" the water with wing dams, detent dams, or side dams, all measures that will increase the effective depth of the stream. You can improve your stream by improving the aerating of the water through any method that will provide splashing of water, either from dropping vertically or being displaced laterally. You can improve your trout stream by preventing the addition of undesirable silt, undesirable fertilizers, or undesirable chemicals such as pesticides or herbicides.

Stabilizing banks by tree planting is perhaps the single most practical step you can take. But remember to fence livestock away from the trout stream, for cloven hooves are hard on trout streams.

Beaver and Trout

Over a large part of the United States, there exists a wonderful symbiotic relationship between the beaver (*Castor canadensis*) and several species of trout.

The beaver cuts down trees that formerly shaded the trout stream, and this raises water temperatures. But the beaver then cuts the trees into workable lengths and uses these pieces to construct a dam, which raises the water level. Making the water deeper lowers the water temperature. The increased water depth makes it possible for trout to live through the winter in northerly areas.

By increasing the water volume of the pond behind the dam, the beaver makes it possible for the trout to benefit from the increased nutrients flooded by the reservoir's advancing waters. This, of course, is good for trout. By slowing running water to a slow walk, the beaver

This venerable stone dam was built by the Civilian Conservation Corps way back in the 1930's. It has completely filled with sand, brought down by springtime runoff waters. Water slowly seeps out of sand near bottom, providing vital moisture for wildlife after half a century. *U.S. Forest Service photo.*

dam causes the load of silt in the water to precipitate, to fall to the bottom, which makes for clearer, cleaner water and this, of course, is good for the trout.

Beaver dams stop soil erosion, bank-undercutting, and gullying, and this is a plus for the entire environment.

Beaver dams eventually fill with silt, and dryland plants eventually gain a foothold on these level, fertile spots. In this way, the final step in the beaver's reworking of a stream bed is a series of fertile terraces, good for almost all kinds of life except trout.

These are all plus factors, things that add up to our naming the beaver a valued co-worker with us in managing a trout stream. But let's look a little farther.

You have a valuable apple orchard within 200 yards of the stream. Beaver suddenly appear, young pairs seeking a place to set up housekeeping. Their dam-building material is apt to be the trunks and branches of your prized apple trees. A negative, surely!

You take your tractor and go out to cut your hay, only to find that the rising waters of the beaver dam have made it impossible for you to ford the stream, inundated your bridge, and even flooded the hayfield. Negative?

The road to town is suddenly impassable, due to beavers damming the creek at a point where no one expected them to operate. Definitely a negative.

The state of Wyoming has had exceptional luck in moving both beavers and a wood supply to feed them and help them build a dam, providing both at the spot where they want the dam built. The Beaver Construction Company promptly goes to work and builds a dam in the proper place, and the work of reclaiming a barren gully has begun. When the beavers

provide the water, the state stocks trout and good fishing often results. Definitely a plus!

Beaver have been known to build a plug for the outflow channel of a fish hatchery, causing water to back up, flood the raceways, and prematurely liberate half a million trout!

Most farmers greet the construction of a new beaver dam by blowing up the dam with dynamite. If they blow up the beavers with it, most consider that an added blessing. If you have beavers on your land, and if they are providing trout fishing, you may consider yourself lucky. However, it is definitely not recommended that you provide beavers to a stream that does not have them. Leave this to the State Conservation Agency.

Let's take a closer look at this interesting engineer of the wild, Mr. Beaver.

An entirely aquatic animal, the beaver has webbed hind feet to help in swimming and a big, broad, flat tail that he whacks against the water in crash-diving, as a danger signal to other beavers. He does *not* use that tail as a trowel to smooth the mud masonry of his dams.

He has an amazing dental arrangement, opposed upper and lower gnawing teeth that grow throughout his lifetime. Incredibly hard, they are kept sharpened by grinding against each other as the beaver cuts down trees as much as 2 feet in diameter. The beaver feeds almost entirely on the bark of trees—preferring aspen and ornamental fruit trees over all other foods. To illustrate just how hard those teeth are, listen to what happened about twenty-five years ago, when the old Branch of Predator and Rodent Control of the Fish and Wildlife Service was busy removing nuisance beaver from the National Forests in South Dakota. Beaver pelts were at a very low price; it didn't pay to skin one.

To help pay for the costs of the program, the Service kept the entire carcass of the animal in cold storage, then auctioned off the entire mess to mink farmers. The mink farmers then ground the entire carcass and shaped the ground meat into chunks to be frozen against the day when they would feed it to the pen-reared mink.

The tool-steel, case-hardened cutter blades of the mink farms grinders hit those teeth, and the tool steel broke. The cutting edges that went through meat, bone, and skin as if it were hot butter couldn't handle the incredibly hard beaver teeth. After that, it became *de rigueur* to cut off the head before grinding the carcass. If these teeth do not find cutting work to be done, the teeth will continue to grow, forming a half-circle and eventually making it impossible for the beaver to eat.

The search for beaver pelts led the mountain men into and through the Rocky Mountains, and the luxurious furs were in great demand for beaver hats and for ladies' coats. Until the styles changed, the beaver was being overtrapped. But prices dropped from as high as $75 per pelt down to the point where the average "skunk house" didn't even quote a price. The beaver population increased markedly with reduced trapping effort, and the beaver became a nuisance in farming country, an inconvenience in the national forests.

Beaver construction is not limited to dams. They also build houses, which are sprawling mounds of wood and mud plastered together, half in and half out of the water. The entrance to such a beaver house is below the water level, often near the floor of the pond so as to make sure

that it is accessible even during periods of thick ice. But the beaver tunnel slopes rapidly upward after the deep entryway is negotiated. The main part of the house is above the water level, providing a warm, almost dry chamber for the beaver to live in during the winter. There is a breathing hole left at the top to allow stale air to escape; the tell-tale bit of "breath" escaping from such a beaver house ventilator is often the only sign of life during the winter months.

Beavers dig lateral canals to allow them to reach food plots and to transport food and building materials back to the pond without exposing themselves to more danger than is necessary. They store food, tender branches stashed in a central place, with some of the butt ends of the branches stuck in the bottom mud or anchored to an existing tree or even to the dam or beaver house. This food patch is the reserve for the winter when ice prevents the beaver from going ashore to cut a fresh dinner.

There are many adaptations about the beaver that make him superbly fitted for his role as watery engineer. He can close his mouth *behind* his cutting teeth, so that he can gnaw under water without getting water down into his throat and lungs. He has a split nail on his foot, which acts as a comb when he grooms that thick, lustrous fur. His flattened tail acts as a stable brace against the ground when he starts to fell a tree, bracing the animal's body so that he can exert tremendous leverage with those cutting teeth.

Contrary to popular opinion, the beaver is not skilled at forecasting just where a tree will fall when he cuts it. This is proven by the recurring tragedy of a beaver being squashed by the very tree he dropped.

He has very poor eyesight, but a discriminating nose, which he relies upon to a great extent. The castors in a beaver's body are used as the basis for scents, even for perfume manufacture. Their purpose in the life of the beaver is not fully understood. Surely they are connected with sexual behavior. By judicious use of the castor scent, a skilled trapper can make sure that his trap set attracts only adult males or only breeding-age females.

And it may become necessary to trap and remove some beaver, if they are interfering with your management of your wildlife resources. The state conservation agency will live-trap and remove nuisance beaver in some states. In other states, this is not economically feasible. If the fur price makes it worthwhile, beaver can bring in a good return to the local trapping expert. They are easily trapped in wintertime.

The most successful trap set is one where a Number 3 or Number 4 Newhouse trap is set on the bottom, at the entrance to the beaver house. The trap must be very strongly fastened down, so that the beaver cannot reach air to breathe once the trap has grabbed him by the foot. In this way, he is quickly drowned, a relatively painless and humane death. If there is enough scope of the trap chain so that he can reach air to breathe, the story will be very different. The beaver has been known to "wring off," breaking the leg bone and twisting the tendons to the point where he actually "wrings off" his own foot and keeps his freedom.

A second effective set is only efficient after permanent ice has blanketed the beaver pond for several months. Then the trap is set on the bottom, about 4 feet below the ice. The hole cut through the ice to allow you to set the trap is then filled with branches of freshly cut aspen, or red willow, or other tasty tree. The ice fills in the hole, securely anchoring the bait. The beaver comes to the fresh bait, stands up to gnaw on it, and catches himself by a back foot. As always, the trap must be securely fastened, for the beaver is very strong and will get away if not drowned quickly.

Often, the nuisance act committed by a beaver can be nullified without destroying the beaver. For example, if the beavers have flooded a road by damming up a drain pipe under a highway, it is possible to (1) remove the plug, (2) use heavy wire mesh to prevent the beaver from getting close to the pipe, or (3) provide another water outlet that will accomplish the same purpose as the road culvert.

Yes, beaver are fascinating creatures, indefatigable engineers and builders, good parents and wood eaters. But they can also play hob with man's best-laid plans. If you have that wonderful combination of beaver and trout, rejoice. But don't try to stock beavers into your creek bed—you will probably live to regret it.

PAN FISH

Bluegill Sunfish, King of Pan Fish

Most bluegills weigh in at less than a third of a pound, yet bluegills provide more pounds of good eating than any other sporting fish in North America. Bluegills are the "first fish" caught by young anglers, they reproduce by the millions, and they are a great treat when fried to a crispy brown. Easily caught on angleworms, the bluegill is also a sporting opponent for the dry fly fisherman—and they put a respectable bend in that long rod, too.

A "bull bluegill" is a strikingly handsome fish, sporting a brilliantly colored orange throat and front of the underbelly, a bit of blue on the back edge of the gill cover (not the gill itself, no matter what the name), a flat plate-shaped body, a big eye, and a small mouth.

Originally native east of the Rockies and south of the Canadian border, the bluegill (*Lepomis macrochirus*) is now found in all the lower forty-eight states. If the water area is somewhat alkaline, the orangebelly doesn't seem to mind. He is suited to any waters with less than 900 parts per million of total alkalinity.

Bluegills get bigger in the southern half of their range than they do in the northern half, for the obvious reason that they eat (and grow) all year long in warmer waters, but eat and grow very little during the winter months up north. To compensate for the fact that they get bigger down south, they live longer up north.

Blessed with a terrific reproductive potential, the bluegill spawns as many as five times per year, with each female laying a tremendous number of eggs. Depending upon the size, physical condition, and age of the parent female, the eggs will number anywhere from 2,500 to 80,000! With reproduction like that, something obviously has to happen to most of the young bluegills or we would surely drown in a sea of bluegills. And a lot of things do happen to most of the young.

When food is scarce, the male bluegill often eats the eggs. He normally eats the first spawn in any case. Aquatic insects eat great numbers of bluegill eggs and bluegill fry, as we call the newly hatched fish. Every fish in the lake or pond seems to relish bluegill eggs, and young bluegills are the meat and potatoes on the menu of the largemouth black bass and many other predatory fish. Wading birds feast on the young bluegills. But let's take a look at the entire process.

When water temperatures near 17°C, the bluegills build a nest on the floor of their watery world, usually in depths of 4 to 10 feet. The chosen location is almost always in direct sunlight, but close to aquatic vegetation. The parents fan out a circular nest, using their fins and caudal fin (tail) to blow the silt off the gravel, leaving a clean place in which to place their eggs. Naturally, this place is far from currents that would move the eggs away. When everything is in readiness, the female and male join in a sort of love-making, which consists of ritualistic circlings, touching, and even butting with their heads to express their undying affection.

The climax of all this emotion is when the female extrudes the eggs, small, round, bee-bees of white to yellowish brown color. Within seconds, the male squirts out the white sperm (called milt), which settles on the eggs like a cloud. The sperm cells must find an egg to penetrate within the first minute and a half, or they die. The eggs can remain receptive to the sperm invader for as long as one hour. Sperm penetrates ova, and the egg is fertilized. It is very soft at first, but quickly hardens at water temperatures and becomes quite solid as it settles into the gravel of the nest.

This is the sensitive time, for the bluegills must drive away all would-be diners who are attracted to the prospective dinner of bluegill caviar. One of the biggest appetites belongs to the father of the eggs. It is strange that the father will often eat the eggs he has fertilized, but most of the time he will defend them aggressively, driving away much larger fish in his zeal to see to it that the eggs have a sporting chance of hatching. He doesn't have long to wait, for the eggs will hatch in about six days, given good conditions. When the eggs do hatch, the young bluegill has no mouth and thus cannot eat at all. This is no problem, for he is attached to a yolk sac, which provides the food he needs while his mouth is developing. Ten days after the eggs are fertilized, the young have absorbed the yolk sac and their mouths have developed.

Daytime diners, the bluegill young feed on minute water organisms and tiny insects for the first few weeks of their lives, gradually switching to the adult bluegill diet, which is insects, small minnows, and some plant life such as algae, supplemented by zooplankton. As they get big enough to inhale a baby crayfish, they do inhale baby crayfish. In fact, a healthy population of adult bluegills may entirely eliminate the crayfish from a small pond.

Bluegills are usually stocked while still very small and have a surprisingly good survival rate.

When only bluegills are placed in virgin waters, with no predators, initial survival rates up to 100 percent can be expected, with perhaps as many as 75 percent surviving until the first fall. When stocked with largemouth black bass, the initial mortality will be about 20 percent, with 80 percent surviving until the first fall.

It is important that you start what you hope to be a balanced fish population all at the same time. Do not stock the black bass one year and the bluegills a year later. If you do, you can expect that the larger black bass will eat up 85 percent of the young bluegills before the first fall, leaving you with a species composition that is already badly out of balance before the first fish has spawned.

Strangely, bluegills seem to do better in a pond with both channel catfish and black bass than they do with the black bass alone. This doesn't seem to make sense, as the channel catfish is a predator on small bluegills, but it is a phenomenon often observed.

Will bluegills do well in your pond? Water temperature is the first consideration. They seem to prefer water at about 28°C. They will do fine in waters that never get higher than 18°C, and they don't seem to mind when temperatures rise to about 33°C, although reproduction stops at that high temperature and the fish are definitely off their feed.

Second consideration, of course, is the matter of dissolved oxygen content in the wintertime. Your state conservation agency can advise you as to what depth of water will be necessary to prevent winter-kill at your latitude.

Bluegills prefer gravel bottoms and will not reproduce on silt bottoms. They like aquatic vegetation, which is a must to provide escape cover for the very young bluegills. But they will not prosper in a pond choked with heavy emergent vegetation.

If there is a constant interchange of water in your pond, through inflowing currents, that is all to the good, as it increases the dissolved oxygen content and brings food with it. But bluegills cannot spawn in a moving water situation, so fast flow is anathema to them.

Easy to produce, fun to catch, and good to eat, the bluegill sunfish is the basic building block for many warm-water fisheries. Substitutes are not readily available, either. The green sunfish and pumpkinseed, the warmouth and goggle-eye cannot take his place, because they are too easily stunted. They simply don't grow big enough to be safe from black bass, thus ensuring their own survival to spawning time.

The black and white crappies are not suited to take the place of the bluegill, as they are inveterate minnow eaters and will decimate schools of young black bass. In addition, they are also prone to overpopulation and subsequent stunting. For further information about pond fish and the ponds they live in, be sure to read carefully chapter 8, on farm ponds, found farther back in this book.

The matter of pond renovation—the process of starting over again—is discussed at more length later in this chapter, but any discussion of bluegill management must be foreworded by saying that there is a danger of overpopulation and subsequent stunting. It is far easier to prevent overpopulation than it is to cure overpopulation.

The warning signs are usually not clear until it is too late. If the average size of your bluegills is not increasing, start watching carefully. If the average size of your bluegills is going down, it is too late, you are in trouble. We must remember that a bluegill is old enough to reproduce his (or her) kind when the second summer season rolls around. The fact that the bluegill may not be more than 3 inches long has very little to do with it. Age, not size, is the determinant in sexual maturity.

Unless you have too few bluegills in your pond, it is a good rule to keep every bluegill that is caught on a hook. If it is big enough to bite a bait, it is big enough to keep. Keep it—not necessarily to eat, for it may be too small. But keep it to reduce the total number of bluegills in your pond. For the good health of your bluegill population, the exact opposite treatment should be given to the biggest

black bass. Do not keep them. Return them to the water to continue their mission in life, which is to eat bluegills. Remember that a bass returned to the water will grow bigger and be more fun to catch the next time you tangle with him.

Young anglers love bluegill fishing, for it requires very little skill and the bluegills are almost always in a biting mood. Encourage the youngsters to keep the bluegills they catch, regardless of size. This will help prevent overpopulation and subsequent stunting.

Lots of Sunfish

There are many kinds of sunfish, and they are all bad news for you in your pond, with the possible exception of the bluegill sunfish. Bluegills grow large enough to eat; they can get large enough to be unavailable to largemouth black bass. In other words, they get big enough to fight back with their secret weapon, the great reproductive potential of the bluegill sunfish.

What's wrong with all the other sunfish? There are always too many of them. There's no such thing as putting just a few green sunfish, or redear sunfish, or redbreast sunfish, into a pond. It's kind of like being a little bit pregnant. Pregnancy doesn't stay little and sunfish don't stay "few." Almost invariably, they overpopulate the waters, which means that the individual sunfish is stunted—too small to be fun to catch, too small to eat—but perfectly able to reproduce some more sunfish.

The redbreast (*Lepomis auritus*) is found in the eastern streams that flow to the Atlantic. Although they have been known to grow to more than a pound, average weight is far below that. They are sporty little devils and will fight hard for their size. But in a small water, they'll almost always overpopulate. Like all true sunfish, they lay their eggs in a shallow water nest fanned out over clean sand or gravel. A water temperature of 68°F is about perfect for spawning redbreasts.

The redear (*Lepomis microlophus*) probably has more local names than any other fish. In its southern homeland, it is known as bream, stumpknocker, yellow brim, and shellcracker. Florida redears have been known to reach weights of 3 pounds, but again, in a small water area, these fertile fish will most often overpopulate. For many years, it held the reputation of being less prolific, and therefore better suited to smaller waters. It was hoped that it would not overpopulate, but my experience has been that it will end up in a population of stunted fish, too small to catch and too small to eat— at least for humans. The body is huskier than most sunfish, so there is something there to eat even when the fish is small in length. This sunfish requires a lot of mollusc food—small crustaceans being the preferred diet—and thus does not compete for insect food with other species of sunfish. However, waters containing sufficient quantities of molluscs are not common, and its preference for large water areas dooms it in the usual farm pond.

The pumpkinseed, *Lepomis gibbosus,* is the sunfish for children. This is the fish most often caught by preschoolers fishing off the end of the dock. It is easily identified by the stiff black gill cover point, which sports an end tipped in orange. During the breeding season, the male has the same bright underbelly and breast as the bluegill sunfish. They've been reported to reach a maximum length of 9 inches. I've never seen one that would top 6 inches. Again, this is a prolific breeder not suited to small farm ponds. In stunted populations, you may have thousands of breeders, all doing their best to keep up the birth rate, and not a single fish measuring more than 2½ inches.

The green sunfish, *Lepomis cyanellus,* is another easily caught, willing striker, willing fighter that doesn't grow to more than 8 or 9 inches maximum. A big female may lay as many as 10,000 eggs at one time, which rules it out in the farm pond where we have to worry about overpopulation.

Can you drain your pond and start all over when you want to? Then you may experiment with the sunfish family, for you have an answer to their overpopulation—remove them! If you cannot drain your ponds, please don't plan on catching them all out of the pond with hook and line. It can't be done.

Crappies

There are two species of crappie, the black, *Pomoxis nigromaculatus,* and the white, *Pomoxis annularis.* Most anglers cannot tell them apart—the real difference is in the number of dorsal spines. Coloration is of little value in separating the two species, for their colors will vary greatly with the color and clearness of the water. The black ranges from Manitoba to Quebec and south through Nebraska and Pennsylvania, on to Florida and up the east coast to the Carolinas. It is a school fish, very sociable, as it travels in great numbers most of its life. It is a minnow specialist and singles out the minnow for its main dish to a greater degree probably than any other fish.

It builds nests on the bottom of the

Light spinning tackle brought this string of crappie from a farm fish pond.

pond, similar to the bluegill sunfish but more apt to be crowded together, for even in spawning the crappie is a social fish. It has been known to deposit as many as 158,000 eggs from one female fish. With that potential for reproduction, the crappie rules itself out of the average farm pond, for it is sure to overpopulate . . . although some authorities say that it is less apt to stunt through overpopulation than is the white crappie.

The black crappie is easily taken, using minnows for bait, when a school is located. However, this may be difficult at times as this fish has a habit of suspending its school in the middle range, halfway to the bottom, and staying there for days.

The white crappie sounds tempting to the person planning a farm pond fishery. It can grow to 5 pounds in suitable waters, although the average is less than half a pound. It is a willing fighter and difficult to land because of its weak mouth, from which the hook is easily torn. It is also good eating, as is its black cousin. The white crappie tolerates turbidity better than does the black, and this makes it a popular reservoir fish in the South. But . . . and this is a big but . . . the white crappie is a prime subject for overpopulation and subsequent stunting. If you can drain your pond and remove them all every four years, you might want to experiment with the white crappie, for it will grow to good size in the first three years, before its own reproduction dooms it to become a population of 5-inchers.

More than any other pond or lake fish, the crappie can be attracted to the right place to be caught by anglers. This is done in two ways. Most common is the practice of sinking a big pile of brush in 15 feet of water. The brush congregates the minnows and aquatic insects, and the crappie goes to that congregation of food where it is most easily caught with the minnow-baited hook.

The second method is to sink a sack of cottonseed in 10 to 20 feet of water, well anchored, of course. As the cottonseed attracts insects, they attract minnows, and the minnows bring in the crappies. Don't overdo this method, for you can so increase the fertility of small ponds that an algal bloom will result—and that you do not want. Your county extension agent can best advise you as to chemical control of algae. It is relatively easy to kill algae, but to kill algae and not harm the fish life—that is quite a different story entirely.

Yellow Perch

Last in our series of fish that you do not want in your pond because of their tremendous reproductive potential is the yellow perch, also known as ring perch and even "convict fish." *Perca flavescens* is the scientific name for this fish, which is common across most of the United States today. It is a delicious eating fish, a willing biter, and a good enough fighter for its size. Problem is that it gives us some of our worst horror stories of overpopulating. A classic example would be the perch population in Spiritwood Lake, North Dakota, in the early 1950s. Despite the presence of goodly numbers of catfish in the 20-pound class, and northern pike in the over-10-pound class, the yellow perch simply filled the lake with their own bodies, most of them measuring less than 4 inches. Some of the fish, which were obviously grandfathers and grandmothers, were less than 3 inches long.

We can only theorize that the hordes of perch ate the eggs of the catfish and northern pike, or consumed the catfish and pike fry so completely that the larger predators couldn't increase in numbers despite the oversupply of good food. Each year the fish population was farther out of balance, with the perch even smaller and more numerous, the predators even scarcer and bigger. Finally, it was necessary to eliminate all fish life in the lovely, spring-fed lake and start over again. Since the chemical elimination of the perch, the North Dakota State Game and Fish Department has introduced walleyes, which have done well, and is experimenting with the tiger muskellunge—an able predator that grows to trophy size.

Walleyes

One of the best-tasting fish in the world, the walleye, or walleyed pike, *Stizostedion vitreum,* is not a pike at all. No pan fish, the walleye has been taken up to 26 pounds—26 pounds of fine eating. He gets his name from the large, opalescent eye, which fits him for nighttime feeding, and which keeps him as far out of the sunlit waters as he can possibly get. This is the largest member of the perch family. It once was a fish of northern waters but has been widely transplanted into large reservoirs in the South. Today the biggest walleyes, on average, are taken from the waters of the Tennessee Valley Authority and other large reservoirs in the mid-South region.

Walleyes are easy to raise in hatcheries and are easily restocked into depleted waters, which makes them a favorite with anglers. They spawn naturally on sandy or rocky bottoms in depths of from 5 to 20 feet, and one female can produce as many as 700,000 eggs, although the av-

Walleyes are not a good choice for farm fish ponds, but they are about the finest eating fish in the nation.

erage would run nearer 25,000. The spawning area can be a rocky ledge in a running stream, or a spot in a lake where the water is in constant movement over the spawners. On some spawning grounds, the action is spectacular as two or three males (the smaller ones always are males) follow one female in a dashing, thrashing, splashing movement across the spawning grounds with clouds of eggs appearing to be fertilized by clouds of white milt. All of the action takes place at night. The adults then leave, providing no protection or care to the eggs or the newly hatched fry, which will appear about sixteen days later. At first the young walleyes feed on their yolk sac, but soon learn to grab minute aquatic organisms and tiny insects. They grow rapidly in clear, clean waters; they do not do well in turbid waters.

There is no finer game and food fish available in North America than the walleye. It will seldom, if ever, reproduce in farm ponds, but the addition of walleyes to the fish population will produce some wonderful sport and good eating—if your pond is clear enough, cool enough, and otherwise to the liking of the walleye.

Northern Pike

One of the most efficient predators in fresh water is the northern pike, *Esox lucius,* an elongated fish with a crocodilian head and jaw, which happens to be well-studded with teeth, the better to hang onto the slippery fish that are its constant prey. Fifty years ago, the northern pike was scorned by most anglers, thought of as a trash fish, and often (to the eternal shame of the anglers) tossed out on the bank to feed a passing raccoon. There were two main reasons for this scorn: The belief that the northern was a killer

of too many good game fish, and the sure knowledge that the long, lean fish was full of tiny bones which made eating his flesh a tedious chore.

Today, the tiny bones are still there, but the northern pike is protected, even nurtured, by fisheries biologists, boat rental operators, and resort owners, as well as fishing guides. His willingness to strike and do battle—when the preferred walleyes are resolutely not striking—has saved the day for many people who earn their living from the lakes of the northern half of this country. He has a never-satisfied appetite for minnows, water dogs, frogs, and other live bait, and will turn away from a juicy minnow to strike a flashing spoon at times. In fact, artificials will consistently outfish northern pike in many waters.

But the northern pike is not a candidate for stocking into most farm ponds. His insatiable appetite gets him in bad all of the time. When he can't get fathead minnows, or golden shiners, or frogs, or freshwater eels, he will readily dine on young northern pike, or any fish slightly smaller than he is. When Dale Henegar first came to manage North Dakota's fisheries, he experimented with putting rapid growth on northern pike by stocking them temporarily into sewage lagoons, which were amazingly fertile, yet which supported fish life very well. It worked! In fact, the first shipment of 3-inchers quickly became 6-inchers, ideal for the waters into which Henegar wished to stock them. But one test didn't turn out so well. The fish went into the lagoon as 3-inchers, fresh from the state's fish hatchery in Lisbon. But when it came time to take them out—one month later—it was not possible for the big, heavy hatchery trucks to approach the sewage lagoons, because heavy rains had soaked the ground to the consistency of soft, soupy mud. It was decided to delay taking the fish out. Three months went by and then the trucks came in to remove the northern pike. Five thousand 3-inch northern pike had gone in. They drained the ponds and recovered one 13-inch northern pike, and he was hungry! In fact, it is quite possible that all 5,000 northern pike were represented in the person of the one survivor.

When television first came to North Dakota, the stations were hungry for anything to show on the air, because they were not yet connected to a network cable to provide programming. We called KFYR-TV in Bismarck and alerted them to the fact that a truck was coming through the city, carrying 5,000 northern pike fingerlings to be stocked into a small lake west of Bismarck. A camera crew met the truck and interviewed Mel Jorgenson, the driver. The announcer type asked, "How many fish in the tank, Mr. Jorgenson?" while the camera zeroed in on the open top of the tank to show the cruising little 3- and 4-inchers. "Five thousand," replied Mel.

As the words left his mouth, one fingerling chopped another in half, right on camera. The two halves each disappeared down the gullets of the nearest northern fingerlings. In the same tone of voice, Mel amended his reply to "Four thousand, nine hundred and ninety-nine." It went over well on the screen.

Northern pike grow to great size, and the record is about 46 pounds, which is a lot of hungry fish to feed. He will tolerate warmer waters and more turbid waters than will the walleye or smallmouth black bass. He will prosper in waters sneered at by any member of the trout family; he will reproduce anywhere there is a stream flowing—or just take advantage of the runoff into a pond to deposit their eggs in the shallows. Hatchability is good, and the young fish live— if allowed to hatch out—until something bigger than they are eats them. The northern pike's catholic tastes in food allow it to feed on almost anything and to grow rapidly, for its sole aim in life is to grow so big that nothing else can eat it.

Northern pike eat fish of all kinds and sizes, frogs, eels, crawfish, baby birds that fall into the water, baby muskrats, small ducklings, tiny turtles, mice that make the mistake of swimming across the top of the northern pike's watery world . . . even a baby beaver was found in one pike's stomach.

Elsewhere in this book, I have told the story of Springer Lake, New Mexico, where northern pike grow big and sassy. They often are found with table-sized rainbow trout in their gullets. However, a northern pike and rainbow trout stocking would hardly make sense, for the northerns will probably eliminate the high-priced trout. They hunt by lying in wait, concealed in weeds where their well-camouflaged bodies disappear against a bottom dappled with sunlight. When the prey comes within range, a sudden lunge— which has been likened to the strike of the rattlesnake by some—grabs the prey, and those spikelike teeth hold on when once clamped together.

At times the northern pike can be used to restore the balance in an overpopulated pond of sunfish or yellow perch. Stocking 100 or 200 5-inch northerns should do the trick. They will eat those sunfish hordes down to size, so that the individual can grow up—if a northern lets him grow up. But this is, at best, a precarious balance and not accepted fishery practice.

It is best to leave the northern out of

most plans for small farm ponds, and that is really too bad, for the once-scorned northern pike is truly a fine game fish.

Bullheads

Over a large part of this nation, the first fish caught by a young angler is the bullhead. Whether you call them yellowbellies, mudfish, eelpouts, or any one of the thousand other names, we are talking about a smaller version of the catfish, with a big head (hence the name), a tapering body, big barbels to better sense food on the bottom, tiny eyes, not much wariness and—well, it's a bullhead, that's all.

On the plus side are these qualities: It is easily caught on a hook baited with angleworms, nightcrawlers, clam bits, crawdad tails, belly skin of other fish, pork or beef or chicken livers, soap, peas, corn, doughballs—almost anything edible and a few things not usually considered edible.

Taken from cold, or at least cool, waters, the bullhead provides a couple of tasty morsels of flesh that are very good. After the waters warm up, the bullhead develops a sort of "muddy" taste, to my palate, and I pass them up from warm-up time until late fall. Just after ice-out, when the water temperatures warm to the point where the bullheads start moving, they are definitely good to eat.

They are very prolific, and a mature pair can fill a warm-water pond with clouds of tiny bullheads in a couple of seasons. The young stay together in tightly packed schools that move through the water like one entity, rather than a thousand tiny bullheads. They provide prime food for birds, fishes, insects, frogs—almost every living organism that frequents the pond environment will feed on bullheads.

Sounds good? Then listen to the one big minus.

Bullheads are strictly bottom feeders, and they have a nasty habit of plowing up the bottom, searching for edible materials. This increases the turbidity of the pond to the point where green plants die out from lack of sunshine. The turbidity slowly settles out, covering the eggs of more desirable fishes and inhibiting reproduction in that manner. This does not seem to inhibit their own reproduction, leading us to the inescapable end result, a muddy pond full of very small bullheads.

If you stock bullheads, or if they are already present in your farm pond, the three best predators to help whittle the bullhead numbers down are the northern pike (but be careful, he may eliminate your other species as well), the channel catfish, and the largemouth black bass. All three dine on bullheads whenever they get the chance.

All in all, the bullhead is not recommended for stocking into your farm pond. If you want them, against professional advice, you will do best with a pond where you can (a) drain the pond to remove excess bullhead numbers, (b) provide a very healthy predator population, such as good-sized northern pike, or (c) catch thousands of them with hook and line—as in a public fishing area close to a large center of population.

BASS

Largemouth Black Bass

More fishermen seek the largemouth black bass than any other species of fish. A cult has grown up around this fish, with tournaments seeking the world's best bass fisherman offering prizes up to $100,000 as of this writing and plans being announced for a million-dollar first prize.

To catch a fat, potbellied member of the sunfish family? Sounds ridiculous, but it is true.

Micropterus salmoides is his scientific name. A long time ago, Dr. Henshall made the mistake of writing that "pound for pound and inch for inch, this is the gamest fish that swims." Unfortunately, that is not correct. I do not profess to know which fish *is* the gamest fish that swims, but I do know that he swims in salt water. Any and all members of the mackerel family, which includes the tuna, will rate a hundred times more accolades for strength and stamina per pound than does the somewhat lazy, ponderous black bass. Bluefish, all members of the jack family, even the spotted "weakfish" rate more sporting qualities, "pound for pound and inch for inch" than the largemouth. Hook up a 7-pound black bass and a 7-pound bluefish, tail to tail, and the bluefish would tow the black bass backwards so fast that he'd rip all the scales off.

Even in fresh water, the largemouth black bass is eclipsed by several other species, if we really mean that "ounce for ounce" bit. The bluegill sunfish fights harder for his size than does the largemouth, so does the white bass, so does the rainbow trout. Now that I have gotten the attention of the bass aficionados and earned myself some new enemies, let's take an *honest* look at why the black bass is America's most popular fish.

His good points are many:

1. He will readily strike artificial lures, which are more fun to fish than bait. At times he hits surface-floating lures, which makes for exciting fishing.

2. He is found almost everywhere, making himself available to more anglers than any other species in the lower forty-eight.

3. He grows to good size, even in small waters.

4. He will occasionally jump when fighting the hook, and this makes for a spectacular struggle although a very short one, compared to really strong battlers.

5. He is edible. He is not delicious, but he is definitely edible when taken from clean, cool waters. If taken from warm waters, his flesh becomes soft, and at times even develops a "muddy" taste. I would rate him far below walleyed pike, rainbow trout, or channel catfish for taste, but he is definitely table fare.

For purposes of developing a self-perpetuating fishery in a warm-water pond or slowly moving river, he is a near-perfect fish. The largemouth is very tolerant of water quality and can enjoy life in waters with total alkalinity up to 900 parts per million. In addition, he can tolerate brackish water and does well in salinity up to 24 parts per million. Remember that the ocean contains only 35 parts per million of salt, and you will see why the largemouth can get along fine in brackish waters such as Pamlico Sound in North Carolina, where he flourishes although the water is definitely saltier than you would expect to find fresh-water fish living in.

The largemouth black bass grows to good size, and the current world's record, caught half a century ago in Georgia, is still 22¼ pounds. Any bass over 5 pounds is a bragging-size fish, and 10-pounders rate headlines over most of the nation, although it takes a 14-pounder to draw the same attention in Florida. Florida-strain bass have been introduced into the western bass fishery to a great extent in the last ten years and have resulted in moving up the state record mark in several states. This is especially true in man-made reservoirs in California and along the Colorado River in Arizona and Utah.

What bass do not eat would make a shorter list than what they do eat. A big bass will swallow anything that moves and that he can fit into his oversized, bucket-shaped mouth. This includes all fish life, crawfish (which he dotes upon), water snakes, minnows, young of all fish including his own, leeches, frogs, salamanders, small ducklings, mice, and young birds unfortunate enough to fall into the water. On at least one occasion—on Lake Lida in Minnesota—I saw a big black bass try for a bird that was sitting innocently on a reed that sagged down to within 4 inches of the water. The bass struck with a "woosh" and knocked the alert red-winged blackbird a foot into the summer air. The bird escaped, but there was no mistaking the black bass's intent. He wanted to dine on bird, feathers and all.

This catholicity of appetite explains why the bass strikes artificials. If it is moving, it is food—that seems to be his opinion.

Black bass fan out nests in nonflowing shallow water to receive their eggs, in a manner reminiscent of bluegills. Like bluegills, they prefer water from 4 to 10 feet deep, clean and sunlit, but near aquatic vegetation. If the bottom is coarse gravel or rock, that will be accepted readily. Fine sand is more often available, thus more often used. They will not spawn successfully on silty bottoms. Water levels and water temperatures must remain fairly constant for successful spawning of black bass.

The bass is a belligerent parent in defense of the nest and strikes artificial lures readily during the few short days when they are guarding the nest. If you wish to protect your black bass from overfishing, close the season during spawning

time. Spawning usually starts when water temperatures come up to about 16°C and speeds up at 18°C. Black bass will tolerate spawning temperatures all the way up to 29°C.

Eighty hours after the eggs are fertilized, the young black bass hatch from the egg. In 192 hours they have developed the necessary mouth to allow them to feed. They are free-swimming after 240 hours and have absorbed the yolk sac after just 312 hours. This fast development was recorded at 19°C water temperature. Nineteen degrees is slightly too cold for best results. At 22°C, hatching took place 48 hours after fertilization and the young were free-swimming after just 168 hours. Given their choice of water temperatures, most black bass will pick areas where the thermometer hovers between 26°C and 32°C.

How many eggs are we talking about? Well, this depends upon size of female, age, and the physical condition of the spawner. All other things being equal, a five-year-old female produces the most eggs, and fish older than seven years cannot brag about their egg production. Fish in topnotch condition produce as many as 100,000 eggs per large female. But the count can also be as low as 20,000.

If thick aquatic vegetation is available, the young bass will quickly learn that you get eaten when away from cover. They grow rapidly, dining on zooplankton and small insects. Those that grow slightly faster than their siblings turn cannibalistic and feed heavily on their own brothers and sisters. When 3 inches long, black bass will start their lifelong job of dining on baby bluegills. Given an even start and correct stocking ratios, black bass and bluegills will often strike a perpetuating balance in numbers.

The greater danger is that the bluegills

may out-produce the bass rather than the other way around. If the bluegills are too numerous, black bass production will stop, leaving you with a very few trophy-sized fish. If bluegill production falls behind, you will have many black bass—all smaller than you wanted.

If fishing brings many small bass to the net, keep them. On the other hand, if your average bass caught is big—but it's too far between bass, return the big fish to the water to spawn again and to eat bluegills. Growth rates of black bass are tied directly to the availability of prey species. In other words, if there is lots of food available, the bass will grow rapidly. But there are other factors in the equation. If there is no harvest of black bass—no bass taken from the pond—the growth rate will be slower than if there is a 20 percent harvest of the black bass population every year. The growth rate will be best when about 40 percent of the adult bass are harvested (caught by anglers) each and every year.

Golden shiners are a favorite food for black bass, but the bass does not seem to be particularly skilled at catching golden shiners. For this reason, bass do better when other food species are stocked, along with the golden shiners. A pond stocked with bass and shiners only will not develop into a good fishing pond.

If plant cover gets too thick, the bass will be severely handicapped in their hunt for food. Removal of some of the aquatic vegetation, under these conditions, will lead to better growth rates for the bass and a healthier balance of species.

The smallest bass pond has everything needed to provide world's record bass. You might have that world's record fish in your small pond. They grow fast with sufficient food.

A properly built, properly stocked, properly managed bass pond will not require supplemental feeding for the sake of the bass. If you go in for supplemental feeding to increase the size of your channel catfish, take it slow and easy. Overfeeding can be fatal to bass and bluegills, because overfeeding results in waste food accumulating on the bottom, increasing the biological oxygen demand and greatly increasing the chances of winter-kill.

Harvest is an important part of management of any bass population. If it is underfished, the end result will probably be thousands of fish, but none longer than 6 inches. No use waiting for those 6-inchers to grow up, they are probably grandfathers already. Catching black bass is part of management.

Bass bite most readily during twilight hours and on dark nights. At times, they will feed voraciously when it is so dark that they must be guided to their prey by sound or vibrations; there's not light enough to see. At such times, they will hit a surface plug worked slowly and noisily over the top of the water. Cast near to any structure that provides cover, for the bass loves to lie in cover, waiting for prey to come to him. After the surface plug lands, let it sit for a long 30 seconds—this is to allow the slow-moving bass time to come over to investigate. Then twitch it, just enough to make it move—to prove it is alive. Be ready! If that doesn't work, try other methods of retrieving—slowly, slower—and as a last resort, try a fast retrieve that makes a wake on the surface.

Surface plugs didn't work? Switch to a plug that dives deeply when retrieved, bobs to the surface when you stop retrieving. Try it close to the bank, close to weed beds, close to any structure. Vary methods of retrieval. If you still have no luck, go to a spinnerbait. These artificial lures are to be retrieved at all possible speeds, with a surprisingly high success ratio going to the relatively fast "sputtering on the surface" retrieve. Something about that lure skittering across the roof of his home sets a bass off.

There are times when nothing seems to work, except persistence. Keep on casting. Work your lure in close to where you think he is lying in wait, and keep on putting it there in close. Sooner or later, you'll goad him into striking.

Still no strikes? And you simply have to catch a black bass? Try the certain method. Hook a 6- or 7-inch-long water dog through the nostrils with a hook that is 6 feet below a good-sized (2-inch-diameter) bobber. Gently lob the whole works out so that the bobber is 15 feet from the bank. The salamander tries to swim to the bottom. The bobber won't let him. He keeps on trying. No big bass can pass this up for long. When he takes the bait, don't be in a hurry to set the hook. He is not going to spit it out, not that big, delicious mouthful. Let him swallow it deeply, for you intend to kill this fish, anyway. Then, when you figure that digestion has started . . . then you rear back on the rod and "cross his eyes!" No method is foolproof, but that one is as close as you can come.

Smallmouth Black Bass

If the back of the mouth extends past a vertical line dropped through the center of the fishes' eye, it is a largemouth. If the back of the mouth does not extend past that vertical line, it is a smallmouth (*Micropterus dolomieu*). There are other ways of telling the fish apart, but that rule of thumb works and is simple.

The two fish are slightly different in habits. The smallmouth is not quite so tolerant of poor water conditions as is his big-mouthed brother. He prefers colder water, in most cases, and is more tolerant of fast-moving water. This makes the smallmouth more of a river fish than the largemouth.

Smallmouth never reach the heavy weights attained by the largemouth. The world's record is far lighter than that 22¼-pound hog taken in Georgia. Smallmouths usually taste better, probably reflecting the cleaner, more highly oxygenated waters they pick to live in. They also fight harder, pound for pound and inch for inch, than the largemouth. Their diet is about the same as the bigger bass's, although I've never heard of one going after a blackbird or young duckling.

It is unlikely that a farm pond will make a good home for the smallmouth, but if your water temperature is low and the water quality is high, you may be fortunate enough to hear the biologist for your state game and fish department recommend the smaller fish. Management is roughly the same as for the largemouth, although the smallmouth is not as big an eater, nor is he so apt to decimate the supply of food fish. It is my opinion that he is slightly harder to tease into striking an artificial. For that reason alone, many farm pond owners would opt for the less discriminating, bigger largemouth.

Spotted Bass

Biologists and anglers now recognize another close relative, the Kentucky or "spotted" black bass. In appearance, he is close to the largemouth but has a series of heavy dark spots along his lateral line, that interesting strip of sensitive skin running from gill cover to tail. We do not really understand the purpose of this sensory organ, but all realize that it does something for the bass. For management purposes, we can lump the spotted bass with the smallmouth and never really know the difference.

White Bass

The white bass (*Roccus chrysops*) is smaller, not even related to the black bass group, looks like a small version of the striped bass (*Roccus saxatilis*), eats minnows like they were going out of style, and really prospers in large reservoirs. He is not a good choice for the small farm pond, which is really too bad because he tastes much better than the black bass group. He is a grand fighter on light tackle and travels in tremendous schools.

CHANNEL CATFISH

The third member of the most-often-used triumvirate of fishes used to stock farm ponds is the channel catfish. Originally native to the eastern half of the United States, from Montana eastward to Quebec and southward to Florida and Old Mexico, the channel cat has been introduced widely and is now found in all of the lower forty-eight states. They grow faster and reach heavier average weights in the southern part of their range.

Ictalurus punctatus is the slimmest, tastiest, sportiest member of the big catfish family. Like all members of the freshwater catfish family, the channel cat sports barbels, or long whiskers below the mouth—whiskers that are used as sensory organs to help the weak-eyed, nocturnal-feeding fish find his food.

Stocked with bluegills and largemouth black bass, the channel cat seems to do well in a separate niche from the other two fishes. He is a bottom feeder; they are midwater and topwater feeders. He is mainly nocturnal; they are 90 percent diurnal feeders. The catfish does not even seem to feed on the very small bluegills, although he is a predator on minnows, crayfish, frogs, and other amphibians that frequent the farm pond.

Because he is a find food fish, and because he is easily raised in small, controllable water areas; because he responds well to supplemental feeding and puts on size and weight like a feedlot steer, the channel cat has been the darling of the fish farm boys. A more complete discussion of fish farming will be found in chapter 8.

Normally, the channel cat does not reproduce well in farm ponds. In fact, it is most easily propagated under hatchery conditions where spawning is brought on by injections of gonadotrophin. This procedure results in controlled spawning, the time being set by the injection. This works well for fish farming enterprises also, but not for the farm pond. The fish mature in about eighteen months in warmer southern climes, but seldom reproduce in the small farm pond.

The channel cat's long slim body sports silvery white below and dark olive-green shading to black on top. He has a deeply forked tail, which differentiates him from the various members of the bullhead and "madtom" families, even when very small. Those silvery sides often carry an assortment of brightly colored dots—reds, greens, and blues.

Contrary to popular belief, the channel catfish is not a scavenger. He will almost always leave smelly bait to go to a meal of fresh fish. Angleworms, chicken livers, small frogs—all are good baits for the channel cat, which has also been taken on coagulated blood baits, cheese balls, and even pieces of soap. However, most of the "stink" baits work better on the larger, slower-moving catfish, the flathead, white, and yellow cats. At times the channel catfish will strike an artificial lure, but this is a rarity. For top results, fish for channel cats at twilight and during the nighttime hours. The list of unusual foods found in channel catfish stomachs, however, is about as long as the same list for largemouth black bass. Identified in the stomach contents were a snake skin, an adult bobwhite quail!—elm seeds— the list is endless. Surprisingly, channel catfish seldom feed on shad, although the other members of the catfish family thrive on them in large reservoirs. Maybe there is something about a shad that turns the cats off. Maybe he cannot catch them, but that seems hardly believable when we know that the flathead catfish dines on shad despite his ponderous bulk and slow moves.

If you are satisfied with the growth rate of your stocked channel catfish, don't change a thing. But if you feel that they should be getting bigger than they are, you will need to go to supplemental feeding. There are many commercially available catfish foods. Some are better than others, but they all work. Be sparing with supplemental feeding. Make sure that you do not feed a greater quantity than will be consumed in ten minutes. Excess food will rot on the bottom, depleting oxygen and increasing turbidity of the water.

MINNOWS AND BAIT FISH

You may wish to introduce smaller species of fish into your pond for the purpose of providing more food for the big ones. This is not a decision to be taken lightly. You will be well advised to get professional advice from a fisheries biologist connected with your state game and fish department.

Do not gather "minnows" from a nearby river or lake and put them into your pond. To do so is to invite unwanted species, such as the carp, for it is very difficult to tell the young of some fishes from the adult minnows.

If your purpose is to provide food for larger fishes only, you will probably be told to use golden shiners or fathead minnows. The fathead is never more than 4 inches and is a favored food of all larger fish. The golden shiner may grow to great size—as much as 9 or even 10 inches— but will seldom exceed 4 inches. The golden is a favored food for larger fish but is also adept at avoiding the predator long enough to grow too big for most fish to eat and finally big enough to reproduce its numbers.

There are other baitfish you may wish to consider. First of these is the gizzard shad, which has become the "most fed-upon" species in western and southern impoundments. This fish is a phytoplankton feeder, which means that it feeds on the tiny stuff that makes your pond water slightly green or yellowish green. If you want a good forage fish that will also double as cleanup species in the green water department, the gizzard shad is your fish. It does best in waters that do not freeze over in the wintertime. But, please, be guided by the recommendations of a fisheries biologist in your choice of forage fishes.

Suckers are fish that grow to greater size than we want, but they are also very hardy and will reproduce well in ponds that have a flowing stream entering them in the springtime. They are an excellent forage fish, and in addition, the lake chubsucker will clean up algae, which is a very big plus in most warm-water ponds. Other suckers, such as the black-tailed redhorse sucker, will do a great job of feeding channel catfish and greatly speed up the catfishes' growth up to the point where you want them on the dinner table.

Another special-purpose forage fish is the mosquito fish. These 2-inch-long fish feed heavily on mosquito larvae and can do a good job of reducing the infestation of mosquitoes coming from breeding areas in your farm pond. They are a good companion species to the channel catfish but are not suited to stocking with the bluegill sunfish, which feeds heavily on the young mosquito fish.

These are the preferred species for stocking as forage fish. Your choice should be based on good scientific reasoning, which is best obtained from a good sound scientist in the field of fisheries.

Minnow Farming

No one knows for sure, but it is estimated that more than two hundred billion minnows are reared and sold as bait in the United States each and every year. And there is usually a ready market for the minnows, at prices ranging from 50¢ to $3 per dozen!

Sound like a gold mine? It is not. It is a hard way to make a dollar, in the testimony of most minnow ranchers. Like every other kind of farming, minnow farming requires lots of hard work, intelligent planning, and good marketing techniques. If you want to try it, get professional help in planning your operation before you begin. After you start it is difficult to change water supplies, pond

dimensions, drainage systems, and many other considerations.

Basically, the most important consideration is the water supply. Spring water, if passed through a shallow holding pond to raise its temperature, is a good source. But spring water, as it comes from the ground, is too cold to promote good growth of the small minnows. Also, spring water may contain dissolved gases harmful to fish life. The holding pond storage of spring water will allow dissolved gases to dissipate.

The imperative thing about your minnow-farming water supply is that it be controllable. If you cannot turn aside spring floods, your ponds will quickly be silted and unusable. If you cannot screen out fish and fish eggs from the incoming water supply, you stand a chance of losing your entire crop to disease or to predation by larger species.

Chlorinated water is unsuited to minnow farming. The chlorine must be eliminated before using city tap water, for example. Best water temperatures are between 60°F and 80°F.

Pond Construction

The basic pond for minnows should be about 25 feet by 75 feet in rectangular measurements. The shallow end should be about 1 foot deep and the deep end should be no more than 4 feet. If you need more pond area than this, go to two ponds, rather than increase the size of the one pond. You want to maintain water areas of manageable dimensions, in order that you can efficiently feed your minnows, and—most important—that you can harvest the crop when it is ready for market and when the market is ready to receive it. If at all possible, you should provide for drainage systems that will allow you to drain the pool down to where the minnows are all concentrated in the deepest part and easier to seine or dip-net out of the pond.

Other considerations enter into this pond-size question. If you intend to hold minnows over winter, you must provide ponds deeper than 4 feet in northern climes. Otherwise ice formation may so severely limit the available water volume that the minnows will find it impossible to find enough oxygen during the cold months. Ponds with 6- to 8-foot depths are successful in the north, but they must have a built-in system to lower the water level to the point where the minnow crop can be harvested.

Because you will not (usually) want to harvest all of your minnow crop at one time, it is best to have several smaller drainable ponds, rather than one big one.

Which species for minnow farming?

The golden shiner is the first choice, because it is so attractive to the buyers of bait minnows. It is hardy, prolific, and a fast grower. Golden shiners can be harvested when small, to serve as crappie or sunfish bait, or they can be kept until the 4-inch size to be sold for walleye and northern pike bait, with a premium market existing in good largemouth bass areas for the 6-inchers—which are the most-desired bait for trophy-sized black bass.

Another good thing about the golden shiner is that it is omnivorous. It can be fed oatmeal, or ground fish, or minced clams, or trout food, or almost anything else. Be careful not to overfeed, for rotting food can quickly poison the waters for even the hardy golden shiner.

One drawback for the golden shiner is the fact that they get soft in warm weather. When harvested in August, they lose scales and develop fungus infections. Not a good bait minnow for the dog-days trade.

Second choice, and in many ways the best choice, is the amazingly prolific fathead minnow. Successful minnow farmers have harvested as many as a million fatheads from one acre of ponds! If fathead minnows are being sold for a $1.50 a dozen, the income would be . . . oh, well, it seldom works out that way. And we ask you to remember that word *successful* before the minnow farmer noun. Most minnow farms fail because of lack of know-how.

The fathead is seldom big enough to satisfy the angler who seeks walleyes or northern pike, but it is a great crappie bait. It seldom exceeds 3 inches in length. They spawn easily on submerged structures, such as cinder blocks or even sunken boards. The female lays the eggs, the male fertilizes them, and then the gallant male guards the eggs until they hatch. It is a good thing that not all of these eggs hatch, or the world's waters would be choked with fathead minnows. A big crop of young fatheads will consume a surprisingly great amount of food. Feeding 15 pounds of soybean meal per acre will usually take care of the dietary requirements of fatheads, and fertilization—within limits—will increase the carrying capacity of the pond for fathead minnows.

Much more able to withstand handling in hot weather than the golden shiner, the fathead would be the perfect bait minnow—if it would only grow another inch longer. But it won't.

There are, of course, many other minnows that work well in minnow farming, but the aforementioned two are the commercially suitable species. If you just want to raise minnows for your own use, or to feed your own pond fish, you might try the many members of the dace family, the common shiners, or the brassy minnow.

Transportation of minnows for sale is a complicated business, requiring aerated tank trucks if the bait is to be moved any great distance. Like any cold-blooded organism, minnows can be killed by changes of temperature that occur too fast for their body to react. For instance, ice blocks in the water will increase the chances of minnows surviving a trip by tank truck. But if they are then poured into warmer waters, the shock will kill them.

As in the case of any other fish farming, minnows offer great potential for profit—but only to the minnow farmer who knows what he is doing. Most small minnow-raising ventures are quickly dropped when the entrepreneur learns what he is up against.

Still interested in minnow farming? Start by studying all the literature you can get your hands on, including that mentioned in chapters 7 and 8. Visit successful minnow farms and ask questions. Have your water supply analyzed for chemical suitability. Monitor the temperature of your water supply throughout the year. Get professional help in designing your ponds and water control structures. Make sure there is a market. Visit that potential market and ask questions as to how many minnows and at what times of the year those markets would soak up your production. It is not like grain farming where you can always get the going price by hauling your grain to the elevator—when *you* want to sell.

Get the help of a fisheries biologist in determining which species of minnow you will attempt to farm. Get advice as to the correct stocking to start with. A properly maintained minnow pond will continue to reproduce itself indefinitely if the feeding is correctly done, if the water quality holds up, if the winter is not too rough, if there is no flooding to ruin ponds and intake structures. There are many "ifs," and you should know all of them before you try minnows for profit.

Control of Rough Fish

In the early 1950s, the North Dakota State Game and Fish Department eradicated all fish life from lovely little Spiritwood Lake, because the lake was overpopulated with stunted yellow perch. The stunted fish were present in teeming millions, and there simply wasn't enough food to be divided by that many hungry mouths.

After the 100 percent successful eradication, the department closed the lake to all fishing for two years, then opened it to fishing with the stipulation that minnows and small fish were not to be used for bait. They did not want the overpopulation of yellow perch to recur. The regulation was strictly enforced.

I had the pleasure of enjoying some good northern pike and walleye fishing there in mid-1984. There were yellow perch in the lake! I tell this tale only to emphasize how hard it is to keep unwanted species out of a fishery. How did the perch return to the lake, which has no outflow and drains only a small area of farmland? No one knows, but there are a few possibilities worth mentioning.

They might have come in as eggs sticking to the feet or feathers of ducks, bitterns, herons, coots, even kingfishers. The yellow perch eggs are very sticky, which makes this a good possibility.

They might have come in with eggs

brought from other hatcheries and hatched out at Spiritwood Lake. Hatchery personnel deal with hundreds of thousands of eggs at one time, and it would be impossible to state that there was not a single perch egg among ten million walleye eggs, for example.

They might have come in in a minnow bucket, for some fishermen are not above breaking the law.

Here are some of the means you can use to prevent the introduction of unwanted fish such as carp, buffalo, perch, or crappies into your waters.

Drawdown and Dry Out

If you can completely drain a pond, you can kill all of the fish. But this is drastic surgery of the fishery, for it kills all fish—the ones you want and the ones you do not want. To be effective, it must stay dry long enough to dry out and kill any fish eggs that may be stuck in the damp vegetation left after the water is gone. Such damp eggs can survive a week without free water in some cases, as long as the vegetation stays damp enough.

Selective Drawdown

It is possible to control carp by lowering the water level after they have deposited their eggs in the shallows. It is easy to tell when carp are spawning, for they thrash about in the shallows at a great rate, making much ado about their romantic efforts. Immediately after the spawning effort is completed, lower the water level to leave the eggs high and dry to be killed by drying out in the sunshine.

Timing is everything in this maneuver. If you draw down the water level too early, some carp will spawn in deeper

waters, and continue to reproduce. If you do it too late, some of the carp eggs will have hatched, which is what we are trying to prevent.

It is also necessary to be careful about drying out bass and bluegill nests. Usually, these are placed at slightly greater depth than those shallows used by the carp. Drop the water level to the right place and you can eliminate an entire year class of carp without harming the fish species you want.

Netting Out

If your pond is so constructed that you can efficiently draw a long seine through the waters, you can net out tons of the undesirable fish while choosing the good fish and putting them back in the pond. This method will never eliminate all of the unwanted species. The law of diminishing returns sets in early here, for seining is hard, cold, wet, muddy work.

However, the removal of ten thousand undersized yellow perch, or crappies, or even bluegills or bass will allow you to divide the available food supply by ten thousand less fish, and this means a bigger food supply per remaining fish. Remember the section in chapter 1 about carrying capacity? If you don't remember it, read it again at this stage of your study. Reduction in fish numbers raises the average size of the remaining fish—always.

Sometimes it is possible to seine out small fish by the ton, and this can be doubly profitable to your farming plan, for the tons of small fish can be spread on your fields, just as any other fertilizer, and it does much to improve yields. It does little to improve the odors riding the afternoon breeze, so we recommend fish-fertilizing only those parts of the farm that are either distant from the home or at least downwind from the home. I know of one enterprising man who grinds a half a ton of bullhead each fall and puts it up in frozen 10-gallon lots. He then uses this ground bullhead to feed to his growing channel catfish the next spring. Works beautifully—but it requires lots of freezer space.

Screening Water Supplies

If you use natural water supplies that contain fish, you should double-screen your water supply. Such screening requires very fine mesh, for fish eggs are not very big. It also requires a "fail-safe" system, which means double-screening of the water supply. This means constant attention to the screens, for they quickly plug up with silt, algae, or floating debris, and then the water goes up and over the screen instead of through it.

If your water supply is pumped from wells or originates in springs, you need not worry about fish eggs or live fish, of course.

Chemical Eradication

The Indians in South American jungles use several native plants to prepare a fish poison that stuns the fish, allowing them to be picked up by hand. This principle was adapted early on in fish control practices. All of the various commercial products available today are based on rotenone. Rotenone is derived from derris root, which is a leguminous plant of the East Indies. Now most of our fish control chemicals are synthetically produced.

In practice, the rotenone is usually mixed with one of the more toxic chemicals that form a basis for our insecticides, such as toxaphene. However, this means that the kill will be more certain, that there will be no chance of a fish living through the poisoning, and that the waters will remain toxic to fish life much longer. It also means that eating the fish killed by this poison is not recommended.

However, when straight rotenone products are used, the fish are killed by suffocation, as the rotenone constricts the blood vessels in the gills. The fish so killed are perfectly good table fare.

In application, the powdered chemical is towed across the surface of the water in burlap sacks. This is done most easily by towing the sack behind a motor boat. As the chemical dissolves out and slowly sinks through the top layers of the water, fish in distress are soon seen. Within ten minutes, many are flurrying on the surface, turning belly up and dying. Fish that customarily inhabit the deeper reaches of the pond are the last to be affected, naturally, but they have two chances, slim and none, as the curtain of deadly water slowly sinks to squeeze them against the bottom and finally to hit their gills.

The water will remain toxic for a very short period of time if the water is warm and if only rotenone is used. But if it is very cold the water will remain lethal to fishes and other gill-breathing animals much longer. When toxaphene is a part of the mixture, the toxicity lasts much longer. In a very cold, deep lake, the toxicity from toxaphene may last for two years! In a farm pond, with warm waters, the toxicity of the chemical is dissipated within two months, on the average.

Before restocking, it is wise to put a test cage in the water and put a sample of your fish to be stocked in it and observe them for several days before risking your entire stock.

Before planning any chemical eradication, be sure to check with state game and fish authorities and with the state livestock board if the waters from your chemically treated pond will escape into other watersheds. Chemical eradication is major surgery. It is seldom needed in small ponds that can be controlled by other means, if the manager (that's you, my landowner friend) is paying attention to his waters and doing what is required.

Preferred Methods

Before we get to the stage where we need chemical eradication, we should have tried several things first. We should try the introduction of predatory species to help with the control job. For example, 100 8-inch northern pike will quickly do a number on an overpopulation of yellow perch, crappies, or sunfish. Eight-inchers are too big to be eaten, and they'll feed heavily and grow remarkably fast. Don't worry about them completely eradicating any species, it simply doesn't happen. When the pickings are too slim, the northern seeks out other prey.

Before considering chemical eradication, we should try trapping and seining to remove numbers of unwanted fish. Chemicals are always fraught with danger to the environment; use them as a last resort!

7

The Farm or Ranch Fish Pond

Properly designed, properly constructed, properly managed, the farm or ranch fish pond can improve the lot of wildlife more than any other one action you can take on your land. It will provide resting and feeding places for migrating waterfowl and water to drink and food to eat for deer, in addition to being a home for fish. Part of its shoreline will provide a watering place for livestock, and its water will encourage the growth that provides nesting and escape cover for grouse and pheasant and quail. Before you start thinking about building a fish pond on your land, seek qualified advice from your County Agricultural Extension Agent. If you wish to read up on the subject, write to the U.S. Department of Agriculture, Washington, DC 20422 and ask for the free bulletins, *Warm Water Fish Ponds,* and *Making Your Farm Pond Safe.*

Then write to your State Conservation Agency (called Game and Fish Department in many states) and ask for their publications that tell about farm ponds, and also ask for their regulations about such ponds, about the availability of fish for stocking such ponds, and any other information that seems appropriate. If your state does not have the kind of informational leaflet you want, try the Missouri Department of Conservation, Box 180, Jefferson City, MO 65102. Ask for their publication, *Fish Farming; What You Should Know.* Try the Illinois Department of Conservation, Springfield, IL 62706, asking for *Pond Fish and Fishing in Illinois.* (See also additional recommended reading in chapter 8.)

A successful farm pond is a grouping of soil, plants, fish, birds, and animals combining to form a complete ecosystem of incredible complexity. The requirements for a successful farm pond vary greatly from one area of the United States to another, depending upon weather, climatic conditions to be experienced, soil types, quality of run-off water, and a hundred other factors.

There are a few generalities that can be applied to all areas. In area, the farm pond should cover at least three acres. Larger is usually better.

Depth is very important. At least 30 percent of the area should have depths of 10 feet or more. Increased depth means increased ability to store dissolved oxygen, preventing loss of aquatic life due to winterkill (or summerkill) when there is not enough dissolved oxygen in the water to sustain desirable fish life. We will be talking at length about this dissolved oxygen business later on, but right now it will suffice to say that depths of 10 to 15 feet are absolutely necessary for success. Water deeper than 15 feet is usually not used by warm-water species such as you will be planting in our farm ponds. Even if it were possible, you would not want to have all of your fish pond composed of 10- to 15-foot-deep water, because the shallows have their own assigned function in the pond's scheme of things. They provide places for vegetation to grow in the sunlit zone, and they provide spawning areas for nest builders, along with escape cover to ensure survival of some young fish out of each crop.

The next requirement is that the basin of your pond be capable of holding water. All ponds will leak when new, but they will usually stop leaking when the underlying soil is soaked up. Sandy soils, however, may leak water permanently as they allow percolation through their layers, even when wet. The local representative of the Soil Conservation Service and your County Extension Agent are best qualified to advise you about the nature of the soil types found on your land. Get their advice before you start, and you will save time and money.

If your soils are so permeable that they will always leak, all is not lost. Leakage can be controlled, to an extent, in many ways. Bentonite may be added to the pond bottom to seal it, although this greatly increases the cost and may not be permanent if there is a great fluctuation in water levels or if there is appreciable wave action on your pond. Sometimes a clay blanket may be bulldozed over the bottom of the pond during the construction phase, which may solve your leakage problem. At the same time, packing of the clay bottom by heavy machinery will do much to slow percolation of water down through the soil. If you can handle the expense involved, there are plastic materials that can be applied to the bottom of a pond to help it hold water.

But let's start our planning at the beginning. Where can you situate a 15-foot-deep pond of more than three acres? First of all, you want it to drain a considerable area, so that its water supply will be sufficient to fill the pond and to keep it at a level that will allow fish to live during the dry months. Obviously, the size of this drainage area will vary greatly between the heavy rainfall areas of Alabama and the bone-dry areas of west Texas. Take a day off and drive around your area, looking at successful stockwater dams and successful farm fish ponds. Pay particular attention to the size of their drainage areas. Then you are ready to talk to your County Agent about locating the pond.

When you've found a drainage area sufficient to provide the water for your pond, the next step is to plan where you will locate the dam itself. For optimum results at minimum cost, your dam should be so located that it can take advantage of existing land contours to flood a considerable acreage with a minimum amount of expensive earth-moving. It should be located where it will be easy to anchor a dam, without leakage occurring around and under the dam itself.

Remembering that you do not hope to stop all of the water running into your pond, you must plan for overflow spillway capacity big enough to allow for the occasional cloudburst or exceptional snow melt without damaging your dam. An ideal situation is one where the spillway is located at a goodly distance from the dam, so that the runoff can be discharged over the spillway without developing damaging water currents at or near the dam. The perfect spillway leads out of the pond at least 100 feet upstream from the dam and allows the runoff water to reach the streambed level—below the dam—without eroding the structure of the dam itself.

Can you plan for an overflow structure that would maintain a constant water level in the pond? A constant water level makes it easy to protect banks from erosion and to establish desirable plant cover and good spawning conditions for nest-building species of fish. At most dams, a 6-inch pipe, located at the desired water level and leading through the dam and discharging well below the dam, will serve this purpose admirably. If that 6-inch pipe leads to a livestock watering tank, so much the better.

If it is possible to plan a reservoir that can be drained quickly and easily, that would be wonderful. There are times when our fish population must be eliminated and we must start over again. This is necessary, for example, when fish populations are badly out of balance, about which more later. It is also possible that we would

want to remove the accumulated silt with a bulldozer. This is only possible in a pond that can be drained.

In your planning, be sure to look ahead to planting time. The living plants that surround your fish pond are as important as the water supply and the following types of plantings must be in place if the pond is to succeed.

1. Plant trees and bushes to form a windbreak. The windbreak will prevent strong winds from striking the surface of the fish pond. Naturally, it should be situated to check the prevailing winds. Plan these plantings to provide shade to water areas, if possible, but do not bring them right to the water's edge. Too close to the water's edge and they will surely inhibit your fishing pleasure later on. You want to reduce the velocity of winds striking your pond's surface to hold wave action down—thus preventing soil erosion from bank undercutting by the waves. Do not plant trees on the dam itself, for the root growth will imperil the stability of the dam structure.

2. Plant the basin scooped out to form your reservoir as soon as you bulldoze it into its final contour. Wheat, oats, or sudan grass will do a good job of stabilizing the loose dirt quickly, making a more solid base for your pond. When flooded, these nurse crops will provide green manure, increasing nutrient supply to the water. Millets do a very good job of protecting reservoir banks, reducing wave-action erosion.

3. Plant a buffer zone all around the drainage area of the reservoir. You should plan for at least 100 feet of good, solid grass cover. This can be planted to orchard grass and lespedeza mix, if your County Agent recommends that mix for your soil and climate. If he has better

ideas, take his word for it and plant grasses that will stabilize the soil, grow a solid sod, and minimize siltation into your newly created reservoir.

4. Next, plant some fence posts. Fence livestock away from the new plantings, away from the banks of the reservoir, away from the dam. Hooves wreak havoc with farm ponds. If it is possible to create a watering *below* the dam, fed by a trickle pipe or "constant level drain" pipe, you have the best of both worlds. If it is necessary that the pond do dual duty by providing a watering for cattle, construct your fences so that the cattle can reach the bank only at one place, not all around the pond.

You can expect to encounter problems with your pond. Almost everyone does. Most ponds encounter problems of tur-

bidity in the water. This is bad because it stops sunlight from penetrating to the plant life that is a part of our newly created ecosystem. You should be able to see your hand under 18 inches of water. If you cannot, look for the reason. Perhaps wave action driven by wind is stirring up the bottom of your pond? This can be cured by increasing the sheltering tree plantings, by getting a more solid deep sod on the drainage area, by further reducing livestock use of the water's edges. If the initial muddiness of the water persists over several months, you may need to go to the more expensive and less permanent treatment of introducing gypsum into the water. This does a good job of precipitating the solids that cause turbidity. Again, check your plans with your County Extension Agent and seek his advice on this treatment. The cleaner and

Note how livestock is fenced away from half of this watering area. This arrangement keeps the water clear and will allow cover for wildlife to grow along edge of pond. *USDA photo.*

clearer your water is, the better luck you will have with your fish when they are finally introduced.

If at all possible, get your original planting stock from your state conservation agency. Seining out a mess of small fish from the nearest river will usually get you a lot of things you don't want, such as carp or gar minnows, even fish diseases and parasites. In a properly managed fish pond, you will only need to stock most species once. Therefore, it is better to go to the expense of buying the fish, if necessary, rather than running the dangers of an unknown source of supply.

COMPATIBLE FISH POPULATIONS

There are many fish species that you do not want in a warm-water fish pond. You do not want carp, because they are bottom feeders who damage vegetation and increase turbidity by roiling the waters. Although they are strong fighters, they are not easily taken on rod and line, making them a poor choice for the farm fish pond.

You do not want crappie or green sunfish. Both species are apt to overpopulate—a common problem with small ponds—and when fish are crowded, they are stunted. A pond full of fish too small to eat but able to reproduce and further complicate the picture—this you do not want. Crappies are also inveterate minnow eaters, which means that a big population of crappies—white or black—will feast on young bass, preventing them from growing up and becoming catchable. Green sunfish, when numerous, are also rough on bass spawn, eating the eggs in the nest before they get a chance to hatch. You do not want bullheads. Although they are particularly tough to kill by reason of winter depletion of oxygen, they are bot-

tom feeders who will keep the waters constantly roiled, with resulting loss of reproduction of the more desirable fish.

One of the most common—because it works—combinations of fish species is known as the bass-bluegill partnership. Bluegills are prolific spawners and will provide a constant stream of tiny bluegills upon which the bass will feed. The bass, in turn, will grow big enough to provide much sport on hook and line. Properly balanced at the beginning, this combination will often prosper for years before too many bluegills destroy all of the bass eggs—or until too many big bass completely eliminate the bluegills. A perfect balance is hard to achieve, but this pairing seems to have the best chance of succeeding for years and years.

A common refinement on this bass-bluegill pairing is the addition of channel catfish to the pond. They do not seem to compete with the bass or the bluegills, yet they will grow to catchable and edible size in the pond and provide excellent food and sport. They will not usually reproduce in a small pond, however, so those fish caught out should be replaced by further stocking. This is easily accomplished, of course, because catfish are readily available for sale from thousands of catfish food farms.

Another variation on the largemouth bass and bluegill story is the substitution of the smallmouth instead of the largemouth. This requires slightly higher quality water, and the smallmouth seems to do better when the water temperatures are lower.

If water temperatures remain low enough all through the year, you can substitute trout in your pond, but you will need much cleaner and colder water. Ask your state conservation agency to recommend a fish species combination for your pond. They will undoubtedly check such things as water depths, the acidity or alkalinity of the water, and the presence or absence of turbidity before making their recommendation.

How many fish will you need for initial stocking of a bass-bluegill-channel cat pond? The Missouri Conservation Department recommends 100 largemouth black bass, 500 bluegill sunfish, and 100 channel catfish per each surface acre. Don't worry about stocking too few fish. If conditions are right, fish have an astounding ability to multiply and fill the available niche. If conditions are not right, heavier stocking simply means that you are wasting more fish than if you had stocked at lower levels.

HARVESTING THE CROP OF FISH

Let's say things are going well and your bass and bluegills both have proved able to reproduce in your pond. Can you promptly catch them all out? Doubtful. Remember that you do not want either species to gain the upper hand in their constantly shifting population balance. To ensure larger fish of both species, go easy on the bass. If you catch them and return them to the pond they will grow bigger and provide more sport next time. Also, the bass you return to the pond will continue to eat bluegills, helping you out in the constant battle against overpopulation and subsequent stunting. I recommend that you keep all bluegills that are big enough to eat—and if they show signs of becoming overpopulated, you should keep all of them, regardless of size, to reduce the numbers.

FEEDING THE FISH

If we are talking only about bass and bluegills, it is not necessary to feed at all.

If you want to get bigger and feistier channel catfish, you may want to feed a prepared catfish food. Here the biggest danger is in overfeeding, which results in rotting food on the bottom, increased oxygen depletion, creation of rotten egg gas, and possible death to your fish population. Feed only what is consumed immediately by the growing catfish. Always broadcast the food in shallow water, so that you can check the bottom to see if it is all consumed.

WINTERKILL

In the northern half of the United States, the greatest danger to fish populations in small ponds is winterkill. This is the result of depleted oxygen content in the water under the ice. Oxygen gets into the water in two important ways. One, by aeration as wave action constantly mixes air and water in splashing motion. Two, growing plants in the water use up carbon dioxide and release oxygen.

Ice changes all that. It completely eliminates aeration as a source of dissolved oxygen. Then ice and snow (which are worse) make it impossible for sunlight to reach the aquatic plants. Without sunlight, the aquatic plants die. Dead plants not only do not produce any oxygen, but they start to decompose and in the process of decomposition they use up oxygen and release carbon dioxide and worse, sulfur dioxide (which we call rotten egg gas). Under a covering blanket of snow and ice, the fish population is entirely dependent upon the stored oxygen in the water. If it lasts till spring breakup, the fish will live. If the oxygen supply is depleted before spring breakup, the fish will die. Some species are more resistant to winterkill than others. Bullheads, for example, have been known to survive when oxygen depletion killed off all the carp, minnows, bass, and bluegills. Trout and salmon are unable to withstand even slightly lowered oxygen content; they need lots of oxygen. This is the main reason why they are poor candidates for small pond life.

Many state conservation agencies have tried many different systems for avoiding winterkill. North Dakota, which has many shallow lakes and which suffers through a long cold winter, began research into this problem in 1950 under the guidance of fisheries biologist Dale Henegar, who later became top man of the entire department.

One of the first projects involved stretching a long plastic hose along the bottom of the lake for 1,500 feet. The hose had small holes in it at regular intervals. The end of the hose that reached the shore was connected to a small air pump, operated by electricity. When ice covered the lake, the pump was started, sending a constant stream of tiny bubbles into the lake. The line of bubbles kept an area of the lake surface free from ice. This allowed wave action to aerate the water, and it also allowed carbon dioxide and sulfur dioxide to escape. This project was successful in avoiding winterkill in some areas, but it was expensive, it required maintenance, and it could not keep the lake open in periods of extreme cold.

One of the latest machines being tested to prevent winterkill is a raft-mounted windmill that sucks water up from the bottom of the lake and splashes it out around the raft. The splashing action helps aerate and helps keep the spot around the raft free from ice. Toxic gases from the lake bottom are also vented at the surface, without displacing bottom sediments. Density currents created by mixing bottom water with surface water then aid in maintaining the circulation of a large area.

Windmill-powered research begun by North Dakota in 1973 is still continuing. The goal is an economical, wind-powered system, which will prevent winterkill and allow marginal lakes to furnish fish and sport for more people.

Ponds that carry fish life through the winter when they are first established may deteriorate to the point where winterkill eliminates the entire fish population. This is caused by the natural process of eutrophication, or aging of the pond. To slow the inevitable process of eutrophication, it is necessary to maintain sufficient depth of water by reducing siltation, by minimizing the fertilizer content reaching the water, by improving the ground cover on the drainage area, and by removing dead vegetation whose decomposition will further exhaust oxygen supplies.

SUMMERKILL

Similar depletion of oxygen contents can occur in the summertime, when water temperatures rise. Warm water cannot hold as much dissolved oxygen in solution (and available to the fish) as can cold water. Elevated water temperatures speed decomposition of organic matter in the water, further exhausting the oxygen supply.

Summerkill can be avoided by lowering water temperatures through shading of the water, by providing deeper water per unit of surface area, or by reducing the amount of organic material in the water.

The best defense against winterkill and summerkill is deeper water.

8

Fish Farming for Profit

Most landowners do a good job of managing their lands to provide maximum returns of whatever crop they are raising. We add fertilizers, herbicides, insecticides; we rotate crops; we summer fallow the land—we do everything we can to allow that soil to produce more.

The same thing can be done with water areas. They can be managed, manipulated, and improved to produce more pounds of fish per acre. And the total poundage of protein produced in water can exceed the total poundage produced on soils. Before pollution reduced its carrying capacity for marine life, the nation's greatest estuary—the Chesapeake Bay—produced more pounds of protein per acre than any land area in Maryland, a state with excellent soils.

If all you want is a bit of sport and food for a few families, the farm fish pond de-

scribed in chapter 7 is just the thing for you. But if you are the managerial type, and you want to get more pounds per acre, then you might go in for fish farming in a big way—which is a big decision. Or you may wish to try your hand in a smaller venture. Let's talk about the graduated steps that lead you from the typical farm pond culture up through the various degrees of investment to the real fish farm.

First of all, consider increasing the production rate of your existing pond. This can best be done by artificial (supplemental) feeding. It is almost never worthwhile to supplement the diet of black bass, sunfish, or crappies above that provided by a healthy pond. But the catfish family are another kettle of fish entirely. Catfish boast of a good conversion factor—i.e. the rate at which they can change food into body weight—and under optimum conditions, it is not unusual for 1½ pounds of good (high protein) food to result in 1 pound of solid catfish flesh.

Commercial catfish foods are available through your feed and seed dealer. It is not advisable to make your own. Pelletized food of the right size and content should be used. There are two kinds of feed, floating and sinking. Floating food costs more, but it is usually worth it. The advantage in using floating food is that you can see what happens to it. You can tell at a glance whether or not it is being cleaned up in fifteen minutes. If it is not cleaned up in fifteen minutes, reduce the amount of feed. Catfish should be fed in 3 to 4 feet of water, at the same time and the same place every time so that the fish become accustomed to feeding when and where you want them to feed. Floating feed will produce quite a show as the catfish feed avidly on the surface, with much splashing as evidence that they enjoy the handout.

Be warned that you are taking on another chore when you start feeding catfish. For best results, they should be fed five or six days out of every week. If you have different age classes (meaning different sizes, of course) you should feed different-size pellets to make the best use of the supplement.

The biggest danger is overfeeding. Feed that is not eaten immediately will sink to the bottom. Even floating feed will sink eventually. On the bottom, it starts to rot, which greatly increases the need for oxygen. If the supply of oxygen is near the marginal point anyway, a bit of excess food will push it over the edge and you will lose all of your fish—not only the catfish, but also the bass and bluegills—from suffocation.

Catfish feed most avidly at tempera-tures between 70°F and 85°F. Watch carefully for signs that the fish are off their feed, which means that they do not splash the surface when feeding, do not clean it all up, do not even seem to be there at all. The most common causes of fish being off their feed are (1) oxygen depletion and (2) temperatures too hot or too cold. If your problem is oxygen depletion, you have an emergency on your hands. Either supply more oxygen in some manner, or lose all of your fish. And it will happen quickly, within a matter of hours. You should be especially careful about the chances of oxygen depletion during and after a prolonged period of cloudy days. Reduced sunlight penetration of the water reduces the amount of oxygen being produced by aquatic vegetation.

In cases of oxygen depletion and in cases of too-warm water, the easiest answer is to introduce more water at once. This will get best results if the water is allowed to splash in, which will increase aeration and add oxygen. The best available source of water usually is your well, from which water can be pumped. However, well water is low in dissolved oxygen. Spraying the water into the air and letting it splash on the surface of the pond can be three or four times as effective as allowing the water to flow in gently. Water that is sprayed and splashed will be cooler and will hold more oxygen.

In the rare cases when your catfish go off their feed because the water is too cold, there is little you can do that is cost-effective. The fish are going into a period of greatly reduced activity, with reduced metabolism, hence, greatly reduced need for food. Just hold off on the food for the period of greatest cold. If you have a normal pond, with correct numbers and sizes of fish, the fish will simply suspend their growth and wait until the water warms up. However, if you have been feeding heavily, you cannot afford to stop feeding entirely. Reduce the amount of food given daily, watch carefully, and keep on adjusting the amount of food to fit the results obtained. In other words, if a handful is still cleaned up, but a bucketful is not, feed the smaller amount and try to keep it in constant adjustment. If your pond freezes over completely, do not feed at all.

CAGED-FISH PRODUCTION

Now that you've learned how supplemental feeding can increase the average size and speed up the growth of channel catfish in your natural pond or stock-water reservoir, you may be interested in seeing how you can improve on nature some more.

Try raising channel catfish in a feedlot. Not a cattle feedlot, for cattle wastes are fatal to a good fish-producing pond. I mean a catfish feedlot, where the same principles apply. The catfish are confined to a small area, fed heavily, and not allowed to work it off. Improved growth rates can be fantastic.

The best way to accomplish this feedlot operation is by using circular fish pens to avoid crowding in corners with subsequent loss of fish, made of screen or wire that allows water to flow through (to bring oxygen and to carry off wastes), about 4 feet deep, and anywhere from 4 to 12 feet across. The entire fish feedlot must float, so there is a temptation to use wood for the frame. This is usually a mistake, because most woods do not last very long in water. If left unpainted, they will soon become waterlogged and sink. If painted, be sure to let the structure age

a long time in water, to avoid accidentally poisoning some of your fish with the paint. It is a much better idea to use Styrofoam for flotation; it doesn't seem to become waterlogged at all and is chemically inert so no harm will befall the fish. The circular fish pen should float and be a couple of feet off the bottom of the pond for best results in carrying off fish wastes, which are considerable in the situation we are describing.

The circular pen must have a bottom, of course, and it should also have a top with a hinged opening to facilitate feeding. When designing the lid, be sure to plan ahead for the day when you want to remove the "fatted fish." If the opening is too small, you will have problems getting them out. Make sure that the opening will accommodate the size of net you will use to dip them out. Use the largest wire mesh you can get away with for the size of fingerlings you are going to stock. Small screen—small mesh sizes—greatly reduces the flow of water through the feed pen. Half-inch to ¾-inch mesh is best, and your catfish used for stocking should be big enough to start with so that this mesh will not allow them to escape. Okay, you have your feedlot floating in good-quality water, and you have allowed it to age for a week, to make sure that any chemical impurities contained in or on the structure have been diluted or washed away. Now you are ready to stock your "feeder" catfish.

The source of the "stocker" catfish is very important. First, check with your state conservation agency to find out what is legal and what is not. It varies considerably from state to state. Second, you want to buy from a producer with a good reputation for (1) freedom from disease, (2) absence of other fish species, and (3) good growth rates and survivability. Talk to other catfish farmers (unless you are the pioneer in your neighborhood) and see what results they have achieved when buying from different sources of supply. Find out what delivery system you will be using. Sometimes it is very easy to ship live fish in plastic sacks with a good oxygen supply to start with, enough for the journey. Maybe you will be going to the source of supply to pick up your fish. Talk to the fish farmer and take his advice as to how you should accomplish the delivery and stocking. He is just as concerned with live arrival as you are, because his reputation depends upon you getting healthy fish.

Next question is how many channel catfish to stock. The rule of thumb in feedlot operations like this is to stock twelve fingerlings of 6 inches or more per cubic foot of water volume. This may sound like a heavy initial stocking, but just remember the cattle feedlot. You can pack a lot of pounds of growing protein in a small area if conditions are right.

When the fish arrive at your pond, ready to put into the feeding cages, you must be very careful in acclimating the fish before dumping them in. The important factor is temperature. If the catfish come in plastic bags, simply place the entire bag in the cage and wait half an hour for temperatures to equalize. Then open the bag and release the fish, and remove the plastic bag entirely.

If your fish come in cream cans, a tank truck, or any other such container, you can equalize the water temperatures gradually by dipping a pailful from the pond and pouring it into the fish container. Wait a few minutes and do it again. This method will slowly change the temperature of the water the fish are riding in to the same temperature they will encounter in the feed cages. Then make the transfer. Although they are tough and hardy fish otherwise, channel catfish can be killed by a sudden temperature change of as little as eight or nine degrees. Equalize water temperatures and safeguard your investment.

Feeding Caged Catfish

Don't experiment with homemade catfish foods. Use a good commercial catfish food that contains at least 32 percent protein. Feed the 3/16-inch pellets at first, and move up to the 1/4-inch pellets as soon as you can. Of course, you will use floating foods only, otherwise a portion of the sinking food will go through the bottom mesh and be unavailable to the hungry catfish.

As in pond feeding, remember that the catfish should clean up all of the available food in fifteen minutes, twenty at the most. If they do not, you are wasting food. The natural fertility of the pond will provide some food—not enough for your concentrated needs, of course, and this should be taken into account. If you simply watch carefully and make sure that they eat it all, you are doing it right. The basic rule is that you provide food equal to 3 percent of the body weight of the catfish you are feeding. Sounds simple, but it involves constant weighing and averaging weights for the big-time commercial catfish farms. You are better served in cage catfish culture by simply feeding enough, but not too much, as evidenced by waste food.

Six to 8-inch channel catfish fingerlings should grow to 1-pound size in a single summer. One-pounders, called fiddlers in some parts of our country, are about the most economical size to harvest. These fiddlers are also the very best eating size. They can be fattened to 2-pound size, but there will be considerable mortality due to overcrowding, disease, and parasites. Also, the larger fish can suffer more from oxygen depletion.

Sickness

Surface feeding of floating foods gives you a good chance to see your growing catfish, to be alert for signs of trouble.

Fish gasping on the surface indicate lack of oxygen. As mentioned before, you need help and you need it quickly. If you can do nothing more than recirculate some of the pond water and let it fall back into the feeding cage through a window screen placed over the top, that will help. The screen breaks up the water into small droplets, increasing the amount of water surface exposed to the air and picking up more oxygen in that way.

White spots on your fish? This is a sign of fungus growth—the result, not the cause. The white spots may simply be proof of mechanical injury to the fish's skin by contact with the wall of the cage. It may be a sign of disease, which can spread like wild fire in a fish cage. Red spots are another sign that you need a fish doctor. Catfish with swollen bellies are sick, so are catfish with badly frayed tails and fins. Seek help at once!

To reduce the chances of losing fish to disease, you should immediately remove any sick or dead fish from the cage. Don't release them into the pond itself, hoping that they will get well. Remove them from the water area entirely.

What Do They Weigh?

On average, a feedlot-produced channel catfish 12 inches long will weigh half a pound. If your water quality is good and your feeding program is correct, it will take five months at 75° to 85°F water temperature for a 6-inch catfish to grow to 1 pound size. That's the best eating size.

Do You Have to Raise Only Catfish?

If you farm catfish, you farm only catfish. Yes, that is good advice. But there are situations when your caged fish producer will be used all year around—catfish in the summertime and rainbow trout in the wintertime!

Do you have 120 days when the water temperature is lower than 70°F and still above 45°F? If so, you can raise rainbow trout in roughly the same way that you raise catfish in the warmer months. Trout need more oxygen than do catfish. Trout consume less food per day than do catfish, but they consume a higher protein food, and it costs more per pound. Trout cannot be stocked as heavily as can catfish. Consult your state Conservation Agency for rules and regulations, for advice on sources of supply of fish that have proved to be suitable for trout farming in your area, for advice on feeding, and for advice on harvesting your fish. If you intend to sell the product, check state regulations. It may not be legal at all.

When it is practical and legal, trout farming in the winter and catfish farming in the summer seems like an ideal crop rotation. It also allows you to produce two crops per year and maximizes the return on your investment in equipment.

FISH FARMING IS ANOTHER MATTER ENTIRELY!

If you have had experience in small-scale raising of fish, you may look at the possible profits to be made in large-scale *farming* of fish and decide that a big operation is for you. This is the time to stop, look, listen, and think it through. The pitfalls are many and varied.

First of all, is there a market for the fish you might raise? This is not a frivolous question but rather your prime consideration. Are there markets that will willingly buy all that you can produce, at all times of the year that you will have fish ready for sale? If not, forget it. Unlike wheat and corn, which have an established world market, fish are sold by prior agreement with potential buyers. You should know where your fish are going to be marketed before you bulldoze the first yard of dirt in a fish-farming operation. Do not take for granted that there will be lots of buyers for your fish. There may not be. Is there a market for small, stocker-size fish? Will that market disappear after one or two years, because they are now producing their own stocker fish? Yes, catfish will reproduce in your ponds, but most of the young will be quickly eaten by their older brethren.

Remember also that your crop may all be ready for market at once. If you can sell 1,000 pounds per month, that does not mean that you can sell the 10,000 pounds of your annual production in the one month when they all reach salable size at the same time. Can you produce salable fish over a long period? Or is your fish-growing season so short that you cannot start till April and must market all the production in October? We cannot emphasize too strongly that you must find a market and be sure of that market before you enter into the business of fish farming. It is not like grain farming, where you simply deliver your crop to the elevator and take your check to the bank. We have used the comparison to a feedlot, but at marketing time the similarity does not exist. You can always sell your

beef or pork on the hoof—the price may not please you, but you *can* always sell it. You may find yourself with tons of catfish and no market.

Do you want to go into the business of preparing, packaging, and marketing your fish as frozen produce? Think it over carefully, for there are great investments in equipment that you will need for a sizable operation. In a small operation, on the other hand, you will not have the economies of scale to help you out, and production and marketing of 500 to 1,000 pounds of catfish may be almost as expensive as production and marketing of 10,000 pounds of catfish.

LOOK BEFORE YOU LEAP

If you are still interested, start studying! Alabama's Auburn University is the foremost authority on the subject of fish farming. They have publications available that will lead you on the right path. Address your request to Agricultural Experiment Station, Auburn University, Auburn, AL 36830. Ask for their free publication, *Preparation of Financial Budget for Fish Production, Catfish Production in Areas with Level Land and Adequate Ground Water.*

For $2 you can receive the publication, *Catfish Farming . . . A Reference Unit*, from Mississippi State University, Curriculum Coordinating Unit, Vocational-Technical Education, State College, MS 39762.

Write to Kansas Agricultural Experimental Station, Kansas State University, Manhattan, KS 66506, and ask for their publication on producing channel catfish in Kansas ponds. It is free.

There are several hardcover textbooks on fish farming, such as *Fish Farming Handbook,* a 391-page book, which can be ordered from AVI Publishing Company, 250 Post Road East, Westport, CT 06880.

Is there an Association of Fish Farmers in your state? You can find out by contacting your state conservation agency. If there is such an organization, you will surely want to join, for it is a good source of valuable information. You should subscribe to *Aquaculture Digest,* a monthly publication from Aquaculture Digest, 9434 Kearny Mesa Road, San Diego, CA 92126. When I last checked, it cost $24 per year.

You can order the free publication, *Channel Catfish Farming*, from Texas Agricultural Extension Service, Texas A & M University, College Station, TX 77843.

What is involved in fish farming, after you determine that there is a market for your production of fish? You will need a pond or ponds with an adequate water supply of good water. By adequate, we mean a water supply that can provide a minimum of 30 gallons per minute for each surface acre of your pond or ponds. Most farm water supplies fall into the category of springs, reservoirs, or wells. Springs and wells both provide water that is free of pollution (we hope) but that must be aerated, as it is low in dissolved oxygen. Let the inflow pipe splash water from a height of at least 3 feet. If it's possible, have the water splash through fine mesh screen to increase aeration. Aeration screens become plugged, requiring labor to clean them at periodic intervals. Remember that your water supply must be available at all times, for fish farming is a year-round business if you want to make it pay off. Aeration is also important, no matter what your primary source, to remove dissolved carbon dioxide, nitrogen, and other gases (especially hydrogen sulphide).

No matter what your water supply, it should be carefully filtered and screened to remove other fish life, silt, and solid particles that help to fill up the pond and thus reduce its carrying capacity. Remember that filters and screens do not remove fish diseases or fish parasites.

If you are sure of your permanent, good-quality water supply, it is time to think about formation of the ponds.

Plan on ponds with perfectly level bottoms, free from stumps, snags, rocks, or other obstructions that make it hard to seine out your production when it is time to go to market. Plan on ponds that are easily filled with water, *and easily drained!* A pond that cannot be drained to facilitate harvest is a decided handicap. In addition, you will want to drain the pond completely after harvest to clean the bottom, to remove silt accumulations, or for chemical rehabilitation. But we must have a pond that can be drained when we want it drained, not one that will drain itself. In other words, the soil must be such that it will retain water without undue loss by seepage. Plan on a pond with depths averaging 6 feet, in order to be safe from oxygen depletion under most conditions. Greater depths will be required the farther north you go. However, catfish farming is really only feasible in temperate climes. If you have to worry about winterkill under the ice, you are too far north to allow for profitable catfish farming.

Profitable? Yes, under ideal conditions, it is possible to produce as much as 10,000 *pounds* of channel catfish per acre on a properly operated catfish farm. Check the price at the local supermarket for packaged frozen catfish and you have an idea of the amounts of money we are talking about. To what extent the farmer will participate in that price depends upon how big a part of the work he is ready to undertake. If he furnishes only the live fish, without cleaning or packaging, his return will be much smaller than if he enters into the marketing process more completely. In other words, the bigger your investment in equipment, the greater the degree of participation in the profits. But we are now talking about large sums of money, both in potential profits and in initial outlay.

MINNOW RANCHING

Still another cash crop that can be grown on your land is the bait minnow. Here the most important consideration is that of finding a market. If sport fishing is a going recreation in your area, check to see if bait minnows are for sale at the resorts on the better fishing waters. In some areas, bait minnows are almost worth their weight in gold. It is now common to pay $2.50 for a dozen large bait minnows in some areas.

Pond requirements and water quality considerations are roughly the same for minnows as for catfish production, but there the similarities end. Of prime consideration to the minnow farmer is the method of harvesting and delivering his crop to market. It is a very labor-intensive business, and the enemies of the growing minnow are many—which makes for many a slip between the profit projection and the actual depositing in the bank.

Your State Extension Service is a good source of information for you as to minnow culture requirements adapted to your area. Your state conservation agency is the source for information about minnow production and sale regulations. In some states, minnow sale is strictly regulated to prevent the seining of young game fish and their sale as minnows. The state conservation agency also has rules governing the use of live minnows in some waters. Their use is often prohibited to prevent the accidental introduction of rough fish into waters now free of carp and other undesirables.

Golden shiners are one of the preferred species used for minnow production because they are desired by fishermen and are relatively hardy. They are not the only species suited to minnow production, however. For more information about minnow farming, send for *Raising Minnows* and *Maintaining Minnows—A Guide for Retailers,* both available free of charge from Texas Agricultural Extension Service, Texas A & M University, College Station, TX 77843.

Farm fish pond for pleasure—caged fish culture—commercial fish farming—commercial minnow production—there are many ways of profiting from farming a water area on your land. But they all require great investments of time and in some cases a great deal of money. Remember that fish are a crop, and production of that crop is not a job for amateurs. It is not something that can be entrusted to luck. Like grain farming or livestock husbandry, the smart farmer is one who knows what he is doing, gets expert help, and goes by the book—instead of flying by the seat of his pants. If you approach the project in a scientific manner, study it thoroughly, and do not fly against the advice of those who know, there's no real reason why you cannot profit from farming the water areas also.

9

Deer

THE WHITE-TAILED DEER

White-tailed deer probably produce more money for landowners than any other form of wildlife that lives on the landowner's land. This income usually comes from the sale of the privilege of trespassing on privately owned land for the purpose of hunting the deer. Fee hunting is common in almost every state in the union. It attains its greatest use in the state of Texas.

Texas is a separate and distinct situation for several reasons. First of all, there is almost no public land in the 262,840 square miles that make up the magnificent empire of Texas. What public land there is, is not usually good deer hunting territory, although there are notable exceptions. Second, trespass laws are strict ever since enactment of the typically

Texan trespass law in 1925. In addition to the tough trespass laws in Texas, there is a psychological attitude in Texas that predisposes the strict obedience to trespass laws. In the southern and western counties of the state there are many stories about the "shoot first and ask who it is later" method of ensuring the sanctity of private land. You simply do not trespass lightly in Texas; the results are apt to be serious.

The nature of the deer environment in the central part of the state, where deerleases are most common, is such that the white-tailed deer may very well be the most economical method of converting plant growth into dollars in the public market. Because deer are browsers, rather than grazers, they can occupy some ranges without competing with domestic cattle for forage. In the thick brush of the Edwards Plateau counties, there is more browse than grass, and some ranches, unsuited to cattle operations, are excellent deer habitat.

There are several ways of charging for the hunting privilege. Most common nationwide is the day lease, or "so much per day" arrangement. This fee may range from a low of $5 to as high as $100 in special areas.

Another way is to sell an annual lease. Customarily, this results in one set fee for the entire acreage and allows hunting of several species. It may include trespass privileges for the entire year. Typically, the lease is paid by one person who represents a group of hunters, or a corporation, or a club of sportsmen. The privileges being sold may vary from (a) the landowner turning over management of the land for wildlife harvest to the person paying the fee, all the way to (b) a strictly spelled out harvest rule system. An example of this second system would allow for ten men to each kill one male white-tailed deer anywhere they wanted to hunt on the 20,000-acre ranch. Income from that lease may range from a low of $500 to as high as $20,000 in 1984 prices.

Another annual lease arrangement is for the landowner to sell the discretionary rights to one individual. For example, an absentee landowner, unable to handle his own leases because he is not there to do it, may accept a flat fee from one person. That person then becomes the entrepreneur and can resell the hunting privileges in whatever form or shape he considers best to maximize the return on his investment.

A variation on the leasing system is the "no kill, no pay" arrangement. Under this system, the hunter is allowed ingress to the land and then pays a set fee—agreed

Artificial deer-hunting blinds, selling here for $230, are used in brush country of south Texas.

upon in advance—for the animal he kills. This type of arrangement is popular with the hunter whose means are limited and to the marginal deer habitat, where success possibilities are "iffy." Because the hunter does not mind paying after he has bagged his game, this system is popular where the landowner has the time or the manpower to keep a close check of the hunters. It is also somewhat popular with the hunter who has only a limited time in which to pursue his game . . . he gladly pays when successful, but is not charged when he fails to connect with a deer.

Variations of these "day lease" and "annual lease" arrangements are infinite, depending upon the nature of the terrain, the quality of hunting offered, the demand for such hunting privileges, the size of the land holding, the distance from centers of population, the ability of the owner to manage hunting on a daily basis, the availability of surplus labor on the landholding, and many other factors. Let us consider how some of these factors affect the lease situation:

If there is a very dense population of deer, it will usually be best to sell "day leases" so that the harvest can be maximized. In this arrangement, when one person, or group of hunters, kill their deer and leave, the landowner then sells the same privilege to another group of hunters and maximizes both his kill and his cash income. Obviously, this requires constant attention and personal management. Do you have an employee who has the time to do this in addition to other duties? Can you keep an accurate census of your deer herd, so that you know when the optimum harvest is being approached

Texas hill-country rancher Byrl Bierschwale poses with deer feeder of a type commonly used in Texas.

and thus shut off hunting before you cut into your herd's ability to sustain its numbers?

If you are not able to keep a watch on the land and the deer hunt, you will be better off selling the annual lease. The nature of that lease would be determined by the number of deer available to harvest. If you have only a few animals, a small herd in good condition that produces trophy bucks, you would want to issue a lease that would allow the harvest of X mature bucks by X hunters, with no chance of additional hunting pressure being brought to bear on your land.

If you are not able to keep watch on the land and the hunt but know that you have a great number of huntable deer, you might be best served by an annual lease issued to one person who would then have discretionary powers as to the size of the harvest to be obtained. Obviously, this can only be done when the landowner has confidence in the integrity of the lessee. If the lessee intends to continue the operation year after year, it will be to his advantage to maximize the sustained yield, just as it will be to your advantage.

How to decide on a price for your lease? No one can advise you, because the "going price" for a lease depends upon so many variables. Is there a good population of deer? Can they be hunted easily, or will it require horses and drives to flush the deer from thick brush? Is your area known as a producer of trophy heads? What is the distance from a big city with its numbers of hunters eager to pay for the lease? How about access roads?

In 1982, the Texas Parks and Wildlife Department conducted a survey of 3,081 hunters who were known to have paid for their hunting privileges through some sort of lease arrangement. The study showed that the average age of a lease buyer was 40, but ranged from 9 to 89 years of age. Eighty percent had finished high school and more than 50 percent had some college education. The average family income was somewhere in the neighborhood of $27,500. Their reason for leasing was usually to hunt white-tailed deer, although in the western end of the state they substitute mule deer for white-tails. In second place after the white-tailed deer hunters (75 percent of all hunters surveyed) came the dove hunters with 54 percent; quail, 43 percent; squirrel, 36 percent; rabbit, 35 percent; and turkey, 25 percent. My educated guess is that the deer was the real reason for the leasing arrangement, with other species as added attractions but not as the determining factor. The average cost of a deer lease, as reported by these hunters, was $393, and this was almost always for an annual lease.

How important to the rural economy is this leasing situation? Three research scientists from Texas A & M University, C. Arden Pope III, Clark E. Adams, and John K. Thomas, summed it up in this terse paragraph:

"It is clear that hunters are willing, able and do pay significantly to obtain access to wildlife in Texas. In the 1981–1982 season, it was estimated that over 300,000 white-tailed deer were harvested by 533,130 hunters. Assuming that 40 percent of these hunters purchased leases at an average cost of $393 per lease, the total amount spent on hunting leases to access white-tailed deer during the 1981–1982 hunting season was approximately $84 million. When the amount spent on leases to hunt dove, quail, mule deer, waterfowl, javelina, and other game species is included, the total amount spent on leases to hunt is conservatively estimated at being over $100 million."

Those Texas leases were based on 1981 prices, with 1981 dollars. You know the rate of inflation since 1981, so update your own figures.

Obviously, Texas, with its land almost entirely in private ownership, is a special case. The extreme opposite would be in the states of Nevada, Wyoming, and Utah with great parcels of land in federal ownership. If the hunter can hunt on the national forest nearby, he is not apt to hunt on privately owned land for a fee.

In the *Journal of Range Management,* September 1965, it was reported that "Harvesting the (Texas) deer at recommended rates based on the net productivity of the deer herd resulted in returns per animal unit equivalent from deer that exceeded the returns from livestock."

The Texas State Property Tax Board in 1981 decided that the net taxable income return from deer leases averaged between $1.00 and $3.00 per acre. They also decided that the capitalized income from deer leases contributes $12.00 to $35.00 per acre to the average price of deer range. If we assume that income from deer leases averages $1.50 per acre (which is conservatively low) then we arrive at a Texas leasing income of $115 million, which corroborates the earlier research findings.

Still not impressed by the value of your deer lease? Try this one for size. In 1982, the net income from deer leases in Texas exceeded the net return from sheep, lamb, mohair, and wool!

What do prospective lease buyers look for in a lease? C. Arden Pope III and John R. Stoll of Texas A & M University summarize the results of a questionnaire sent to Texas hunters and found that lease buyers look for many things. Very surprising to me is the fact that the privilege of bringing the family along on the hunt rated second highest in a list of desirable factors. Here are the results of the poll:

Qualities	Number of Times Mentioned	Percent
Lots of game	253	69
Ability to bring family	235	64
Different kinds of game	227	62
Trophy animals	163	44
Camping privileges	158	43
Good facilities (road, blinds, etc.)	148	40
Ability to bring guests	139	38
Cabin with conveniences	136	37
Visually pleasing habitat	133	36
Game feeders	132	36
Fishing privileges	125	34
Cabin without conveniences	59	16
Trailer hookups	26	7
Target range	19	5
Good service, drop off, pickup, cleaning game	18	5
Airplane landing strip	9	2
Luxury cabin with conveniences	8	2

What Do We Know About Whitetails?

Easily the most important big game animal in the United States, the white-tailed deer (*Odocoileus virginianus*) inhabits woods and the edges of woods, thick forest, prairie lands, swamps, and almost every other kind of habitat known to exist. His range runs from southern Canada—about 700 miles up into Canada in Manitoba and Ontario—all the way south to Colombia and Venezuela in South America. His place is taken through most of the western states by the mule deer, in the desert southwest by the Coues deer, and in the Pacific states by the blacktail. He is absent from most of Alaska, but there are excellent populations of Sitka whitetails in the panhandle of that great land.

The whitetail numbers more than thirty subspecies, but they are all variations on a theme. As a general rule, northern whitetails are larger than southern whitetails, with the very biggest being those lordly bucks of the lands where the northern lights snap and crackle in January's cold. The whitetail is one of the most successful and adaptable of all big game animals. He coexists with man in close proximity, if not happily. Deer tolerate men, but their aims are at swords' points most of the time, so the relationship is a grudging acceptance, one of the other.

Those giant north country bucks measure 39 inches at the shoulder and weigh 160 pounds or more when alive. Remember we're talking about average weights, and many of the big busters go far above the average. How far above the average? The biggest recorded was a Minnesota buck that was killed in 1926. This monster dressed out at 402 pounds and was estimated to weigh 511 pounds when alive and on the hoof. That one is a matter of record, and I have to admit that I do not believe it. That's too much for my mind to comprehend. Wisconsin has reported two bucks of 386 and 378 pounds hog-dressed weights. Maine lists a 355-pound (hog-dressed) buck taken in that state. A Georgia buck weighed in at 355 pounds hog-dressed. Iowa cornfields produced a buck in 1962 that weighed 440 pounds at 4½ years of age.

Why are average weights so much below maximum weights? Simply because we shoot most bucks long before they can reach maturity. It is doubtful if the average buck reaches three full years of age. During his short lifetime, the white-tailed deer is a marvel of grace and agility. Although it seldom exceeds 35 miles per hour, its graceful leaps over windfalls and fences make it seem to be moving at twice that speed. Dodging and twisting as it jumps, the whitetail can outdistance any other form of life in the short chase through woodland habitat. Its endurance is not great, however, and it is run down quite easily by packs of wolves, especially during late winter months when the deer's resistance is lowered by poor diet.

Antlers

Antlers grow larger each year through the first six years of a buck's life, if he is in good condition. After growing his fifth set of headgear, the buck will probably produce a smaller, less symmetrical set of antlers in the declining years. Well-fed deer produce larger antlers, naturally, than less well nourished deer. Certain areas, which provide a highly mineralized diet, seem to have a propensity for producing large-sized antlers. Such an area is the Jicarilla Apache Indian Reservation in New Mexico, which has produced an inordinate percentage of the state's big racks. However, in late years, the Jicarillas have been maximizing their cash flow by allowing more and more hunters. Hard-hunted, the reservation no longer produces those very big racks.

Antlers begin growing in March or April depending upon geographical location. At first the antlers are covered by a material we call velvet, covering a complex system of blood vessels to carry in the materials from which the antlers are formed. As the antler grows, it is extremely sensitive. Injury at this stage can result in misshapen "freak" antlers. Hormones secreted by endocrine glands in the buck's body regulate the growth of antlers, and other secretions later on stop that growth and harden the antlers into the potent weapons they will need to be in the rutting season. Then the bucks rub the itching antlers against brush and trees to scrape off the tattered remains of the velvet. The antlers are carried proudly during the breeding season. When that autumnal madness is over, the testosterone levels in the bucks' blood drop and the antlers are shed. Antlers are dropped naturally and are eaten by gnawing rodents that seek the salt and trace minerals found in them.

Successful and adaptable? There are many more deer in the lower forty-eight now than there were when only the Indian hunted the white-tailed deer. Deer were hunted very hard from the beginning of colonial days, and the colonists early recognized that they needed some protection if deer were to survive. In 1646, the colony of Rhode Island passed legislation that set aside open-season and closed-season times for deer. Connecticut and Massachusetts followed soon after and the deer now is completely "managed" insofar as when it is legal and when it is illegal to shoot deer.

Texas boasts of some three million whitetails, which surely puts that state in first place. But Michigan can claim 300,000 of the white-tailed animal; Pennsylvania and Alabama have big herds. Even prairie states like North Dakota, with less than 1 percent of its land being forested, are good deer country, with a high hunter success ratio and an intelligent program of management. The greatest concentration of whitetails I have ever seen in one place was on the Old Badger Homestead in the Black Hills of South Dakota back in 1957. We counted 317 deer in one cornfield at 5:30 P.M. of a winter day.

The whitetail has greatly increased his numbers since 1919, when the last states gave him effective protection from year-round shooting. Before that time, market hunters had almost eliminated the whitetail in some states. Savannah, Georgia, shipped 600,000 deer hides to Merrie Olde England in 1775–1778. Similar stories came from all parts of the states east of the Mississippi, and a rack of venison was a prime item on the menu of most restaurants prior to World War I.

Deer have a tremendous reproductive potential. Well-nourished does will breed their first year, but if they are not in good condition, they will wait till their second fall. Whitetail does usually produce a single fawn their first pregnancy, then produce twins from then on into old age, which is about six years of age. After that first pregnancy, the chances of a doe producing triplets is always present. In the case of multiple births, the fawns usually arrive about one hour apart. However, there is a poor survival rate for the third

Whitetail doe with two young bucks that have antlers in velvet. *U.S. Fish & Wildlife photo.*

Whitetail doe with twin fawns. First birth is almost always a single. After that, twins are the rule. *U.S. Fish & Wildlife photo.*

fawn. But in normal twin births, survival rate for fawns from well-fed does runs better than 90 percent. A white-tailed doe produces milk that is three times as rich in fat and protein as the milk of a Jersey cow. A good parent, the white-tailed doe keeps her fawn or fawns with her until their second birthday.

Definitely polygamous, the white-tailed buck copulates with as many does as he possibly can during the whirlwind excitement of the fall breeding season. Conception among white-tailed does in the wild runs near the 99 percent mark, and it is a rarity for a doe to go through estrus without being bred. However, if it should happen that she misses being bred in the first heat, she will come into season about five weeks later and will be bred then. Competition for does is very intense, with a lot of pushing and shoving matches tak-

ing place as younger bucks test the mettle of the reigning monarch. While His Lordship is fighting off one young buck, another young buck may sneak in and breed one of his does. Fights are almost never fatal, although both bucks can be badly scratched and bruised.

The gestation period averages 202 days, with extremes ranging from 195 to 212 days. The better-fed does have shorter gestation periods.

On very rare occasions, battling white-tailed bucks lock antlers. When this happens, it may result in double starvation, with both bucks losing their lives. I remember one late fall day when we found two bucks locked together just south of the baseball park in the south side of Bismarck, North Dakota. Although solidly hooked together, they were still able to avoid four men on foot. Chief Game Warden Walter Moore used a scope-sighted .270-caliber rifle to shoot off one of the antlers. Both bucks ran off, seemingly healthy, but I think both of them had a headache for a few days. Upon another occasion, I saw two beautiful mature white-tailed bucks frozen into a chunk of ice that came floating down the Missouri River during spring breakup. They had locked antlers and drowned while trying to get loose.

Just how good that reproductive potential is was well illustrated at South Fox Island in Michigan. In September of 1962 6 bucks and 11 does were stocked onto its 3,000 acres. Two died, leaving 15 animals to start the herd. In 1969, after hunters had killed at least 40 deer, the herd numbered at least 500, so a regular season was introduced. In that season, 188 deer were killed! In 1970, a hunting season bagged 382 deer of all ages and both sexes. Without hunting, a herd can double each year. Although hunters killed 620, in eight years the 15 grew to 250 animals.

This ability to populate its range is a mixed blessing. Unless the herd is cropped by sport hunting, whitetails will literally eat themselves out of house and home, and starvation will do the job of cropping the herd, bringing it back into balance with the available food.

An understanding of white-tailed deer population dynamics is vital to managing the herd. Let's imagine a closed population, which cannot admit deer from outside, nor lose any of its deer to the outside. Let's say that our population unit holds 100,000 deer. We can expect to add another 100,000 fawns in the April and May (in most states) fawning season. With normal high survival of fawns, we now have 200,000 whitetails in June, when living is easy and there is lots of food. Deer diet is varied and wide-ranging. One Pennsylvania study identified ninety-eight different plant species. Fifty-seven of these were tree, shrub, or vine species, and forty-one were herbaceous plants. Tender leaves and twigs make up most of the diet in spring, when new growth

White-tailed deer on the Aransas National Wildlife Refuge, Texas. *U.S. Fish & Wildlife photo.*

Fawn of the white-tailed is very vulnerable to predation by feral dogs in the first weeks of its life.

is available. As they become available, apples, oak acorns, and other mast crops are greedily consumed.

There are many mortality factors. Road kills have taken as many as 8,000 deer in Pennsylvania in one year alone! Packs of dogs may now be the most important predator on whitetails, and they kill many. Let's allow for a loss of 40,000 fawns in the period from May to November. That still leaves us with 160,000 deer in our management unit the first of November.

Now if we kill 25,000 deer during the hunting season, we will still have 135,000 deer after the season is over. Winter is the hungry time, the starvation time in the northern part of its range when winter snows are exceptionally deep or remain overly long into what should be spring. But we also lose whitetails to just plain cold weather—a sudden drop to abnormally cold temperatures will kill many whitetails if they are not in prime shape to start with. This is amply demonstrated

in the Edwards Plateau of Texas, where poorly nourished, very small whitetails will die like flies when the temperature takes a sudden nosedive, even if that dive is only from 40° to 20°F. Tejanos call this a "blue norther" when it happens, blaming the cold weather on the damnyankees (which most Texans consider to be one word). In the Spanish-speaking parts of Texas, such a cold wind and drop in temperature is known as a "matacabra" or "goat killer."

It is realistic to expect a winter die-off *averaging* about 35,000 animals out of our postseason population of 135,000.

This leaves us with 100,000 animals again, same as we had a year earlier at the same month of the year.

Perhaps you think that hunters will take more than the predicted 25,000 whitetails during the hunting season? Maybe, but history has shown that hunters don't do a very good job of killing white-tailed deer. In that South Fox Island example we have talked about, Michigan officials decided to reduce that herd. So they issued 612 permits in 1970, and each permit allowed the hunter to take as many deer as he wanted to take. But outdoor writer Glen Helgeland puts it correctly when he writes that the white-tailed deer is a full-time wild animal and the average deer hunter is only a part-time hunter.

There was a population density of more than 100 deer per square mile. Surely all the hunters would bag deer? Well, 54 percent (more than half) of the hunters failed to kill a deer! The season was nine weeks long, yet less than half of the hunters bagged a whitetail, despite having 100 targets per section. The kill totaled 382. This included 108 bucks, 134 does, and 140 fawns.

This teaches us a fundamental lesson of white-tailed deer management. If you kill bucks only, your herd will continue to increase. Let's look at the arithmetic again. We have 100 does and 100 bucks in our hypothetical area—this results in 100 pregnancies, with a production of perhaps 135 fawns.

Now let's kill off 90 bucks in our area. We now have 10 bucks and 100 does going into the breeding season, and this results in 100 pregnancies with production of probably 135 fawns! We can kill *most* of the bucks every season and we will still have nearly 100 percent pregnant does that winter.

But overpopulation inevitably leads to disease and to starvation. Starvation is not as merciful as the hunter's bullet. It takes a long time for a starving deer to die, and it is not pretty to watch. Fawns die first, does second, and the stronger and bigger bucks die last. So starvation does exactly the opposite of the hunting season. Starvation kills off the weaker

sex—and deer numbers can drop catastrophically.

Let's say that we have 100 bucks and 100 does, and we have a starvation situation that kills off half of the does and only 10 percent of the bucks. That leaves us with 50 does and 90 bucks to go into the breeding season, resulting in 50 pregnancies and a fawn crop of probably 60 youngsters. I predicate the lowered percentage of twins on the obvious fact that the starving deer is not in good condition by the time it comes around to breeding, hence produces fewer twins.

Every rancher knows that the male animal (the bull) is half of his cattle herd. We must remember that the male animal (the buck deer) is half of his deer herd. This half is expendable. Every buck removed from the wintering herd makes room for a fawn or a doe to survive through the hungry time.

Obviously, fewer deer die when winter foods are abundant. What foods? White cedar is perhaps best in northern latitudes, with aspen and jack pine, maple, sumac, ash, and basswood coming along behind. Both yellow and black birch are used, but are not "best-liked" foods. Although deer eat lots of fresh green grass in springtime, and seem to need it, the sere brown grasses of winter can be listed as useless.

In the winter of 1983–1984, many states fed deer herds artificially during the hungry months, because their usual foods were buried beneath the deep snows. Almost without exception this is time and money wasted. The sad fact is that a deer can fill its belly with grass twice a day in the wintertime and die of starvation, for its stomach is not designed to utilize grass when it is dry.

Deer do most of their traveling in early

winter and late fall months, but they do not seem to be expert at seeking out foods that will carry them through the winter months. Deer "yard up" in traditional places and seek out those same places the next year, even after many of the herd died off in the "traditional" place. Most whitetails live out their lives within one or two sections of land, the same sections of land where they were born. If food supplies are good in the wintertime, it is almost impossible to drive deer out.

Corn on the stalk is a strange and wonderful new food for most whitetails. They do not know it as being good to eat, but when one deer finds the yellow delicacy on the stalk, they all learn quickly. Wintering deer thrive on corn, unfortunately for the corn farmer.

In the other three seasons of the year, deer are fastidious feeders, nipping a bite here and a second bite over there, almost never eating one plant to its death. When food is scarce, the opposite is true, of course, and deer can browse even scrub oak into oblivion. More than 600 species of woody plant have been identified in deer stomachs. Along with the tender leaves and twigs, deer love many fruits and nuts—especially acorns, which are perhaps their best source of fat to tide them through the winter months. They eat mushrooms but never seem to try the deadly ones, like *Amanita verna,* which kills humans.

When it comes to the necessities of life, the worst enemy the white-tailed deer ever had was the movie "Bambi." Its totally unrealistic propaganda against hunting—which is a necessary management tool now that large predators are scarce—has doomed a million whitetails to a slow, lingering death by starvation in the winter months when they have ov-

erpopulated their habitat. Walt Disney never intended his beautiful fairy tale to have this effect, but it grabbed the imagination of an entire generation, teaching them that the hunter was the deer's enemy. It would have been far better to teach them that "Each man kills the thing he loves" for the hunter does love the whitetail and he does the herd a favor when he removes some of its members. That is not sentimental, but it is accurate.

In the long run, the best friends the white-tailed deer ever has are the logger, who harvests the big forest and encourages edible second growth; the hunter, who takes enough animals so that the remainder can find enough food in the winter time; and the wild fire, which promotes second growth in the burned-over area.

In the millennia before man started his Smoky the Bear campaign to eliminate wild fire, the whitetail got along just famously. Where man has determined that all fire is bad, the whitetail population went down.

While we are deciding what things are good and what bad for our deer herd, let's talk about a couple more mortality factors—road crossings and dogs. Whitetails never seem to learn about roads. They come up to the side of the road and watch traffic for half an hour, then leap out in front of a speeding automobile and lose their life. It happens so often that it is not a rarity, but a recognized cause of significant deer mortality.

The mountain lion is the most efficient predator on North American deer, but his numbers have thinned greatly as man moved into his home, crowding him into less and less area of the higher mountains and more isolated areas. The coyote kills large numbers of fawns, as proved by studies in Oregon and elsewhere. The coyote is most deadly during periods of deep snows, when the deer's mobility is restricted to a far greater degree than that of the coyote.

The domestic dog is now the most important single predator on white-tailed deer, after man himself. Our pampered pets are well-fed and strong during the winter, when deer are weak and vulnerable. A healthy whitetail has nothing to fear from a single dog when the snow is not hampering the deer. But given a 3-foot snow drift and a pack of six or seven dogs, and the deer has what Dizzy Dean called two chances, slim and none.

The dogs that do this killing are seldom "gone wild" or feral dogs. They are our well-fed, domestic pets—dogs we can trust with the baby—dogs that wouldn't think of chasing farm cows or chickens. Chasing something that flees is second nature to the dog family—and deer are severely hurt by domestic dogs in almost every state in the Union.

Diseases are not important to well-fed, well-sheltered deer herds. When populations rise above the carrying capacity of the range, diseases wreak fearful havoc with the weakened herd. As with humans, prevention is much more practical than curing the disease. Parasites are commonly found in almost every deer, but these parasites do not contribute to the death of the animal, unless the deer is weakened by malnutrition first.

Most common parasites are lungworms, *Leptostrongylus alpenae,* which hatch in the lungs. As the worms mature, they move up to the throat or are coughed up there. The deer then swallows the worm and it is passed out along with the feces. This enables it to start the life cycle all over again with a mature fly, which again lays eggs in the deer's nostrils.

Second most common are liver flukes, *Fasciolides magna,* which have an interesting life history on their way to and from the deer's liver. Their intermediate host is the snail, which is often eaten by the deer. The tasty snack results in a liver infestation, but not one that seems to harm the otherwise healthy animal. Neither parasite poses any danger to man.

Albinism is very rare in the white-tailed deer family. Nature does not treat the white individual very kindly. It stands out against almost any background in spring and summer and is unable to hide as a normal fawn would—by simply lying still. The white coloration might be of some help in avoiding detection against the white snows of winter—but the white fawn seldom lives long enough to see snow.

Management for the White-tailed Deer

Here are a few truths about white-tailed deer, which you will want to take into account when managing your deer herd:

1. White-tailed deer fawns are almost never abandoned by their mother. The "abandoned" fawn is simply doing what its mother told it to do—lie still and don't move. Its mother is usually close by, at a higher elevation, watching the fawn. If we touch the fawn, we leave our odor on the youngster and this *may* cause the doe to refuse to let it nurse. Leave the abandoned fawn alone. Its mother is nearby, even if you can't see her.

2. You cannot overshoot the bucks. No matter how few the bucks are, they will be sufficient to get the job done. For about 363 days out of the year, a white-tailed doe is the model of modesty and prudishness. But for those other two days,

she is a willing lover, a hoyden who never says no—and she *will* find a sexual partner.

3. To reduce the numbers of a deer population, you must shoot some females.

4. Left to their own resources, modern-day white-tailed deer will always increase to the point of overpopulating the carrying capacity of the range.

5. Winter starvation is a cruel way to die; the hunter's bullet is far more merciful, and no deer lives forever.

6. Hay is a lousy deer food. Starving deer will die with their bellies full of grass hay.

7. If you must use supplemental feeders, use cracked corn and other grain foods, rather than hay. Don't overdo the feeding, for it concentrates and weakens the deer herd.

8. Watch for a browse line, where you can plainly see the top limit of the deer's browsing. If you can see a plain line, your deer are in deep, serious trouble, for they are eating more food than the habitat is producing each year.

The best management tool to improve the lot of the white-tailed deer is the proper management of the woodlot. If mature trees can be cropped in such a way as to provide succulent second-growth vegetation for the deer to use as both food and escape cover, the whitetail will usually prosper.

Second most important habitat development measure (not in the south) is the plantings of conifers to provide dense winter cover. These need not be large plantings, as few as sixty trees in the proper grouping will do the job. These are called clump plantings, and they are most effective if placed on south slopes or in spots where they will be out of the wind as much as possible.

Intelligent management of white-tailed deer must include removal of mature animals to keep the herd within the carrying capacity of the habitat. This removal of mature animals is best accomplished by sport hunting. It is a pleasant fact of life that landowner regulation of the hunt can be both wise management and a source of landowner revenue.

The most basic fact of deer management is this: You must remove females from the population to decrease the size of the herd. Shooting bucks only will never reduce the total population from one year to the next.

THE MULE DEER

Wildlife managers have had to revise many of their accepted notions about mule deer in the last twenty years. We used to think of the mule deer as being a resident of the Rocky Mountains and west, but he has proved more adaptable than we thought and is extending his range eastward as far as Minnesota. In my native state of North Dakota, we once thought of the Missouri River as being the dividing line between whitetails to the east and mule deer to the west.

Now, near Grassy Butte, in western North Dakota, I watched sixteen deer choose their bedding spots in one willow bar along a stream. Nine were mule deer, seven were whitetails. Biologists used to say that whitetails and mules occupied different niches, even though in the same general area. In this case, both species bedded down in exactly the same niche. Perhaps this change has something to do with the fact that hybridization between whitetail and mule, while still exceedingly rare, is much more common than previously thought. In addition, beautiful, big mule deer are now putting in an appearance far to the east of the wide Missouri.

Another accepted truth that is no longer true was the oft-repeated theorem that mule deer were not as smart as whitetails. True, both species had a bad habit of stopping to look back when they were startled into flight. But the whitetail usually got himself into cover and then stopped to look back, while the mule stopped before he reached safe cover. This stopping to look back resulted in death for many mules, it is true, for the experienced mule deer hunter waited till the deer stopped, then took a shot at a standing target. But the mule deer has learned. Today he is the equal of the whitetail in escaping from the hunter, although his methods are different. The trait of stopping for a look back is being bred out of the species—for the mule deer that stops to take a last look no longer lives long enough to pass on his genes.

We used to think that the mule deer was a browser. Now, food habits studies have shown that the mule is a browser *and* a grazer. One Colorado research project identified 673 different plants that the mule deer used as food. There seemingly is no end to the list of plants upon which the mule deer can feed, and certainly there is a tremendous difference in diet between the mule deer buck living on arid Tiburon Island in the Sea of Cortez and the muley inhabiting the lush rain forest of British Columbia. What do we know about mule deer?

If we are willing to classify the Columbian blacktail, or the Sitka blacktail as being merely subspecies of the *Odocoileus hemionus* family, we have a very adaptable animal that occupies most of a range from the far northern place where British Columbia meets Alaska, all the way down to the blazing hot high desert lands of Central Mexico, from North Dakota's grainfields to the southern end of the Baja California peninsula in Mexico. In Canada, the mule is found in all of British Columbia, Alberta, and in parts of Manitoba and even parts of the Yukon territory, where the winter conditions are so rough that the whitetail cannot gain a foothold.

He is bigger on average than the whitetail, but the maximum weights recorded for mules are not as great as the maximum weights recorded for whitetails. He looks a lot like the white-tailed deer when he is standing still, with only the large ears (which give him his name) and the antler difference giving away the fact that this is a mule deer. But when he starts to move, the differences are great. Instead of the bouncing white flag tail of the whitetail, the muley has to get along with a black-tipped wisp of a white and gray tail, which does nothing for his appearance. In addition, instead of the flowing grace of the running whitetail, superbly adapted to bounding through deadfalls and over and around downed trees, the mule deer has a pogo stick gait, with all four feet landing at once and the deer bouncing rather than running. This gait is surprisingly efficient, however, and in rough or broken ground, the mule can probably outdistance the whitetail.

It is difficult to describe the difference in antler formation, but once seen, it is a never-failing method for differentiating between male mule and male whitetail. The whitetail features a single beam on each side, from which two or more spikes rise; the mule deer features an antler beam which forks, and then each fork forks again. The inside spread measurement of antlers shows the mule occasionally reaching a width of more than 34 inches, while it is a very large whitetail that will measure 24 inches, inside spread.

Deer are what they eat, and they have a complicated four-chamber stomach to help them handle the low-nutrient foods that make up such a large part of their diet. Where there is lots of high-quality food, the deer will be larger than where they are forced to subsist on marginal food supplies. For this reason, mule deer in farming country will average heavier than mules in strictly forest country. The reason is undoubtedly found in the excellent nutrition obtained from cornfields, alfalfa patches, and other cultivated plants. Deer have incisor teeth in the lower jaw but not in the upper. The upper jaw has a pad of gristle that is used to hold the food while the incisors cut through it.

Antlers are grown in the summer, with the actual schedule varying with the latitude. Antlers develop in the same way they do on whitetails, although the shape is different. The antlers are used for the battles between bucks in the rutting season. Fawns are born anytime from May to September, varying with the latitude and the climate. In semidesert areas, where summer rainfall is very scarce, fawns aren't dropped till late August or even into September. This produces the fawns at the time when the vegetation is beginning to benefit from the rains—if any—of late summer, and there is more succulent food available for fawns and lactating does.

Slightly more than 60 percent of adult does in good health will produce twins, with an occasional set of triplets thrown in for good measure. As in the whitetail family, a virgin doe usually produces only one fawn on her first attempt. After the first-born, twins are definitely the rule. Given good conditions, mule deer show the same very high reproductive potential as whitetails. In near-starvation situations, even the mature doe will have only a single fawn 90 percent of the time.

Although colors vary widely from summer to winter, and from different parts of the sprawling mule deer range, the coat is an overall grayish brown. The deer has a light patch, almost white, on the top of his snout—and a pronounced white rump patch, which tries to take the place of the waving flag tail of the whitetail. The brisket line running down the front of the chest and between the front legs is often a pronounced black, and the brisket hairs point forward—while all the other hairs on the animal's body point backward. Why? Darned if I know.

Mules have a larger home range than do whitetails. In addition to having a larger

Mule-deer doe in New Mexico.

Young mule-deer fawn. Some people take fawns from the wild in the mistaken belief that their mother has abandoned them. Leave fawns strictly alone. Human scent causes doe to abandon youngster. *U.S. Fish & Wildlife photo.*

home area in summer, the mule deer often migrates as much as fifty miles from summer range to reach wintering range. This migration usually, but not always, takes the form of a trek from higher elevations down into lower. During migrations, mule deer follow set paths, and blocking one of these migration routes can have serious effects upon the future of the deer herd.

Because the overall trend in mule deer populations has been upward since about 1910, we can be optimistic about the future of the herd. However, the encroachment of humanity on suitable mule deer range continues as man's seemingly uncontrollable population explosion contin-

ues. Obviously, the solution would be to limit the growth of human populations. As this seems to be impossible, given the present state of man's efforts to become civilized, there is grave cause for concern about the long-term future of our mule deer herds.

Historically, the mountain lion was the chief cause of mule deer mortality. This was graphically demonstrated, in reverse, in the case of the Kaibab mule deer herd in Arizona. Predator control on the million-acre Kaibab plateau almost completely eliminated the mountain lion. In addition to this, the U.S. Forest Service, which administered the newly created game preserve, used guns, traps, and poi-

A fine pair of Montana mule-deer bucks. *U.S. Fish & Wildlife photo.*

sons to eliminate 4,889 cougars, 20 wolves, and a few bears. The Kaibab deer herd, which had been estimated as about 4,000 animals, began to explode. Remember that there was no hunting allowed in the area. The deer herd increased to approximately 100,000 animals! Alarmed by the damage deer were doing to the available food supply, the Forest Service proposed to have hunting allowed again on the Kaibab. The governor of Arizona said that he would have his wardens arrest anyone coming off this federal land with a deer.

Although limited numbers of deer were killed by federal employees, the population increased. Finally, reason took the place of sentiment, and sport hunting was reinstituted. No effect—the population exploded in an irruption that demonstrated the species' ability to reproduce itself. The deer herd grew to the point where it had badly overgrazed and over-browsed its habitat. Wholesale starvation began to reduce its numbers by thousands each and every winter. As many as 60,000 deer starved in the winter of 1925. The great outdoor writer, Zane Grey, advised that cowboys should get together and "herd" the excess mule deer off the Kaibab plateau and onto public and private lands nearby, where there was no overpopulation of mule deer. The advice was followed, with predictably humorous results. Despite the best efforts of the great roundup participants, no mule deer were "herded" off the Kaibab. Stubborn as a mule, the mules refused to leave their home range, doubled back, and escaped through the lines of riders. Those deer that were moved a few miles from their preferred spot doubled back at night and went back into their starvation habitat. Not a single deer was herded off the Kaibab.

Naturally, Nature had an answer for the overpopulation. Disease and starvation dropped the Kaibab herd back to within the reduced carrying capacity of the land, and the situation once again came into some sort of a dynamic balance. Three lessons were learned. One, the mountain lion may be doing the herd a favor by killing some of them. Two, you cannot herd mule deer on horseback. Three, hunting is a part of good mule deer management. Today, scars of the damage to the browse are still apparent, but intelligent deer management, including liberal hunting seasons, has restored the Kaibab mule deer herd to health.

Today, the only other mammalian predator of importance across most of the mule deer range is the coyote. Research in Oregon has shown that coyotes take a fearfully high percentage of the fawn crop where coyote numbers are high. Control measures, especially shooting coyotes from a helicopter, proved effective in increasing mule deer numbers.

Although it was starvation that cut back the Kaibab herd, starvation is seldom the cause of mortality for a well-managed mule deer herd. Human predation takes the place of the lion, and the mule deer numbers are kept within the carrying capacity of the land. Modern-day mule deer management consists almost entirely of regulating the harvest. Hunters keep the deer herd well within the carrying capacity of the habitat.

But there are ways of improving the carrying capacity of the land. Forest fires are not a calamity to the deer herd, unless too great an area is burned at one time. The burned-over area comes back in lush second-growth vegetation, which is excellent mule deer food. This results in higher incidence of twin fawns due to improved physical condition of the breeding does. Selective clear-cutting can have the same effect, with less danger to other wildlife and to the forest itself. Maximum improvement in deer food occurs in the five-year period from five to ten years after a burn or a clear-cutting operation. However, the benefits are felt for a quarter of a century, until the climax succession again results in a mature forest that provides very little food for deer.

A management technique that is quite effective in the semiarid southwest is the provision of water where water was not available before. This spreads deer use, eliminates damage to food plants near the rare watering places, and makes a larger part of the forest into "deer range." In my home state of New Mexico, I have searched in vain for signs of mule deer in a dry section of the Gila National Forest and found mules only near the permanent streams. Deer will not live away from free water supplies, although they go into fringe areas of the desert. If we multiply the area of suitable habitat by providing free water where it did not exist before, we should multiply the mule deer numbers by the same factor, and experience has borne this out. On the Cabeza Prieta Desert Game Range, mule deer are found near the very few waterings—such as Antelope Wells and Charlie Bell Well. They can get a large part of their water from succulent plants, but they must have free water somewhere on their range, or they will disappear.

Severe winters, such as that of 1983–1984, can be very harmful to deer herds. Weakened by long months of subsisting on less than nutritious foods, mule deer fall victim to winter storms and deep snows, especially if those storms come late in the year. Well-meant efforts to winter-feed deer herds during such periods are almost always wasted. The same snows that keep mule deer away from subsistence foods also keep their human rescuers from getting into the critical wintering areas. Also, the amount of food that humans are able to provide can be divided by the number of hungry deer, and we will arrive at the inescapable conclusion that there wasn't one stomachful of artificially provided food for each deer in the wintering herd.

Wintering cover, or escape cover, is seldom a problem for mule deer. They will make do in the sparse thickets of prairie country and get along just fine in the cactus and mesquite habitat of Arizona's deserts. They prosper in second growth, as opposed to mature forest, but that is a matter of food availability, not cover.

There is little the individual landowner can do to manage a herd of mule deer, other than controlling the mortality by hunting. In the rare instances where too-numerous coyotes are cutting heavily into fawn production, predator control can help, but it must be conducted on a larger area than is usually enclosed by the fences of just one landowner.

PROPER CARE OF VENISON

The main thing about deer meat is that it must be taken care of properly if you want to have tasty eating. Given the same care as you would give a steer carcass, venison is prime to choice. But you do not transport a steer two hundred miles on top of your car without dressing it out, without cooling it out, without protecting it from flies. Why, then, do so many people treat venison in that manner?

It is important to get the blood out—

Mule deer commonly gather in groups during cold weather. In late winter and spring, mature bucks will usually be solitary or in pairs. *U.S. Fish & Wildlife photo.*

but modern bullets, fired from modern guns, often do a good job of that. A deer may be completely "bled out" internally. Cutting into the chest cavity will release all of the blood at once. I was with Dr. Harry Wheeler, an excellent physician from Mandan, North Dakota, when he shot his first deer with the bow. The arrow sliced completely through the lungs, through the heart and buried itself up to the feathers in the rocky stream bed. The deer crumpled quickly, but not a drop of blood showed. As the surgeon sliced into the chest cavity, all the blood in that carcass poured forth and the learned doctor remarked in surprise, "Look at that, completely exsanguinated." Whether or not you use such terminology, it is correct procedure to (1) get the blood out of the carcass, (2) get the viscera out of the

How many deer do you see in this Wyoming scene? Good bedding cover is essential to good mule-deer populations.

carcass, (3) get the hide off the animal to allow it to cool out properly and quickly, and (4) cover the carcass securely with a fly-proof "game bag," which will ensure that air can circulate around the carcass, but house flies and other insect pests cannot get to the meat. You will notice that I did not suggest that you cut out the scent glands found on the deer's legs. I have never felt this to be necessary. Properly cared for, the carcass will have its legs cut off below the joint, for there is no meat to speak of on that lowest part leading past the scent glands and down to the hoof.

Once the carcass is properly cared for and properly protected against insects, it is time to hang it in a cool place—the cooler the better as long as it does not freeze.

Unless you are an expert, let a butcher cut your deer into proper pieces and

package it for the freezer. It is money well spent. Whether you do it yourself or have it carved for you, you'll end up with roasts, steaks, chops, stew meat, and a bunch of hamburger—everything that didn't fit into one of the other categories will be ground up for venison burgers.

Everything we have to say about whitetailed deer applies equally well to mule deer, to the coastal blacktail, even to the tiny Coues deer. What the deer is feeding upon has more to do with that hard-to-define quality of flavor than does the species delineation.

Cooking Venison

Fried Venison Liver

Your first meal should be the liver, which is delicious. It should be sliced thin, fried quickly on a hot skillet, and eaten right away. If you sauté a bunch of onions in the pan first and serve them alongside the slices of liver, you'll find that your guests will ask for more. Don't overdo the cooking, for there's nothing worse than venison liver fried to a crisp. My favorite cook dredges the thinly sliced liver in flour before it hits the skillet, and I can't say that the meat is hurt by this treatment. The heat must be turned up high, for you want to seal those juices in, not stew them out.

Venison Roast

A larger roast will turn out better than a smaller one, all other things being equal. If the roast has loose ends, tie it to make a more compact package. Sprinkle with salt and pepper to taste after wiping it down with a sliced-open clove of garlic. Discard the garlic. Place the roast in a greased roasting pan, and sprinkle all over with flour. Pop into a preheated oven for about 15 minutes at 500°F to sear the outside. Then reduce the heat to 225°F and roast slowly, allowing 40 minutes per pound. The roast will end up slightly pink inside. If you want it done more, give it another shot in the oven at about 325°F, but don't dry it out, for venison has very little marbling—with notable exceptions found in deer raised on corn in Iowa and the Dakotas.

Swiss-Steaked Venison

Dredge steaks in flour and sear quickly in hot pan. Then place in deep cooking vessel on top of the contents of a can of stewed tomatoes, some diced onion, and two large bell peppers, sliced thinly. Discard the white interiors of the bell peppers, naturally. Add a package of dried onion soup and a can of cream of mush-room soup. Cover and simmer slowly for hours . . . it won't overcook. When tender to the fork, serve it piping hot. If you're cooking a lot of steaks you may have to double the quantity of mushroom soup, but don't overdo the onion soup mix. Carrots and celery added to the cooking mixture won't hurt a thing.

Venison Barbecue

Cut the tougher pieces of venison up into small cubes, less than 2 inches each way. Brown in shortening or in bacon dripping; either one will do as long as it is piping hot. Set aside.

Mix 1 cup catsup; ½ tablespoon Worcestershire sauce; 3 cloves garlic, minced finely; ½ cup wine vinegar; about 10 drops Tabasco red sauce; ½ cup brown sugar; juice of 1 big lemon, and 1 teaspoon each salt and pepper. Stir it all together and start it to simmering on the back burner. Sauté some onion rings, cut thin. When onions are translucent, add them to the venison and the simmered barbecue sauce. Cover and cook slowly until meat is tender.

Venison Stew

Cut venison into 1-inch cubes and brown on all sides. Add whatever you'd add to a beef stew, giving it a slightly more generous supply of onions, and cook until meat is tender.

Venison Burgers

We usually form the hamburger into meat loaf, adding nothing but meat, and freeze it that way. Then we use the meat saw to cut off the required number of burger steaks. Cook as you would beef burgers, but remember that the venison is usually not as fat as beef and that it should not be dried out.

A slightly better system is to add one part of pork sausage to every three parts of venison and mix it well, before you freeze it into venison loaf. Incidentally, venison makes good sausages, if you remember to use enough pork to supply the fat that venison does not have.

Hunters' Venison Stew

> 2 *pounds venison stew meat, in*
> *small cubes*
> 2 *tbsp. butter*
> 3 *big carrots, cut up into 1-inch*
> *pieces*
> 3 *stalks celery, cut up*
> 3 *medium-size onions, cut up*
> 2 *big potatoes, cut into chunks*
> 1 *tsp. sugar*
> *salt and pepper to taste*

Brown the meat cubes in a skillet. Put into slow cooker with all vegetables. Cover and simmer for 2 hours, or longer if not tender after 2 hours. You know your own slow cooker better than I do.

Venison Sauerbraten

Marinate a 3-pound venison roast in a glass bowl with 3 sliced onions, a couple of bay leaves, 12 peppercorns, 6 whole cloves, 2 tsps. salt, 2 cups red wine vinegar, and enough boiling water to cover the meat. The bowl should be allowed to cool and should then be covered with plastic wrap and left in refrigerator for three days (four won't hurt). Turn the meat over occasionally, using a wooden spoon.

Drain the meat, but keep the marinade. Get some shortening sizzling hot in a cast-iron skillet, and brown the meat quickly on all sides. Return the marinade mixture to cover the browned meat, cover, and simmer slowly until meat is tender. Remove meat and onions and keep them hot while you make up some excellent gingersnap gravy with the juices in the cooking pan. It will take about 12 big gingersnaps, crumbled fine, to do the job.

Venison Casserole

Brown 1 pound of venison burger in skillet with a little shortening and set it aside. Cook 4 ounces macaroni and drain. Mix the meat, the macaroni, 1 can cream of celery soup, 1 cup milk, ¾ cup catsup, 1 cup grated cheddar cheese, and 1 cup minced green bell pepper and onion well mixed together in an ungreased casserole dish, about 2-quart capacity. Forty minutes to 1 hour in a 350°F oven and it's ready to delight the diners.

Venison Heart Deluxe

> 1 *pint tomato juice*
> 1 *pint water*
> ½ *tsp. sweet basil*
> 1 *pinch cinnamon*
> 1 *bay leaf*
> 5 *whole cloves*
> 1 *deer heart*
> 5 *strips bacon*

Place tomato juice, water, and spices in the bottom of a steamer kettle. In the top of the steamer place the heart with the bacon strips on top of it. Cover tightly and steam slowly for 3 hours, or until fork comes out easily. Drain the heart and chill it in refrigerator. Slice thin and serve cold. Goes great with a red wine or even with beer. This recipe is courtesy of the South Dakota Game, Fish and Parks Department.

10

Other Big Game Animals

THE PRONGHORN ANTELOPE

Found nowhere else in the world and without any close relatives, the pronghorn antelope is typically North American—he was here before any of us. He belongs on the wide plains and prairies, and he's doing quite well, thank you.

When the first Europeans set foot on this continent, there were at least 40 million pronghorns here. Some estimates say that there were at least 100 million! But he was sympatric with the tremendous herds of buffalo (bison), and his fate seemed to be destined. The reason was simple but little understood until about 1930. The herds of bison grazed on grass. This grazing prevented the grass from taking over the land's forbs and bushes. The antelope ate forbs; his diet is less than 2 percent grass!

When the bison was eliminated for all practical purposes, grass grew tall, and the forbs were eliminated from much of the historic range of the antelope. Add to this the fact that the settlers dined heavily on antelope steaks all through the year, and we have the makings of extermination for the antelope. It was close; as long ago as 1910 antelope numbers were estimated as low as 20,000 in the United States, with another pitifully few thousands in Canada and in northern Mexico. Then mankind made another big mistake.

Cattle and sheep took over the Great Plains, and greed prompted overgrazing. As cattle destroyed the lush fields of grass, forbs returned and the pronghorn was rescued from the brink—a classic case of a wrong making a right. Its numbers slowly grew but were still too low to allow much hunting opportunity by 1940, although several states had open seasons at that time. Then another action by man, aimed at protecting domestic sheep and goats, gave the pronghorn its biggest boost. Compound 1080, a remarkably specific poison aimed at coyotes, proved effective beyond any stockman's fondest dreams. Coyotes had been the limiting factor on antelope herds, causing heavy mortality in the fawn crop. In some areas, coyotes took 60 percent of the fawns, which effectively stopped any increase in the herd's numbers. It is true that the antelope existed side by side with the coyote for millennia before the development of Compound 1080. However, man's actions had concentrated the antelope into smaller areas, where he was vulnerable to coyote predation on his fawns. In addition, the unit value of each fawn was far greater now that we were hoping to increase the herd. Compound 1080, alone among coyote control measures, really did reduce coyote numbers. The antelope population took off in a wonderful explosion of numbers. Every year, we now legally shoot more antelope in the top state—Wyoming—than existed in the entire world before Compound 1080.

State after state reopened antelope hunting in areas that had been closed since the 1920s or even earlier. Today, this graceful speedster is found in North and South Dakota, Nebraska, Kansas, Oklahoma, Texas, New Mexico, Arizona, Utah, Nevada, Idaho, Montana, Oregon, California—and topping them all, in wide, wonderful Wyoming. Remnant populations are to be found south of the border, but they are not growing and would seem to have a poor future.

Let's take a good look at this remarkable animal, only representative of the genus *Antilocapra*. He grows horns, not antlers. Antlers are bone, horns are hair. But of all horned animals, he is the only one that sheds his horns every year! The sheath of hair turned into horn grows anew each year on a bony core. The horns are positioned directly above the eyes, and curve their tips inward, or sometimes outward, sometimes forward, sometimes back. In addition to the curved central beam, this horn growth has a prong jutting frontward near the top. This gives the animal its name of "pronghorn." The record antelope head measured just over 20 inches in length of horn, but only that one has ever been measured over 20. Anything over 16 inches is trophy class.

Just below those unique horns are the antelope's eyes, biggest in the mammal kingdom for the size of the animal. Antelope have eyesight better than any other game animal, in this man's humble opinion. The combination of exceptionally good eyesight and great speed of foot is

Typical pronghorned-antelope bucks. *U.S. Fish & Wildlife photo.*

the defense of the pronghorn antelope. He feels that he can see you and outrun you, so he stays right out in the open without any attempt to hide.

Brilliantly colored and strikingly marked, he is unusually difficult to see although he stays out in the open. An overall light tan color, with white underbelly and white and black markings on his neck, he has a white rump of erectile hairs. Using his ability to erect those bright white hairs, he has a heliograph, or mirror, right on his behind. When alarmed, he erects that mirror and flashes a signal that can be seen for miles across the flat plains country that he loves.

Smaller than either mule deer or whitetail, a mature pronghorn buck is not likely to weigh more than 125 pounds live weight, and about 110 field-dressed. Does are much smaller. Like the bucks, does grow horns, but they are much smaller and more slender.

Does and young bucks carry their head high, with the neck almost perpendicular to the line of the backbone. Older bucks,

and especially the trophy animals, run with the head held well out in front of them, as if the weight of their horns was too much to bear. And run is what they do best.

Many observers have credited young doe antelope—the fastest—with speeds in excess of 70 miles an hour, as recorded on the speedometer of the speeding car that was racing the antelope. Pronghorns know that they are the fastest runners, and they will often challenge a car by running alongside it for a way, then turning on the afterburner and crossing ahead of the car as if to say, "Take that, slowpoke!" Not only are they fast sprinters, but they can keep it up for as much as 4 miles at a clip estimated at 35 miles per hour.

Their generally slim build is a delusion. The slim leg bones have a breaking strength superior to that of a 1,000-pound steer. Although their coat is composed of hollow hairs and doesn't seem to offer much protection from the winter blizzards, this is an animal that does well on

Pronghorned antelope in winter snows. *U.S. Fish & Wildlife photo.*

the windswept plains of Wyoming, enduring the blizzards with equanimity. The pronghorn is one tough customer. The only chink in their armor is when the kids are first dropped. Like deer, they usually have twins, which can do a wonderful job of hiding the first week of their lives. After that danger time, the coyote can no longer catch them, and they have only man and his machines to fear. Especially man's fences and high-powered rifles.

Scorning the soft, tender meal of grass, the antelope seems to prefer sagebrush, greasewood, rabbitbrush, juniper, bitterbrush, chicory, larkspur, dandelion, and wild onions. Obviously, they do not compete with cattle for food. In fact, they will prosper on pastures that cattle have overgrazed. At times they are destructive of farm crops, being especially fond of ripe flax, where they nip off the full heads and leave the straw standing.

Wary antelope, ready to leap into high gear in New Mexico.

Management for the Pronghorn

As is often the case, wise management of the land is wise management for the pronghorn antelope. Grazing by cattle keeps the grasses down to where the forbs prosper. Antelope browse on the forbs, keeping them from shading out the grass. If antelope numbers are controlled by wise management (which means sport hunting), the cattle will prosper in the same field with them. And if man unwisely overgrazes the land, hurting the grass upon which his livelihood depends, the antelope will still do well in that overgrazed pasture and will not slow the restoration of ranch grasses by his presence.

Snow will take the place of water in the wintertime, but in the summer, antelope like to visit free water twice daily

and will go long distances to drink from a stockwater dam or tank supplied by a windmill-operated pump. Antelope have no objection to watering along with domestic livestock and often feed right alongside the ranch cattle, although the two species are eating two different types of food. Any management plan for antelope must include access to water twice daily. Whenever possible, three-strand barbed-wire fences should be used, as they pose no barrier to antelope. When possible, make the bottom strand of the fence out of plain wire—no barbs. This prevents loss of antelope by hanging up on the fence, which happens oftener than one would think. Sheep-tight woven wire fences, however, seem to be impassable to antelope, which seldom jump over anything. Traditionally, antelope herds drift great distances before a winter storm. An antelope-tight fence that stops this drifting can result in loss of an entire herd.

Although they can jump quite well, antelope prefer to go down on their bellies and slide under a barbed-wire fence. I have seen herds of a hundred or more go under a fence in one fluid slide, without seeming to lose any speed in the maneuver, down and up again still running.

Highly gregarious at all times, the antelope travels in herds, which makes them that much harder to stalk. Mature bucks gather small harems of receptive does during the rutting season, seldom having control of more than three or four does at one time. These mature bucks do most of the breeding, obviously, and almost every doe is pregnant when the breeding season is over. They carry the young for about 240 days.

To summarize—management of the pronghorn means regulation of the harvest of antelope, intelligent livestock operations, providing free water in the summertime, and above all, heeding the antelope's plea of "Don't fence me in!"

THE ELK

As I found out one sunny, warm day in northern New Mexico, the fun of elk hunting is all over when you kill the animal. Then the work starts, and work it is. A bull elk with average antler growth, say a five-year-old, may weigh as much as 1,100 pounds! Bulls on Afognak Island in Alaska have been weighed in at nearly 1,500 pounds, but the average for the Rocky Mountain elk would run much closer to 900 pounds per bull. And that is a lot of bull if you intend to cut it up and pack the parts out over a couple of mountain ridges and change elevation above sea level by as much as 1,000 feet—up! I have never been that fatigued again, nor do I want to be.

The biggest elk rival moose in size. The smallest, the tule elk, are outweighed by some of the world's record white-tailed deer that have been taken on this continent. But if you are carrying part of him on your back, any elk is a large animal.

He was once our most widespread big game animal, being found from northern Quebec south to Mexico, from Florida to California and Washington, and on up north, almost to Alaska when the white man came. The only place he was not found was in the desert areas of Nevada, California, Utah, and Arizona. Across this tremendous range, the elk was at home on the prairies, in the woods, in the lush swamps of Alabama and Florida, in the semiarid pinyon mountains of New Mexico and Arizona, in the rain forests of Oregon, and in the dry, rolling hills of eastern Oregon. He was extremely tolerant of his surroundings, but basically

Chuck Cadieux with good antelope buck he took in northeastern New Mexico.

Bull elk on Niobrara National Wildlife Refuge. *U.S. Fish & Wildlife photo.*

upon man for food in the worst of the winter. The Yellowstone Park Herd and the herd that comes out of the Thorofare region of northwestern Montana winter in the Jackson Hole Country. The National Elk Refuge was established there on the outskirts of the city of Jackson, Wyoming, to feed the wintering thousands. All summer long, the crews of the National Elk Refuge, operated by the Bureau of Sport Fisheries and Wildlife, cut and hauled hay to the barns located on the refuge. They had to be ready for the hungry time.

The elk cows and calves arrived on the refuge first; the fiercely independent bulls were the last to come into the grasp of civilization, forced to be beggars and stand in line for their handout of hay.

Once when I was filming the National Elk Refuge to make a movie about the feeding operation, I had the opportunity to record the movement of a big part of the wintering herd, probably 9,000 animals, all coming over the snow-covered hill into view of the camera. They were running at an easy lope, and the steam from their breath and from their warm bodies stood up like a solid cloud of white over the black animals. They filled the viewfinder from horizon to horizon and the living sea of black, snorting and blowing, moved on past the camera until we ran out of film—and still they came. I've never been privileged to see the great game herds of East Africa, but I think I know what they might look like. However, the crowding and poor natural forage of the overcrowded winter range led to necrotic stomatitis, a stomach disease brought on by poor condition and usually associated with browsing on coarse foods, foods of last resort. This disease caused great losses in the wintering herds, and the whole

he was a plains animal. This comes as a surprise to many, for the elk has retreated before the advance of European settlement, until he is now found only in the most beautiful part of our nation, the high mountains—the Rockies and the Coastal Range. Oh, yes, I know that reintroduced elk are doing well in parts of Oklahoma, Michigan, and Minnesota, and even on the prairies of North Dakota—but the big herds, the 99 percent of our elk, are in the Rockies and in the Coastal Range and Sierra Nevadas. He has moved back to the places where man affects him the least—the places where he is hardest to find.

But even in his mountain fastnesses, the mighty elk is sometimes dependent matter of artificial feeding was again under the microscope.

Today, the Fish and Wildlife Service is attempting to make the elk herd live within the capacity of the forage production on their winter range, without the artificial feeding. This means, of course, that we must be satisfied with fewer elk, in the long run, than we had while we were dumping the baled hay off the horse-drawn sleds on the feeding grounds.

This artificial feeding operation was a good place to see elk up close, but they are not really at their best while they are existing on charity. The shed antlers on the National Elk Refuge are collected each year by the Boy Scouts of America who then sell them at auction to a bunch of ancient Orientals who think that the powdered antler has aphrodisiac qualities. The powdered antler probably does nothing for the Chinaman's love life, but it did a lot for the bull elk while he was wearing it.

During the breeding season, the bull elk is a thing gone berserk, an insane male that thinks of nothing but his harem of cows for more than one month at a time. He goes without eating, he drinks the urine from receptive cows, he rolls in puddles of urine and even eats the urine-soaked mud that he has rolled in! He is the very embodiment of the mating urge. But it is during this madness that the bull elk produces one of the most fascinating and exciting sounds ever heard in the wild.

We call it elk bugling, but it is more like a whistle. First, you hear—"as if from distance borne"—this unbelievably high-pitched, squealing whistle, sustained for a long time. If you answer with your artificial bull elk call, the bull may come toward you. Or if you work closer to him, you will hear the entire calling sequence.

It starts out with a couple of deep, coughing grunts, in a real bass voice. Then the squealing whistle starts with the baritone notes and goes on up the scales, through wildlife tenor into the soprano range, and ends in the dying whistle—the C above high C. It may or may not be followed by another one or two of the deep grunts.

Watched at close range, the bugling is even more exciting, the sound even harder to describe. It arouses something atavistic in all but the most effete humans, and I confess to feeling the hairs prickle up on the back of my neck every time I hear it. It is part of nature's symphony, a majestic solo delivered in the most beautiful amphitheater in the world—a valley in the high Rocky Mountains.

When the rut is in full swing, the bull is very busy. He must keep his harem rounded up, and that is not easy, for they have a tendency to roam. He must also withstand frequent challenges from other bulls who feel that they can beat him and thus own his hard-won harem of brown-eyed beauties. On the Vermejo Park territory in northeastern New Mexico, we watched a harem master for four hours one afternoon. He bugled almost constantly, and got answering challenges from every point of the compass. He patrolled the perimeter of a little area he had decided was home for his harem, constantly on the move to keep his cows rounded up and within reach when the time for breeding came.

During that time, two bulls came to challenge him. One was a youngster, obviously one or two years away from being a match for the monarch who was King of the Mountain this autumn. That young bull merely clashed antlers once in a formalized challenge, then took off running with the herdmaster snorting close behind him—close but not catching up. The sole aim of the herdmaster was to drive him away, not to do him bodily harm.

The second challenge was from an old bull, one with even bigger antlers than the herdmaster displayed. But he was leaner, obviously past his muscular prime. His swollen neck was half the size of the herdmaster's, and he seemed doomed to failure as he charged into the clearing in front of the nine cows and faced the herdmaster with a challenging toss of those magnificent antlers.

Four times they separated and charged each other again, clashing the huge racks and twisting, turning, trying to force the opponent off balance or get his neck twisted far to one side. The herdmaster finally got the clear advantage and raked his antlers in a punishing smash against the ribs of the oldster. Then he caught the older bull in the belly with a full frontal attack and the issue was decided. Squealing with rage and unrequited lust, the older bull ran right past us and disappeared into the forest. The herdmaster sent his challenge ringing out over the valley once again, and then returned to the never-ending job of corralling the cows. The defeated oldster stood in the shadows a quarter of a mile away and squealed his rage as he smashed his antlers from side to side, beating hell out of a small conifer. Battles between bull elk of equally matched antlers and body size are not a ritual show. They are deadly combat and it is not at all unusual for one or the other to die from the effects of the battle.

The antlers that determine most elk battles start to grow in May and reach their full glory by the end of September. The world's record head, taken way back in 1899 by John Plute in Dark Canyon, Colorado, had main antler beams of more than 55 and more than 59 inches. Its greatest inside spread was 45½ inches, but the #3 all-time wapiti trophy measured 53 inches inside spread. The way a big bull elk runs through the forest without touching those magnificent antlers to anything is a marvel to behold. But I think it must be a great relief when they finally drop off in late February or early March. "What a load off my mind," he must say.

But the result of carrying those antlers into battle is the privilege of breeding the cows. The cows carry the calf for more than eight months, and most Rocky Mountain elk calves are dropped in May and June. The newborn calf hides like a whitetail fawn and does an excellent job of holding perfectly still and not making a sound. One calf above Jackson in the beautiful Wyoming high country let me take a photograph from less than 6 feet, but when I moved in to 5 feet, it panicked and ran away. Less than one week old, it could easily outrun any man.

Given their choice, elk are grazers rather

Bull elk. *U.S. Fish & Wildlife photo.*

than browsers. Given their choice, 90 percent of their intake would be grass. This gets them in bad with the rancher who would gladly tolerate mule deer and antelope, which are mainly browsers and do not compete with domestic cattle. But if the grass is in short supply, elk will begin browsing and will get their nutrition from twigs and leaves, even standing on their hind legs to feed from the higher branches. They'll go into the water to feed on lush weed growth, à la the biggest deer, the moose. From cactus to willow twigs, from grass to black sage, from cottonwood to mesquite—elk will eat almost anything that grows. But given a choice, they'll take grass. Given a choice in the grass category, they'll choose bluegrass.

What Happened to the Elk?

Once there were 9 or 9½ million elk. Once they were found across almost all of the forty-eight contiguous states. By the year 1850, the eastern elk were gone, for all practical purposes. By 1900 all elk had been driven from the prairies and plains; the surviving herds were in the most remote mountain fastnesses, hiding from man. Elk meat was delicious and market hunters supplied elk meat for the mines of Colorado, for the railroad building crews, for the pioneer families that conquered the West—conquered and almost destroyed the land.

By 1905 there were only 50,000 elk, by most estimates, and their range had shrunk from forty-eight states to only parts of seven states. The craze for showing an elk's tooth fob on the watch chain faded out when it became illegal to kill elk, but the majestic animal almost disappeared into the shadows because "tooth hunters" could make good money shooting elk, and it was easy to hide the teeth and transport them to market.

America's ecological conscience showed the first signs of stirring about this time, and laws were enacted to protect the remnant herds. Of even more importance, game law enforcement began! It took a long time to learn the fact that wildlife protection demanded enforcement of wildlife laws. Man is not innately good, it seems, and fear of being caught was all that stopped the slaughter of elk in some areas.

Restocking began about 1905, and elk were transplanted into many parts of their former range. By 1910 elk numbered 60,000, according to most experts. By 1941 there were more than 200,000 elk roaming the forested mountains of Colorado, Wyoming, New Mexico, Montana, Idaho, Washington, and Oregon. And we must remember that it is an ill wind that blows nobody good . . . as amply demonstrated by the fact that forest fires of catastrophic proportions renewed much of the primitive elk range during these years. Regeneration of second growth produced unlimited elk forage and the herds prospered.

By the 1950s the elk herd had recovered to the point where it was outstripping the habitat's ability to grow forage. In Yellowstone National Park, shortsighted park officials watched thousands of elk die of starvation in the wintertime, yet refused to allow sport hunting, which might have helped to replace the natural predation. The cougar was scarce, the grizzly even scarcer. Most important of all, the timber wolf was gone from most of the elk's range, leaving the elk without any natural enemies worthy of note.

Faced with the incontrovertible fact that

Wintering elk on the National Elk Rufuge, Jackson, Wyoming. Artificial feeding has been necessary because of dwindling winter habitat. *U.S. Fish & Wildlife photo.*

the Yellowstone Park herd had to be reduced in numbers, the park officials resorted to having park rangers shoot the animals—as many as 4,000 were commercially butchered by park rangers in one year alone—and tried ridiculous schemes to drive the elk out of the park, forcing them to run past firing lines of hunters. In that "hunt," a pair of track shoes served the hunter better than a scope-sighted rifle. It mattered not who shot the animal, it only mattered who got there first with the game tag accepted as proof of ownership.

The controversy about hunting in the national parks is not yet over. Even today, National Park Service officials refer to the "historic concept which has never allowed hunting within the park areas," despite the obvious fact that the next national park to the south, the majestic Grand

Teton National Park, has always allowed elk hunting since its inception, with no damage to the "historic park concept." In fairness, it must be reported that sport hunting in Grand Teton has never controlled the explosion in elk numbers there, either. There can never be a justification for letting elk—or deer, for that matter—starve. To its credit, the park service went the extra mile to cooperate with conservation authorities who wanted elk for restocking, and Yellowstone Park elk are the basis of thriving herds from Michigan to California.

Elk are not timid about raiding farmers' haystacks when they get hungry. Elk damage to crops in storage has led to insurance programs in some states and to serious attempts to keep herds within population bounds. I remember one state game department biologist who tested

African lion urine collected from a zoo as a repellent. He reported that it worked better than anything tried previously, but doubted the sufficiency of the supply.

At the present time, the United States probably has as many elk as it can support, given today's conditions. The Yellowstone Park herd is a sore spot, and it is doubtful that any solution is in sight, short of the obvious very unpalatable solution of letting nature take its course. That would mean that the elk herd would seriously damage the browse plants in the park and suffer a population explosion with subsequent die-off from starvation. It is doubtful if enlightened public opinion today would stand for that course of action, for a major elk starvation in a severely damaged national park would surely make the ten o'clock news and be graphically portrayed on television. Outraged public opinion would override considerations of sound wildlife management. Given the difficult terrain of Yellowstone Park, it is also doubtful that sport hunting could handle the problem without access roads being constructed into the back country. I am definitely not in favor of building roads in Yellowstone, so I guess we'll leave that problem in the hands of the National Park Service.

Management for the Elk

If you can provide more habitat, America can provide the elk to stock that habitat. But land is the one thing they're not making more of anymore. It is one man's opinion that we have all the elk we can have under today's conditions. For most landowners, the problem is that of preventing elk depredations, not of producing more elk. It is shameful to have to admit it, but we have taken his native America away from the elk, and homeless, he cannot return to his former abundance. This nation could no more harbor ten million elk again than it could tolerate the return of *Tyrannosaurus rex* to the New Jersey Turnpike at rush hour next Friday afternoon.

THE MOOSE

Largest member of the deer family, the awkward, ungainly, and strangely beautiful, majestic animal is almost entirely unmanageable from the point of view of the individual landowner.

Sometimes described as a "horse designed by a committee," the moose may be as big as a riding horse, with weights up to 1,200 pounds. Forequarters are higher than hindquarters—in fact, his hind legs seem entirely inadequate for the job. Moose antlers are wide-spreading, spatulate growths, which may extend as much as 70 inches in width.

His eyes and brain seem to be slightly weak, but there is nothing wrong with his hearing or powers of smell. He's the preferred winter meat of Alaskans and once was a staple of diet in the lower forty-eight. Today the moose seems to be making a comeback in some places. Maine recently reopened a hunting season on moose that had been closed for decades. The moose has ventured onto the wide prairies of North Dakota, voluntarily crossing the border from Canada, and North Dakota promptly opened a limited season on the big deer. Under wise management, the moose is holding its own in Wyoming and Montana. This is the Shiras variety in the vicinity of Yellowstone National Park, a slightly smaller moose with

Young bull moose on the Kenai Moose Range, Alaska. *U.S. Fish & Wildlife photo.*

much smaller headgear than the lordly Alaska-Yukon moose. Canada and Alaska have no shortage of moose, and they are hunted every year without diminishing the population.

Moose are primarily browsers, as opposed to grazers, although they eat their share of tender grass and love the vegetation that grows in the water.

Near Denali National Park in Alaska, I watched a cow moose submerge completely, time after time, to come up with

Moose calf. *U.S. Fish & Wildlife photo.*

big mouthfuls of succulent vegetation, which she would then chew up at her leisure, then go back under for another load.

Unpredictability seems to be the only characteristic which moose have in common. I've met bull moose on a trout stream in Montana that put me up a tree and kept me there for more than an hour, then wandered off as if he had forgotten why he was mad at me in the first place. I've known of bull moose—sex-maddened in the rutting season—that tried to make love to a saddled horse, a gelding at that. The gelding promptly landed a pair of shod feet square on the jaw of the amorous bull, and that seemed to settle that.

Willows and alders are high on the list of edibles for the moose, along with a bewildering array of water plants and other succulent bushes on the dry side. Food is seldom a problem for the big animals.

In fact, since the virtual elimination of the gray wolf, the moose has no real enemies other than man and disease. Management of moose herds in our country seems to be entirely a matter of regulating the harvest to keep the herd within the "tolerance capacity" of the range. In other words, it is not how much food is available that limits the moose population, but rather how much the human population will put up with from the big deer.

For the individual landowner, the problem is simple. If you have moose on your land, enjoy their presence. If you want to keep all of them, you can bar hunters from your land. If you want to get rid of a few moose, or all your resident moose, invite hunters in. But actual management is more a function of the State Game and Fish Department. Their decisions are based on what is best for the moose herd—statewide—and this may not always seem to be what is best for the individual moose, or small herd, that you have on your land.

Cooking Moose

Moose meat is tasty, and there is so much of it on one moose. In Alaska, they jokingly refer to rabbits as "low bush moose." This is a sarcastic reference to a hard winter during which they must subsist on rabbits instead of moose during the long hard winter.

Make no mistake, moose meat is good. Here is one of the best ways of preparing it.

Moose Round Steak with Onions

Slice moose rounds into 1-inch steaks. Sprinkle half a package of dried onion soup on the heavy foil. Put the moose steak atop the sprinkled onions. Add the rest of the dry onion soup on top along with ½ cup water. Then fold the foil tightly to keep most of the juices in while the steak broils in the heat of a campfire that has been allowed to burn down to the coals. It is not necessary to turn the meat while it cooks. When it is tender to the fork, about 1½ hours, you may salt and pepper to taste and have at it.

All of the usual methods of cooking beef can be adapted to moose cookery, and I especially like the Swiss steak moose and the Moose Stroganoff.

11

Exotic Big Game as a Cash Crop

It is difficult to locate the beginnings of the exotic game program in the United States. Probably about two hundred years ago, wealthy landowners imported European and Asian game animals as display animals on their lands. Eventually, the progeny of these animals escaped or were deliberately turned loose to increase and multiply. Many species, not suited to the environment they found themselves liberated in, simply disappeared. Others did increase and multiply. But this hit-and-miss business was not the start of the thriving programs of the 1980s. Today's exotic game rancher is a scientist; he has to be to survive.

Today the hunter who is willing to shell out substantial sums of money for the privilege can hunt a tremendous list of foreign game animals without leaving the United States! If you want to hunt addax, aoudad, axis deer, fallow deer, Catalina or Spanish goats, feral hogs or Russian boars, ibex, nilgai, scimitar-horned oryx, red deer or Sika deer, Armenian red sheep, Barbados sheep, black Corsican sheep, Corsican sheep, four-horned sheep, Hawaiian black sheep, mouflon, snow-white Corsican, Stumberg-Argali sheep, or blackbuck antelope, you can find them all on ranches in Texas.

At first glance, the prices charged to hunt these exotic game animals here at home may seem outlandish enough to make preserve hunting a prerogative of the rich. However, if you subtract the air fare to Africa or Asia, which you do not pay, from the cost of your hunt, then subtract the cost of safari personnel that you do not have to pay, you find that the exotic game animal hunt in Texas is far cheaper than it could ever be to hunt the same animal overseas.

Typical fees charged for hunting exotic

Hunts for exotic big game are for sale on many Texas ranches.

game, at the time this book went to press, averaged as follows:

Elk	$5,000
Red deer	2,500
Scimitar oryx	2,500
Buffalo	2,000
Nilgai antelope	1,200
Aoudad sheep	1,000
Stumberg sheep	1,000
Axis deer	900
Blackbuck	900
Fallow deer	900
White-tailed buck	850
Asiatic ibex	750
Mouflon sheep	750
Hawaiian black ram	650
Sika deer	650
Texas dall sheep	650
Corsican sheep	500
Javelina	300
Catalina goat	250
Turkey	150
White-tailed doe	75

Wounded and lost charge is usually 75 percent of base trophy fees. In addition, you'll pay about $75 per day for the guide, and you do need a guide on most of these exotic big-game hunting ranches.

In some cases, you can hunt exotic game in Texas that can no longer be hunted in its original habitat. Many species were unlucky enough to live in Third World countries that have not been able to raise their human population above the starvation level of existence, much less spend scarce resources trying to manage their big-game stocks. As a result, the only sensible chance to shoot some species is now on a big-game ranch.

Although our emphasis has been on Texas, there are big-game-shooting exotic ranches in other states as well. However, Texas far outnumbers all of the other forty-nine for several reasons. (1) The laws in Texas favor such commercialization of privately owned exotic game animals. A man's land is a man's land in Texas, and the law cares little what the man does with his land, as long as he doesn't harm his neighbor. (2) Texas has great expanses of rocky hill land, covered with native scrub brush, which is not suited to crop farming nor to profitable cattle operations. Some exotic game animals fill this environmental niche amazingly well. (3) Texas is far enough south to avoid the prolonged bitter cold weather that prohibits importation of tropical or semitropical game animals to much of the United States. (4) Texans have a history of "risk-taking" that is conducive to the very expensive business of starting an exotic-game-shooting operation. (5) Texas people have a long history of paying for the hunting privilege, as well as a hunting clientele available in Dallas, Houston, and the other oil-rich cities of Texas—enough to furnish customers for the exotic game operation.

A listing of exotic-game-animal hunting opportunities follows. A ranch may discontinue such hunting without notice.

Bamberger Ranch
7046 Callaghan Road
San Antonio, TX 78229
Phone: 512-868-7563

Broken Arrow Ranch
P.O. Box 61
Ingram, TX 78025
Phone: 512-367-5871

Corazon Ranch
Box 588
Bracketville, TX 78832
Phone: 512-563-2390

Cottonwood Springs Ranch
2610 Curtis
Amarillo, TX 79109
Phone: 806-359-5466

Dolan Creek Ranch
Box 1549
Del Rio, TX 78840
Phone: 512-775-3129

El Rincon Del Rey
Route 9, Box 124-C
Canyon Lake, TX 78130
Phone: 512-899-2501

Exotic Game Breeders, Inc.
Box 8093
Fredericksburg, TX 78624
Phone: 512-997-4377

Forest Ranch
Route 3, Box 695
Bandera, TX 78003
Phone: 512-796-4470

Flying "A" Ranch
Route 1, Box 60
Bandera, TX 78003
Phone: 512-796-4750

Greenwood Valley Ranch
Route 1, Box 75
Mountain Home, TX 78058
Phone: 512-683-3411

Hatch Ranch
Route 1, Box 54
Mountain Home, TX 78058
Phone: 512-640-3268

Honey Creek Ranch
P.O. Box 136
Hunt, TX 78024
Phone: 512-238-4625

Inks Ranch
P.O. Box 186
Llano, TX 78643
Phone: 915-247-5011

Johnson Farms, Inc.
RFD 1
Bucklin, Missouri 64631
Phone: 816-376-3543

Packsaddle Ranch
Click Route, Box 36
Llano, TX 78643
Phone: 915-388-4001

Priour Ranch
Box 401
Ingram, TX 78025
Phone: 512-267-5324

Rockycrest Ranch
4203 Woodcock, Suite 105
San Antonio, TX 78228
Phone: 512-735-9293

777 Game Ranch
203 West Nakoma
San Antonio, TX 78216
Phone: 512-342-9438

Texas Exotic Game Ranch
Route 1, Box 10
Santo, TX 76472
Phone: 817-769-3515

Texotic Wildlife, Inc.
P.O. Box 181
Mountain Home, TX 78058
Phone: 512-367-5069

Tommy Thompson Ranch
Route 1, Box 52
Medina, TX 78055
Phone: 512-589-7703

Trophy Class, Inc.
P.O. Box 100
Mountain Home, TX 78058
Phone: 512-640-3351

Turkey Spring Exotics
Menard Route, Box 8
Mason, TX 76856
Phone: 915-265-4356

Valdina Farms
Utopia, TX 78884
Phone: 512-966-3517

West Kerr Ranch
Box W
Palacios, TX 77465
Phone: 512-972-2537

Whiskey Canyon Ranch
Box 13197
Houston, TX 77019
Phone: 713-529-0900

Wild Country Hunt Club
P.O. Box 224
Unionville, Missouri 63565
Phone: 816-947-2624

Wildlife Safaris, Inc.
Fredericksburg Route, Box 33-B
Llano, TX 78643
Phone: 915-247-3476

Woodcliff Big Game Ranch
Route 2
Fremont, Nebraska 68025
Phone: 402-721-7616

Y O Ranch
Mountain Home, TX 78058
Phone: 512-640-3222

All of the exotic game producers listed above are members of the Exotic Wildlife Association, 1811-A Junction Highway, Kerrville, TX 78028. Their phone number is 512-895-4288. A glance at the classified section of any of our hunting and fishing-oriented magazines will reveal that there are very many other opportunities to hunt exotic game, especially in California.

The decision to stock exotic game animals on your land should not be made on the spur of the moment. The introduction of any exotic should be reason for soul-searching of the most probing nature. The history of the introduction of such exotics has been a history of failure for the most part. These failures were caused by a misunderstanding of the animal's needs and requirements, an inability to understand the problems that can be caused by ill-planned introductions of exotic species, failure to conform to State Game and Fish Department rules and regulations governing such introductions, failure to know and understand the requirements of the State Livestock Sanitary Board, or other state organization dealing with the prevention of livestock diseases, lack of business management skills necessary to operate a commercial venture, inadequate range in which to liberate the animals, cooperation or lack of it from neighboring landowners, presence of a market for what you are to sell—

Blackbuck antelope taken by Nancy Klepper on exotic-game farm in Texas. *Dan Klepper photo.*

the hunting privilege. Obviously, residents of Texas would be much more ready to pay for the privilege of hunting big-game animals than would the residents of Montana or Wyoming, where there are herds of big-game animals available on public lands.

GETTING INTO THE EXOTICS BUSINESS

If you are interested in getting into the exotic big-game hunting business, I would advise you first of all to study the situation as thoroughly as is possible.

Visit several successful operations, not

just one. Find several operations where the terrain, climate, and plant growth are similar to the area you have in mind for your operation. Talk to the operators; most of them are friendly rancher types. Find out which species they chose, and WHY! If you have ideas for different species, tell them about your plans. It may be that they've already traveled that road and know the pitfalls.

Once you have formulated a plan for your land, which names the species you intend to stock and naming your potential source of supply, present your plan to the State Game and Fish Department of your state. I do not mean that you should talk it over with your local game warden, but rather that you visit the state headquarters and talk to those who will be responsible for enforcing state laws governing exotic game animals. Then go home and write out a proposal for exactly what you intend to do, and send it to the Director of the State Game and Fish Department, asking him for a written statement as to whether or not his department has any objections. He will undoubtedly run your proposal past the Attorney General of the state to see if there are any objections. Try to satisfy any complaints he may have about your plan, and amend your proposal if necessary, but get his support, or at least his permission. Then . . .

Submit your proposal, as amended, to the State Livestock agency, which goes by different names in different states. You want to reach the people who are concerned with the health of domestic livestock in your state. Get their permission, in writing. This will not be easy, unless the exotic hunting business is well established in your state. They will be especially concerned with the source of the

exotics you intend to import for stocking your pastures. They will want to make sure that these animals come from Bangs-free and brucellosis-free areas. If, after fighting your way through all of this red tape and bureaucratic correspondence, it seems feasible to you that you go ahead with your plans, get together with your neighbors and talk it over with them. If they have worries about fence-jumpers, or about livestock diseases that may be transmitted from exotic game to domestic livestock, now is the time to allay these fears.

Next step, and a very important one, is to check the status of your checking account. Buying and transporting your exotic breeding stock is going to be very expensive. The cash flow is going to be all outgo and no income for several years, until you have established a herd—or herds—that contain trophy individuals that should be harvested by the hunter.

Before you introduce the first animals, you will have special cash outlays for fencing, for creation of watering places that will spread animal use all over the range—a very desirable point for the ranch that intends to charge for the hunting privilege. Will special mineral supplements be needed, different salt blocks, different foods that will provide the necessary nutrition to produce healthy animals and trophy heads?

After all preparations and plans have been finalized, then go back to the exotic game ranches that you visited, the successful ones. If it is possible in any way, sit down with the successful exotic rancher and talk over your plans with him. After that session, if all looks well— go ahead!

Exotic-game-animal ranching for shooting purposes is a fascinating busi-

ness and a challenge to a successful livestock rancher to see if he can learn how
to raise a completely different animal, to
see if he can manage a commercial venture that makes him wait years for his
first cash crop, to see if he likes the idea
of having strangers come to his ranch to
kill the animals he has so lovingly raised—

animals he feels a certain affection for,
no matter how strongly he has worked to
keep them wild.

It is a fascinating business, but not one
to be undertaken without knowing what
you are doing. Study well before you
invest!

12

Managing Nongame Birds on Your Land

There is great enjoyment to be gained from the very fact that our closest neighbors are birds. Some of them sing beautifully, like the robin, the mockingbird, the wood thrush, and a hundred others. One of the most beautiful sounds in nature is the clear, crystal song of a western meadowlark, sounding as if his heart would burst with happiness as he greets the morning on the Dakota prairie.

Other birds give us countless hours of enjoyment just watching their antics. House wrens, cactus wrens, flycatchers, and kingbirds fall into this category, as do a hundred others. The comical roadrunner delights the eye with his loping gait, disconnected movements, and all-around gawkiness. Nevertheless that bird is so quick that it can easily avoid the strike of a snake and will often kill and eat small poisonous snakes—with no ill effects.

Hummingbirds are probably the greatest fliers of all, able to fly backward, hover in stationary flight, zip straight up or down, shift into top speed from a standstill start; they have a thousand ways to amaze us with their agility.

Many birds perform miracles in insect control. A local population of purple martins, residing in a condominium built close to your home, will do much to clear the air of mosquitoes on a humid summer evening. All of the swallow family are excellent flying insect traps—be they the bluebacked, orange-fronted barn swallow or one of the black-backed and white-underbellied cliff swallows. The chimney swift, using alternate strokes of his wings instead of flapping them both at once, is an expert acrobat of the city and country skies and eats his own weight in insects every three days. The nighthawk matches this feat.

Woodpeckers searching for worms in dead trees hollow out cavities that are used by many other forms of life, from small birds to large wood ducks, from flying squirrels to tree frogs.

All raptors eat small rodents, but the owls are by far the most efficient killers in this line. One good pair of barn owls—the ones that gave birth to the description "with an owlish expression"—do a great job of rat control. The rat is nocturnal and so are the owls, and no other predator eats as many per night.

Ospreys are fish hawks, and they expertly grab fish out of the water, as does the bald eagle, America's national emblem. When I was a child, we called all buteo hawks "chicken hawks" and thought that these slow-moving, broad-winged hawks were a real threat to our Leghorns. Almost every farmer took a

Barn owls, like this one in Oklahoma, are wonderful rat catchers. *U.S. Fish & Wildlife photo.*

shotgun to any hawk he saw. Thank goodness, that attitude is gone now, and almost everyone knows that hawks are excellent mousers, that the larger ones kill and eat rabbits, that the smaller ones feast on grasshoppers—that all hawks are to be considered pluses to the community.

It is relatively easy for the landowner to influence the population and the species composition of the bird life on his land. In other chapters of this book, I describe specific measures for increasing the populations of specific game birds, such as the quails, the partridges, the grouse, the pheasants, and waterfowl, with emphasis on wood ducks.

But right now our mission is to discuss the means by which you can increase the populations of birds that will:

1. Sing for you.
2. Eat insects that eat you or your crops.
3. Eat rodents that eat the crops you raise.
4. Amuse you with their antics.
5. Eat millions of weed seeds before they have a chance to sprout in your crop fields.

Robins are one of America's most numerous and certainly most loved songbirds. I remember a poem from some long ago reading—

I wish that those who say there is no one,
To rule from beyond the distant sun.
Would somehow take a needed warning,
From the robin's prayer in early morning.
Like sweet-voiced choristers chanting Latin,
The robin sings his early matin.

Can't remember any more of it. But I'll never forget the song of the robin redbreast, the harbinger of spring where I grew up, the sign of a hard winter—now that we live in the southwest, where many robins winter.

Because the robin is a specialist in earthworms, there is very little you can do to improve his food supply, except to maintain a good lawn, which means a well-watered lawn filled with earthworms. The robin eats many other insects, of course, but you do not want to increase the number of bugs, so you'll have to leave the food supply up to the robin. It is seldom a problem to them, anyway. One thing you can do that will greatly help the robin, and that is to keep your house cats in the house. House cats are important predators on robin nests and on the adult birds, also. Feral cats are a menace to all birds, game birds and nongame as well. Your house pet, which loves to be petted as it curls up on your lap, often becomes an efficient predator as soon as it leaves the house.

In San Antonio, Texas, there are many chinaberry trees. Robins like to eat the berries after they have fermented on the tree! How this insect eater ever got started on the alcoholic frozen chinaberries, I'll never know. But they do get drunk and perform ridiculous feats, such as swinging by their feet under a wire clothesline perch, instead of roosting on top of it. They also fly drunkenly and have been known to crash into the side of the house when on a binge.

Purple Martins are the largest member of the swallow family. This 8-inch-long insect trap has decided that it likes to live close to people, and if you put up a martin house—an apartment dwelling, with separate entrances into about twenty separate nesting boxes, you are almost assured of having a good martin population. And they will work wonders on reducing an insect population.

Hummingbirds can be attracted to your land by placing feeders near the flowers they normally visit in search of nectar, which is their primary food. You can buy the feeders from any pet store, most discount stores, and even grocery stores in suburban areas. You provide the food by dissolving as much sugar in tap water as it will hold. That super-saturated sugar solution is food to the hummers, and they'll visit the feeders regularly all day long. But be sure to keep the feeder filled, for it would be cruel to get the hummingbirds depending upon you and then go away and leave them. You can spend countless hours watching the incredible flying feats of these tiny bits of feathered diamond.

Bluebirds are insect eaters and lovely additions to the biota of your land. They lost out in competition with the introduced starling—one of our worst mistakes—and almost disappeared from their familiar haunts around human homes. However, nesting boxes seem to be bringing them back. If you put up nesting boxes near your house, you should notice a remarkable decrease in grasshoppers, caterpillars, and beetles, all insects that can be taken on foot, not flying. But make sure that the two nasty imports—starlings and English sparrows—don't usurp the nesting boxes. It pays to be ruthless in dumping out starling and sparrow nests, for it is possible to keep them out and keep the boxes ready for the bluebirds.

Wrens will also respond to the establishment of nesting boxes, but it is easier to keep the sparrows out. Simply make the entrance hole so small that a sparrow can't shove his big head through it. The wren can still easily scoot in and out. Its singing will reward you for the gift of the nesting house.

Blue Jays—well, I have mixed feelings about blue jays. They are lovable rascals, beautifully colored in blues, grays, whites, and blacks. Their strident call, which to me sounds like "thief, thief," is not unpleasant, and their antics are always worth watching. They take readily to bird feeders that contain seeds of all kinds, cracked grains, suet, even corn.

Blue jays have a bad side, however, for they are inveterate "egg eaters" and are not above eating both eggs and newly hatched young of the robin, bluebird, brown creeper, thrush, mourning dove, and almost any other nesting bird. It would be silly to criticize the blue jay for this, he is just doing what comes naturally, and he certainly does not perceive his actions as being either right or wrong. They are just part of the bird. But, unless your winters are very rough, he may stay with you all year around, and you can ensure this by maintaining a well-filled feeder available to him. He may, of course, drive all smaller birds away from it, but that is part of his charm.

Cardinals, the "red birds" of a large part of the United States, are not usually migratory. If food is available year around, you should have cardinals year around. What kind of food? The typical seed-eater's beak of the cardinal is your clue. Give him seeds, almost any seeds, and he'll stay with you when others have proved themselves fair weather friends by flying south.

Catbirds are about 8 inches long, slate gray with shiny black cap and tail. They are usually secretive, preferring to flit about in low shrubbery or dense foliage,

out of sight. They are melodious singers and like to interrupt their song with a mewing sound, very much like that of a cat, which gives them their name. They feed on both insects and seeds, but prefers fruits to seeds. If raisins, grapes, cherries, or chopped apples are presented on a bird feeder, the catbirds will often get in the habit of having breakfast with you. Because they nest in low bushes, they are frequently victims of marauding house cats. Get rid of the cats and you'll be much more apt to enjoy the sounds and the sights of catbirds.

Woodpeckers, especially two smallish species, the hairy and the downy, are real friends of mankind. They diligently hunt out and eat the boring insects that are the worst enemies of orchard trees. They like beef suet, so you should provide this food, up out of reach of cats and dogs, during the cooler months. These woodpeckers do not kill the tree they feed upon. They do excavate a hole in a *dead* branch or tree trunk to form their own home.

Flickers, one of my favorite birds, are larger cousins of the woodpeckers. They are more than a foot long from tip of beak to tip of tail, easily recognized by the small but very visible round spot of red on top of the head, the dark band across their throat like an undersized bib, the yellow underbelly with its solid black spots. The flicker is the best ant "eater" among our North American birds. They will readily accept an artificial nesting box, if hung in a safe position and kept free of sparrow and starling intruders. You'll enjoy the loud ringing cry of this bird and enjoy watching it pick its insect food out of low vegetation and decaying wood. When it braces its stiff tail feathers against the trunk of the tree and beats out a tattoo, you'll hear it all across the land. Definitely a bird worth cultivating on your land.

Goldfinches are small, 4-inch-long birds. The male is the only small yellow bird with black wings. Their flight is extremely undulating, like a flash of yellow fire through the greenery. They are usually late nesters, often starting their seasonal effort after most other birds have completed maternal chores. Perhaps this is so the young will be born into a world that contains a multitude of edible seeds? They are often called "wild canaries," which is a tribute to their musical ability. They like flowers and prefer to nest in low shrubbery or along the hedgerows of flower gardens. Don't worry; they'll eat a thousand weed seeds for every flower seed they steal. A colorful and welcome addition to your bird population.

Grackles come in several sizes and form several species, but the most common is the purple grackle in the north and the "boat-tailed" grackle in the southern part of our country. That is a misnomer—it should be "oar-tailed" instead of boat-tailed grackle. Both species like to nest in close proximity, one with the other, and they often congregate in city parks and other places that provide the type of nesting tree they prefer. They are definitely not music makers, as their calls consist of a series of squawks; squeals; and rasping, grunting sounds—which may be music to another grackle's ears, but not to mine. These rascals do quite a bit of damage, eating the eggs and young of songbirds, but they are definitely beneficial when it comes to destroying great quantities of insects—especially harmful insects like the weevils and white grubs and caterpillars. This presents a problem best solved by maintaining lots of nesting cover for the more desirable birds. This enables them to spread out their nests and to conceal them better, which will prevent much grackle predation. However, if you are seriously trying to increase your populations of mourning or white-winged doves, you must take steps to reduce or eliminate the grackle population from around your dove nesting areas, because the doves never learn to conceal their nests and the grackles really feast on dove eggs.

Killdeers are common birds over most of the nation, nesting in pastures, gravel pits, stone piles, or other places, but almost always near rivers, marshes, or lakes. No menace to deer, the bird gets its peculiar name from its call, which sounds like "kill-dee, kill-dee" to my ears. White underbelly, brownish tan back, with two bands of black across the underside of its neck, it is very easy to recognize.

Definitely a beneficial bird, the killdeer is a selective insect eater—and the insects it selects are our worst enemies, including mosquitoes and mosquito larvae, flies, ticks, weevils, and beetles. When it places its eggs on gravel nests, they simply disappear, as they are perfectly camouflaged by their color. Feral cats are a danger to this bird, although the cat is often fooled by the old "broken-wing caper," which the killdeer works to near perfection. It will drag one wing on the ground, make feeble attempts to fly, all the while screaming in distress. The enemy is fooled into pursuing an apparently easy meal, while the bird lures you away from its nest. However, the deception breaks down if the enemy doesn't follow the crippled (*looks* crippled, anyway) bird away from the nest area. When that happens the bird *flies* back to the spot and again goes into its broken-wing act.

Red-Winged Blackbirds prefer to build their nests in rushes or other emergent vegetation, over water. They are beautiful birds, with the bright red shield on the wings edged with bright yellow being their identifying mark. They are gregarious birds, preferring to live in good-sized flocks, even during nesting time. They are beneficial birds in that they eat tremendous numbers of insects, especially during the time when they are feeding young. However, they do a lot of damage to corn and maize in the milk stage, and thus are hated by many farmers with good reason. Large flocks of redwings mixed with cowbirds, descending on grainfields at the right time, will cause great financial loss. Most landowners like redwings for their bright beauty and for their strange but musical call. Landowners who raise grain crops that are fed upon by hordes of redwings do not like the birds.

Obviously, there are hundreds of other birds that you will see on or near your lands. We cannot describe them all, nor is there any reason to do so. But we can talk a bit about how to attract and keep nongame bird populations. With some species, there is very little we can do. For example, the killdeer is always welcome, but he is an independent cuss and will not take advantage of food supplies that man makes available for his use. All we can do to help him is to leave him strictly alone during the nesting season. Keeping cattle off gravelly spots near water would help, but the killdeer fails to recognize your effort to help him and stubbornly puts his eggs in a dangerous spot, like between the car tracks in a farm road. The sparrow hawk, one of the most beautiful and smallest of all hawks, is a very beneficial bird. His biggest diet item is grasshoppers, followed by small field

Great horned owl, one of nature's most expert killers. *U.S. Fish & Wildlife photo.*

mice, grubs, and beetles. There is almost nothing we can do to help him, but he doesn't seem to be needing any help.

Many birds that winter in the northern half of the country welcome supplemental feeding in the wintertime. This is especially true when we provide missing elements of the winter diet, such as suet, which is relished by very many species. When exceptionally heavy winter snows and ice storms cover its usual weed-seed diet, the mourning dove welcomes a trip or two to the bird feeder for grains and small seeds. A bird feeder should contain bread crumbs, crackers, cheese, chopped hard-boiled eggs, mealworms, coconut meat, broken dog biscuits, hominy, peppers, pumpkin and squash seeds, earthworms, ant eggs, bananas, cooked rice, doughnuts, grapes, oranges, apples, raisins, and peanut butter, according to Don Pfitzer and Thurman W. Booth, the au-

Baby great horned owls in Virginia. *U.S. Fish & Wildlife photo.*

thors of the excellent leaflet *Attracting and Feeding Birds,* published by the U.S. Fish and Wildlife Service.

Many bird lovers are surprised to see peanut butter on the list of desirable bird foods, but it is relished by more species than perhaps anything you could provide for birds. Do not put out more food than will be cleaned up quickly, for the birds will pass up rotten food. Remember that small grit particles will be very attractive to almost all species of birds. If you use a compartmented feeder of some kind or another, you will be able to see which foods, or grits, are your preferred offerings. Crushed eggshells will be used by many species, especially in the breeding season, when the small females have the big job of generating enough egg shell for their own brood. Suet, the uncooked fat trimmed off your roast, will also be welcomed in wintertime. And above all, make sure that water is available during the summer months and up until freeze-up.

Many birds bathe in the water; all need it to drink. Other species of birds do their bathing in dust, but they will find that dusting place by themselves.

Many shrubs are worthwhile additions to your plantings, simply because they provide food for nongame birds. Among these are the following: winterberry, vi-

Leg-banding an indigo bunting, taken in a mist net as part of effort to unravel the mysteries of a migration. *U.S. Fish & Wildlife photo.*

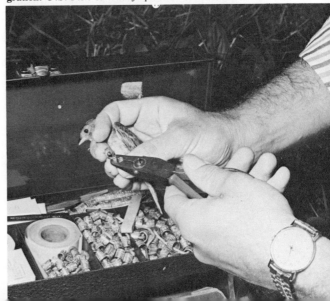

burnum, sumac, spicebush, snowberry, pyracantha, privet, pokeberry, elderberry, blueberry, blackberry, bayberry, and althea.

Vines used by birds for food include Virginia creeper, greenbrier, honeysuckle, trumpet vine, and wild grapes.

But there are many other practices—other than feeding—that make your land more attractive to the birds. Provision of *undisturbed* nesting cover is perhaps the most important. Short trees and shrubbery are optimum nest spots for many species. Can you afford to fence livestock out of a small bit of shelterbelt, or tree claim, or forested corner? Successful nesting will double when trees and shrubs are not damaged by cattle. Bird use of undisturbed cover will surprise you, when you compare it with a grove of trees where cattle have eliminated the ground grass cover and rubbed the trees shiny with their itching flanks.

If you are planting a shelterbelt or windbreak, consider the needs of the birds. Talk to your county agent and ask what combinations of trees will do the best combined job of conserving moisture and providing nesting cover for the birds—both ground nesters and tree nesters. Properly placed to slow winter winds, a shelterbelt can do much to lower fuel bills in your home during northern winters. A windbreak dense enough to slow winds, or divert them upward and away from your home, will also provide nesting cover for many species. The row or two of con-

ifers mixed in to provide denser windbreak in the winter will also provide nesting cover for many species that seem to prefer the conifer over the deciduous tree for raising a family.

How about tree plantings with lots of food for fruit and berry-eating birds? It is part of planning to attract birds.

To sum up, we can increase populations of singing nongame birds, by:

1. Providing nest boxes for species that will use them.
2. Improving nesting cover by planting trees and shrubs and by fencing cattle out of nesting cover.
3. Choosing tree and shrub species that provide food for songbirds.
4. Curbing the activities of house cats, feral or tame.
5. Providing supplemental food at all seasons of the year.
6. Providing survival food in wintertime, such as suet and seeds for cardinals, blue jays, chickadees, nuthatches, mourning doves, etc.
7. Try to make life miserable for starlings and house sparrows, chase them out of nest boxes intended for more desirable species.

You'll never have better neighbors than songbirds. Try to be a good neighbor and repay them for removing the millions of insects, the trillions of weed seeds that they eat on your land.

13

Predator Control

So the foxes are getting your pheasants, and you want to kill them all off because it is as evident as the nose on my face that reducing the numbers of pheasant-eating foxes will automatically increase the supply of pheasants.

Sorry, my friend, it simply doesn't work that way.

Written in the winter snows, you see the unmistakable evidence that coyotes, working as a pair, tore down and killed a mature, healthy, white-tailed doe last January. So you want to reduce the number of coyotes, which will automatically increase the number of deer.

Sorry again, my friend, but it simply doesn't work that way.

In the second chapter of this book I discussed at length the so-called balance of nature. I said that predator species eat prey species, true, but that they do not control the numbers of prey species. Exactly the opposite is true; the numbers of prey species available controls the numbers of predators. If the table is set for twenty coyotes, they will come to dinner. But if there is only food enough for one coyote, the other nineteen will be absent.

Consider a few fundamental facts:

1. Predators have been eating prey species for a million years, but they have not eliminated those prey species.

2. If you eliminate one meat eater species from your land, another meat eater species will almost automatically become more numerous, filling the void that was created by removal of the big carnivore. For example, when Compound 1080 does such a good job of eliminating 90 percent of the coyote population, badger, bobcat, raccoon, and skunk all increase in num-

Thirteen-lined ground squirrel, the flickertail of the Dakotas. *Luther Goldman, U.S. Fish & Wildlife photo.*

bers in the area under consideration. Conversely, if there is a huge rodent (or game bird) population in an area, meat eaters will show up, out of nowhere, it seems, to take advantage of the opportunity. Just try starting a game farm to raise pheasant and quail and see how quickly the great horned owls find your location. Watch how quickly the fox comes slinking around the edges of the fencing, looking for a way to take advantage of the new opportunity.

3. Predators fill a necessary niche in the web of life. For example, when government trappers almost eliminated the mountain lion on the Kaibab in Arizona, deer numbers exploded to the point where the deer outstripped their available food and starved by the thousands.

4. Reduction of numbers of a particular species to protect another species almost never works. If the cost of removing a unit of predation is considered, then we must be dealing with a prey species that has a high value per unit. Otherwise, we are wasting money and time. However, when the unit cost of the species we seek to protect is very high—aha! Now we are approaching the realm of possibility.

5. If we are trying to protect a newly stocked population, then predator control is justified. First of all, the introduced stock does not have its feet on the ground; they are not ready to fend for themselves in a new environment. While they are getting accustomed to the environment, we must protect them or our original investment will be gone. If you are releasing pheasants on your land, yes, you should try to eliminate the larger predators to give your expensive stock a chance to get used to life in the wild. But remember that your efforts will not reduce the total "meat-eating capacity" of the mammals and raptors on your land; you will simply shift from foxes and coyotes, which are good pheasant predators, to skunk and badger, which are not as efficient on pheasants, but more efficient on some rodents.

6. At certain times, for limited purposes, predator control pays big dividends. Intensive aerial hunting of coyotes during antelope and mule deer-fawning seasons proved very effective in improving juvenile survivability in several western states. The value received per dollar expended for predator control will be much bigger at those times when the prey species is most vulnerable. Two months later, the value received for that same dollar of control work will be much less because the prey is less vulnerable.

7. Removal of a particular predator, or pair of predators, can be economically justified. The reduction of an entire population over the land area of a county can almost never be justified. In other words, aim your control method directly at the

offending individuals, whenever possible, not at the whole population.

How can you do your own predator control work? The State of Missouri finances an Extension Trapper Service, which will come to the Missouri farm and actually teach the farmer how to trap. The State of Missouri says that the system works well. Critics say that it simply has raised the level of predation loss the farmer will tolerate without screaming. An efficient steel trap will catch lots of fox, coyote, bobcat, mountain lion, raccoon, badger, skunk, and opossum—the rank amateur will go through several years of trial-and-error efforts before he is catching enough fur to pay for the gasoline for one trip to town.

If you are having lots of predation on game bird nests, you might want to set out a few dummy nests containing strychnine eggs. However, restrictive laws and difficulty of finding a source of supply for the strychnine make this a difficult row to hoe. However, the eggs, each containing half a tablet of strychnine alkaloid, used to be a remarkably specific and remarkably quick method of eliminating a local population of coons or skunks. Check with your County Agent to find out if such control methods are legal in your area and to see who can furnish the quick-acting, humane, strychnine.

Although many pest control operators in small towns advertise a certain ability in controlling predators, very few of them are really able to help out much. A farm boy who learned his trapping skills on the local muskrats and skunks will be better able to provide predator control—right where it is needed.

If raccoons are your troublemakers, it might pay to see if the local coonhound boys want to stage a nocturnal romp or two. They make the night air hideous with the sounds of yowling hounds, but they do put the coon up a tree where it can be shot out of the beam of light from a strong flashlight. Check on state laws before trying this one, though. No two states are alike.

Coyotes do the most damage during the early spring when they are feeding pups. At that time, it is possible to locate the coyote's den, toss a few smoke cartridges down it, and then fill the entrances—all of them—with dirt. The coyotes trapped below suffocate quickly. Same goes for foxes. A helpful bit of information about finding coyote dens is based on the fact that a hunting animal takes a meandering course, investigating each clump of grass that sticks up out of the snow, checking each scent post, smelling of every rock to see what has passed by. And when that same hunting animal has caught dinner, it heads *directly* for the den. So it follows that you find a straight line, note which way the animal is going, then head toward the den. If you lose the track, you swing out in a wide circle and find another direct track leading to the den. The intersection of those two lines of position will be very near the den. With coyotes it is well to remember that the mother moves the pups often, sometimes from nervousness, sometimes to escape the tremendous numbers of fleas and ticks that build up in the interior of the burrow.

Speaking of dens, it is well to remember that the evidence around a predatory animal's burrow may be very misleading. For example, a fox has a curious habit of picking up things and bringing them along home to the den. A rural home in North Dakota threw out eleven chicken heads, complete with beak, comb, and feathers. A week later, I found them all in a fox den. The foxes hadn't eaten them, but they had carried them along home. Now, if I hadn't recognized the source of those white Leghorns, I would have thought that those particular foxes were dining royally on white Leghorns to the great financial loss of the nearby farmer.

Coyotes often dine on carrion, and in the process, bring some of it home to the pups. The presence of a lamb's skull in the den may or may not mean that the coyotes have killed a lamb. The chances are at least fifty-fifty that the coyote dined on a lamb that died of other causes, then brought the incriminating evidence along home.

If the predator you seek to kill is a gray or red fox, or a coyote, you might wish to try your hand at calling them to within gun range. It is fairly easily done, if the animals have not been exposed to this danger before. If they haven't heard a predator call, they will surely come— once! You must make that first shot count, for it is increasingly difficult to fool the call-wise coyote or fox the second time. Tape-recorded calls will do a fine job of teaching you how to make the sounds you want to make. Electronic callers are available, but they are illegal in some states. Check the laws carefully on this. If you want to buy some of the tape recordings to teach yourself or to be used in an electronic caller, we heartily recommend dealing with Johnny Stewart Game Calls, Inc., P.O. Box 7594, Waco,

TX 76710. Not only does he sell a quality product, but Johnny Stewart is a practical field man who has developed his calls and his methods in the wild. He makes them work and he can tell you how to make them work.

For a much more detailed description of predator control methods and an evaluation of the role of predators in the natural scheme, you may wish to read my book, *Coyotes: Predators and Survivors,* which was published by Stone Wall Press in 1983. Your librarian or bookseller can find it easily by its ISBN number, ISBN 0-913276-42-1, or by its Library of Congress Card Number, 82-062895.

To sum up my personal beliefs, based on fifty years of being close to the problem, I would only repeat:

1. It is almost never worthwhile to attempt to reduce the numbers of a predator species in the hopes that it will increase the numbers of a prey population. Quail have existed with foxes for millennia—unless we bollix it up too badly, they will continue to coexist with foxes.

2. To protect high-value prey species, it *is* often worthwhile to aim control measures at one individual animal, or at one breeding pair, or even at one farm or ranch. The ideal is to *get* the offending individual, not to try to exterminate a species.

3. Given good nesting and escape cover, the avian species will not be seriously hurt by a predator population. Habitat is the key!

14

Crawfish as a Farm Crop

When the English forced the French colonists out of their homes in Acadia—the Maritime Provinces of Eastern Canada—they took with them a love of good eating and a fond remembrance of crustacea, which had formed a part of their diet in France centuries ago and in Acadia.

These Acadians settled in Louisiana and are called Cajuns (a corruption of Acadian) to this day. They also rank among the finest cooks in the world, specializing in seafoods and fresh-water crustaceans. "Fresh-water crustaceans" is a fancy way of saying crayfish, or crawfish, or crawdads, or mud bugs.

No matter what you call the diminutive lobster of the swampy waters of Louisiana, he is the basis for crawfish *etouffe*, crawfish *bisque*, and a hundred other dishes—and that, my friend, is eating!

They have been harvested from the wild for more than 100 years, but their cultivation as a farm crop is relatively new, dating only to 1959, when a Louisiana Department of Wildlife and Fisheries biologist named Percy Viosca built the first experimental crawfish-rearing pond. It would have been hard to predict what has happened since! Today we have around 1,500 crawfish-farming operations, raising as much as 3,000 pounds of crawfish per acre and adding up to a cash crop in the neighborhood of sixty million dollars. There are approximately 100,000 acres devoted to crawfish farming in Louisiana. Let's take a look at the gourmet crustacean that is the basis for all of this activity.

There are more than 300 species of crawfish in the world; about 100 species in the United States. For our purposes, however, there are only two—the Red

Youngsters take a close look at the small fresh-water lobster that has a big reputation in Louisiana. *Bob Dennie photo.*

Swamp crawfish and the White River Crawfish. Both species find conditions most to their liking in the Sportsman's Paradise state of Louisiana. To be specific, they prefer the Atchafalaya Basin of Louisiana, where natural conditions have prepared the world's greatest crawfish farm.

Louisiana's Department of Wildlife and Fisheries has continued their interest in the development of the crawfish re-

Here are the basic ingredients for all sorts of delicious eating. *Bob Dennie photo.*

source, ably aided and abetted by the research units of LSU, the University of Southwestern Louisiana and Southern University.

The Cooperative Extension Service of Louisiana is well versed in the lore of the crawdad, and more and more farmers are learning that there is more than a tasty meal to be had in the crawfish swamps, there is also a good profit in cash money. The Extension Service provides information to Louisiana farmers, showing them how to add another cash crop to their farming rotation of rice, soybeans, or sugar cane.

Because Louisiana is a great rice-producing area, the marshy fields were already there, and crawfish and rice go together in the swamp as well as they do on the table of epicures.

The Red Swamp variety shares the ancestral paradise of crawdads, the Atchafalaya Basin, with the White River species. The Red has proved itself slightly more tolerant of high-water temperatures and low dissolved oxygen conditions, so it is now the preferred species for commercial farming. The Red variety now makes up about 90 percent of the commercial catch and is preferred because of its dark red color after boiling and because the edible fat is a good yellow-orange color.

THROUGH THE YEAR WITH THE CRAWFISH

Breeding occurs year around, with waves of recruitment in September, January, and March. The male deposits sperm in the external receptacle of the female. The sperm are held in this receptacle until the eggs are laid. Shortly after the breeding, a few crawfish females will go out on shore and "dig in" to form their burrows. At this time they are very vulnerable to raccoons, wading birds, and many other predators, each of which has its own recipe for *etouffe*.

Under farming conditions, the ponds are drained slowly in May and June. As the water levels go down, the females dig in and form their burrows, as much as 36 inches deep. Sometimes the more amorous males will accompany a female into a burrow, and it is thought that additional breeding takes place at that time, although it does not seem to be necessary for the successful fertilization of the female's eggs.

For several months the female rests in that burrow, safe from all predation, awaiting the return of the water levels to soften the mud plug she has placed on top of her burrow and allow her to come back into the watery world.

The crawfish ponds are flooded again in September. Eggs are laid in the burrows. Fertilized eggs are held under the female's tail, stuck on by a gluey substance called glair during the first recruitment of the summer.

Crawdad eggs hatch in fourteen to twenty-one days, depending upon water temperatures. Fertility is high, and the red crawfish spawn numbers range from 200 to 900, depending upon the size of the spawning female. Each of the crawbabies is less than half an inch in length and about as big around as a pencil lead.

The successful crawfish farm now provides an abundance of water, essential for good survival of the young. The young immediately begin to feed and to grow at a fast rate.Microscopic organisms form a large part of the diet at this stage, although vegetation is a necessity at all stages of crawfish life.

During this growing stage, pond temperatures ideally are maintained at 70°F to 85°F. Under optimum conditions of water temperature and abundant food, young crawfish reach market size sixty to ninety days after hatching.

Mortality is heavy during the adolescent period. Fish of all sizes feed heavily on them; small sunfish eating the newly hatched, bass loving the intermediate size and even tackling the fully grown adults. Bullfrogs dine heavily on the small young, along with herons, bitterns, snakes, grackles, rails, coots, and almost every other organism that lives in or near the water. Raccoons are expert fishermen for the crawdads when they frequent the shallow waters close to the banks of the pond, along with crows and other opportunistic diners of the wild. Aquatic insects and beetles are also significant predators on the tiny crawfish at this stage of their development.

Food Requirements

Crawfish will eat dead and living plant and animal matter. While they seem to be ingesting only plant material at some stages, there are hundreds of varieties of aquatic organisms that are feeding on the plant growth and are taken in along with the plant food. They do not seem to prefer rotten food; they will leave it to go to fresh meat or fish almost every time. Big plants, such as cattails and water hyacinth, are not utilized at all and are actually harmful in the crawfish pond. Decaying vegetation is a bad thing, as it uses up the available oxygen (which may already be in short supply due to high water temperatures) and causes the crawfish to climb out of the water and breathe air for long periods. At this stage, losses to predators are very heavy. The crawdad *can* breathe out of water, but he is an aquatic animal.

Water Quality

There is much ongoing research into the qualities a water area must have for optimum crawdad production. Good crops have been obtained in waters varying from acid (pH of 5.8) to alkaline (pH of 8.2). Dissolved oxygen content should also stay well above 1.5 parts per million and most crawfish operators begin recirculating and reaerating water when the dissolved oxygen content drops to 3 parts per million.

Remember always that the bulk of crawfish food is vegetable in nature.

When it is necessary to provide more water to the ponds, a lot of caution is required. Water from a deep well is usually just what the crawfish ordered, but if the supply is a free-flowing bayou or irrigation ditch, the crawfish farmer must be certain that this supply does not contain pesticides that will kill the required emergent vegetation and that it is free of any toxicants that will kill the crawfish itself.

It used to be true that treated seed could not be used to start rice crops in areas destined for crawfish production. However, today's improved methods of treating seeds have removed this worry.

Timing of the crawfish commercial crop is very important. Every crawfish farmer knows that he will get a better price if his crop is ready before the wild crop is harvested, but that he will face lower prices and a reduced demand if his crop comes off at the same time that thousands of Louisiana gourmets are out harvesting the bounty of the Atchafalaya Basin, using dip nets in the roadside ditches, traps in

the deeper waters—at times it seems like everyone in Louisiana is seining or netting the delicious 'dads.

Want to Try Crawfish Farming?

Although Louisiana-style crawfish farming has spread to neighboring states and across the seas to Spain (with initial brood stock from Cajun Country), the hard facts are that Louisiana is singularly blessed with the right combination of long growing season, lack of killing frosts, rich alluvial soil, water everywhere, and the best foods for crawfish growing wild. It would seem that the Sportsman's Paradise has very nearly a monopoly on crawfish farming. Crawfish farming is the largest commercial crustacean aquaculture operation in the world. But if you feel that the conditions on your land are near enough to the Louisiana ideal to give it a try, here are a few recommendations:

1. Get in touch with the Louisiana Department of Wildlife and Fisheries, Box 15570, Baton Rouge, LA 70895, and ask for the publication entitled *Crawfish Farming*. Read it carefully. Contact your County Agent for an on-site survey of your potential pond site. If you still feel like trying your hand—

2. Design a pond of 40 to 60 acres, which can be drained and refilled easily with "safe" water.

3. Try to eliminate large water plants such as water hyacinth and cattail.

4. Plan ahead, so that *when* the crawfish farming is a success, you'll be able to expand the operation into something that is economically viable. Remember, there is a very large labor requirement in crawfish farming, and this limits the size of the operation you can handle.

5. Talk to successful crawfish farmers, visit their operations, and listen and learn—this is not an easy farming operation you are about to get into. It has to be done right to succeed.

If you still want to get into the business, more power to you.

Cooking the Crawfish

After you harvest your crustaceans, here are some good ideas of what to do with them, courtesy of the magazine

Louisiana Conservationist: Recipes by Marian "Pie" Pendley:

Crawfish Pie
> 2 lbs. crawfish tails
> 1 cup chopped onions
> 1 cup chopped celery
> 2 cloves garlic, minced
> 1 stick margarine
> 1 can cream of mushroom soup
> 1 large can evaporated milk
> 1 tsp. cornstarch
> 2 tbsps. minced green onions
> 2 tbsps. minced parsley
> salt and pepper to taste
> 1 unbaked piecrust and top

Peel crawfish tails, set aside. Saute onions, celery, and garlic in margarine until thoroughly cooked. Add soup, milk, and cornstarch that has been diluted in a little water. Cook about 10 minutes, stirring occasionally. Add crawfish tails, green onions, and parsley and cook until tender. Pour filling over bottom crust. Cover with top crust and cut slits in top. Bake at 350°F for about 15 minutes. Reduce heat to 300°F and bake until golden brown. MMMMMMMMM!

Crawfish Etouffe

> 2 lbs. crawfish tails
> 2 large onions
> 1 stalk celery
> 2 cloves garlic
> 2 medium-size bell peppers
> 1 stick butter, melted
> 1 tbsp. flour
> 1 cup water
> 2 tbsps. chopped parsley
> 2 tbsps. chopped onion tops
> salt and cayenne pepper to taste.

Mince onions, celery, garlic, and bell peppers. Saute minced vegetables in melted butter until soft and clear. Stir in flour. Add crawfish tails and fat (if available). Season with salt and cayenne pepper. Add one cup of hot water according to desired thickness of gravy. Let simmer in a covered pot until tails are tender. Add parsley and onion tops. Serve over rice.

Boiled Crawfish

> 25 pounds (approximately) crawfish per pot
> 2 boxes salt
> 3 lemons, halved
> 3 onions, halved
> 2 boxes crab boil
> small, unpeeled red potatoes (optional)
> five ears of corn (optional)

Got all of that ready? Wash the crawfish and discard any dead ones. In a 10-gallon pot, bring to rolling boil about 4 gallons of water with all ingredients except crawfish. Add crawfish, cover and heat until steam escapes from underneath the lid (12 to 15 minutes). If not quite tender, steam a few more minutes, but do not overcook.

You can cook approximately 25 pounds per pot and a second batch can be cooked in the same water. The potatoes and corn are delicious when eaten along with the crawfish.

Crawfish Dip

  2 cups boiled crawfish tails
½ pint sour cream
  1 8-ounce package cream cheese
½ cup celery
½ cup finely minced onions
   salt and pepper to taste
   juice of 1 lemon
   paprika

Mince crawfish tails and set aside. Combine sour cream with cream cheese. Add celery, onions, salt, pepper, and lemon juice to taste. Add the minced crawfish to the cheese mixture. Sprinkle with paprika on top and serve.

Although my family name is French, it is not Acadian French. I cannot legitimately lay claim to any knowledge of crawfish or the Cajun magic used to prepare memorable meals out of these succulent little "mud bugs." For their help in preparing this chapter, I gratefully wish to thank my good friends, Bob and Gail Dennie, legitimate Louisiana residents, at whose table I ate the finest crawfish cooking it has ever been my privilege to batten upon. I also wish to acknowledge the contribution I have drawn from the writings of Dr. Larry de la Bretonne, who is an acknowledged expert on crawfish. He and his colleagues at the Louisiana Cooperative Extension Service did much to fill in the very large gaps in my knowledge of crawfish.

15

State and National Departments and Agencies

THE UNITED STATES FISH AND WILDLIFE SERVICE

Strictly speaking, the U.S. Fish and Wildlife Service is the agency set up to handle the management of migratory waterfowl and to enforce regulations that have to do with crossing state lines. For example, the Lacey Act puts the federal government right in the middle of enforcing laws concerning transportation of game across state lines.

However, over the years the federal agency has assumed a far greater role in the management of fish and game resources. This has been made possible because the agency that controls the purse strings also controls the spending of that money. When the state agency has to depend upon the federal government for supplies of fish for stocking, it is easy for

the federal agency to control policy with regard to fish stocking. The federal excise tax on sporting arms and ammunition (Pittman-Robertson funds) is disbursed by the U.S. Fish and Wildlife Service in actuality, because the Fish and Wildlife Service will only okay for 75 percent reimbursement those previously approved projects that conform to federal notions of good wildlife management.

Several national administrations have attempted to turn back to the states some parts of this federal agency's work. For example, there is a recurring attempt to turn over to the states the administration of the national fish hatcheries. This has failed in the past for the simple reason that most of the states could not afford to operate those hatcheries. As long as Uncle Sam has the money to produce fish, the states want those fish in their management plans, but they cannot afford to raise the fish themselves. If the federal government could return the fish hatcheries to state control, along with a source of funding, it would be a popular move, despite the excellent job done by the federal hatcheries—but there seems to be little chance of that happening.

Regional Offices

Speaking as one who spent a large part of my working life in the employ of the U.S. Fish and Wildlife Service, I must admit that this is a singularly hard-to-contact agency. Your best bet is to work through their regional offices.

These regional offices are located in Boston, Minneapolis, Atlanta, Portland, Denver, and Albuquerque, with a slightly less than regional setup in Anchorage to handle the great state of Alaska.

Region 1, U.S. Fish and Wildlife Service
500 N.E. Multnomah Street
Portland, OR 97232
This office supervises the agencies' operations in Washington, Oregon, California, Nevada, Idaho, and Hawaii.

Region 2, U.S. Fish and Wildlife Service
500 Gold Avenue SW
Albuquerque, NM 87103
This office supervises the agencies' operations in New Mexico, Arizona, Texas, and Oklahoma.

Region 3, U.S. Fish and Wildlife Service
Federal Building, Fort Snelling
Twin Cities, MN 55111
This office supervises the agencies' operations in Iowa, Minnesota, Illinois, In-

diana, Ohio, Michigan, Missouri, and Wisconsin.

Region 4, U.S. Fish and Wildlife Service
Richard B. Russell Federal Building
Atlanta, GA 30303
This office supervises the agencies' operations in Alabama, Arkansas, Florida, Georgia, Kentucky, Louisiana, Mississippi, North Carolina, South Carolina, Tennessee, and the Virgin Islands.

Region 5, U.S. Fish and Wildlife Service
One Gateway Center
Newton Corner, MA 02158
This office supervises the agencies' operations in Massachusetts, Delaware, Connecticut, Vermont, New Hampshire, Maine, Rhode Island, New York, Pennsylvania, Virginia, New Jersey, Maryland, and West Virginia.

Region 6, U.S. Fish and Wildlife Service
Box 25486, Denver Federal Center
Denver, CO 80225
This office supervises the agencies' operations in Colorado, Kansas, Montana, North Dakota, Nebraska, South Dakota, Utah, and Wyoming.
The national office in Washington is addressed simply:

U.S. Fish and Wildlife Service
Department of the Interior
Washington, DC 20240

Matters concerning you as a landowner may be referred to very many different parts of the federal agency. For this reason it is best to direct your inquiry first to the Public Affairs Officer of your regional office, and ask him to help you contact the appropriate office.

STATE CONSERVATION AGENCIES

Some states call it the Game and Fish Department; others refer to the State Conservation Department; and still others call it the Department of Natural Resources. No matter what its name is, here is the correct address—at the time this book went to press—for you to contact if you want the wildlife managers of your state.

ALABAMA

Department of Conservation and
   Natural Resources
64 North Union Street
Montgomery, AL 36130
Telephone: 205-832-6300

ALASKA

Department of Fish and Game
Box 3-2000
Juneau, AK 99802
Telephone: 907-465-4100

ARIZONA

Game and Fish Department
2222 West Greenway
Phoenix, AZ 85023
Telephone: 602-942-3000

ARKANSAS

Game and Fish Commission
#2 Natural Resources Drive
Little Rock, AR 72205
Telephone: 501-223-6300

CALIFORNIA

California Department of Fish and
   Game
1416 Ninth Street
Sacramento, CA 95814
Telephone: 916-445-3531

COLORADO

Division of Wildlife
6060 Broadway
Denver, CO 80216
Telephone: 303-825-1192

CONNECTICUT

Department of Environmental
   Protection
State Office Building
165 Capitol Avenue
Hartford, CT 06115
Telephone: 203-566-5599

DELAWARE

Division of Fish and Wildlife
P.O. Box 1401
Dover, DE 19901
Telephone: 302-736-4431

FLORIDA

Game and Fresh Water Fish
   Commission
620 South Meridian Street
Tallahassee, FL 32301
Telephone: 904-488-1960

GEORGIA

Department of Natural Resources
270 Washington Street SW
Atlanta, GA 30334
Telephone: 404-656-3530

HAWAII

Division of Forestry and Wildlife
1151 Punchbowl Street
Honolulu, Hawaii 96813
Telephone: 808-548-2861

IDAHO

Fish and Game Department
Box 25

Boise, ID 83707
Telephone: 208-334-3700

ILLINOIS

Department of Conservation
Lincoln Tower Plaza
524 S. Second Street
Springfield, IL 62706
Telephone: 217-782-6302

INDIANA

Department of Natural Resources
608 State Office Building
Indianapolis, IN 46204
Telephone: 317-232-4200

IOWA

State Conservation Commission
Wallace State Office Building
Des Moines, IA 50319
Telephone: 515-281-5145

KANSAS

Fish and Game Commission
Box 54A, Route 2
Pratt, KS 67124
Telephone: 316-672-5911

KENTUCKY

Department of Fish and Wildlife
  Resources
#1 State Game Farm Road
Frankfort, KY 40601
Telephone: 502-564-3400

LOUISIANA

Department of Wildlife and Fisheries
400 Royal Street
New Orleans, LA 70130
Telephone: 504-568-5612

MAINE

Department of Inland Fisheries and
  Wildlife

284 State Street Station #41
Augusta, ME 04333
Telephone: 207-289-2766

MARYLAND

Department of Natural Resources
Tawes State Office Building
Annapolis, MD 21401
Telephone: 301-269-2752

MASSACHUSETTS

Department of Fisheries, Wildlife, and
  Recreational Vehicles
100 Cambridge Street
Boston, MA 02202
Telephone: 617-727-3141

MICHIGAN

Department of Natural Resources
Box 30028
Lansing, MI 48909
Telephone: 517-373-1214

MINNESOTA

Department of Natural Resources
300 Centennial Building
658 Cedar Street
St. Paul, MN 55155
Telephone: 612-296-3336

MISSISSIPPI

Department of Wildlife Conservation
P.O. Box 451
Jackson, MS 39205
Telephone: 601-961-5311

MISSOURI

Department of Conservation
Box 180
Jefferson City, MO 65102
Telephone: 314-751-4115

MONTANA

Department of Fish Wildlife and Parks

1420 E. Sixth Street
Helena, MT 59601
Telephone: 406-449-2535

NEBRASKA
Game and Parks Commission
Box 30370
Lincoln, NE 68503
Telephone: 402-464-0641

NEVADA
Department of Wildlife
Box 10678
Reno, NV 89520
Telephone: 702-784-6214

NEW HAMPSHIRE
Fish and Game Department
34 Bridge Street
Concord, NH 03301
Telephone: 603-271-3421

NEW JERSEY
Division of Fish Game and Wildlife
CN 400
Trenton, NJ 08625
Telephone: 609-292-9450

NEW MEXICO
Game and Fish Department
Villagra Building
Santa Fe, NM 87503
Telephone: 505-827-7911

NEW YORK
Department of Environmental
  Conservation
50 Wolf Road
Albany, NY 12233
Telephone: 518-457-5400

NORTH CAROLINA
Wildlife Resources Commission
512 N. Salisbury

Raleigh, NC 27611
Telephone: 919-733-3391

NORTH DAKOTA
State Game and Fish Department
2121 Lovett Avenue
Bismarck, ND 58505
Telephone: 701-224-2180

OHIO
Department of Natural Resources
Fountain Square
Columbus, OH 43224
Telephone: 614-265-6300

OKLAHOMA
Department of Wildlife Conservation
Box 53465
Oklahoma City, OK 73152
Telephone: 405-521-3851

OREGON
Department of Fish and Wildlife
Box 3503
Portland, OR 97208
Telephone: 503-229-5551

PENNSYLVANIA
Game Commission
Box 1567
Harrisburg, PA 17120
Telephone: 717-787-3633
                    and/or
Fish Commission
Box 1673
Harrisburg, PA 17105
Telephone: 717-787-2579

RHODE ISLAND
Department of Environmental
  Management
83 Park Street
Providence, RI 02903
Telephone: 401-277-6800

SOUTH CAROLINA

Wildlife and Marine Resources
    Department
Box 167
Columbia, SC 29202
Telephone: 803-758-0059

SOUTH DAKOTA

Game, Fish and Parks Department
445 E. Capitol
Pierre, SD 57501-3185
Telephone: 605-773-3485

TENNESSEE

Wildlife Resources Agency
Box 40747
Nashville, TN 37204
Telephone: 615-741-1512

TEXAS

Parks and Wildlife Department
4200 Smith School Road
Austin, TX 78744
Telephone: 512-479-4800

UTAH

Division of Wildlife Resources
1596 W.N. Temple
Salt Lake City, UT 84116
Telephone: 801-533-9333

VERMONT

Fish and Game Department
Montpelier, VT 05602
Telephone: 802-828-3371

VIRGINIA

Commission of Game and Inland
    Fisheries
Box 11104
Richmond, VA 23230
Telephone: 804-257-1000

WASHINGTON

Department of Game
600 N. Capitol Way
Olympia, WA 98504
Telephone: 206-753-5700

WEST VIRGINIA

Department of Natural Resources
1800 Washington Street E
Charleston, WV 25305
Telephone: 304-348-2754

WISCONSIN

Department of Natural Resources
Box 7921
Madison, WI 53707
Telephone: 608-266-2621

WYOMING

Game and Fish Department
Cheyenne, WY 82002
Telephone: 307-777-7631

OTHER SOURCES OF INFORMATION

When you need answers to questions, when you do not know which path is the better one—where do you turn for more information?

1. Ask your County Agricultural Extension Agent. He is choice number one.

2. Contact your State Game and Fish Department, or State Conservation Department, or whatever they call it in your state. No matter what the name, this is the agency with the responsiblity for managing your state's fish and wildlife. Always ask if there is a publication available to answer your questions. Many state conservation agencies have worked up a great library of information to help them spread the gospel of good wildlife man-

agement. They may have a leaflet devoted to just exactly what you want to know.

3. Talk to landowners who have succeeded in doing what you plan to do. If you intend to stock quail on your land, get the names and addresses of others who have received such planting stock. Visit them in person, and ask a lot of questions.

4. Subscribe to the magazine of your state game and fish department.

5. Read! Read everything you can get your hands on about the subject of wildlife management. University libraries are excellent sources of information, and today's modern information retrieval systems will greatly facilitate your search for exactly the right information.

It is wise to do some reading on the subject before you contact the expert and ask for his advice. He will appreciate the fact that you have taken the trouble to get yourself acquainted with the basics of the problem, because that will reduce the time he will have to spend with you going over the basics.

There is a tremendous library of writing about the management of fish and wildlife. Here is our attempt to list some of the best reference works available for your consideration, grouped roughly according to subject matter.

Suggested Reading

Attracting Songbirds

Attracting and Feeding Birds, Conservation Bulletin Number 1. Order from U.S. Fish and Wildlife Service, Department of the Interior, Washington, DC 20240.

Attracting Birds: From the Prairies to the Atlantic, by Vernon Davison. Published by Thomas Y. Crowell Company, New York. Check your local library for this one.

Audubon Guide to Attracting Birds. Published by Doubleday.

Beginner's Guide to Attracting Birds, by Leon A. Hausman. Cornerstone Library, New York. In your library?

Bird Houses, Baths and Feeding Shelters. Cranbrook Institute, Bloomfield Hills, Michigan.

Birds of North America, by Robins, Brunn, and Zim. Golden Press, New York.

Guide to Birds, by Roger Tory Peterson. Houghton Mifflin Company, Boston, Mass.

How to Attract Birds, by Robert S. Lemmon. The Country Life Press, Garden City, New York.

How to Watch Birds, by Roger Barton. McGraw Hill Book Company, New York.

Big Game Animals

The Elk of North America, by Olaus Murie. The Stackpole Company, Harrisburg, Pa.

Hunting Pronghorned Antelope, by Bert Popowski. The Stackpole Company, Harrisburg, Pa.

The Deer of North America, edited by Walter P. Harris. The Stackpole Company, Harrisburg, Pa.

Big Game of North America. Obtainable from the Wildlife Management Institute.

Small Game Animals

John Madson's excellent leaflet of 56 pages is easily the best thing around. Entitled simply *The Cottontail Rabbit*, it was published by the Conservation Department of Olin Mathieson Chemical Corporation, the parent company for Winchester. It is no longer available from that source, but good libraries have a copy of it.

Coyotes: Predators and Survivors, by Charles L. Cadieux. Distributed by Winchester Press, New York. Good discussion of the effects of coyote predation upon other forms of wildlife, including deer, antelope, and upland game birds.

Upland Game Birds

Improving Your Forested Lands for Ruffed Grouse, by Gordon W. Gullion. Published by the Ruffed Grouse Society, Coraopolis, Pa. Perhaps the best short course in ruffed grouse management.

The Mourning Dove, by John Madson for the Olin Mathieson Chemical Corporation. No longer available from the publisher, but still the best thing ever done on mourning doves. Check with a good library. This is another in the classic series that John produced while working for the parent company of Winchester.

Pheasants in North America, edited by Durward Allen. Published by the Stackpole Company, Harrisburg, Pa.

The Ruffed Grouse, by Gardiner Bump and Walter Crissey. Available from the New York Conservation Department.

Waterfowl

Goosehunting, by Charles L. Cadieux. Available from Winchester Press in hardcover and from Stoegers in paperback.

Waterfowl Tomorrow. Published by the U.S. Fish and Wildlife Service, Department of the Interior. Now out of print, but found in most big libraries.

Wildlife Management in General

Game Management, by Aldo Leopold. Charles Scribners Sons, New York. This ancient classic belongs in every wildlifer's library.

A Sand County Almanac, by Aldo Leopold. Oxford University Press. This is mostly good philosophy; it will not give you guidance in management itself but will supply the philosophical basis for today's management.

Practical Wildlife Management, by George V. Burger. Winchester Press, New York.

Wildlife Management Techniques, by Robert Giles. The Wildlife Society, Washington, D.C. Costs $15, but worth more.

Our Wildlife Legacy, by Durward L. Allen. Published by Funk and Wagnalls, New York. One of my favorite source books.

The Arena of Life, by Milne, Lorus, and Margery. Doubleday Natural History Press.

Waterfowl Tomorrow, sort of a yearbook assembled by the U.S. Fish and Wildlife Service long time ago, but still pertinent.

These Are the Endangered, by Charles L. Cadieux. Available from Winchester Press; treats of the endangered species of wildlife in North America, including thorough discussions of the legislation that affects the future of these endangered species.

16

Trapping

You may decide to trap fur bearers on your land for several reasons. The most common and most logical is to make a buck or two. The prices for furs fluctuate greatly—I have sold beaver pelts for $54 and for $6. And the $6 furs were better quality than the $54 ones.

The second reason for trapping fur bearers is to remove meat eaters that you feel are beating you to the game birds or animals that you wanted to eat. This is just another way of saying "predator control," of course.

A third reason for steel trapping is to remove nuisance animals, such as the beaver that cut down your apple trees and dam up streams that then flood your hay meadows. Or it may mean removing a badger that has been digging big holes in your pastures, holes that a high-priced horse might step into and break a leg.

The most commonly trapped fur bearer is the muskrat, which has financed the first dates for many farm boys. If you can avoid cutting into muskrat houses to do your trapping, you will be well advised to do so. Cutting into them may cause loss of your muskrat population, and that is not a wise idea for anyone who hopes to have a continuing income from the 'skrats. Of course, if you can locate the underwater entrance to the house and place a trap there—that's fine.

As a school boy, I had great luck with the carrot bank set. Using #2 traps—in good condition they are plenty big for any muskrat—I placed a carrot high on the upper end of an emerging log or sloping bank, then placed the trap below it where the 'skrat would have to put his heavy foot enroute to the carrot dinner. I had a heavy rock—about the size of your head—wired to the trap frame from the bottom. When the startled muskrat felt the trap grab him around the leg, he instinctively dove in, heading for deep water and safety. But the big rock fell into the water with him, of course, and held him under where he quickly drowned. No, I do not claim that drowning is humane and painless, but neither are long hours sitting in a trap, trying to chew off the foot. The drowning is quick and it saves the catch for me to skin and market, and that is the name of the game. Skinning a muskrat is about as easy as peeling off a sock. The moves are strikingly similar and both end up inside out. The muskrat should be stretched over a board, fur side in, and left to dry in a cool—but not sunlit— place. Scrape away all fat and blood while the pelt is still fresh to avoid "burning" the pelt as it dries.

Most landowners control the right of trespass on their lands to trap. If you are going to do your own trapping, be sure to wait until furs are prime and you will get the best return for your money. Cropping muskrat marshes is not easy work. You can safely remove as many as half of the muskrats each winter and still have a good, self-sustaining population, for the muskrat is a ready producer.

Mink are usually travelers and seldom stick to one small wintering area. However, if you know that a mink is using your water areas, you can often do well with blind sets of #2 traps placed where they will force the mink to pass between two stones and, in so doing, put his foot in a trap. The muskrat is one of the natural foods of the mink, and you may have to trap your mink early to preserve the harvestable muskrats. However, one mink pelt in good condition will pay for the loss of a dozen good muskrats.

Their natural curiosity can be used against the raccoon and the bobcat, but in completely different ways. The raccoon is apt to investigate any shiny object placed in the water, where he can reach it. In getting into position to reach for it, the coon is maneuvered into stepping on a trap, which should be a #3 Victor or Newhouse, as big boar coons are very strong. Coon trappers also take advantage of the coon's own cleverness in reaching in to get things. They build a small opening in the rock, or in boards, into which the coon will reach, in an attempt to reach a piece of corn, or a frog impaled on a stick, or a piece of sardine (right out of the can). When he reaches in, the trap snaps shuts on the reaching "hand" and the coon is yours.

One of my favorite sets for bobcats takes advantage of curiosity also. The bobcat doesn't trust his nose but is a hunter who depends upon his excellent eyesight. I hang a chicken wing on a string, over the trap, just out of reach for a big bobcat. Intrigued by the wing floating in the air, turning and twisting in the wind, the bobcat attempts to get close enough to swat at it with a front paw. In so doing, he steps in the correctly placed trap.

Bobcats seldom fight a trap but will usually sit calmly waiting for the trapper to come. Once I got a real scare. I found the trap gone and the trap chain in plain sight 10 feet ahead of me on the trail. I moved toward the trap chain and saw that the drag was buried tightly against some stout branches where it could not be pulled free. Then my eyes followed the chain, up and over a branch and back toward me. Slowly I turned my head to the right and met the bobcat eyeball to eyeball, about 18 inches distant. He never made a sound. I let out my pent-up breath in a soft "Whewwww!" then shot him behind the ear with my .22 rifle.

Beaver can be trapped easily under the ice. Simply find a logical place to chop a hole through the ice and lower a trap to the bottom, under the food cache. The beaver swims to this underwater food storage and stands up to start chewing off the tender branch. He steps on the trap. The trap chain, if long enough, can be led up through another hole and fastened to a crossbar frozen across the entry hole in the ice. Beaver can also be trapped routinely by finding the entrance to the beaver lodge and setting a trap at the spot where he stops swimming and puts his foot down to start walking up the tunnel into his lodge. These sets have the advantage of quickly drowning the beaver. An expert can use beaver castors—the scent-manufacturing glands that perform some unknown sexual function for the beaver, and that serve as the basis for some perfumes—not only to catch beaver but actually to determine which sex and which age beaver he will take in the trap. Professional trapper Dean Badger proved this to me many winters ago in South Dakota. On a bet, he took an old male in one trap, a young male in a second, and a female in the third—just as he said he would. The castor from an old beaver was used to bring the old patriarch on the run to fight off an intruder in his watery domain. The scent of a young female brought the young male to investigate, even though it was not breeding time. The third set, which took a female beaver, was baited with "different male" castor, according to Dean. I can't explain the complexities of beaver castors, but I do know that they do attract beaver in wondrous ways.

Number 3 Newhouse and #3 Victor traps will handle almost all trapping chores. Those with offset jaws are more apt to retain the animal taken than those with straight jaws. The offset jaw does not often break the bone in either front or back leg, but still grabs securely. The broken bone is often wrung off, twisted off, or chewed off, allowing the animals to escape and become exceedingly trap-shy. Both beavers and coyotes are good at regaining their freedom in this way.

Out my way, trappers describe an ugly woman as being "coyote ugly." That means that the poor woman is so ugly that a man, upon waking in the morning with this ugly gal sleeping on his arm, will chew off his own arm, rather than wake her up by moving. Now, friends, *that* is ugly!

In addition to the steel leghold trap, there are four other possibilities that have a place in your trapping plans. Number one is the ancient, tried, and still effective, snare. Made of strong wire, the easily made snare is highly effective against coyotes that have learned to avoid steel traps. Placed where the coyote enters a "sheep-proof" fence, it takes its share of coyotes.

Second, you should think about the Conibear trap, which is more difficult to conceal and more difficult to set, but which has the advantage of killing its victim with a humane blow, rather than with a lingering death in the trap. It has never gained full acceptance by commercial trappers, although some swear by it. In the larger sizes, it is dangerous to children and should not be used in heavily populated areas. However, where the trap will not be within reach of children, it is a possibility. Another drawback of the Conibear is that you can release a house cat, a domestic dog, or even an unwanted wild animal from a leghold trap, but when the Conibear is operating properly, it is not possible to release the animal—that animal is dead.

The third possibility is only recommended for beaver. It is the clamshell trap, which is baited in the center of the clamshell, which is lying out flat. The beaver trips the trigger when he starts to eat the bait, and the clamshell springs shut. The big advantage is that the clamshell seldom injures the animal, and that animal is a good prospect for transplanting to an area that suits him better. It is not advised for quicker, more agile animals. It will usually catch a lightning-quick fox or an agile coyote in its jaws, rather than completely inside. The coyote then either is killed or fights its way out of the trap. Because the clamshell trap is cumbersome and expensive, it is not recommended for purchase. However, your state game and fish department may use them for trapping and transplanting beaver. For that one job they are perfect.

Havahart traps are simply a refinement of the old "figure 4" box trap we set for squirrels when we were kids. We seldom caught the squirrels, and the Havahart does not have a high percentage of success when compared with either the Conibear or the leghold trap. The reason is that most animals are leery of entering a confined space, and this they must do for the Havahart to work properly. It has the very great advantage of not causing any pain or suffering to any animal. The animal so taken can be moved safely, without the trapper worrying about being bitten by the trapped animal. It is possible to trap skunks and remove them to a distant place and turn them loose, if that is your aim, and if you are willing to risk the chance of being hit with the skunk's very effective first line of defense—which is very offensive. If you wish to trap for cash income, the steel leghold trap is the answer. None of the others, with the exception of the wire snare, is worth the time and trouble. The steel leghold will out-trap the other kinds five or ten to one.

Fur trapping is an ancient and honorable profession. Trappers were the mountain men who opened the west to colonization. By necessity, the trapper is a good outdoorsman, a keen observer, and a student of animal behavior. Trapping is not easily learned. A day on the trapline with an expert is worth a hundred books of instruction. However, instruction books are available, and a subscription to the magazine *Fur-Fish-Game* is a good investment for the amateur trapper.

17

Posting Land Against Trespass

There are many different answers to the question, "How should I post my land?"

These answers range from ABSOLUTELY NO HUNTING OR FISHING UNDER ANY CIRCUMSTANCES, EVER. KEEP OUT! THIS MEANS YOU

to

NO HUNTING OR FISHING WITHOUT WRITTEN PERMISSION OF THE OWNER.

to

NO HUNTING OR FISHING WITHOUT PERMISSION.

to

HUNTING OR FISHING WITH PERMISSION ONLY.

to

PARK YOUR CAR IN MY FARMYARD AND ASK. MAYBE I'LL LET YOU HUNT OR FISH.

to

HUNTERS WELCOME. PLEASE RESPECT PRIVATE PROPERTY.

to

HUNTERS AND FISHERMEN WELCOME.

That last sign is almost extinct now. It was popular during the years when the South Dakota farmer felt that the pheasant was a nuisance that was destroying his crops. It was also popular when crow roosts blackened the December trees in southern Iowa and Missouri, years back.

Sad to say, those tough signs are becoming more popular each year. Slob hunters have made themselves very unwelcome on private property. What kind of a reception do you think the farmer would get if he drove into town, drove his pickup right up on the lawn of a fancy home, got out his picnic paraphernalia, and had a picnic on the city dweller's lawn? How about if he left paper napkins

285

and litter lying all about, lit a big bonfire and tried to cut down green trees to feed into the bonfire, left open the gates to the backyard, and turned the city dweller's dog out of his run to go loose? After all, that is the way many city hunters and fishermen treat the farmer's property. But it must be noted, even if only in passing, that the slob hunter (while too damned numerous) is only a small percentage of the total hunting and fishing fraternity. It is not right to punish the good hunter for the sins of his slob counterpart.

But there is also no reason why the landowner should allow hunters and anglers on his property. What's in it for me? That is the watchword for most of us these days. Wyoming and a few other states compensate the landowner for every antelope shot on his property. This set fee is part of the license fee collected from the hunter. It makes the hunter far more welcome on the land of a private rancher. New Mexico and some other states handle the situation differently. They provide a set percentage of all big game permits to the landowner. He can then sell access to his land for hunting privileges. Only when the prospective hunter can show a receipt from the landowner–that he has paid for the right of trespass to hunt—only then will the state agency issue his permit to hunt on that land.

Let me repeat: There is no reason why the landowner should allow free hunting or fishing on his land. Why should he? Of course, it is the hunter's and fisherman's license fees that pay for all of the game enhancement work done in the state. It is the sportsman's money, through the Pittman-Robertson excise tax on sporting arms and ammunition, that pays for acquisition of waterfowl refuges. Without this wildlife enhancement work, and without the wildlife refuges, there would not be populations of some species to be hunted—by sportsman and landowner alike. That is true. But the individual landowner finds it hard to be altruistic, to allow trespass that will harm his land, for he knows that the refuges will still be there if he posts against trespass; the wildlife enhancement work will still go on even if he does not allow trespass on his land.

Free hunting and fishing? What's in it for me? is the logical question being asked by most landowners. And unless there is a cash return to the landowner, the truthful answer should seem to be: There's no reason why the landowner should allow free hunting or fishing trespass.

This situation has long been recognized in Europe, where wild game is really a property of the landowner, salable to sportsmen who recognize that they must pay for the privilege. There are still great areas of the western United States where free hunting and fishing, even on private land, is the recognized norm. But that situation is disappearing fast. The state agencies can use all of their federal monies, and much of their license fees, to buy public access to hunting and fishing. Many are doing so. More will come around to this point of view as ever-increasing numbers of *Homo sapiens* put ever-increasing pressure on an ever-decreasing land base. The hard fact is that all hunting and fishing will soon carry a price tag. State and federal lands may remain open to trespass for sport, but that trespass will have to be self-supporting in terms of money if it is to continue. More and more private lands will be opened only on a ''pay for play'' basis.

This is not entirely bad.

For the landowner it will be a definite

improvement, for with the right to collect entry fees, we have the right to control harvest and to minimize disturbance to the human and to the wildlife environment.

Enforcing the laws against trespass varies from easy in Texas, where there is a long and strong tradition that a man's land is his, and trespassers are apt to be shot first and questioned later, all the way to almost impossible in the flat prairies where land ownings are big, section line roads run everywhere, and it is possible for a man to trespass, shoot, and get out quickly. Grain country often lacks fences, and this further complicates enforcement of No Trespassing bans.

If you do not want to take on the arduous chore of enforcing the ban on trespassing yourself, you may want to consider the possibility of selling your hunting and fishing rights to a club or to an individual. That will transfer most of the job of enforcing to the club or individual with whom you have made the agreement. He doesn't want to see others enjoy, for free, that which he paid for.

I regret the passing of the frontier. I am sorry that we cannot simply go out in the country and go hunting, as we always did when I was growing up in the Dakotas. But today's crowds of hunters and anglers exert too much pressure on landowners, and the free and easy day is gone. The fact that its disappearance was hastened by slob hunters is a cause for sorrow in the hunting and fishing fraternity. But the development of an outdoor ethic would have only delayed, not prevented, the coming of the pay-for-play system.

You are the landowner; you have the final say in the harvest of fish and game. Handle your role wisely, please, for much depends upon you. The future of hunting and fishing depends upon you!

18

Censusing Wildlife

HOW MANY HAVE YOU GOT?

Wildlife species will seldom hold still to be counted, so wildlife censusing is seldom easy. There are exceptions, of course. For example, it is relatively easy to count pronghorn antelope. They never hide and can be spotted at a distance by a competent observer who has learned how to pick out their strikingly marked (for which read "camouflaged") bodies against the background of the western plains. Counting the channel catfish in a lake is another matter entirely.

Wildlife management biologists have gotten around this problem to a degree by deciding that they do not *need* to know how many they have. Far more important is the *trend*. Do we have more than we had a year ago? Then things are going nicely. Do we have fewer animals than we had a year ago? Then we had better find out why, and do it quickly.

In preceding chapters, we have discussed the cock-crowing counts for pheasant managers, and the dove-calling counts for dove managers. Each of these counting systems gives a reliable *trend* in the bird's population—tells us whether the population is increasing or decreasing.

As a landowner, you usually have a better idea of numbers than any outside observer could come up with. You are the Good Shepherd and you know yours, etc . . . . Usually.

Here are a few censusing methods used today in wildlife management. Most of them are obvious, some may be new to you.

Aerial Counts of Deer or Elk

A fixed-wing aircraft, operated at low level and at slow speed, gives you a good look down at the white-tailed deer and the elk. Whitetails are especially easy to count in this manner, as they run with that name-giving big white flag whipping back and forth, and they can be seen very easily. Whitetails always seem to fear a low-level plane and they all run, therefore most of them are counted. Mule deer are another story entirely. Most mule deer will hold perfectly still, looking upward at the roaring plane but not giving their position away by running. Even when they do run, they are not as easily spotted as their whitetail cousins.

There are several drawbacks to aerial censusing of deer. One is high cost, another is danger. To do the job accurately, it is necessary to get down low, and low-level flight carries with it a certain risk that cannot be avoided.

Helicopters eliminate some of the danger of low-level flying, but they increase the size of that other drawback—cost.

Helicopter charter is very expensive, however, it remains the best way to census big game animals. You simply fly down and count them; they cannot escape.

For small landowner's holdings, it is usually enough to keep track of the condition of your deer browse plants. If there is a definite, easily seen "line" where the deer have eaten all the new growth up to the highest food they can reach easily, your range is in trouble. Deer populations should be drastically reduced to allow the browse plants to make a comeback.

Aerial Counts of Fur Bearers

We often get our population trends for muskrat and beaver populations by the same method. Flying at low level we count—not muskrats and beaver—but

Running antelope are easily counted from low-flying aircraft or helicopter. *Bureau of Land Management photo.*

muskrat houses and beaver dams and houses. For most landowners, however, aerial observation of these two fur bearers is not really needed. You know what is on your land and you can better estimate the muskrat or beaver population by eyeball count, after you have learned to recognize active and inactive beaver or muskrat houses.

We discussed the aerial censusing of waterfowl at some length in the chapters on ducks and geese. Another species, sandhill cranes, have been censused very accurately using the airplane. While they are on their migration, they are aerial-counted along the Platte River in Nebraska. This can be done to the point where we obtain an actual number count rather than an estimate. In addition, they are routinely counted on their wintering grounds. Aerial observations made by human observers have been checked against actual bird-by-bird counts of birds on large-scale photographs. The counts have been remarkably accurate, but I doubt if any one landowner will have a reason to know the actual number of cranes on his land.

Counting Grouse

Grouse are most easily censused when they lose their native caution in the spring breeding season. Sage grouse, pinnates, and sharptails all congregate on dancing grounds or "booming" grounds in the springtime. These meeting places are called leks by biologists, and their location seldom changes. If you are fortunate enough to have one or more leks on your land, you can easily get an estimate of your breeding population by quietly visiting the lek and watching and listening. In addition to checking on your popula-

tion trend, you will be treated to one of wildlife's most entertaining shows. Remember that the show starts just before sunrise.

Ruffed grouse are a different matter. The males set up their own booming (or drumming) sites, and these are usually solo performances. However, their drumming can be heard for great distances, and it is a good idea to get out on the land at daybreak during the drumming season. Listen for three mornings, five days apart, during the height of the season, and you should be able to form a good idea as to how many birds are available for spring breeding duties. Game bird populations fluctuate greatly over the year, but the only important figure is the figure that tells you how many will be reproducing their kind in the spring.

Fish Index

One of the more complex methods of estimating a population is the index commonly used for estimating fish populations. We net out 100 black bass, carefully mark them, and release them back into the pond. This marking can be done easiest and without expense by simply cutting a notch out of a pectoral fin, always on the same side of the fish. Then we keep a close count of how many fish are caught from the lake in the next six months. We have no reason to believe that the marked fish will be caught at a greater or lesser rate than the unmarked black bass in the same pond. So if we come up with a total catch of 1,576 bass, for example, and 16 of them are marked fish, we have all the information we need to compute the black bass population of the entire pond.

You see, we caught 16 out of 100 marked

bass. That means we caught 16 percent of the marked bass. We can postulate that we also caught 16 percent of all the bass in the pond. Right? If 1,576 bass were 16 percent of the total number of bass in the pond, then the total number available to be caught must be 9,850.

This index method can be used to estimate the population of any fish species that can readily be caught on hook and line. It will not work to find a population estimate of fingerling walleyes, for example, nor does it work well on large catfish.

This method of computing a fish population was invented way back in 1893. It is often called a Lincoln Index, or a Peterson Index, or any one of a dozen other names. It may have certain refinements added to it, but it remains a basic mark-and-recapture system for finding out (approximately) how many fish we have to count.

Another way to get an idea of what is under the surface is simply to pull a seine through the water, and check the contents. But there are drawbacks here, too. The seine is more apt to take the species that like the shallows and to miss the species that love the depths. For example, you are much more apt to seine out the small crappies that school in the shallows and to miss the adult flathead catfish that lies on the deepest bottom. You are also apt to miss the bass, which dart off to deeper water when you enter the pond with the seine. But it does help to give you some idea of the fish population of your pond, even if only a very imperfect, rough idea.

For the manager of the small farm pond, it is usually enough just to know that (1) the average bass is getting bigger, or (2) the average bluegill is getting smaller, or

(3) we don't seem to be catching many catfish at all any more. This type of information is enough to manage a fish population in a small water.

Waterfowl

Wildlife managers are justifiably derisive in their comments about windshield surveys. By windshield survey, I mean the situation where a person drives through a waterfowl breeding area and formulates an opinion about the breeding success for that year. For example "I drove more than 600 miles in Saskatchewan's best duck areas and I can tell you first-hand that it will be mighty slim pickings this fall. There are very few breeding ducks." The wildlife professional knows that 600 miles is but a drop in the bucket in the immense breeding range of ducks. He also knows that observations must be qualified and quantified by factors such as: increase or decrease in total water areas or height of emergent vegetation, which makes a lot of difference in seeing or not seeing duck broods. He also wants to know if the observations were made by the same personnel on the same dates for the last ten consecutive years, so that he can evaluate the results properly. He also wants to know about the weather conditions which obtained on the observation days, for this makes a great difference in the numbers seen.

We must all be careful with windshield observations. For example, "I don't see as many rabbits on the trip to town as I usually do," is not a good indication that the rabbit hunting will be poor. Too many factors must be taken into account. "I sure am seeing a lot of pheasants this summer," doesn't necessarily mean that the pheasant hunting three months later will be good.

FOR WHAT IT'S WORTH DEPARTMENT

If you can imitate the hoot of an owl, just at sunset, the turkey gobblers are apt to gobble back at you, just to show their defiance of the owls.

Slamming a car door will sometimes cause the toms to gobble.

Just as your tame dogs howl when the police or ambulance siren assaults their ears, so a coyote will answer the wailing of a siren, giving away their position if not their numbers.

WORTHLESS TRIVIA

I don't have any idea of how you can use this bit of information, but I found it interesting. A seismograph crew strung their recorders across a section of South Dakota farmland, placed their charges, and set it off. As the seismic echoes penetrated into the earth to map the oil formations below, every pheasant in the section leaped up into the air! Evidently the explosion set off vibrations in their feet that they did not like. In addition to jumping 6 feet in the air, the roosters also set off a crowing, as if to shout their defiance of the foot tickler, whoever or whatever it might have been.

19

Trees and Wildlife

Anyone who has watched the agricultural scene on the Great Plains over the last fifty years has witnessed a revolution. Yet that revolution has been so quiet, so much a slowly creeping thing, that it may have gone unnoticed.

I refer, of course, to the change in the appearance of the land as trees sprouted to break the barren skyline, as shelterbelts have made winter life more pleasant in farm homes, as new wildlife species have moved in to occupy the niche formed by the new tree plantings, as soil moisture has been augmented by the snow retention qualities of the tree plantings. Nothing could have made a bigger change in the appearance of the Great Plains than the shift from bare prairie, protected only by occasional tall grass hayfields, to the present picture, with trees in sight almost everywhere.

In the Dakotas and Nebraska, parts of Montana and parts of Minnesota, the shelterbelts are of primary importance in slowing winds, forcing them to drop their load of drifting snow. As a side benefit, shelterbelts have made it possible for ring-necked pheasants to endure the northern winters with their heavy snowfalls and worse, the horizontal blizzards of drifting snows. The existence of trees has enticed the fox squirrel to invade whole states where he was not found before the tree plantings.

Farther south, the increase in woody cover in Kansas, Oklahoma, and Texas has improved the lot of bobwhite quail and pinnated and sharp-tailed grouse, as well as extended the southern limit of the ringneck's range. As is the case of the shelterbelts farther north, moisture conservation is an important reason for planting the shelterbelt.

I know of no other action of man, any-

Windbreak tree plantings such as this one in South Dakota conserve moisture and improve crop yields. They also provide homes for wildlife. *U.S. Forest Service photo.*

where in the world, that has done so much to change the nature of the land as the Shelterbelt Program, sponsored by the federal government's Department of Agriculture through the Soil Conservation Service. The program began as a make-work project in the early years of the 1932–1939 Dust Bowl. The real value of the project soon became apparent, and the scope of the work greatly widened. Even without government subsidy, the work would have gone ahead in some areas where it was obviously one of the solutions to the Dust Bowl problems.

The archetypical shelterbelt planting of the earliest days consisted of one or two rows of short, dense plants on the outside lines, usually, but not always, conifer-

Typical northern Great Plains shelterbelt, viewed from end. The tall trees, dense enough to stop most of the surface blizzard snows, force the wind to leapfrog up and over farm croplands.

ous. Then came one or two rows of medium-height trees, a row or two of tall trees in the center lines and then the sequence repeated in reverse order down to the outside rows of conifers again. Obviously, the first purpose was to make the winter blizzards leapfrog up and over the tree plantings. The selection of which species of trees to use varied greatly with the latitude of the farmland receiving the planting, with the severity of the winter, with the availability of (or lack of) suitable groundwater to sustain tree life. In my native North Dakota, the first plantings consisted of tall cottonwoods (a poor choice for wind slowing and worthless for wildlife foods) in the center, flanked by box elder, which did not grow as tall as the cottonwoods. Then came Russian olive, which was a good wildlife plant, and many different coniferous plants on the outer edges.

Farther south, osage orange played an important part in the tree plantings, as did the excellent multiflora rose, which provided food and cover for small game birds and animals as well as excellent nesting cover for songbirds. Eastern red cedar and blackberry entered the picture early on in southern climes, and the basic southern shelterbelt provided more food for wildlife than did the basic northern shelterbelt, where choice of species was dictated by their ability to handle the severe winter.

Tree plantings are of vital importance for wildlife. It is almost impossible to find a species that does not benefit from a properly placed tree planting. Deer browse on the tender leaves and twigs and use the planting as escape cover. All game birds seem to enjoy tree plantings as sources of food in all seasons of the year and as escape cover and winter cover during the cold months. Songbirds nest in them and feed on the berries of the

This low windbreak of conifers does a good job of starting the snowdrift well away from the farmstead, but it does not provide food or cover for wildlife.

many "food tree" species that are used today.

In the period from 1984 through 2000, the shelterbelt, which transformed the Great Plains, will face a serious crisis. The trees have now all matured and many of them are dying from old age. Whether or not these aged plantings will be replaced is the question of greatest importance for wildlife. In these days of a great pinch on farm income, with every acre of land having a great cash value, it is hard for the farmer to resist the chance to remove dead trees, plow up the land, and enjoy a short-term gain in total cash productivity. The smart farmer is busily replacing his trees, usually with shorter, more multipurpose, trees. Autumn olive, for example, is worth much more than the box elder which it replaces. The trend is toward more fruit and berry trees, toward more escape cover and away from the purely ornamental, and away from the very tall trees. Where soil and water conditions will allow it, there is a switch toward hardwoods, which will endure for many years and provide valuable food and cover for squirrels, deer, and turkeys. But over much of the Great Plains, there is going to be a severe loss of trees, and this is a modern-day tragedy for wildlife.

Your County Extension Agent is the best source of information as to how to design a tree planting, where to locate it, and which species of plants to use in the planting. He may refer you, in some states, to State Forestry people, who are specialists in trees rather than being generalists as the County Agent must be. In some states, it is possible to get financial assistance for tree plantings from the State Game and Fish Department. In other states, it is possible to get the tree-planting stock itself from the State Game and Fish Department. Check into the situation in your state, and take advantage of the expert help offered.

SOME WILDLIFE-PREFERRED TREES

Autumn Olive

Autumn olive is a wonderful choice, one that the Department of Agriculture is high on. Let me quote directly from the publication, *Autumn Olive, for Wildlife and Other Conservation Uses*, which is available through your County Agent.

"Thickets or rows of fully grown autumn olive furnish good protective cover for many kinds of wildlife—both birds and mammals. Songbirds find the branches excellent places for their nests, and game birds and rabbits find shelter under the wide spreading branches. Raccoons, skunks, opossums, and even black bears feed upon the berries. But it is as a producer of food for birds that the autumn olive is most outstanding.

"Birds eat the fruit (berries) of autumn olive from ripening time in September to late winter. Robins have been known to winter north of their normal range despite snows and severe cold when there were plenty of autumn olive berries. Other birds that eat the berries are cardinals, catbirds, cedar waxwings, common grackles, evening grosbeaks, fox sparrows, hermit thrushes, house sparrows, mallards, mockingbirds, myrtle warblers, purple finches, rufous-sided towhees, song sparrows, starlings, tree swallows and veerys.

"Bobwhite quail, ruffed grouse, mourning doves, ring-necked pheasants, and wild turkeys find autumn olive fruit highly attractive food. . . .

"It takes at least 100 autumn olive plants to be certain of having enough food for both game birds and songbirds."

We would like to suggest that plantings of small conifers be interspersed with the autumn olive to make it doubly attractive as winter cover and as protected feeding areas, close to nesting sites. The autumn olive is an excellent plant to use as a windbreak and a good controller of gully erosion and sheet erosion when planted on slopes. One of its greatest attractions is the fact that it is a nitrogen-fixing plant and does well in reclaiming such "hard-to-handle" spots as strip-mined spoil piles, badly eroded hillsides, and old gravel pits.

This wonderful plant has proved itself across the north central part of our nation, from Massachusetts south to North Carolina and westward to Wisconsin, Iowa, and Missouri.

Osage Orange

Growing as high as 45 feet, the osage orange, also called horse apple or hedge apple, is a hardy plant, of medium value as a windbreak, an excellent songbird nesting cover, and a wildlife food for squirrels and rabbits. Its wood is strong and durable and used for many purposes.

Jack Pine

A dense, hardy plant, the jack pine is well suited to form the leading edge of a windbreak, and it provides excellent nesting cover for smaller birds. It can exist on poor soils, especially sandy soils, and helps in erosion control, but does nothing to provide food for wildlife. On good soils will grow to nearly 40-foot height.

Eastern Red Cedar

A dense conifer, the Eastern red cedar grows to heights of 50 feet and provides

Hedgerow of Osage orange makes an excellent windbreak and provides shelter for small gamebirds and animals. *U.S. Forest Service photo.*

These cedar strips, planted as windbreaks in Nebraska, hold snow and conserve soil moisture. *U.S. Forest Service photo.*

a blue-colored berry that is a good food for songbirds and turkeys. The foliage, while not a prime food for deer, is utilized by these browsers to some extent. An exceptionally good wind stopper, it does well on limestone-rich lands, which makes it a good choice for some worn-out farmlands and steep hillsides.

Sumac

There are many sumacs, but the one we prefer for wildlife use is the aromatic sumac, also called the fragrant sumac. It seldom reaches a height of as much as 6 feet, and this is good, because it keeps the food supply close to wildlife. The small red fruit matures in July or August and is relished by ruffed grouse and wild turkey. The twigs are browsed by white-tailed deer. It does well as a field border plant and will make out on rocky hillsides.

Blackberry

Another short plant, with good food value to wildlife and to man. But you'll have to hurry to beat the birds, turkeys, and deer to the blackberries. Needs full sunlight, but is an excellent addition to your tree plantings.

Russian Olive

The shiny gray leaves identify this plant, which has become the mainstay of wildlife plantings in the northern Great Plains area. It grows to a height of about 20 feet and can tolerate almost any soil type. It produces a small yellow fruit, which is relished by almost all songbirds, by grouse and by deer. Its branches are dense enough to give it good value as a windbreak tree, and it does provide good nesting sites for songbirds. This plant will handle the northern climate much better than its relative, the autumn olive.

Multiflora Rose

Advertised a few decades ago as being "horse-high, hog-tight, and bull-strong" the multiflora rose was imported to this country to provide a tough, strong hedge, which produced lots of food for wildlife and provided perhaps the best escape cover for quail and rabbits in the entire world. It has an annoying habit of spreading to where you didn't plan to have it. The seeds, passed through the digestive system of birds and livestock, germinated in strange places. However, this volunteer growth is easily controlled by chemical herbicides and the value to wildlife of the tough tangles cannot be overstated. Ask your County Agent if it will handle the climate on your land. If so, you may have a real winner in this plant.

Silver Maple

Growing to a height of 80 feet, the silver maple produces many seeds, which are relished by birds and deer. Its twigs and leaves are eaten by deer. It lives to a ripe old age and provides den trees for cavity-nesting birds and for squirrels. It is a fast-growing tree, but is subject to insect damage. Check with a forestry advisor before choosing this lovely tree, it might not be advisable in your area.

Black Walnut

If it will handle the winter in your area, the black walnut is one of the prizes for the tree planter. It grows to great heights, even to 85 feet. Produces great quantities of black walnuts, which are used by squirrels, but which are protected by one of the hardest, most difficult-to-open shells in the entire nutty world. Once opened, the nut meat is delicious, and much used by humans stubborn enough to fight their way in to the meat. It is a very valuable tree for wood production, in fact, it has tempted many ruthless persons to steal entire trees because the saw logs are worth so much money.

Pecan

Another tree in the same class with the black walnut, this beautiful, big (more than 100 feet tall when fully grown on good soil) fruit-bearing tree is one of the very best for wildlife food production. The delicious nuts are relished by squirrels, wood ducks, turkey, and deer. Some selected varieties are used as commercial nut producers for human food; others, which produce smaller nuts, are to be preferred if you are thinking solely of wildlife foods. In some parts of Texas they have a saying, "Take care of your pecans when you are young and they'll take care of you when you're old," which refers to the value of the cash crop of pecans from a mature tree. This tree needs very good soil in full sunlight and will not do well on rocky soils.

Oaks

There are four big oak trees, all of which are valued for food production (acorns) and as den sites for squirrels. These are the Northern red oak, the pin oak, the bur oak and the lordly white oak. All reach heights of nearly 100 feet on good soils. All produce acorns, which are a top-choice food for turkeys, wood ducks, squirrels, deer, and many large birds. All are wonderful shade trees and excellent choices for the center of a big windbreak, if space permits. It is wise to plant more than one variety of oak tree, to make sure that you will have a mast crop (acorns) of one variety or another every year. Again, your County Agent can advise on this.

As we mentioned earlier, the choice of

which trees to plant is dictated by soil and climate restrictions. However, in addition to the few trees described above, we would like to ask you to consider the following, if they fill the bill for your climate and soils.

Conifers—the pines—shortleaf, loblolly, scotch, white, and Austrian.

Larger trees—such as the green ash, shagbark hickory, yellow poplar, cypress, black cherry, mulberry, black alder, and hackberry.

Among the shorter plants, in addition to those we have described, you might want to take a look at these good wildlife food-producing plants: Nanking cherry, wild plum, persimmon, dogwood, shrub lespedeza, holly, hawthorn, button bush, serviceberry, chokecherry, hazelnut, bittersweet, pyracantha, ninebark, honeysuckle, crabapple, sassafras, and gooseberry.

If you live in Missouri or one of the states bordering it, we suggest you ask the Missouri Conservation Department for a copy of their excellent publication: *Conservation Trees and Shrubs for Missouri.* It is one of the very best source materials on wildlife tree plantings.

MANAGING THE WOODLOT

Depending upon the purpose of your tree planting, the management will be very different. For example, if your primary aim is the production of fuelwood, you will harvest your trees at different time intervals than if you intend them strictly for wildlife cover.

If you want to produce commercial timber, you would probably go to a monoculture, growing only marketable trees. But I am assuming that you are interested in the wildlife potential of your

tree lot, so I will assume that you will allow hardwoods to mature—that you will not cut down aged hardwoods, because you know that they are excellent den sites. If you are forced to remove a den tree, it is wise to replace the lost dens with artificial den boxes, which are inexpensively made and will do almost as good a job as the natural opening.

In livestock range, the most important thing you can do to manage a woodlot is to fence livestock out. We know that the cattle like a chance to chew their cud in the shade, and it is nice to have both "cow shade" and wildlife cover, but they are seldom found on the same bit of ground.

Fire is a big minus in wildlife tree plantings, because it temporarily destroys the understory, eliminates the grassy cover, and kills some trees. We know that wildfire in deer habitat is considered a plus as it encourages the growth of second-growth plants, which are excellent deer food. In a small area, wildfire is a catastrophe. Be careful.

As we have explained in the chapters on wild turkey and white-tailed deer and quail, the edge of the woods is an important transitional zone for wildlife. If tree lots are bordered by tall grass cover, their value to wildlife is greatly enhanced. The preferred nesting sites for many game bird species is in the tall grass close to the woods.

Clean cultivation is a necessity to get a good start for your trees for the first two years after planting . . . longer for the slower-growing trees. Weed control is a must to protect new trees. Chemical herbicides are a second choice after cultivation by machine or by hand. Mulching around the plants with hay, ground corn cobs, commercial bark preparations, or rotten sawdust will do much to retard weed growth and to conserve moisture. Cultivation must be shallow to avoid damage to tree roots.

However, cultivation under the trees removes about half of the wildlife value of the trees and should be discontinued after the plantings have become established. The understory is valuable; preserve it.

When you crop your woodlot, removing salable timber or fuelwood, it is wise management to leave the unsalable branches and toppings in the area. Do not burn them. Turkeys love these spots for nesting, so do quail, and they are the number one escape cover for rabbits.

Providing water in close proximity to woodlots will greatly increase the wildlife use of that woodlot.

Habitat is the most important word in the wildlife manager's dictionary. Habitat includes food, water, and a place to live. The woodlot that provides these essentials is a home to wildlife. Wise management of a woodlot is wise management of wildlife.

SUGGESTED READING

If you wish to go into the subject of managing woodlots for wildlife to a greater degree, we recommend the following publications:

Landowner's Guide to Woodlot Management in the Northeast, by Sepik, Owen, and Coulter. University of Maine, Life Science and Agricultural Experiment Station, Report 253, 23 pages.

Aspens, Phoenix Trees of the Great Lakes Region, by Graham, Harrison, and Westell. University of Michigan Press. This one may be out of print now.

Improving Your Forested Lands for Ruffed Grouse, by G. W. Gullion. The Ruffed Grouse Society, Coraopolis, Pa., 1972.

Introduction to Forest Science, edited by R. A. Young. John Wiley and Sons, New York, 1982.

Manager's Handbook for Aspen in the North Central States. U.S. Forest Service Technical Report NC-36, 1977.

Quaking Aspen, Silvics and Management in the Lakes States, by Brinkman and Roe. U.S. Forest Service Handbook 486, 1975.

Practical Wildlife Management, by George Burger. Winchester Press, 1973.

Gardening with Wildlife. Published by the National Wildlife Federation, Washington, D.C., 1974.

Let's Plant a Tree. Free from the Consumer Information Center, Pueblo, Colorado. This is a Johnny Horizon publication of the U.S. Department of the Interior.

Plant a Tree; A Working Guide to Regreening America, by Michael A. Weiner. Collier Books, 1975.

If you are trying to produce both wood for heating purposes and wildlife on your woodlot, you will want to know which wood is the best for heating, as well as which woods are the best for wildlife.

Courtesy of the University of Minnesota Extension Service, Bulletin 436, here is the comparative heating value of various woods. The heating value is expressed in millions of Btu per cord of wood.

COMPARATIVE HEATING VALUE

Hickory	15.2
Ironwood	15.0
Apple	14.6

White oak	14.1	Box elder	9.8
Beech	13.2	Jack pine	9.4
Sugar maple	13.2	Hemlock	8.7
Yellow birch	13.0	Black spruce	8.7
White ash	13.0	Aspen	8.1
Paper birch	11.2	White pine	7.9
Cherry	11.0	Balsam fir	7.9
American elm	10.7	Basswood	7.4
Black ash	10.5	White cedar	6.7
Red maple	10.3		

20

About Scientific Names

Because there has been so much confusion about the "correct" names for wildlife species, scientists have resorted to a system of assigning Latin names to them. This can be very confusing, as we will see shortly. However, it does have a lot of value, because the scientific name system acts as the real authority in determining that we are both talking about the same species.

In some parts of the United States, a big wild cat is called a puma, in others a catamount, a panther, a painter—but they are all names describing *Felis concolor*. We italicize the scientific name simply because it is written in a foreign language.

Felis concolor tells us quite a lot. The first word—which is always capitalized, by the way, tells us that this is a member of the grouping known as felines. Our word *feline* came from the same Latin root word, *Felis*, obviously. The second word, *concolor* is a somewhat clumsy way of telling us that the mountain lion is about the same color all over. The second word, and third word if there is one, is never capitalized.

Some scientific names—such as *Felis concolor*—are a sincere attempt at describing the animal. Others are attempts to honor the man who discovered it, or described it, or simply the name of a man the biologist doing the naming happened to like. For example, we refer to a small Canadian goose as being a Hutchison's goose, which comes from its scientific name, which ends in *hutchisonii*. The Mearns' quail is another example; its scientific name in Latin ends with the word *mearnsii*. Sometimes the scientific name is less than complimentary. For example, our beloved robin red breast is known as

Turdus migratorius, and I object to call-ing this lovely songster a migratory turd. The starling, yclept *Sturnus vulgaris*, certainly does have a vulgar stern, if that's what the taxonomist meant.

If this were a perfect world, the first part of a scientific name would tell you which family grouping it belongs to. But this is not a perfect world. For example, all of the North American quail species are of one family, obviously. But their scientific names start with *Colinus*, with *Callipepla*, and with a few others.

Sometimes the taxonomist who la-beled the species is trying to tell us some-thing about it. For example, the rattle-snake bears the cognomen of *Crotalus horridus*, which is certainly a statement of opinion. Another would be the label attached to the grizzly bear, *Ursus hor-ribilis*. If you've ever been close enough to an uncaged grizzly to taste the acid of fear in your mouth, you'll probably agree with the label attached to the magnificent bear.

Sometimes taxonomists get downright poetic. One labeled the snow goose *Chen hyperborea*, which translates into "goose from beyond the north wind." Poetic and accurate. At one time we labeled the blue phase of the snow goose with *Chen caer-ulescens*, which translated into "quar-relsome goose." Then we learned that the blue and the snow were only color phases of the same species, and those descriptive terms were abandoned.

Some scientific terms tell us a lot. The blue grouse is called *Dendragapus ob-scurus*, which means "tree-loving dark bird"—an apt description.

Others don't tell us much. William Warner's beautiful book about the life of the crab fisherman in Chesapeake Bay takes its name, *Beautiful Swimmer*, from the scientific name of the blue crab. Now it is true that the crab is a swimmer, but he is beautiful only in the eyes of another crab.

Scientific names have to change oc-casionally, when the taxonomists find out that they were wrong in placing a species in a certain genus. Sometimes they have to admit mistakes and change scientific names. We won't try to understand sci-entific names. We will list some of the more common names, in order that you may look them up and make sure that you and the biologist are talking about the same species. We'll list them under birds, animals, and freshwater fish, and not try to be fancy about it.

BIRDS

Dove, mourning	*Zenaidura macroura*
Dove, white-tailed	*Zenaidura asiatica*
Duck, mallard	*Anas platyrhynchos*
Goose, Canada	*Branta canadensis*
Goose, white-fronted	*Anser albifrons*
Grouse, blue	*Dendragapus obscurus*
Grouse, pinnated, greater	*Tympanuchus cupido*
Grouse, pinnated, lesser	*Tympanuchus pallidicinctus*
Grouse, ruffed	*Bonasa umbellus*
Grouse, sage	*Centrocercius urophasianus*
Grouse, spruce	*Dendragapus canadensis*

Partridge, chukar	*Alectoris graeca*
Partridge, Hungarian	*Perdix perdix*
Pheasant, ring-necked	*Phasianus colchicus*
Quail, bobwhite	*Colinus virginianus*
Quail, masked bobwhite	*Colinus virginianus ridgewayii*
Quail, California	*Lophortyx californica*
Quail, Gambel's	*Lophortyx gambelii*
Quail, Mearns'	*Certonyx montezumae mearnsii*
Quail, mountain	*Oreortyx picta*
Quail, scaled	*Callipepla squamata*
Turkey, wild	*Meleagris gallopavo*

ANIMALS

Antelope, pronghorn	*Antilocapra americana*
Badger	*Taxidea taxus*
Beaver	*Castor canadensis*
Bear, black	*Euarctos americanus*
Bobcat	*Lynx rufus*
Coyote	*Canis latrans*
Deer, mule	*Odocoileus hemionus*
Deer, white-tailed	*Odocoileus virginianus*
Elk	*Cervus canadensis*
Fox, red	*Vulpes vulpes*
Jackrabbit, black-tailed	*Lepus californicus*
Jackrabbit, white-tailed	*Lepus townsendii*
Mink	*Mustela vison*
Moose, Alaskan	*Alces alces*
Moose, Wyoming style	*Alces shirasi*
Rabbit, cottontail	*Sylvilagus* (many subspecies recognized)
Rabbit, snowshoe	*Lepus americanus*
Raccoon	*Procyon lotor*
Skunk	*Mephitis mephitis*
Squirrel, flying, northern	*Glaucomys sabrinus*
Squirrel, flying, southern	*Glaucomys volans*
Squirrel, fox	*Sciurus niger*
Squirrel, gray	*Sciurus carolinensis*
Wapiti	*Cervus canadensis*

FRESH-WATER FISHES

Bass, largemouth black	*Micropterus salmoides*
Bass, rock	*Ambloplites rupestris*
Bass, smallmouth black	*Micropterus dolomieu*

Bass, striped	*Roccus saxatilis*
Bass, white	*Roccus chrysops*
Bullhead, black	*Ictalurus melas*
Bullhead, brown	*Ictalurus nebulosus*
Bullhead, yellow	*Ictalurus natalis*
Catfish, channel	*Ictalurus punctatus*
Catfish, blue	*Ictalurus furcatus*
Catfish, flathead	*Pylodictus olivaris*
Catfish, white	*Ictalurus catus*
Crappie, black	*Pomoxis migromaculatus*
Crappie, white	*Pomoxis annularis*
Goldfish	*Carassius auratus*
Muskellunge	*Esox masquinongy*
Perch, yellow	*Perca flavescens*
Pickerel, chain	*Esox vermiculatus*
Pickerel, redfin	*Esox americanus*
Pike, northern	*Esox lucius*
Sauger	*Stizostedion canadense*
Sunfish, bluegill	*Lepomis macrochirus*
Sunfish, green	*Lepomis cyanellus*
Sunfish, longear	*Lepomis megalotis*
Sunfish, orange-spotted	*Lepomis humilis*
Sunfish, pumpkinseed	*Lepomis gibbosus*
Sunfish, redbreast	*Lepomis auritus*
Sunfish, redear	*Lepomis microlophus*
Sunfish, warmouth	*Chaenobryttus gulosus*
Sunfish, yellowbelly	*Lepomis auritus*
Trout, brook	*Salvelinus fontinalis*
Trout, brown	*Salmo trutta*
Trout, cutthroat	*Salmo clarkii*
Trout, lake	*Salvelinus namaycush*
Trout, rainbow	*Salmo gairdnerii*
Walleye	*Stizostedion vitreum*

Index

A

Age ratio, definition of, 1
Aleutian goose, 104
Allowable harvest, definition of, 1–2
Altricial, definition of, 2
Arctic plovers, 127
Attwater's prairie chicken, 45, 61, 62–63
Autumn olive, 296–97

B

Bag limit, definition of, 128
Bait fish, 190–91
Baiting of migratory birds, 129–31
Baits for: bullheads, 184; channel catfish, 189–90;
    crappies, 180; largemouth black bass, 187–88;
    rainbow trout, 162
Balance of nature, definition of, 2
Baldpate ducks, 114
Band-tailed pigeons: clutch size of, 98; description of,
    97; food of, 97–98; migrations of, 98; nesting of, 98;
    predators of, 98; range of, 97
Bass: compatible with bluegills, 201; largemouth black,
    184–88; smallmouth black, 188; spotted, 188–89;
    white, 189
Beavers: aerial counts of, 289–90; trapping of, 283; trout
    and, 172–75
Bentonite in ponds, 198
Biota, definition of, 2
Birds: how to manage nongame, 255–62; how to
    replenish game, 13, 15; migration of, 124–28; needs
    of game, 14–15; scientific names for, 304–5. *See
    also* name of bird
Blackberry, 298
Black walnut, 299
Bluebirds, how to manage, 257
Bluegill sunfish, 175–78, 201
Blue grouse: clutch size of, 54; courtship of, 53–54;
    description of, 53; food of, 53; habitat of, 52, 53;
    hooting of, 53–54; incubation of, 54; management
    of, 54–55; mortality and, 53; nesting of, 54; other
    names for, 52; predators of, 53; range of, 52–53
Blue jays, how to manage, 258
Bobcat, trapping of, 282–83
Bobwhite quail: clutch size of, 18; covey of, 19; food of,
    21–23; freezing of, 19; habitat of, 22, 23;
    hybridization and, 17; incubation and, 18; mortality
    and, 19; nesting of, 17–19; predators of, 19; range
    of, 16; renesting of, 19; weight of, 16

Booming grounds of grouse, 58, 63
Botulism, effects of wildlife, 132–33
Brook trout, 163–64
Brown trout, 164–65
Browse, definition of, 2
Bullheads, 184, 201

C

California quail, 28–29
Canada geese: breeding of, 108–9; clutch size of, 106;
    description of, 104; effects of management on, 101,
    105–6; food of, 107–8; habitat of, 109–10; how to
    cook, 110–12; nesting of, 107; shortstopping of, 101,
    105–6; weight of, 104
Canvasback ducks, 101, 102, 124, 127
Capon, definition of, 2
Cardinals, how to manage, 258
Carnivorous, definition of, 2–3
Carrying capacity, definition of, 3
Catbirds, how to manage, 258
Catfish, channel, 189–90, 201, 206–8
Chemicals: effects on trout, 169–70; effects on wildlife,
    11; used in eradicating fish, 195–96
Chlorine and effects on minnow farming, 191
Chukar partridges, 73–75, 76
Climax species, definition of, 3–4
Climax succession, 4
Commensal, definition of, 4
Coots, 126
Copraphagy, rabbits and, 147
Cottontops. *See* Scaled quail
Cover, definition of, 4
Crappies, 179–80, 201
Crawfish: breeding of, 268–69; farming of, 270–71; food
    of, 269; how to cook, 271–72; mortality and, 269;
    predators of, 269; species of, 267–68; water quality
    and, 270
Crazy flight, of the ruffed grouse, 50
Cutthroat trout, 165–66
Cyclic, definition of, 4

D

Dabblers: management of, 116–18; types of, 102; origin
    of name, 102, 112
Dams, use of, 167–69, 173
DDT, effects on wildlife, 11, 127

Deer: aerial counts of, 288–89; how to care for venison, 231–32; how to cook venison, 232–34; mule, 225–31; white-tailed, 212–25

Depredation, definition of, 4

Diving ducks, 101–2, 103

Doves: how to cook, 96–97; mourning, 85–91; white-winged, 91–96

Drumming, of grouse, 47–48

Ducks, wild: effects of management on, 101–3; how to cook, 119–20; management for dabblers and mallards, 116–18; survey of breeding grounds, 112–15; use of dogs in banding, 113–14; wood, 120–24

E

Eastern red cedar, 297–98

Ecology, definition of, 4

Ecosystem, definition of, 4

Edge, definition of, 4–5

Elk: aerial counts of, 288–89; antlers of, 242; artificial feeding of, 240–41; breeding and, 241–42; bugling of, 241; food of, 243, 244; management of, 243–45; range of, 239–40; restocking of, 243; weight of, 239

Environment, definition of, 5

Eutrophication, definition of, 5

Exotic game: factors to consider before going into the business of, 252–53; fees for hunting, 248–50; list of exotic game ranches, 250–52

F

Fathead minnows, 192

Feeding of, artificial/supplemental: bobwhite quail, 23; caged catfish, 207–8; channel catfish, 190, 202, 204–5; elk, 240–41; fish in ponds, 202, 204–5; golden shiners, 192; nongame birds, 260–61; turkeys, 83; white-tailed deer, 225

Feeding versus baiting of migratory birds, 129–31

Feedlot, fish, 206

Feral, definition of, 5

Fish: census taking of, 290–91; scientific names for, 305–6

Fish farming: caged-fish production, 206–8; of catfish, 204–8; diseases, 208; factors to consider before, 208–9, 210–11; of minnows, 211; sources of information on, 209–10, 211; supplemental feeding, 204–5; of trout, 208; when fish are off their feed, 205–6

Flickers, how to manage, 258–59

Flying squirrels, 140–41

Food chain, definition of, 5–6

Fool grouse. *See* Ruffed grouse

Fox squirrel: description of, 134; differences between a gray squirrel and a, 136, 138; food of, 138–39; habitat of, 136; how to cook, 139–40; mortality and, 136; range of, 136, 137–38; reproduction of, 137; weight of, 134

Fry, definition of, 161

G

Gadwall, 102, 114

Gallinaceous, definition of, 6

Gallinaceous guzzlers, 29, 74–75

Gambel's quail: difference between mountain quail and, 23–24; grazing and effects on, 25–26; habitat of, 25; range of, 25; reproduction of, 25

Gizzard shad, 190

Golden shiners, 190, 192, 211

Goldfinches, how to manage, 259

Grackles, how to manage, 259

Gray partridge. *See* Hungarian partridges

Gray squirrel: description of, 134–35; differences between a fox squirrel and a, 136, 138; food of, 138–39; habitat of, 136; how to cook, 139–40; mortality and, 136; range of, 135–36, 137–38; reproduction of, 137; weight of, 134

Grazing, effects on: Gambel's quail, 25–26; harlequin quail, 30; sage grouse, 57–58; scaled quail, 27, 28

Green sunfish, 179, 201

Grouse: blue, 52–55; census taking of, 290; how to cook, 70–71; pinnated, 60–65; ruffed, 45–52; sage, 57–60; sharp-tailed, 65–71; spruce, 55–57

H

Harlequin quail, 29–30

Harvest, definition of, 6

Herbivorous, definition of, 6

Hibernation, definition of, 6

Hummingbirds, how to manage, 257

Hungarian partridges: clutch size of, 73; description of, 72; food of, 72; habitat of, 73; how to cook, 75–76; predators of, 72; range of, 72

Hybridization: bobwhite quail and, 17; ring-necked pheasant and, 35; squirrels and, 136; white-tailed and mule deer and, 225

I

Irruption, definition of, 6

J

Jack pine, 297

Johnny Stewart Game Calls, 266

K

Kaibab squirrels, 141

Kamloops, 161

Killdeers, how to manage, 259

Kirtland's warblers, 127

L

Lake trout, 166

Largemouth black bass, 184–88, 201

Lead poisoning, 131–32

Lek, definition of, 6

Lincoln Index, 291

M

Mallards, management of, 102, 116–18

Mast, definition of, 6

Mearns' quail. *See* Harlequin quail

Mink, trapping of, 282
Minnows, 190, 191, 192–93, 211
Monogamous, definition of, 6–7
Montezuma's quail. *See* Harlequin quail
Moose: antlers of, 245; food of, 246; how to cook, 247; management of, 246–47; range of, 245–46; weight of, 245
Mosquito fish, 191
Mountain quail: clutch size of, 24; difference between Gambel's quail and, 23–24; food of, 24; habitat of, 24; migration of, 24; predators of, 25; range of, 24
Mourning doves: call counts of, 87–88; clutch size of, 86; courtship of, 87; description of, 85; food of, 88–89, 90–91; incubation and, 86, 88; management of, 91; mortality and, 89–90; nesting of, 88; pigeon's milk, 88–89; range of, 85; renesting of, 89
Mule deer: antlers of, 226–27; differences between white-tailed deer and, 226–27; management of, 230, 231; mortality and, 228–31; range of, 225–26, 227–28; reproductive potential of, 227; weight of, 226
Multiflora rose, 298–99
Muskrats: aerial counts of, 289–90; trapping of, 281–82

N

Nest boxes for: squirrels, 142–43; wood ducks, 122, 124
Northern pike, 182–84

O

Oaks, 299
Ocellated turkey, 78
Omnivorous, definition of, 7
Osage orange, 297

P

Pair bond, definition of, 7
Pan fish: bluegill sunfish, 175–78; bullheads, 184; crappies, 179–80; northern pike, 182–84; sunfish, 178–79; walleyes, 181–82; yellow perch, 180–81
Partridges: chukar, 73–75; how to cook, 75–76; Hungarian, 72–73
"Patridges," 45
Pecan, 299
Pen-raised animals versus wild-trapped animals for restocking, 15
Peterson Index, 291
Pigeons, band-tailed, 97–98
Pigeon's milk, 88–89
Pinnated grouse: booming grounds of, 63; clutch size of, 65; compared with sharp-tailed grouse, 65–66; courtship of, 63, 65; coveys of, 63; description of, 63; food of, 63; how to cook, 70–71; incubation and, 65; leks and, 63; management of, 65; range of, 61–63
Pintail duck, 102, 125, 127
Pittman-Robertson Act, 100, 121
Pittman-Robertson bird. *See* Mourning dove
Polygamous, definition of, 7
Ponds: compatible fish in, 201–2; construction of, 191–92; feeding fish in, 202; for fish farming, 210–11; how many fish are necessary in, 202; how to control fish in, 193–96; how to stop leaks in, 198;

livestock and, 200; location of, 198–99; overflow spillway for, 199; planting of trees and bushes around, 199–200; problems of turbidity in, 200–201; size and depth of, 198; soils of, 198; sources of information on, 197; summerkill in, 203; when to harvest fish in, 202; winterkill in, 202–3
Prairie chicken. *See* Pinnated grouse
Precocial, definition of, 7
Predators: definition of, 7; how to control, 263–66
Prey, definition of, 7
Pronghorn antelope: description of, 236–37; food of, 238; horns of, 236; management of, 238–39; predators of, 236; range of, 235; weight of, 237
Pumpkinseed sunfish, 179
Purple martins, how to manage, 257

Q

Quail: bobwhite, 15–23; California, 28–29; food for, 21–22; Gambel's, 25–26; harlequin, 29–30; how to cook, 30–31; mountain, 23–25; scaled, 26–28; what makes a good habitat for, 22–23
Quiet release method used on ring-necked pheasant, 34

R

Rabbits, cottontail: food of, 147; how to cook, 151–53; management of, 147–49; predators of, 145–46, 149; range of, 143; reproductive potential of, 146; restocking of, 145, 149–50; tularemia and, 150; warbles and, 150–51; weight of, 144
Raccoons: food of, 156; how to control, 154–55, 265; how to cook, 156–57; range of, 153
Rainbow trout, 160–63
Raptor, definition of, 7
Redbreast sunfish, 178–79
Redear sunfish, 179
Redhead ducks, 101
Red squirrels, 140
Red-winged blackbirds, how to manage, 260
Reproductive potential, definition of, 7–8
Ring-necked pheasant: black Mongolian strain of, 34; clutch size of, 36; description of, 35; food of, 36, 37; how to cook, 43–45; hybridization and, 35; incubation and, 36; management of, 38–39, 41–42; mortality and, 36, 37, 38, 42; nesting of, 35–36, 38; predators of, 42; range of, 33; renesting of, 36; reproduction and, 35; stocking of, 32–33, 40; winter cover and, 36–38, 41
Rio Grande subspecies of turkey, 77, 78, 79
Robins, how to manage, 257
Rotenone, fish control and, 195
Ruffed grouse: annual cycle of, 51; boom-and-bust cycle of, 51; clutch size of, 50; courtship of, 47–48; crazy flight of, 50; description of, 47; food of, 50–51; habitat of, 51; incubation and, 50; mortality and, 50, 51; nesting of, 50; predators of, 51; range of, 46–47; renesting of, 50; weight of, 47
Russian olive, 298

S

Sage grouse: clutch size of, 60; courtship of, 57, 58; description of, 57; food of, 60; grazing and effects on, 57–58; incubation and, 60; leks and, 58;

Sage grouse (*continued*)
    management of, 60; nesting of, 60; predators of, 60;
    range of, 57; weight of, 57
Scaled quail: clutch size of, 27; coveys of, 27;
    description of, 26; grazing and effects on, 27, 28;
    incubation and, 27; mortality and, 28; nesting of, 27,
    28; origin of name, 26; range of, 26; renesting of,
    27; reproduction and, 27; weight of, 27
Scientific names, lists of, 304–6
Seining, use of, 194–95
Sex ratio, definition of, 8
Sharp-tailed grouse: clutch size of, 68; compared with
    pinnates, 65–66; courtship of, 68; coveys of, 68;
    description of, 61, 65; food of, 66, 67; habitat of, 67;
    how to cook, 70–71; incubation and, 68; leks and,
    68; management of, 68, 70; plains, 67; prairie, 67;
    range of, 66–67; types of, 67
Shelterbelts: effects on fox squirrels, 136; effects on
    mourning doves, 90; program, 294–96
Shortstopping of Canada geese, 101, 105–6
Silver maple, 299
Smallmouth black bass, 188, 201
Sources of information, 278–80
Spoonbill duck, 117
Spotted bass, 188–89
Spruce grouse: clutch size of, 56; courtship of, 56;
    description of, 55–56; food of, 56; habitat of, 56;
    management of, 56–57; nesting of, 56; range of, 55;
    renesting of, 56
Squaretails, 163
Squirrels: flying, 140–41; fox and gray, 134–40; Kaibab,
    141; management of, 141–43; red, 140; tassel-eared,
    141
State conservation agencies, list of, 275–78
Steel shot program, 131–32
Stocking of: bluegill sunfish, 177; brook trout, 164;
    channel catfish, 207; rainbow trout, 162
Stockpiling, definition of, 8
Stratification, definition of, 8
Suckers, 190–91
Sumac, 298
Summerkill, 203
Sunfish, 178–79
Sustained yield, definition of, 8–9
Sympatric, definition of, 9

T

Tassel-eared squirrels, 141
Teal ducks, 102, 114, 117, 125
Thermocline, definition of, 9
Toxaphene, used in eradicating fish, 195
Trapping, 281–84
Trees and wildlife, 293–96: management of, 300–301;
    sources of information, 301; wildlife-preferred trees,
    list of, 296–300
Trespassing and posted signs, 285–87
Trout: beavers and, 172–75; brook, 163–64; brown,
    164–65; chemicals and, 169–70; cutthroat, 165–66;
    fish farming of, 208; how to improve a trout stream,
    166–72; lake, 166; rainbow, 160–63; reasons for
    having, 160; for your pond, 201–2
Tularemia, rabbits and, 150–51

Turkey, wild: clutch size of, 78; compared with tame
    turkey, 77; food of, 79; how to buy, 80; incubation
    and, 78; management of, 81–82, 83–85; mortality
    and, 82–83; predators of, 83; range of, 76–77;
    renesting of, 83; restocking of, 80–81; sources of
    information on, 84–85; subspecies of, 77;
    supplemental feeding for, 83; weight of, 77–78

U

United States Fish and Wildlife Service, 273: regional
    offices of, 274

V

Valley quail. *See* California quail

W

Walleyes, 181–82
Warbles: definition of, 9; in rabbits, 150–51; in squirrels,
    137
Waterfowl, migratory: botulism and, 132–33; Canada
    goose, 103–12; census taking of, 291–92; feeding
    versus baiting of, 129–31; lead poisoning and,
    131–32; management of, 99–103; migration of,
    124–28; wild ducks, 112–24
Water supplies, screening of, 195
White bass, 189
White-tailed deer: antlers of, 217; as browsers, 212–13;
    food of, 220–21, 222–23; habitat of, 216;
    management of, 224–25; money from hunting,
    212–16; mortality and, 221–24; numbers of, 217–18;
    range of, 216; reproductive potential of, 218–19,
    220; weight of, 216–17
White-winged doves: clutch size of, 93; description of,
    91–92; food of, 94–95; incubation and, 93;
    management of, 95–96; mortality and, 93–94;
    nesting of, 92, 93; range of, 92–93; predators of, 94
Widgeon ducks, 102, 124–25
Wildlife management, principles of: changes in the
    environment and, 11; chemicals and, 11; gains
    versus losses in, 10–11; interrelation of action/steps
    taken, 11; official prayer of the Outdoor Writers
    Association, 12; ownership of wildlife, 12; role of
    landowner and, 10
Wild-trapped animals versus pen-raised animals for
    restocking, 15
Winterkill, 202–3
Wood ducks: clutch size of, 122; description of, 120;
    food of, 121–22; habitat of, 120–21; management of,
    103, 124; nesting of, 120, 122; range of, 121
Woodpeckers, how to manage, 258
Wrens, how to manage, 257–58

Y

Yellow perch, 180–81